BIOLOGY
OF THE
REPTILIA

BIOLOGY
OF THE
REPTILIA

Edited by

CARL GANS

The University of Michigan
Ann Arbor, Michigan, U.S.A.

VOLUME 10

NEUROLOGY B

Coeditors for this volume

R. GLENN NORTHCUTT

The University of Michigan
Ann Arbor, Michigan, U.S.A.

and

PHILIP ULINSKI

University of Chicago
Chicago, Illinois, U.S.A.

1979

ACADEMIC PRESS

LONDON NEW YORK SAN FRANCISCO

A Subsidiary of Harcourt Brace Jovanovich, Publishers

ACADEMIC PRESS INC. (LONDON) LTD
24/28 Oval Road
London NW1 7DX

United States Edition published by
ACADEMIC PRESS INC.
111 Fifth Avenue
New York, New York 10003

British Library Cataloguing in Publication Data
Biology of the Reptilia.
Vol. 10: Neurology B
1. Reptiles
I. Gans, Carl   II. Northcutt, R Glenn
III. Ulinski, Philip
598.1   QL641   68–9113
ISBN 0–12–274610–4

Text set in 11/12 pt Monotype Ehrhardt, printed by letterpress,
and bound in Great Britain at The Pitman Press, Bath

Contributors to Volume 10

M. G. Belekhova, *Sechenov Institute of Evolutionary Physiology and Biochemistry, U.S.S.R. Academy of Sciences, 44 Thorez pr., Leningrad, 194 223, U.S.S.R.*

P. J. Berger, *Department of Zoology, University of Melbourne, Parkville, Victoria, Australia 3052.*

G. Burnstock, *Department of Zoology, University of Melbourne, Parkville, Victoria, Australia 3052.* (Present address: *Department of Anatomy and Embryology, University College, London WC1E 6BT*).

William L. R. Cruce, *Neurobiology Department, Northeastern Ohio Universities College of Medicine, Rootstown, Ohio 44272, U.S.A.*

H. J. ten Donkelaar, *Laboratorium voor Anatomie, Katholieke Universiteit, Nijmegen, The Netherlands.*

A. Kusuma, *Laboratorium voor Anatomie, Katholieke Universiteit, Nijmegen, The Netherlands.*

Rudolph Nieuwenhuys, *Laboratorium voor Anatomie, Katholieke Universiteit, Nijmegen, The Netherlands.*

André Parent, *Laboratoire de Neurobiologie, Faculté de Medecine, Université Laval, Quebec 10e, Canada G1K 7P4.*

M. E. Schwab, *Max Planck Institute for Psychiatry, Department of Neurochemistry, D-8033 Martinsried, Munich, Federal Republic of Germany.*

Preface

This is the second volume of our coverage of the reptilian nervous system. It continues the pattern of the first and starts the analysis of characteristics and pathways of the brain itself.

The volume begins with an analysis of the structure and physiology of the autonomic nerves and the pattern of the regions that they supply. This is followed by four contributions dealing with the pathways of the spinal cord and brainstem; one of these reports concentrates on tegu lizards, as the level of information on these forms is at this moment significantly much greater than that for any other reptile. These chapters are followed by a discussion of the monoamine systems of the brain, utilizing the new histochemical approaches. Finally, there is a very significant discussion of experimental work on the forebrain; this chapter is particularly welcome as it incorporates a summary of the Russian literature, which is difficult of access and consequently has sometimes been ignored.

We have again been fortunate in being able to interest major authorities in contributing these several chapters on topics to which they have made significant contributions. We appreciate their willingness to have us match the style and extent of their chapters to those of others. Beyond this, we are grateful to many colleagues for discussions and advice regarding the subject matter to be covered in the present volume. Drs M. R. Braford, Jr., G. Burnstock, A. B. Butler, C. B. G. Campbell, W. L. R. Cruce, S. O. E. Ebbesson, F. F. Ebner, M. Halpern, B. Jones, A. H. M. Lohman, P. F. A. Maderson, Malcolm R. Miller, R. Nieuwenhuys, E. C. Olson, E. H. Peterson, C. L. Prossor, W. B. Quay, D. G. Senn, and R. H. Webber reviewed individual manuscripts and Drs G. Zug and H. Wermuth critically read the entire set of manuscripts and checked the proofs for current usage and accuracy of the Latin names employed. I thank my co-editors for their efforts in handling editorial chores and Mary Sue Northcutt for aid with the complex problems of some of our manuscripts. The index was compiled by P. Ulinski. The Division of Biological Sciences of The University of Michigan and the Department of Anatomy. The University of Chicago contributed part of the considerable bills for postage.

May, 1978   Carl Gans

Contents

5. Variation in the Rhombencephalon

Martin Ernst Schwab

CHAPTER 1

Autonomic Nervous System

P. J. BERGER and G. BURNSTOCK*

Department of Zoology,
University of Melbourne,
Parkville,
Victoria, Australia

I. Introduction

Autonomic nervous system (ANS) is the term given to all those efferent nerve outflows which control involuntary tissues, such as glands, the striated muscle of the heart, and all smooth muscle including that of the viscera and vasculature. The term ANS was introduced by Langley (1898) to replace the confusing terminology which had been used up to that time.

There has never been a comprehensive review of the autonomic nervous system of reptiles, so this chapter discusses the available literature in detail. The chapter attempts to resolve conflict in the work of different authors and to point to the many areas where further work is needed. The fact that there is so little to discuss in several sections emphasizes that research can still be done in virtually unexplored areas in reptiles. Throughout this chapter the reptiles have been regarded as a homogeneous group. The justification for this approach is that, from the available data, there seem to be very few differences in the physiological and pharmacological features of the ANS in the different orders. The reality of this observation, however, remains to be determined.

II. Anatomy

A. GENERAL DESCRIPTION OF THE MAMMALIAN ANS

The anatomy of the mammalian ANS is well documented, but a brief description of its basic features will provide a useful prelude to a discussion of the reptilian ANS in sections that follow. The view of the mammalian ANS presented here conforms largely to that outlined by Langley (1921) and repeated in more recent textbooks (e.g. Kuntz, 1953); however, some

*Present address: Department of Anatomy & Embryology, University College, London WC1E 6BT.

important recent findings have also been included (see Campbell, 1970; Burnstock, 1972). The ANS is characterized by a two-cell design: a pre-ganglionic fibre, with its cell body located in the central nervous system, synapses with a peripherally placed neuron which terminates in the inner-vated tissue. Autonomic outflows may leave the brain via nerves III, VII, IX, X and XI and via the spinal cord in the thoracolumbar and sacral regions.

The pre- and postganglionic fibres of the thoracolumbar outflows make up the sympathetic part of the ANS. The preganglionic fibres leave the spinal cord in the ventral roots and run in the white rami communicates either to synapse in the paravertebral ganglia of the sympathetic trunks, or to pass through the paravertebral ganglia and synapse in a system of prevertebral ganglia. In most cases the postganglionic cell body lies at some distance from the innervated tissue. Although the preganglionic fibres arise from a restricted part of the spinal cord, sympathetic ganglia extend from the upper cervical region to the sacral region. Postganglionic fibres may reach their target tissue without joining other nerve trunks, as in the renal and cardiac nerves, or they may join the peripheral tracts of the spinal and cranial nerves.

The cranial and sacral outflows were shown by Langley to differ pharma-cologically from the sympathetic outflows so he grouped them together as a separate part of the system. Langley recognized that the craniosacral fibres often had actions which were antagonistic to the actions of the sym-pathetic nerves. He therefore called the craniosacral outflows the parasym-pathetic nervous system. While the two subsystems are not completely antagonistic, the distinction between sympathetic and parasympathetic nerves is a valuable one because of the differing anatomical features of the two: the craniosacral outflows are separated from the sympathetic outflows by the somatic outflows of the limbs, and in contrast to the sympathetic system the postganglionic fibres of parasympathetic nerves generally lie close to or within the innervated tissue.

Langley identified the enteric nervous system as a third division of the ANS. This division is made up of cell bodies and fibres situated within the gut wall. It is capable of mediating integrated activity in a section of the gut with its connections to the central nervous system completely severed. It is not known whether the myenteric plexus of reptiles is capable of mediating such integrated activity.

In the early part of this century it was considered that postganglionic sympathetic neurons mediated their actions by the release of noradrenaline, while postganglionic parasympathetic nerves were considered to release acetylcholine. Later work has shown that these views are inadequate. While most sympathetic fibres do release noradrenaline, sympathetic cholinergic vasodilator fibres are known to exist. Some postganglionic parasympathetic fibres do release acetylcholine but is debatable whether, for instance, the pelvic innervation of the bladder is cholinergic. Moreover, it has been established that the vagally mediated inhibitory response of the gut does not result from stimulation of cholinergic or even adrenergic fibres. Instead, there is evidence that the inhibitory response could result from stimulation of nerves releasing a third transmitter substance, adenosine triphosphate (ATP) (see Burnstock, 1972).

B. ANATOMICAL PLAN OF THE REPTILIAN ANS

1. General

The essential features of the discussion to follow are represented diagrammatically in Fig. 1. The figure is a composite and was taken from the diagrams and descriptions of Hirt (1921), Stiemens (1934), Adams (1942) and Burnstock and Wood (1967a). The descriptions of Willard (1915) and Oelrich (1956) also contributed to the representation of the cranial parasympathetic nerves and the extensions of the sympathetic nerves into the head.

It is probably true to say that the reptilian ANS is very similar to that of mammals. However, much of our knowledge comes from gross anatomical work of the nineteenth and early twentieth century, so that it is often impossible to make a firm judgement on the points at which preganglionic fibres synapse, particularly in the cranial and sacral outflows. Nevertheless it is clear that myelinated preganglionic fibres issue from ventral roots between the limb plexuses and then run within the rami communicantes to the bilateral trunks. Unmyelinated fibres then run from the ganglia of the trunks to the innervated tissues. By analogy with the mammalian ANS, this system may be termed the sympathetic nervous system. Sympathetic ganglia are present on the paravertebral trunks above and below the levels at which preganglionic sympathetic fibres emerge in the ventral roots, e.g. sympathetic ganglia can be found as far anteriorly as the upper neck and as far caudally as the tail. It seems that reptiles lack anatomically distinct prevertebral ganglia (Stiemens, 1934). Sympathetic neurones do, however, form diffuse prevertebral plexuses in the region posterior to the adrenal glands in the turtle *Caretta caretta* (Kuntz, 1911). At least anterior to the adrenal glands, then, any splanchnic nerves are probably comprised of nerves that are entirely preganglionic. Autonomic outflows also leave the CNS in certain of the sacral nerves and in cranial nerves III and X and, probably, VII and IX; these outflows contain preganglionic fibres which probably synapse near to, or within, the innervated tissues. Thus, reptiles have a parasympathetic nervous system similar to that of mammals. Whether there are autonomic fibres in cranial nerve XI of reptiles is unknown.

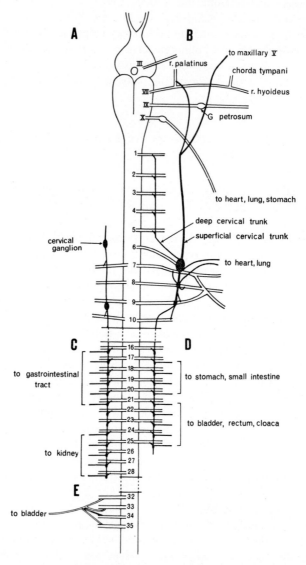

FIG. 1. A composite diagram of the autonomic nervous system in Sauria. The cranial and cervical regions are included in parts (A) and (B), while (C) and (D) include the abdominal and lumbar regions, and (E) represents the sacral region. Parts (A) and (C) were taken from Stiemens (1934) and represent the sympathetic system in *Tupinambis teguixin*, parts (B) and (D) were taken largely from Hirt (1921) and Adams (1942) and represent the parasympathetic and sympathetic nervous systems in *Lacerta agilis* and *L. viridis*. Part (B) also conforms to the descriptions of Willard (1915) and Oelrich (1956). The sacral autonomic outflow (E) was taken from Burnstock and Wood (1967a).

The general pattern of the ANS is similar in all the orders of reptiles, but it is only in lizards that a complete picture can be pieced together. Insufficient work has been done to allow a detailed description of the outflows and distribution of autonomic fibres in turtles, snakes, crocodiles and *Sphenodon*, but there is no reason to suspect that basic differences exist between the orders. We intend therefore to construct our description on the framework of the anatomy of lizards, while using details gleaned from all reptilian orders where pertinent. Further partial information concerning the anatomy in other orders can be found in the following references (Osawa, 1898; Kuntz, 1911; Ogushi, 1913a, b; Shiino, 1914; Fedele, 1937; Bellairs and Shute, 1953; Soliman, 1964). A useful paper is that of Stiemens (1934), who considers in detail the gross anatomy of the sympathetic nervous system in a lizard, a turtle, a crocodilian and *Sphenodon*. This paper also includes a painstakingly complete account of the sympathetic system in a python.

The gross anatomy of the cervical and cranial autonomic nerves of lizards was first studied in detail by Fischer (1852) while the major contributions since that time have come from the work of Willard (1915) and Oelrich (1956). Three particularly useful papers on the thoracolumbar regions are those of Hirt (1921), Reibnitz (1923) and Adams (1942). Unfortunately the sacral nerves have received very little attention; most published accounts deal only with the cervical and cranial outflows.

Before starting the discussion it will be useful to state some criteria which establish that autonomic fibres are present in a nerve. If a nerve has an autonomic component, fine fibres should be present in the roots leaving the CNS. Any fine fibres could, however, be sensory so one should observe the effects of electrical stimulation of the roots on likely target organs. This technique does not rule out the possibility that antidromic stimulation of sensory fibres could be responsible for any observed response. To establish that the fibre is efferent, degeneration studies should be performed; section of the roots proximal to the sensory ganglion will result in degeneration of efferent fibres only. Degenerating fibres can then be sought histologically in the peripheral nerve. Peripheral stimulation after degenerative section can cause responses only via activation of afferent fibres. The peripheral connections made by nerves with an autonomic component can then serve as a guide as to which nerve branches carry autonomic fibres. Once again, however, only degenerative section and electrical stimulation can prove beyond doubt that a nerve carries autonomic fibres. Note that a nerve branch in the periphery could contain preganglionic or postganglionic fibres; the former are usually myelinated and the latter are usually non-myelinated.

The criteria described above are seldom fulfilled even in the extensively studied mammalian ANS. In practice, if electrical stimulation of a nerve causes a response in a tissue which could be expected to receive an autonomic innervation, the nerve can be considered to carry autonomic fibres. In studies of the reptilian ANS even these criteria are often not satisfied. An assessment must often be made on the existence or absence of fine fibres in the nerve roots leaving the CNS, and the peripheral connections made by autonomic fibres so defined. When, however, these criteria are coupled with the observation that the nerve runs to a tissue which could be expected to receive an autonomic innervation, the case is somewhat strengthened. As will be seen later it is on such a basis that VII and IX are considered to carry autonomic fibres in reptiles.

2. *Parasympathetic Nervous System*

a. *Nervus terminalis*. Larsell (1919) found that the nervus terminalis arises as several small roots from the ventromesial surface of the forebrain in the turtle *Chrysemys picta*. The left and right nerves unite and run to a ganglion which Larsell considered to be autonomic. The ganglion distributes fibres to the snout in company with the olfactory, vomeronasal and ophthalmic nerves. Nothing is known about the physiological actions of the nerve, but it is the only example of an autonomic outflow from the chordate forebrain.

b. *Oculomotor nerve III*. The short root of the oculomotor nerve of *Anolis* contains fine myelinated fibres which synapse with postganglionic neurons in the ciliary ganglion (Willard, 1915). The postganglionic neurons are myelinated and reach the eyeball in the short ciliary nerves where they can be traced as far as the ciliary body in a gecko (Evans and Minckler, 1938). A branch of the ophthalmic division of the trigeminal nerve is known to enter the ciliary ganglion or the short ciliary nerves of reptiles (Lenhossek, 1912; Bellairs and Shute, 1953; Oelrich, 1956; Santamaria-Arnaiz, 1959) and the fact that some of the fibres contained in this branch are non-myelinated in lizards (Willard, 1915) suggests that this is a route through which sympathetic fibres could reach the eyeball.

Where physiological work has been done it supports the anatomical and histological evidence that preganglionic fibres are present in the short root of the oculomotor nerve of turtles and crocodilians (Koppanyi and Sun, 1926; Iske, 1929). There is no reason to suspect that the situation would be different in lizards. Electrical stimulation of the ophthalmic branch to the ciliary nerves causes no iridial response in either the alligator or turtle (Iske, 1929). Therefore any sympathetic fibres in the ophthalmic branch must have some other function in the eye.

c. *Facial nerve VII*. Many fine myelinated fibres are present in the facial nerve as it leaves the brain. These fibres, presumably autonomic, are distributed either in the palatine branch (Willard, 1915) or in the chorda tympani (Oelrich, 1956). No data are available on the physiological actions of either the palatine or chorda tympani branches of VII.

The palatine branch bears two ganglia in lizards; situated proximally, the very small palatine ganglion and, near the junction of the palatine and ophthalmic nerves, the ethmoidal (Willard, 1915) or sphenethmoidal (Oelrich, 1956) ganglion. It is likely, in *Varanus* at least, that some autonomic palatine fibres are distributed in the branches of the trigeminal nerve (Bellairs, 1949). It is interesting that Watkinson (1906), in contrast to Bellairs (1949), did not find a sphenethmoidal ganglion in *Varanus*. Watkinson however, like several other workers, did not section her material, an omission which reduces the usefulness of a large part of the neuroanatomical work available in reptiles. A sphenethmoidal ganglion is not found in crocodilians (Bellairs and Shute, 1953), but appears to exist in turtles (Soliman, 1964). Another ganglion which possibly contains postganglionic palatine cell bodies is the infraorbital ganglion which lies on maxillary V, near where branches of palatine VII and the lateral cranial sympathetic trunk join that nerve (Oelrich, 1956). Autonomic palatine fibres have an extensive distribution to the glands of the mouth and also innervate the Harderian, lacrimal and nasal glands (Gaupp, 1888; Oelrich, 1956).

A chorda tympani is present in almost all reptiles and certainly exists in lizards. Note that, although a chorda tympani, was not found in the turtle *Eretmochelys imbricata*, it is present in many other turtles (see Soliman, 1964). The chorda tympani of lizards bears a ganglion, the mandibular ganglion, near its junction with the mandibular branch of the trigeminal nerve (Willard, 1915; Oelrich, 1956). Fibres from the chorda tympani supply glandular tissues of the lower jaw (Gaupp, 1888; Goodrich, 1915; Oelrich, 1956).

d. *Glossopharyngeal nerve IX.* Whether parasympathic fibres of glossopharyngeal origin exist in reptiles has not been established with certainty; the effects of electrical stimulation of IX have never been reported. Fine fibres are present in the outflow of IX in *Anolis* but their peripheral distribution is only vaguely known. Willard (1915) states that the fine fibres might join the ramus palatinus VII along with the medial cranial branch of the sympathetic nerve in what is known as Jacobson's anastomosis. On the other hand, the claim that the lingual glands are innervated by IX (Gaupp, 1888), via its lingual ramus, would require that some fibres remain in the glossopharyngeal nerve distal to Jacobson's anastomosis. A judgement of whether fibres follow one or both these routes will be possible only when the peripheral distribution of the fine fibres present in the glossopharyngeal outflow is established with the techniques described earlier. Note that a parasympathetic otic ganglion, as seen in mammals, is absent from all reptiles so far studied (Bellairs and Shute, 1953).

e. *Vagus nerve X.* Of all the parasympathetic nerves, the vagus has received most attention. Preganglionic fibres leave the brain in the vagal roots and run to the heart, trachea, lungs, pulmonary and coronary vasculature, thymus, thyroid and gut. A large volume of physiological work is available on the vagus nerve but physiologists disagree as to the points at which vagal fibres synapse. Some physiological work suggests that synapses occur in the innervated tissue itself, whereas other work suggests that postganglionic cells lie in the vagus trunk. Gaskell (1886) has suggested that, in crocodilians, postganglionic neurons to the stomach have their cell bodies in the ganglion of the vagal trunk, which is presumably homologous to the ganglion nodosum, and which lies in the lower neck of reptiles. Unfortunately there is no satisfactory anatomical work which could resolve the controversy. However, Kuntz (1911) has reported that during development neurons of vagal origin form cardiac and pulmonary plexuses and give rise to the submucous and myenteric plexuses of the esophagus and stomach in *Caretta*. Whether these neurons receive a preganglionic vagal supply, however, cannot be decided from his work.

f. *Sacral nerves.* Pelvic parasympathetic nerves are known to arise in the sacral region of reptiles but they have never been studied in detail. The pelvic parasympathetic innervation of the lizard and turtle bladder has been studied physiologically and anatomically (Snyder and Light, 1928; Burnstock and Wood, 1967a) but the pelvic innervation of the anal end of the alimentary canal has not been studied anatomically and histologically. Ogushi (1913a) depicted a pelvic innervation of the penis of turtles, and multi-polar nerve cells have been found in the lizard hemipenis (Majupuria, 1969). However, there is no physiological information available on the parasympathetic innervation of the genitalia.

3. *Sympathetic Nervous System*

Hirt (1921) was the first to propose that the preganglionic outflow to the sympathetic trunk of lizards is restricted to the ventral roots between the limb plexuses. He came to this conclusion on the basis of a study of adult specimens of four species of lizards, although he was also influenced by Langley's work on birds and mammals. Hirt's conclusion was confirmed by Reibnitz (1923) in an embryological study of *Lacerta agilis*, and later by Adams (1942) in the adult of *Lacerta viridis*. The two later studies show that preganglionic fibres leave the cord in spinal nerves 9 to 24, and that the rami connecting sympathetic ganglia and spinal nerves above or below these two levels are composed entirely of postganglionic fibres. The rami communicantes of spinal nerves 9 to 24 are mixed, being composed of both myelinated preganglionic and non-myelinated postganglionic fibres (Hirt, 1921; Adams, 1942).

Anterior to the 11th spinal nerve in *Lacerta viridis* the rami run cranially so their distribution is to the heart, lungs and anterior tissues. The rami below the 11th spinal nerve run anally and the preganglionic fibres synapse with the cell bodies of fibres which run through the mesentery to the alimentary canal, spleen and urinogenital system (Adams, 1942). Some fibres from all levels rejoin the spinal nerves as postganglionic neurons and are distributed to peripheral blood vessels and, in chameleons, the dermal chromatophores. It is significant that the abdominal sympathetic trunk of *L. viridis* is very fine, making it difficult to follow in dissection, in contrast to the trunk above the 10th spinal nerve which generally equals the thickness of the vagus nerve (Adams, 1942).

Although preganglionic fibres arise only from the spinal nerves between the limb plexuses, the sympathetic trunk extends the length of the body. The bilateral trunks in *Lacerta agilis* continue caudally to the tail where the ganglion impar, the fused left and right 27th ganglion, is found (Hirt, 1921). The trunks then continue as fine strands into the tail (Hirt, 1921). Anteriorly the situation is not quite so clear. The most anterior ganglion which can definitely be called sympathetic lies slightly cranial to the brachial plexus. However, if this is the most anterior of the sympathetic ganglia we must conclude that the myelinated fibres of the cervical sympathetic trunk (Adams, 1942) are postganglionic. In that it is usual for sympathetic postganglionic fibres to be unmyelinated it is possible that the ganglia seen on the cranial nerves (e.g. sphenethmoidal, palatine) could be partly or wholly sympathetic. Before analyzing the possibility it is necessary to describe the cranial extensions of the sympathetic nervous system.

At the level of the brachial plexus in *Lacerta* three sympathetic ganglia are usually seen (Hirt, 1921; Adams, 1942). From the most anterior of these ganglia an unequal division occurs. One or two fine branches pass medially and dorsally and communicate with each of the spinal nerves of the neck. This is the deep cervical sympathetic nerve (Hirt, 1921) and it probably supplies postganglionic fibres to the cervical nerves (Terni, 1931) and most likely lacks a cranial distribution (Adams, 1942; but see Hirt, 1921). The major branch continues as the superficial cervical trunk (Hirt, 1921) to the head in close proximity to the vagus nerve. In some lizards the vagus and sympathetic nerves are totally separate in the neck (Hirt, 1921; Adams, 1942) although in others the nerves are very closely apposed (see Fischer, 1852). Small branches are given off from the superficial cervical trunk to the vagus, carotid arch and thymus (Terni, 1931; Adams, 1942; Oelrich, 1956), while the main branch continues to the upper cervical region where it divides into medial and lateral cranial sympathetic branches.

The medial branch makes contact with the glossopharyngeal nerve (Watkinson, 1906) and possibly receives some fibres from that nerve (Willard, 1915) before joining the palatine ramus of VII with which it is then distributed. The lateral branch joins the hyomandibular branch of VII, but whether sympathetic fibres join this nerve is debatable (compare Oelrich, 1956 with Willard, 1915 and Adams, 1942). The lateral cranial sympathetic continues rostrally to join the maxillary nerve (Adams, 1942) at which point lies the infraorbital ganglion (Willard, 1915). Oelrich (1956) observed a further branch of the lateral cranial sympathetic joining the ophthalmic nerve in a plexus from which fibres ran to the lacrimal gland and the glandular tissue of the upper eyelid. While sympathetic fibres have been traced as far as their junction with various cranial nerves, there is as yet no anatomical or physiological information on the effector tissues innervated by cranial sympathetics. On the basis of their distribution in mammals, cranial sympathetic fibres probably innervate blood vessels and the glands of the reptilian head.

It is now possible to return to a discussion of the ganglia of the cranial autonomic nerves. The chorda tympani probably carries no sympathetic fibres, so the mandibular ganglion, which lies at the junction of the chorda tympani and mandibular nerve, is probably parasympathetic. Sympathetic myelinated fibres run with the palatine nerve and also join the maxillary nerve, so the ganglia associated with these nerves could be sympathetic. The ganglia in question are the infraorbital, the palatine and sphenethmoidal. This extreme possibility is unlikely because the parasympathetic glandular fibres of the palatine nerve are likely to synapse in one or all of these ganglia. It is nevertheless still possible that fibres in the cervical sympathetic nerve synapse in one or more of the cranial ganglia, and the existence of myelinated fibres in the cervical sympathetic nerve seems to support this suggestion. However, postganglionic myelinated fibres do exist, e.g. as mentioned earlier the postganglionic neurons in the short ciliary nerves of the lizard are myelinated. Myelination therefore is only a partially reliable criterion on which to identify a fibre as preganglionic. Solution of the problem of the autonomic ganglia of the head must therefore await the results of experiments using such techniques as degeneration and electrophysiological mapping of pathways.

Having discussed the anatomy of the reptilian sympathetic system the question of the identity of the transmitter substance released by the nerves still remains. From studies using the technique of fluorescent histochemical localization of monoamines (Falck, 1962) it is clear that saurian sympathetic nerves contain a primary monoamine, probably noradrenaline (McLean and Burnstock, 1967a, b; Furness and Moore, 1970). Further evidence that noradrenaline is the sympathetic transmitter substance comes from assay studies which show that noradrenaline is the predominant catecholamine in the heart of lizards and turtles (Friedman and Bhagat, 1962; Azuma et al., 1965; Cooper et al., 1965) and tortoise vas deferens (Sjöstrand, 1965). As yet, no information is available on Sphenodon, but in Crocodylus fluorescent adrenergic fibres have been observed in the heart and mesenteric blood vessels (see Figs 2 and 8). The available information therefore suggests that noradrenaline is the sympathetic neurotransmitter in the reptiles. The mammalian and avian sympathetic transmitter is also known to be noradrenaline, whereas in at least the anuran amphibians it is adrenaline (see Burnstock, 1969 for a summary of monoamine levels in all the vertebrate classes).

C. SUMMARY

1. Parasympathetic fibres are present in cranial nerves III and X, and probably in VII and IX of all reptiles, and there is also clear evidence of a sacral system of parasympathetic nerves.

2. A bilateral system of segmentally arranged sympathetic ganglia is found in reptiles and the preganglionic outflows are restricted to the thoracolumbar spinal outflows between the limb plexuses. Postganglionic sympathetic fibres distribute over the whole of the body, joining the peripheral tracts of cranial nerves in the head. The transmitter substance of postganglionic sympathetic nerves is probably noradrenaline in all reptiles.

3. The parasympathetic or sympathetic status of the autonomic ganglia of the head cannot be decided with certainty from the literature. However, the fact that fibres from the ganglia innervate glands suggests that the ganglia are at least partially parasympathetic.

III. Control of Effector Organs

A. HEART

1. *General*

Autonomic nerves innervate the hearts of all vertebrates with the exception of myxinoids. The vagus nerve mediates predominantly excitatory effects in the petromyzontid heart, whereas from the elasmobranchs to the mammals the vagus has an inhibitory action on the heart mediated by cholinergic nerves. A sympathetic cardiac innervation is first seen in some species of teleosts (Gannon and Burnstock, 1969; Gannon, 1971) although other species do not have a sympathetic cardiac innervation (e.g. Falck *et al.*, 1966; Cobb and Santer, 1972, 1973). In the amphibians, birds, and mammals, the heart is invariably innervated by sympathetic adrenergic excitatory fibres (see review by Burnstock, 1969).

In view of its importance in the physiology of the heart, some mention should be made of the mechanism of conduction of excitation in reptilian hearts. Although there is no atrioventricular node or bundle in reptiles, it is clear that some specialization must be present at the auriculoventricular (AV) junction to explain the time lag between auricular and ventricular contraction (Gaskell, 1883; Alanis *et al.*, 1973). Indeed, muscle fibres tend to circle the AV junction before crossing from the auricles to the ventricle (Alanis *et al.*, 1973) thereby increasing the fibre length over which impulses must travel to cross the junction. Alternatively, the time lag could be the result of AV conduction being carried out by specialized cells with a reduced speed of conduction; this suggestion is basically that proposed by Gaskell (1883) and it is supported by the observation that the cells at the AV junction differ histologically (Robb, 1953) and ultrastructurally (Alanis *et al.*, 1973) from auricular and ventricular cells. These fibres could have a function similar to the atrioventricular bundle of mammals, and the fact that Robb (1953) reported that the fibres crossing the AV junction finally disappeared among ventricular muscle fibres adds to the similarity. Recent work indicates that there are probably two conduction pathways between the auricles and ventricle in *Testudo* and *Pseudemys*, one leading to the left side of the ventricle and the other to the right (Burggren, 1978). During periods of apnea, ventricular contraction begins on the left side of the ventricle indicating that AV conduction is inherently faster in the pathway leading to that side. During breathing, or following efferent stimulation of the vagus nerve, or application of acetylcholine to the ventricle, contraction first occurs on the right side of the ventricle. Burggren suggests that during breathing cholinergic vagal fibres reduce the speed of conduction in the left pathway so that the right pathway now conducts more quickly, and therefore initiates contraction.

2. *Chronotropic Effects*

a. *General.* The pacemaker of the reptilian heart lies at the sinus venosus, or in the right precaval vein near the sinus (Mills, 1884; Garrey, 1911a; Meek and Eyster, 1912). It might be thought that any change in heart rate implies a change in the rate of depolarization of the sinus. Indeed, an increase in heart rate would appear to have no other reasonable explanation, although the stimulating agent might have caused a region of the heart remote from the sinus to assume the function of the pacemaker. There is no evidence that this occurs, so a nerve-mediated increase in heart rate can be taken as evidence that the nerve innervates the sinus, and that the transmitter substance released from the nerves increases the rate of pacemaker depolarization. In contrast, a nerve mediated decrease in heart rate can be accounted for in two ways. The first is by the inhibitory action of neurotransmitter released close to pacemaker cells, and the second by the action of neurotransmitter released onto cells conducting the depolarization from the pacemaker to the auricles. The two mechanisms act in different ways; the first inhibits impulse generation, the second inhibits impulse propagation. As a result of either mechanism the auricles and ventricle would beat less frequently, or cease to beat altogether. These two mechanisms must be remembered when assessing whether inhibitory nerves innervate the sinus.

b. *Vagus—depressor fibres*. It is well known that vagal stimulation causes a fall in heart rate in reptiles (Crocodilia: Gaskell, 1884; Couvreur and Duculty, 1924; Testudines: Meyer, 1869; Gaskell, 1883; Mills, 1884; Guyenot, 1907; Stewart, 1909; Garrey, 1911b; Sauria: Khalil and Malek, 1952a; Lande *et al.*, 1962; Serpentes: Gaskell, 1883; Acolat, 1955). The negative chronotropic response results from stimulation of vagal C fibres (Heinebecker, 1931), it is blocked by atropine (e.g. Gaskell, 1883) and is therefore cholinergic as in all other gnathostomes. Vagal stimulation and exogenously applied acetylcholine increase the potassium permeability of cardiac muscle cells (Lehnartz, 1936; Harris and Hutter, 1956), as in mammals. It is noteworthy that the testudinian heart may be stopped for well over one hour by continuous vagal stimulation (Mills, 1885; Hough, 1895) in contrast to the mammalian heart which escapes from vagal inhibition after a short time.

The two ways in which vagal stimulation could decrease heart rate were described above. The first method, via reduction in the depolarization rate of the sinus, was shown to play a role in cardiac control by the observation that vagal stimulation hyperpolarizes sinus cells (Hutter and Trautwein, 1956) and prevents contraction of the pacemaker (Garrey, 1911a). As could be predicted, therefore, acetylcholine prevents action potential firing in the sinus of turtles (Bozler, 1943). The right vagus has a more potent inhibitory effect on the sinus than the left vagus (Meyer, 1869; Mills, 1885; Garrey, 1911a). Aside from the physiological evidence of a vagal innervation of the sinus, ultrastructural studies have demonstrated cholinergic axon profiles in close proximity to sinus cells in turtles (Yamauchi, 1969). The second method, via blockade of conduction between the pacemaker and the auricles, could also be a means of regulating the heart rate because the contraction rate of the sinus may remain unaffected even when contraction of the auricles ceases in response to vagal stimulation (Lee, 1935; Fischer, 1936).

c. *Vagus—accelerator fibres*. In a few studies an increase in heart rate has been reported to occur in response to vagal stimulation in reptiles. There are three possible explanations of this phenomenon. The first is that parasympathetic accelerator fibres exist in the species studied, the second that vagal tachycardia is a myogenic reaction to the preceding inhibition of cardiac muscle cells, the third, to be discussed in Section 2d, that cardiac sympathetic fibres join the vagus nerve peripheral to its exit from the brain.

Mills (1885) reported one experiment in which stimulation of an intracranial (presumably vagal) root caused only an increase in heart rate, an observation which suggests that parasympathetic cardioaccelerator fibres do exist. However, this was the only instance, in nine experiments, in which he recorded a primary increase in heart rate when stimulating vagal roots or the medulla oblongata. More persuasive evidence must be presented before one accepts that cardiac accelerator fibres are present in the vagal outflow. It is interesting to note that there are reports of pure cardiac acceleration and augmentation in response to vagal root (e.g. Okinaka et al., 1951) and medulla oblongata (Weiss and Priola, 1972) stimulation in dogs.

The tachycardia caused by cervical vagal stimulation in turtles (Gaskell, 1883; Mills, 1885; Stewart, 1892) and lizards (Khalil and Malek, 1952b; Berger, 1971) appeared only at the end of a period of stimulation. In any one species the vagally mediated tachycardia is seen only sometimes and Berger (1971) has reported that vagal stimulation did not consistently cause tachycardia even within a single preparation of the heart of Trachydosaurus. Thus, if vagal cardioaccelerator fibres exist in reptiles, they are present infrequently in any species and, even when present, they only sometimes mediate a cardiac response when electrically stimulated. Such fibres are likely to play only an insignificant role in cardiac regulation. It seems more likely that the tachycardia caused by vagal stimulation is a reaction of cardiac muscle cells to the preceding inhibition of the heart. Consistent with this proposal, tachycardia was never observed in response to cervical vagal stimulation after treatment with doses of hyoscine which prevent cardio-inhibition (Berger, 1971). The question of vagal cardiac augmentor and accelerator fibres in mammals has been fully discussed by Campbell (1970).

d. *Sympathetic—accelerator fibres.* Cardiac sympathetic fibres originate in ganglia in the brachial region and stimulation of the trunk, or of fibres running from the trunk to the anterior vena cava, causes cardiac acceleration (Crocodilia: Gaskell, 1884; Couvreur and Duculty, 1924; Testudines: Gaskell and Gadow, 1884; Mills, 1884; Fedele, 1937; Sauria: Khalil and Malek, 1952b; Berger, 1971). Thus, in reptiles as in mammals, a group of sympathetic fibres runs directly to the heart from the nearby sympathetic trunk and innervates the pacemaker. Fluorescent adrenergic fibres have been demonstrated histochemically in the sinus venosus of the lizard Trachydosaurus (Furness and Moore, 1970). The sympathetically mediated response is mimicked by adrenaline (Heinekamp, 1919; Dimond, 1959) and noradrenaline (Lande et al., 1962) and abolished by bretylium (Berger, 1971).

Anatomical studies suggest a second possible pathway by which sympathetic fibres could reach the heart. In the cervical region the vagus and sympathetic nerves often have points of communication where cardiac sympathetic fibres might enter the vagal trunk. If this occurs, stimulation of the peripheral stump of the cervical sympathetic nerve, or of the vagus in a preparation treated with hyoscine, should increase the force and rate of beating of the heart. Mills (1885) performed experiments of the former type in *Pseudemys* and observed acceleration of the heart in some specimens, but in most specimens there was no communicating branch between the lower cervical vagus and sympathetic nerves. Unfortunately this type of experiment has not been performed with any other species. In experiments of the latter type, excitatory cardiac responses sensitive to blockade by bretylium were elicited by vagal stimulation in *Trachydosaurus*, but only if the electrodes were very close to the heart (Lande *et al.*, 1962; Berger, 1971). Sympathetic cardiac fibres appear therefore to be absent from the upper cervical vagus of *Pseudemys* and *Trachydosaurus* but approach and possibly enter the vagus in the lower cervical region.

Since the cervical vagus and sympathetic nerves are often closely associated it is possible that some vagal fibres reach the heart after joining the sympathetic trunk. In fact Khalil and Malek (1952b) observed that heart rate initially decreased then increased during stimulation of cardiac sympathetic nerves in the lizard *Uromastyx*. While it is possible that the decreased heart rate resulted from stimulation of vagal fibres which had actually passed through the sympathetic trunk, it is equally likely that stray vagal fibres in the vicinity of the trunk had been stimulated.

3. Inotropic Effects

a. *General.* Inotropic responses are mediated by a direct influence of neurotransmitter upon cardiac muscle cells. Consequently, a study of the alteration in force of beating in response to nerve stimulation provides evidence of whether the nerve directly innervates the region or chamber being studied.

b. *Auricles.* i. Vagus. A great deal of evidence demonstrates that the auricles receive a vagal innervation. The early observation that the vagi mediate negative inotropic effects in the auricles (Gaskell, 1883, 1884) has been confirmed abundantly by later workers (Garrey, 1911a, b; Ashman and Garrey, 1931; Gilson, 1932; Khalil and Malek, 1952a, b; Lande *et al.*, 1962; Berger, 1971). Predictably, acetylcholine inhibits auricular contractions (Garrey and Chastain, 1937a; Fredericq, 1951; Appert and Friedman, 1955; Dimond, 1959). Although it is clear that both vagi innervate both auricles, there is a preferentially ipsilateral distribution of each vagus (Garrey, 1911a; Fredericq and Garrey, 1930).

ii. Sympathetic. Sympathetic stimulation causes an increase in the force of beating of the auricles (Bottazzi, 1900; Fano and Bodano, 1900) and the response is blocked by bretylium (Berger, 1971). Catecholamine-containing fibres have been observed histochemically in the auricles of *Trachydosaurus* (Furness and Moore, 1970) and *Crocodylus* (Fig. 2) and adrenaline causes

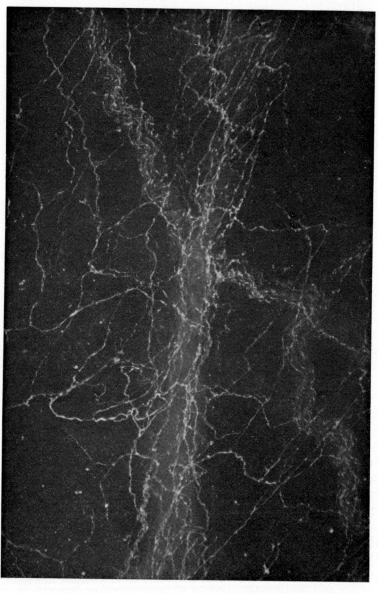

FIG. 2. A fluorescence histochemical study of the left auricle of the crocodile *Crocodylus johnstoni*. A thin region of the auricular wall is shown in a stretch preparation. A muscle bundle running across the figure is covered by a network of small bundles of adrenergic nerves and by single varicose fibres. A large fluorescent trunk containing varicose fibres passes across this muscle bundle. The thin, non-muscular regions of the wall are also covered by a light network of very small adrenergic nerve bundles and single varicose fibres. (× 180.) (Courtesy of Joanne Moore, Dept. of Zoology, Unversity of Melbourne.)

positive inotropic effects in reptilian auricles (Heinekamp, 1919; Lande *et al.*, 1962). There is no evidence indicating whether sympathetic fibres are ipsilaterally or bilaterally distributed to the auricles.

c. *Ventricle.* Until recently, there has been virtually no physiological evidence for innervation of the reptilian ventricle by autonomic fibres. It must be remembered, however, that Gaskell (1884) is the only person to have investigated the possibility of a sympathetic innervation of the ventricle. In contrast, several studies appear to establish that vagal fibres have no influence on ventricular contraction.

When studying whether the ventricle is vagally innervated, it must be remembered that changes in heart rate could have passive effects on the force of beating of the ventricle. Ideally then, only those experiments carried out at a constant rate of ventricular beating can provide critical information about the possibility of a vagal innervation of the ventricle. By selecting a low intensity of vagal stimulation, it is possible to avoid a change in the rate of beating of the heart. Under these conditions, vagal stimulation produces no effect whatever on the force of ventricular contraction, even though the force of auricular contraction is greatly diminished (Gaskell, 1883; Garrey, 1912). As an alternative experimental approach, if the ventricle is electrically driven with impulses of low voltage and long duration, and at a frequency slightly greater than the resting rate, the heart-beat sequence is reversed, i.e. ventricle to auricles to pacemaker. Stimulation of either vagus, with weak or strong impulses, now inhibits auricular contractions, but has no effect on the amplitude of the induced ventricular contractions (Garrey, 1911b).

To conclude that the vagus does not innervate the ventricle would seem to be inescapable on the basis of the evidence outlined above. The fact that the ventricle is reported to be insensitive to acetylcholine (Garrey and Chastain, 1937b; Knowlton, 1942; Appert and Friedman, 1955) would further imply that any vagal fibres present in the ventricle would be superfluous. Nevertheless, there is good anatomical, histological and ultrastructural evidence that cholinergic vagal fibres are present in the ventricular myocardium (Gaskell, 1883; Okita, 1971; Yamauchi and Chiba, 1973). In an attempt to resolve the conflict between physiologists and anatomists, a study was undertaken of the effects of vagal and sympathetic stimulation on the lizard ventricle, and the results are presented below.

The whole heart and the right and left vagi and sympathetic cardiac nerves were dissected from the lizard *Trachydosaurus rugosus* and placed in a jacketed organ bath. The ventricle was electrically driven via two platinum leads attached to it, and recordings of auricular and ventricular tension were taken. As a result of the driving technique the ventricle was the first chamber to beat, followed by the auricles and sinus. To test the effects of agonist drugs a strip of ventricle was set up in an organ bath and electrically driven as above.

The typical effects of nerve stimulation, and of the addition of drugs, are shown in Fig. 3. Simultaneous stimulation of both vagi caused a slight negative inotropic effect in the ventricle while strongly inhibiting auricular contractions. Stimulation of either the left or right sympathetic nerve caused a powerful positive inotropic effect in the ventricle and auricles (Fig. 3). As would be anticipated, acetylcholine caused a feeble negative inotropic effect in the ventricle, and noradrenaline caused a strong positive inotropic effect (Fig. 3).

The results presented above clearly contradict previous physiological findings. Quite possibly the techniques used by earlier workers were not sensitive enough to record slight negative inotropic effects such as those in Fig. 3. Alternatively, vagal stimulation might be without effect on the ventricle of Testudines, the group used in all previous studies. It is also possible that previous workers observed slight negative inotropic responses to vagal stimulation or applied acetylcholine, but considered the responses insignificant. Note that contrary to all the workers cited above, Dufour et al. (1956) observed that acetylcholine caused a very slight negative inotropic effect in the testudinian ventricle.

The fact that sympathetic fibres innervate the reptilian ventricle is in no way surprising. Adrenaline is known to cause a positive inotropic effect in the turtle ventricle (Hiatt and Garrey, 1943; Dufour et al., 1956; Hardman and Reynolds, 1965) which is mediated via β-receptors (Meester et al., 1965; van Harn et al., 1973). Furthermore, catecholamines occur in the ventricle of turtles (Friedman and Bhagat, 1962; Azuma et al., 1965) and fluorescent adrenergic fibres have been demonstrated histochemically in the ventricle of Trachydosaurus (Furness and Moore, 1970). In addition, fibre profiles containing vesicles typical of adrenergic nerves have been observed ultrastructurally in the ventricular myocardium of turtles (Yamauchi, 1969; Yamauchi and Chiba, 1973).

Although axon profiles containing granules typical of cholinergic fibres have been demonstrated ultrastructurally in the ventricular myocardium, the role of the fibres has been a puzzle until recently. As acetylcholine and vagal stimulation have only a feeble inotropic effect on the ventricle, the fibres could be of little use in controlling the force of ventricular contraction. Fredericq (1928) argued that vagal fibres altered the excitability of ventricular muscle cells, but Garrey and Ashman (1931) demonstrated that Fredericq's experimental results were the passive effects of vagal action elsewhere in the heart. Perhaps the first indication of the role played by the ventricular cholinergic fibres came from the work of Alanis et al. (1973). They showed that acetylcholine reduced conduction velocity and finally

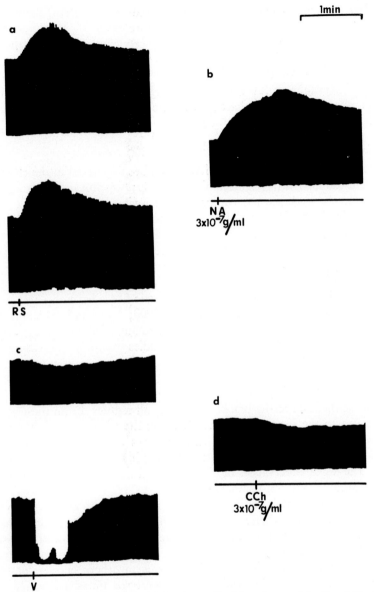

FIG. 3. Responses of the chambers of the electrically driven heart of the lizard *Trachydo-saurus rugosus* to nerve stimulation and to injected carbachol (CCh) and noradrenaline (NA). In panels (a) and (c) the upper trace is from the ventricle and the lower trace is from the auricles. Panels (b) and (d) show the effects of drug application on an electrically driven strip of ventricle. Panel (a) shows responses to stimulation of the right sympathetic nerve with 10 Hz for 15 s, and in panel (c) the left and right vagi were stimulated for 30 s with 20 Hz. Time marker 1 min. (From Berger, 1974.)

blocked conduction between the auricles and ventricle, and between the ventricle and bulbus cordis in turtles. More recently, Burggren (1978) demonstrated that vagal stimulation and acetylcholine reduced the conduction velocity in the ventricle of turtles while having little effect on the force of ventricular contraction. Coupled with his demonstration of the effect of the vagus on AV conduction, Burggren's work establishes that the vagus plays a very important role in the physiology of the ventricle of turtles.

4. *Tonus Effects*

Slow rhythmic length changes have often been observed in the chambers of the testudinian heart (e.g. Loomis *et al.*, 1930; Appelrot and Carlson, 1930; for the early work see the comprehensive review of Meek, 1927). These changes in the resting tone of the heart are presumably brought about by contraction and relaxation of the extravascular smooth muscle known to be present in all chambers of the testudinian heart (Rosenzweig, 1903; Shaner, 1923; Robb, 1953). There is some evidence that changes in auricular tone have a regulating effect on ventricular filling, and therefore stroke volume (Gesell, 1915), and that vagal and sympathetic fibres have an effect on the resting tone of the chambers (Bottazzi, 1900; Fano and Badano, 1900; Oinuma, 1910). Such a mechanism of controlling stroke volume would be novel, and if only for this reason further studies would be of great interest.

5. *Summary*

a. The postganglionic sympathetic innervation of the heart arises from ganglia at the level of the brachial plexus in all reptiles. From these ganglia fibres run to the heart predominantly along the venae cavae, although in some species some sympathetic cardiac fibres appear to join the lower cervical vagus with which they then reach the heart.

b. The vagal innervation of the sinus and auricles is distributed in a preferentially ipsilateral manner.

c. The sinus venosus and auricles are innervated by cholinergic vagal, and adrenergic sympathetic fibres. New physiological evidence presented in this section demonstrates that sympathetic fibres exert a powerful control, and vagal fibres a feeble control, over the force of beating of the ventricle.

d. The evidence for the existence of parasympathetic accelerator fibres is scanty while the little evidence that depressor fibres are mixed with sympathetic fibres is open to an alternative explanation.

e. Cholinergic vagal fibres reduce the speed of conduction in the ventricle of turtles and also inhibit AV conduction, at least in the pathway leading to the left side of the ventricle.

f. Extravascular smooth muscle is known to be present in the testudinian heart and there is some evidence that changes in its tone may be brought about by the action of autonomic nerves on this muscle.

B. GASTROINTESTINAL TRACT

1. *General*

Autonomic nerves have three separate functions in the alimentary canal, namely the control of motility, the control of digestive juice secretion and the control of blood flow. The little that is known about the neurogenic control of blood flow in the reptilian gut will be considered later (see Section D).

2. *Control of Motility*

Recent work has shown that in addition to the classic cholinergic excitatory response, the mammalian vagus also mediates an inhibition of the stomach via non-adrenergic fibres (Martinson, 1965; Campbell, 1966). There is ample evidence that vagal stimulation causes similar responses in the reptilian stomach. Low frequency vagal stimulation causes either a pure contraction (Veach, 1925) or relaxation (Bercovitz and Rogers, 1921a; Rogers and Bercovitz, 1921) of the stomach of turtles, whereas stimulation at higher frequencies causes compound excitatory and inhibitory responses. The excitatory responses are abolished by atropine in turtles (Bercovitz and Rogers, 1921b) and by hyoscine in lizards (Fig. 4) and therefore must be mediated by cholinergic fibres. While all the vagally mediated contractions of the reptilian stomach reported in the literature are likely to have been mediated by cholinergic fibres, it is possible that some of the responses are of the "rebound" type described by Bennett (1966) and Campbell (1966); at the end of a period of hyperpolarization induced by stimulating inhibitory nerves, the membrane of the gut muscle often overshoots the resting potential leading to action potential firing resulting in rebound contraction. In this situation, contraction results from stimulation of inhibitory nerve fibres. Many of the contractions of the vertebrate gut reported in the literature have been interpreted as rebound by Campbell and Burnstock (1968). In some of the early work on the reptilian stomach it is impossible to judge whether the contraction occurred during or after the period of stimulation, so the possibility exists that some reported contractions might be rebound, e.g. the contraction in response to low frequency vagal stimulation reported by Veach (1925). Nevertheless, the results obtained with muscarinic antagonists firmly establish that vagal stimulation causes a cholinergic contraction of the reptilian stomach.

The vagally mediated inhibition of the stomach of lizards is resistant to adrenergic neuron blocking agents such as bretylium (Fig. 5) and therefore

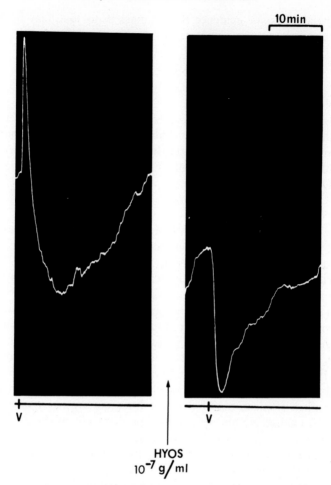

FIG. 4. Kymograph recording of the length changes of the stomach of the lizard *Trachydo-saurus rugosus* to stimulation of the vagus nerve at V at a frequency of 20 Hz for 10 s. Between the two panels the addition of hyoscine (10^{-7} g/ml) to the organ bath abolished the excitatory phase of the response. Time marker 10 min. (From Berger, 1974.)

resembles the vagally mediated inhibition of the stomach of mammals, birds and anuran amphibians. The identity of the transmitter substance mediating the response in each class is unknown. However, it is highly likely that the transmitter substance is the same in each class. It has recently been suggested that adenosine triphosphate, or a related substance, could be the inhibitory transmitter substance released by vagal stimulation of the

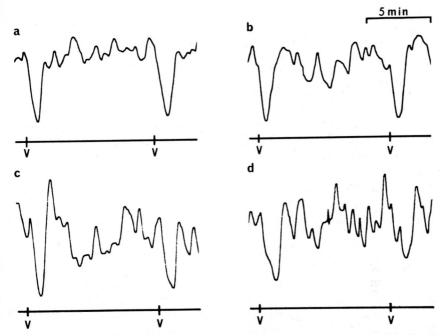

F$_{IG}$. 5. Tension changes caused by vagal stimulation at V of the stomach of the lizard *Trachydosaurus rugosus* vascularly perfused at a constant pressure of about 5 cm H_2O. The preparation had already been treated with hyoscine (10^{-7} g/ml). Panel (a) shows control responses to stimulation with 5 Hz for 30 s. Between panels (a) and (b) bretylium (3×10^{-6} g/ml) was added to the perfusion fluid. Panel (b) shows responses to vagal stimulation 40 min after the estimated time of arrival of bretylium at the preparation. Panel (c) shows responses taken 40 min after the estimated time of arrival of bretylium (3×10^{-5} g/ml) at the preparation. Panel (d) shows responses taken 50 min after the estimated time of arrival of bretylium (3×10^{-4} g/ml) at the preparation. Note that bretylium had little effect on the inhibitory response. Time marker 5 min. (From Berger, 1974.)

amphibian and mammalian stomach (Burnstock *et al.*, 1970; see Burnstock, 1972, for review).

The point at which gastric vagal fibres synapse in reptiles has received little attention although it seems that excitatory fibres synapse in the stomach of turtles (Noon, 1900; Veach, 1925). Gaskell (1886) sectioned the cervical vagus and allowed degeneration to occur in *Crocodylus* and *Alligator*. Subsequent stimulation above the ganglion of the vagal trunk had no effect on gastric motility whereas stimulation below the ganglion caused a contraction. He concluded that vagal fibres synapse with excitatory gastric fibres in the ganglion of the vagal trunk. However, the contraction is weaker, and has a longer latency than a control response; thus some fibres could synapse more peripherally. Whether the vagal fibres which cause inhibition of the stomach of turtles are pre- or postganglionic is uncertain; nicotine has been reported to block (Veach, 1925) or to have no effect upon the inhibitory response (Bercovitz and Rogers, 1921b).

Gaskell (1886) reported that vagal stimulation caused contraction of the crocodilian esophagus. However, the report is probably based upon visual observation, so the response could well be of the rebound type. The testudinian esophagus is relaxed by vagal stimulation (Carlson and Luckhardt, 1921). The response persists after treatment with atropine, while adrenaline causes contraction. Thus the inhibitory fibres resemble those in the vagal supply to the stomach.

There is no information on how far vagal fibres travel down the gut. Likewise, the pelvic parasympathetic innervation of the gut has yet to be studied.

The stomach and intestine also receive an innervation from the splanchnic sympathetic nerves. Unfortunately, practically no physiological data are available on the action of the splanchnic nerves. It has been shown that in the presence of hyoscine and guanethidine, transmural or splanchnic nerve stimulation causes a contraction of the ileum of lizards (Burnstock, Satchell and Smythe, 1972). In view of the antagonists present, the fibres are neither cholinergic nor adrenergic. It has been suggested that the excitatory response of the ileum is mediated by ATP released from the splanchnic nerves (Sneddon et al., 1973). Whatever the transmitter substance released by the nerves, they bear a pharmacological resemblance to the excitatory splanchnic fibres which innervate the amphibian gut. In the Amphibia, excitatory splanchnic fibres have their cell bodies in the dorsal root ganglion and lack direct connection with the spinal cord (Bishop and O'Leary, 1938). The origin of these fibres in lizards is unknown. There is no evidence that similar fibres are present in the splanchnic nerves of mammals. Although physiological confirmation is lacking, the splanchnic nerves obviously supply the gut with adrenergic fibres. Fluorescent adrenergic nerves have been histochemically demonstrated in the myenteric plexus of the lizards (Read and Burnstock, 1968) but are virtually absent from the muscularis externa of the gut (Read and Burnstock, 1969). This distribution is similar to that of the adrenergic splanchnic nerves of the mammalian gut, a similarity which suggests that the adrenergic innervation of the lizard gut is likely to modify the activity of enteric neurons as in mammals (see Furness and Costa, 1973).

3. *Control of Secretion*

a. *Gastric Glands.* The gastric glands of the reptilian stomach have often been described and it seems likely that a single cell combines the functions of the chief and parietal cells of mammals (see Wright *et al.*, 1957). Very little is known about the physiology of gastric secretion in reptiles so this section will examine the information to see whether reptiles employ any of the mechanisms of secretion demonstrated in mammals. No mention will be made of the properties of reptilian gastric juice or of the effects of temperature on secretion; this information will be readily found through references quoted. The control of gastric secretion in lower vertebrates, including reptiles, has recently been reviewed (Smit, 1968).

The first phase of gastric secretion in mammals, the "cephalic phase", refers to the secretion of large quantities of acid and pepsin in response to tasting, smelling, chewing and swallowing food. The secretion is mediated by efferent impulses in the vagus and occurs even if food is diverted from the stomach through an oesophageal fistula. Whether a similar cephalic phase occurs in reptiles has not been directly tested, but Wright *et al.* (1957) have shown that vagal stimulation causes secretion of gastric juice with high acidity and pepsin content in the tortoise *Testudo graeca* and the lizard, *Trachydosaurus rugosus*. However, the volume of juice released by vagal stimulation was very small so the cephalic phase, even if it occurs, could be of only minor importance in reptilian digestion.

The second phase of mammalian secretion is the "gastric phase" and is contributed to by vagovagal and local reflexes. If the results of Wright *et al.* (1957) on the weak secretory response to vagal stimulation are accepted, then vagovagal reflexes could contribute little towards secretion. Yet potent mechanisms of secretion are obviously brought into play during digestion because large quantities of acid and pepsin are secreted after ingestion of a meal in the snake *Natrix* (Skoczylas, 1970). Furthermore, intragastric fluid with high acidity has been demonstrated in the digesting stomach of the alligator (Staley, 1925), tortoises and lizards (Wright *et al.*, 1957) and turtles (Fox and Musacchia, 1959). Presumably, secretion is largely under the influence of local enteric reflexes initiated by distension.

The gastric secretory response in mammals involves a muscarinic receptor. In reptiles, injection of carbachol causes secretion of acid and pepsin (Wright *et al.*, 1957) and pilocarpine reduces the intensity of pepsinogen staining in gastric gland cells (Kahle, 1913). However, the fact that muscarinic stimulants can cause gastric secretion does not necessarily mean that secretion is mediated by enteric cholinergic nerves. To determine whether cholinergic nerves do mediate secretion *in vivo* one would need to study the effect of a muscarinic antagonist on physiologically induced secretion.

Acid and pepsin secretions in mammals are powerfully stimulated by the direct action of the hormone gastrin on the secretory cells. Gastrin has yet to be demonstrated in the reptilian gastric mucosa, and in fact Keeton *et al.*

(1920) did not observe a secretory response in the turtle stomach to injections of crude gastrin extract. However, their results are open to question for they also failed to observe secretion in response to histamine injection, whereas Wright *et al.* (1957) obtained a clear secretory response to histamine in tortoises and lizards.

b. *Salivary glands.* A number of salivary glands lie in the upper and lower jaws of reptiles, including distinct poison glands in some groups (see Gaupp, 1888; West, 1898; Smith and Bellairs, 1947; Kochva, 1978). Secretion is obviously induced by the presence of food in the mouth (Skoczylas, 1970) but the nerves carrying the efferent fibres which promote secretion have not been investigated physiologically. The early anatomical work establishes that parasympathetic fibres are probably present in the palatine and chorda tympani branches of the facial nerve (Gaupp, 1888; Goodrich, 1915; Oelrich, 1956) and in the lingual branch of the glossopharyngeal nerve (Gaupp, 1888). Sympathetic fibres are also present in certain of the cranial nerves. However, physiological confirmation that these nerves carry secreto-motor fibres is still awaited.

c. *Exocrine pancreas.* Although virtually no ultrastructural work has been done on the reptilian pancreas, cholinergic nerve profiles have been observed close to exocrine cells in the snake *Elaphe quadrivirgata* (Watari, 1968). Possibly, then, the secretion of juice and enzymes is promoted by cholinergic vagal fibres as in mammals (e.g. Lenninger and Ohlin, 1971).

d. *Gall bladder.* Nothing is known about the neural control of the reptilian gall bladder.

4. *Summary*

a. The visceral muscle of the stomach is supplied with vagal cholinergic excitatory fibres as well as inhibitory fibres the transmitter substance of which is unknown. It has been proposed that similar vagal inhibitory fibres to the mammalian stomach release ATP. How far vagal fibres travel down the gut is unknown.

b. Splanchnic nerves supply non-cholinergic, non-adrenergic fibres to the ileum of lizards but the splanchnic innervation of the stomach has not been studied physiologically. Fluorescent adrenergic fibres, presumably of splanchnic origin, are found in the myenteric plexus of lizards.

c. The pelvic innervation of the gut has not been studied.

d. The neurogenic control of gastric secretion in reptiles is an almost totally unexplored field, but the little evidence available suggests that local reflexes due to distension account for the bulk of secretion. Vagal stimulation has only a weak secretomotor effect.

e. Neural participation in pancreatic and bile secretion has not been studied.

C. Lung

1. *General*

Although the lungs of all vertebrates have an embryologically common origin from the foregut, it is not clear whether the smooth muscle of the reptilian lung is strictly homologous with mammalian bronchial muscle (Bronkhorst and Dijkstra, 1940). It would be unwise therefore to make predictions about the physiology of the lungs of one class from a knowledge of the other. Nevertheless, similarities in the innervation of the lungs of the two groups raise the possibility that pulmonary muscle serves the same function in reptiles and mammals.

2. *Vagus*

a. *Excitatory fibres.* In the first reported study of the autonomic innervation of the reptilian lung Bert (1870) demonstrated that stimulation of the vagus nerve in *Lacerta lepida* caused a contraction of the lung. Excitatory pulmonary fibres were later demonstrated in the vagus nerve of other groups (Testudines: François-Franck, 1908; Jackson and Pelz, 1918; Luckhardt and Carlson, 1921a, b; Serpentes: Carlson and Luckhardt, 1920a) and further confirmed in Sauria (François-Franck, 1909; Burnstock and Wood, 1967b). This finding has never been contradicted. The excitatory vagal fibres in turtles (Coombs, 1920) and lizards (Berger, 1973) have been shown to arise from the brainstem and are therefore truly parasympathetic. In turtles the vagus nerve supplies excitatory fibres to the ipsilateral lung only (François-Franck, 1908; Carlson and Luckhardt, 1920a; Coombs, 1920). Although Bert (1870) failed to observe contralateral distribution of pulmonary vagal fibres in *Lacerta lepida*, such a distribution was observed by François-Frank (1909) in some well-designed experiments using the same species, and by Burnstock and Wood (1967b) in *Trachydosaurus rugosus*.

The vagally mediated excitatory response of the reptilian lung is abolished by the muscarinic antagonists atropine (e.g. François-Franck, 1908; Prevost and Saloz, 1909; Luckhardt and Carlson, 1921a, b; Kleitman, 1922; Burnstock and Wood, 1967b) and hyoscine (Berger, 1973) indicating that the fibres are cholinergic. An excitatory cholinergic innervation of the visceral musculature of the mammalian (see Widdicombe, 1963) and amphibian lungs (see Campbell, 1971) has also been demonstrated. The excitatory pathway originates in the brain of mammals as in reptiles, but it probably has a spinal origin in anuran amphibians in which the excitatory fibres are present in the cervical sympathetic nerve.

b. *Inhibitory fibres.* It was not until 1925 that it was proposed that the vagus carries inhibitory fibres to the reptilian lung. In that year Veach showed that vagal stimulation sometimes caused almost a pure inhibition of the turtle lung. An inhibitory vagal innervation was later demonstrated in the lizard lung (Burnstock and Wood, 1967b). Before 1925 it was universally considered that the vagus supplied only an excitatory innervation of the reptilian lung, because an inhibitory response was not revealed even after abolition of the excitatory response with atropine. Either species differences exist, or the reported lack of inhibitory responses in the early literature can be attributed to technical causes. Burnstock and Wood (1967b) suggested that inhibitory responses were not recorded by early workers because of some inadequacy in their recording conditions. Indeed, much of the early work was done with the water manometer, an apparatus which Carlson and Luckhardt (1920a) admit to be less sensitive than the air tambour. But this alone is unlikely to account for the inability to record inhibitions of the lung for similar apparatus was used in successfully observing inhibitions of the amphibian lung (e.g. Carlson and Luckhardt, 1920b).

An explanation appears on comparison of the amphibian and reptilian lungs. The amphibian lung is tonically inhibited by impulses passing down the vagus, so that section of the vagus results in a lung with high tone (e.g. Luckhardt and Carlson, 1921a). It is well established that section of the reptilian vagus does not result in a rise in tone (Carlson and Luckhardt, 1920a; Luckhardt and Carlson, 1921a). In fact, Fano and Fasola (1894) have reported that the lung of *Emys* is in a state of elevated tone dependent partially upon the extrinsic innervation. Thus inhibition will be more readily recorded in the high tone amphibian lung than in the reptilian lung. This explanation is supported by three observations from the literature. Luckhardt and Carlson (1921a) mention that vagally mediated inhibition of the lung was observed in preparations with high tone. An inhibitory phase in the response to vagal stimulation can be seen in Fig. 3 of Jackson and Pelz (1918) in what must have been a high tone preparation for a profound inhibition was elicited by sympathetic stimulation. Paradoxically these two groups of workers claimed that the vagus was purely excitatory to the lung. Finally, Veach (1925) recorded pure contraction of the turtle lung when the tone of the preparations was low, but as tone rose during the experiment an inhibition became the predominant response to vagal stimulation.

A similar interpretation of the literature concerning an inhibitory vagal innervation of the reptilian lung has been proposed by Berger (1973). This interpretation strongly implies that the lungs of the Testudines, Sauria and Serpentes receive an inhibitory vagal innervation. It was pointed out earlier that the excitatory fibres in the vagus nerve are truly parasympathetic (i.e. they originate in the brain). It is likely that at least some of the inhibitory fibres present in the cervical vagus of lizards also arise from the brain, because stimulation of the intracranial vagal roots causes an inhibition of the lung (Berger, 1973). However, in reptiles the vagus and sympathetic trunks run close together and are often joined by branches in the cervical region. Thus the cervical vagus might carry some inhibitory pulmonary fibres which have a sympathetic origin. There is virtually no evidence which supports this possibility (see Section 3 below), so the inhibitory fibres present in the cervical vagus of reptiles are probably entirely parasympathetic.

The vagally mediated inhibitory response of the lizard lung is virtually unaltered by the adrenergic neuron blocking agent bretylium, or the β-adrenoceptor antagonist propranolol, in concentrations which abolished the inhibitory response to sympathetic stimulation (Berger, 1973). The inhibitory fibres in the vagus nerve are therefore probably all of a non-adrenergic type. Although a non-adrenergic vagal innervation has not been demonstrated in the mammalian or avian lung, it is the sole parasympathetic innervation of the lung of anuran amphibians (Schnizer et al., 1968; Campbell, 1971). Non-adrenergic inhibitory fibres were recently demonstrated in mammalian tracheal smooth muscle (Coburn and Tomita, 1973), suggesting that carefully planned experiments might also find an inhibitory parasympathetic innervation of the mammalian lung itself.

The presence and site of a synaptic relay in the vagal innervation of the reptilian lung cannot be decided from the literature. Histological evidence is compatible with a relay, for groups of ganglionic cells have been demonstrated at the base of the lung in turtles, lizards and snakes (Jones, 1926; McLean and Burnstock, 1967a). Moreover the ganglion cells migrate from the hindbrain and vagal ganglia during development (Kuntz, 1911) so they might be expected to have synaptic connection with vagal preganglionic fibres. However, the results obtained with nicotinic antagonists are confusing. Luckhardt and Carlson (1921b) reported that nicotine blocked contractions of the lung of snakes, but not of turtles. In contrast, Veach (1925), also working with turtles, found that nicotine abolished the vagally mediated contraction and relaxation of the lung. With more recently introduced nicotinic antagonists the situation becomes no clearer. Burnstock and Wood (1967b) found that the vagally mediated contraction and relaxation of the lizard lung were unaffected by pentolinium, while mecamylamine caused only a reduction in both phases of the response. It could be that the ganglion blockers used in these studies have a weak affinity for the receptors at the reptilian ganglionic synapse.

The evidence therefore points to an excitatory and inhibitory vagal innervation of the reptilian lung. However, no work has been published yet on the autonomic innervation of the lungs of Sphenodon or the crocodilians. On the basis of only one preparation studied in this laboratory, vagal stimulation elicited a contraction followed by a relaxation of the lung of Crocodylus johnstoni. The contraction was abolished by hyoscine while the inhibition persisted after perfusion of bretylium and propranolol (Fig. 6) in concentrations which effectively abolished the sympathetic relaxation of the lizard lung (see below). Thus the crocodilian vagus carries fibres which are physiologically and pharmacologically like those of the lizard *Trachydosaurus*.

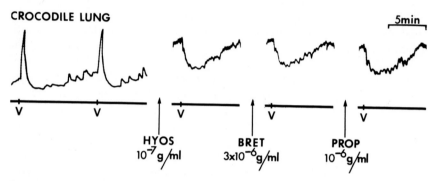

FIG. 6. Tension changes caused by vagal stimulation (at V for 15 s with 10 Hz) of the perfused lung of the crocodile *Crocodylus johnstoni*. Between the first two panels the addition of hyoscine (10^{-7} g/ml) to the perfusion fluid quickly abolished the vagally mediated contraction. The addition of breylium (3×10^{-6} g/ml) to the perfusion fluid between the second and third panels had little effect on the vagally mediated relaxation of the lung 60 min later. Likewise, the addition of propranolol to the perfusion fluid between the third and fourth panels had little effect on the relaxation 30 min later. Time marker 5 min. (From Berger, 1974.)

3. Sympathetic

A sympathetic innervation of the reptilian lung has been physiologically demonstrated only twice. Jackson and Pelz (1918) observed a relaxation of the lung in response to weak stimulation of the sympathetic trunk in the region of the brachial plexus in turtles. The efferent impulses were obviously carried by fibres seen running to the lung from sympathetic ganglia lying in the brachial region. In the second study it was shown that the sympathetic innervation of the lung of the lizard *Trachydosaurus rugosus* arises from ganglia homologous with those stimulated by Jackson and Pelz in turtles (Berger, 1973). These ganglia have been referred to as the "stellate complex" (Berger, 1971). Stimulation of these ganglia, or of the sympathetic trunk caudal, but not rostral, to the complex, causes a relaxation of the lung. Thus the efferent fibres are present in the sympathetic trunk just caudal to and at the level of the stellate complex, but do not loop or arise rostral to the complex. An inhibitory sympathetic innervation is also found in mammalian bronchial muscle (Widdicombe, 1963).

Anatomical studies supply the only other evidence that the lungs of reptiles receive a sympathetic innervation. Gaskell and Gadow (1884) observed fibres running to the alligator lung from sympathetic ganglia in the brachial region. The origin of pulmonary sympathetic fibres from ganglia in the brachial region of turtles has been questioned by Carlson and Luckhardt (1920a). They claimed that they could not find the fibres responsible for the inhibition of the lung reported by Jackson and Pelz (1918) even though they did observe fibres running from the brachial region to the lung. These fibres were considered to innervate a skeletal muscle bundle on the anterodorsal border of the lung. If the fibres were somatomotor, they would be expected to run to the lung without passing through the sympathetic trunk. Yet, in their neuroanatomical diagram Carlson and Luckhardt (1920a) depict the nerves which run towards the lung as originating in sympathetic ganglia. Such fibres are almost certain to be sympathetic. Thus, in at least those species which have been studied physiologically or anatomically, a sympathetic innervation of the lung invariably arises from ganglia near the brachial plexus and passes directly to the lung.

A second possible route by which sympathetic fibres could reach the lung has been mentioned already. Anastomoses frequently join the cervical vagus and sympathetic nerves and it is possible that sympathetic fibres join the vagus at these points. However, stimulation of the cervical sympathetic is without effect on the lung of turtles (Carlson and Luckhardt, 1920a) or lizards (Burnstock and Wood, 1967b; Berger, 1973). These observations conflict with the finding that cervical sympathetic stimulation causes a contraction and a relaxation of the lungs of "freshwater American turtles" (Jackson and Pelz, 1918). Remembering that excitatory and inhibitory fibres are present in the nearby vagus, it is possible that these results could be accounted for by current spread to the vagus nerve. It is perhaps more than coincidental that cervical sympathetic stimulation sometimes "ends in failure"; it could be that on those occasions the electrode was too far from the vagus to allow current spread to excite vagal fibres. It also seems unlikely that the vagus and sympathetic nerves would each carry excitatory and inhibitory pulmonary fibres. Considering that crucial aspects of the study of Jackson and Pelz are questionable, it is reasonable to propose that present evidence indicates there are no pulmonary fibres in the reptilian cervical sympathetic trunk.

It has been shown that the sympathetically mediated relaxation of the lizard lung is abolished by the adrenergic neuron blocking agent bretylium, and either blocked or sometimes reversed to a contraction by the β-receptor antagonist propranolol (Berger, 1973). When a sympathetically mediated contraction of the lung occurs after propranolol it is rapidly abolished by the α-receptor antagonist phenoxybenzamine (Berger, 1973). Thus the sympathetic innervation of lizard lungs is adrenergic and, while β-receptors mediating inhibition predominate, there are also some α-receptors mediating contraction of the lung. All these antagonists blocked sympathetic responses of the lung at concentrations which barely affected vagally mediated inhibitions of the lung, thereby pharmacologically distinguishing the two sets of nerves.

No pharmacological work has been carried out on the sympathetic innervation of the lungs of any reptilian group other than lizards.

4. Summary

a. The vagus nerve supplies the visceral muscle of the lung with cholinergic excitatory and non-adrenergic inhibitory fibres.

b. Sympathetic adrenergic fibres from the stellate complex usually mediate an inhibition of the lung via β-receptors but some α-receptors mediating contraction are also present. The possibility that pulmonary sympathetic fibres join the cervical vagus can probably be discounted.

D. VASCULATURE

1. General

It is generally considered that arterioles are the major sites at which changes in vascular resistance are brought about in mammals. As will be shown below, it is mainly constriction of the extrinsic pulmonary artery which raises vascular resistance in the pulmonary circulation of turtles and lizards. This observation raises the possibility that vascular resistance is controlled at the level of distributing arteries in lower vertebrates. It is noteworthy in this respect that Langley and Orbeli (1911) observed complete closure of the mesenteric arteries in response to splanchnic nerve stimulation in the frog.

2. Pulmonary Circuit

a. *General.* This section will be split into two major topics; a description of the responses to autonomic nerve stimulation of the whole pulmonary circuit, followed by an attempt to localize the sites at which resistance change occurs.

b. *Neural effects on the whole pulmonary circuit.* i. Sympathetic. The pulmonary vasculature of the lizard *Trachydosaurus* is innervated by sympathetic adrenergic fibres which usually mediate vasodilator responses via β-receptors, but constrictor responses mediated via α-receptors are sometimes seen (Berger, 1973). The sympathetic innervation arises from ganglia in the brachial region and fibres generally run directly to the lung in *Trachydosaurus.* In Testudines, cervical sympathetic stimulation, although causing positive inotropic and chronotropic effects in the heart, has no effect on the pulmonary vasculature (Burggren, 1977; Milsom *et al.*, 1977). Adrenaline causes dilatation of the pulmonary arteries in *Testudo* and *Pseudemys* (Burggren, 1977) but has no effect in *Pseudemys* (Milsom *et al.*, 1977).

ii. Vagus. In turtles the vagus nerve carries tonically active vasoconstrictor fibres to the lung (Maar, 1902; Krogh, 1910) and atropine blocks the vagally mediated vasoconstriction (Luckhardt and Carlson, 1921a). Likewise, the saurian vagus supplies excitatory cholinergic fibres to the pulmonary vasculature (Berger, 1973). Although the pulmonary arteries of snakes and crocodilians are constricted by acetylcholine, vagal stimulation has no effect in crocodilians and causes only a feeble constriction in snakes (Smith and Macintyre, 1977). After hyoscine treatment a fall in perfusion resistance is usually seen in response to vagal stimulation of the lung of lizards, and the effect is resistant to adrenergic neuron blocking agents and adrenoreceptor antagonists (Berger, 1973). While the fall in resistance might be a passive result of relaxation of the lung (see below), if the response were active it would be one of the few non-cholinergic, non-adrenergic vascular responses known.

c. *Sites of nerve-mediated resistance change.* The extrinsic pulmonary artery of *Trachydosaurus* is constricted and dilated by vagal and sympathetic stimulation respectively (Berger, 1972) so the observation of similar responses when the whole circuit is perfused could be expected. The question now arises as to whether intrinsic vessels also respond to nerve stimulation. Sympathetic fibres have only a vasodilator action on the extrinsic artery (Berger, 1972) yet sometimes mediate vasoconstriction in the perfused intact lung (Berger, 1973). Intrinsic vessels must therefore have been responsible for the vasoconstrictor response. Since intrinsic vessels are able to constrict to sympathetic stimulation, it is possible that they also contribute to all other neurogenically mediated responses of the perfused lung.

The pulmonary circuit may be studied in such a way as to determine the individual contribution of the extrinsic and intrinsic vessels to the response to vagal stimulation of pulmonary vasoconstrictors. If the pulmonary vasculature is perfused with a constant flow of nutrient solution, resistance changes in any part of the vascular tree will be reflected as pressure changes measured proximal to the lung, i.e. inflow pressure. Because the intrinsic pulmonary vasculature is a set of vessels or resistances in parallel with one another, a cannula in any intrinsic artery will record virtually the total response of the intrinsic vessels to vagal stimulation. Alterations of resistance in the extrinsic vessel, under conditions of constant perfusion fluid flow, can have no effect on the pressure recorded from the intrinsic vessels at rest or during nerve stimulation. By measuring inflow pressure, and the pressure from an intrinsic artery, it is therefore possible to assess how much the extrinsic and intrinsic vessels contribute to the vagally mediated vasoconstriction of the lung. In experiments of this type it has been shown that about 85% of the total pulmonary vasoconstriction to vagal stimulation is attributable to constriction of the extrinsic artery in *Trachydosaurus* (Berger, 1974). In similar experiments the extrinsic pulmonary artery was also found to be responsible for the major part of the constrictor response of the pulmonary circuit in the agamid lizard *Amphibolurus barbatus* and the tortoise *Chelodina longicollis* (see Fig. 7). In contrast, it was shown that vagal

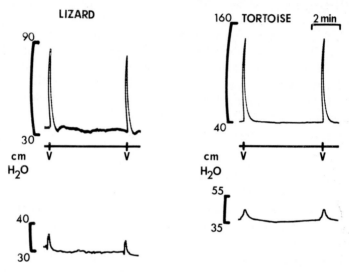

FIG. 7. Recording of inflow pressure (upper trace) and the pressure from an intrinsic artery (lower trace) of the lung of the lizard *Amphibolurus barbatus*, and tortoise *Chelodina longicollis*, perfused at a constant flow rate. The vagus was stimulated at the points indicated on the baseline with 10 Hz for 10 s in both parts. Note that the pressure change recorded from the intrinsic artery is only a small proportion of the inflow pressure response. Time marker 2 min. (From Berger, 1974.)

stimulation and injected acetylcholine have no effect on the extrinsic artery of *Crocodylus johnstoni*. Obviously the earlier report (Berger, 1972) that vagal stimulation caused only a feeble constriction in the extrinsic artery of *Chelodina* is in error. Better techniques in the later experiments might explain the difference in results, except for the observation that a constriction to injected acetylcholine was highly tachyphylactic in the early experiments. Alternatively, seasonal differences might exist, for the early work was done with animals captured and used in summer whereas in the later work captive animals were studied in winter. Subsequent work has confirmed that vagal stimulation causes a powerful constriction of the pulmonary vasculature in testudines and that the extrinsic artery is the major site of constriction (Burggren, 1977; Milsom *et al.*, 1977).

3. *Systemic Circuit*

a. *General.* Excitatory adrenergic and cholinergic nerves innervate the systemic arch of lizards (Kirby and Burnstock, 1969a), and acetylcholine and noradrenaline have been shown to increase the frequency of spontaneously generated action potentials in the testudinian systemic arch and aorta (Roddie, 1962). The origin of the cholinergic nerves is of interest for they might be the only example of sympathetic cholinergic fibres in reptiles.

The smaller systemic vessels have also been shown to receive a sympathetic innervation (Tiegs, 1932; Furness and Moore, 1970) and injected noradrenaline raises peripheral resistance in reptiles (Kirby and Burnstock, 1969b; Akers and Peiss, 1963; Reite, 1970). A reflex control of systemic vascular resistance is therefore probable, and the fact that thermal stimulation of the hypothalamus causes changes in blood pressure in turtles (Heath *et al.*, 1968) implies that the hypothalamus is an important cardiovascular control centre. However, in most of the available cardiovascular work no serious attempt has been made to establish reflex responses involve systemic vasomotor mechanisms. For instance, Fedele (1937) showed that central stimulation of nerves which innervate the truncus arteriosus of turtles causes a fall in blood pressure, but this effect could simply result from the observed fall in heart rate. Little is known about what happens to systemic resistance during diving, although it is obvious that pulmonary vascular resistance rises considerably (White and Ross, 1966; White, 1969, 1976).

The literature does provide one unequivocal demonstration of reflex control of the systemic vasculature. When placed in hot or cold surroundings some species of reptiles heat more quickly than they cool, whereas the reverse is true of other species (see Spray and May, 1972). Cardiovascular adjustments contribute to the difference in heating and cooling rates, and the vascular responses appear to have passive and active components. While the heat-induced cutaneous responses are passive (see Section 3e), the vasoconstriction of the hindlimb skeletal muscle bed in response to heating in lizards is a reflex response (Weathers *et al.*, 1970). Presumably the afferent arm of the reflex arc is a cutaneous thermoreceptor fibre. Cutaneous thermoreceptors are known to initiate the reflex cardiovascular responses to heating and cooling in turtles (Spray and May, 1972). Whether heating and cooling initiate reflex resistance changes in other than skeletal muscle beds is unknown.

There is no physiological information on vascular beds which have not been discussed below apart from what can be inferred from the fluorescence histochemistry study of Furness and Moore (1970). This study also includes work on the venous system but the veins will not be considered in this review because no physiological information is available.

b. *Cerebral bed.* The cerebral arteries of snakes and turtles are innervated by adrenergic and cholinergic fibres but the physiological action of the nerves is unknown (Iijima, 1977; Iijima *et al.*, 1977).

c. *Skeletal bed.* When lizards are heated, blood flow through skeletal muscle is reduced even though dorsal aortic blood flow increases, and the fall in skeletal muscle perfusion is blocked by dibenamine (Weathers *et al.*, 1970). Thus the efferent fibres involved in the reflex vasoconstriction are adrenergic and probably sympathetic. Fluorescent adrenergic fibres have been reported to surround the skeletal blood vessels of the hindlimb of lizards (Furness and Moore, 1970).

d. *Coronary bed.* A coronary circulation exists in all reptiles but it has been studied physiologically only in Testudines. In this group, coronary vessels are restricted to the outer part of the ventricular wall so that only a small percentage of the total ventricular mass is vascularized by the coronary system; 10% of the mass according to Brady and Dubkin (1964) and Ošťádal and Schiebler (1971) or from 25–30% according to Juhasz-Nagy *et al.* (1963). The rest of the ventricular tissue is supplied by nutritive vessels in connection with the ventricular cavity (Juhasz-Nagy *et al.*, 1963).

Vagal stimulation causes dilatation of the tortoise coronary vasculature (Drury and Smith, 1924) which is mimicked by injected acetylcholine and blocked by atropine (Sumbal, 1924). The response is therefore cholinergic. On the other hand, stimulation of the sympathetic ganglia of the brachial region causes a vasoconstriction (Dogiel and Archangelsky, 1907) which is mimicked by adrenaline (Drury and Sumbal, 1924); this evidence implies that the sympathetic fibres are adrenergic. Note that the coronary nerve, which runs beside the coronary vein, seems to contain sympathetic and vagal fibres (Drury and Sumbal, 1924). Fluorescent adrenergic fibres have been reported around branches of the coronary arteries of the lizard *Trachydosaurus* (Furness and Moore, 1970) suggesting that the coronary vasculature of lizards is also sympathetically innervated.

e. *Splanchnic bed.* Edwards (1914) recorded an increase in blood pressure in response to stimulation of the splanchnic nerves in intact turtles. Unfortunately, the stimulated nerves had not been sectioned, and only the forebrain of the animal had been pithed, so that part of the response could have been caused by reflex constriction of other than the intestinal vasculature. Nevertheless, some of the increase in pressure is likely to have been caused by stimulation of splanchnic vasomotor fibres because fluorescent adrenergic fibres have been seen around mesenteric vessels in lizards (Furness and Moore, 1970), and might be expected to exist in turtles.

Consistent with this view, adrenaline is known to cause constriction of intestinal vessels in the turtle (Hartman *et al.*, 1918).

Although nothing is known about the physiological actions of splanchnic nerves in crocodilians, large fluorescent trunks can be seen running towards the superior mesenteric artery in *Crocodylus johnstoni*, and a dense adrenergic innervation of this vessel is also observed (Fig. 8).

f. *Cutaneous bed.* Heating the integument of reptiles causes a vasodilatation, and cooling causes a vasoconstriction (Morgareidge and White, 1969a; Weathers and White, 1971). These responses could result either from reflexes initiated by receptors in the integument, or from a direct effect of temperature change on the tone of the smooth muscle of the cutaneous blood vessels. Since the responses occur only in the region being stimulated, the afferent and efferent arms of a postulated reflex would have to lie very close together. While this is possible it would seem more likely that the vascular responses are the result of direct temperature effects on blood vessels. Indeed, because the responses are not abolished by application of local anaesthetic to the heated or cooled area (Morgareidge and White, 1969b), or by intravenous injection of atropine, pentolinium or bretylium (Weathers and Morgareidge, 1971), neurons probably play no role in the responses.

Even though heating and cooling do not appear to evoke reflex responses in cutaneous vessels, an autonomic innervation of these vessels could exist. Note that heating and cooling have a direct effect on vessel diameter in mammalian skin and that cutaneous vessels are also autonomically innervated.

g. *Spleen.* Furness and Moore (1970) observed a dense adrenergic innervation of the capsular smooth muscle of the lizard spleen. The adrenergic innervation of the mammalian spleen has long been used as a model to study the physiology of adrenergic neurons (e.g. Brown and Gillespie, 1957; Blakeley *et al.*, 1963; Dearnaley and Geffen, 1966; Fillenz, 1970; Kirpekar *et al.*, 1972). An interesting comparison would be possible if similar studies were performed on the adrenergic innervation of the reptilian spleen.

4. *Summary*

a. The pulmonary vasculature of lizards and turtles receives a cholinergic vasoconstrictor innervation from the vagus nerve and while the extrinsic artery is the major site of constriction, the intrinsic vessels also constrict feebly. In the lizard *Trachydosaurus* sympathetic fibres mediate predominantly vasodilator responses via β-receptors although α-receptors mediating constriction are also present in the intrinsic vessels.

b. The aortic arch and dorsal aorta are innervated by excitatory cholinergic and adrenergic fibres. The blood vessels of skeletal muscle also receive an excitatory adrenergic innervation.

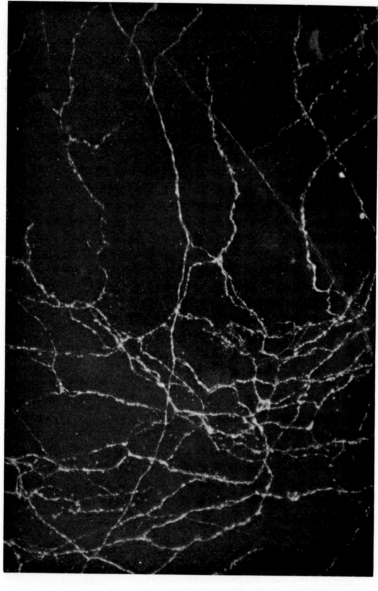

FIG. 8. A stretch preparation of a lightly innervated region of the superior mesenteric artery of the crocodile *Crocodylus johnstoni*. Small bundles of adrenergic nerves and single fibres with terminal branching run around the vessel. (× 180.) (Courtesy of Joanne Moore, Dept. of Zoology, University of Melbourne.)

c. The coronary vessels of turtles are innervated by inhibitory cholinergic fibres from the vagus nerve and excitatory adrenergic fibres from the sympathetic trunk.

d. Splanchnic blood vessels are probably innervated by excitatory adrenergic fibres from the splanchnic nerves.

e. At present there is no evidence for an efferent innervation of the blood vessels of the integument.

f. As yet nothing is known about the physiological actions of the adrenergic and cholinergic innervation of the spleen of lizards or of the adrenergic and cholinergic innervation of the cerebral arteries of snakes and turtles.

E. URINOGENITAL SYSTEM

1. *Bladder*

The testudinian bladder is innervated by sacral parasympathetic nerves which spring from spinal nerves 12 and 13 and travel to the bladder along with the vesical artery (Snyder and Light, 1928). No mention was made in this study of a sympathetic innervation, but the existence of other fibre pathways was not excluded. Stimulation of the vesical nerves caused a contraction of the bladder (Snyder and Light, 1928) which has never been studied pharmacologically.

The lizard bladder is also innervated by sacral parasympathetic fibres which arise predominantly from spinal nerves 33 to 35 in *Trachydosaurus* (Burnstock and Wood, 1967a). As in the turtle, no anatomical description of a sympathetic innervation has been published, but fluorescent adrenergic fibres are known to innervate the smooth muscle of the lizard bladder (McLean and Burnstock, 1967b). Stimulation of the vesical nerves caused contraction in all but one of the bladder preparations, and a relaxation followed in 70% of preparations (Burnstock and Wood, 1967a). While the responses clearly suggest an excitatory and inhibitory innervation via pelvic nerves, attempts to identify the neurotransmitters present us with a pharmacological nightmare. All results quoted below come from Burnstock and Wood (1967a).

The contraction of the bladder in response to vesical nerve stimulation was enhanced by eserine. Treatment with atropine usually reduced the contraction by only 20–60%, but in two cases the contraction was entirely obliterated. Thus the contraction can be enhanced by treatment with an anticholinesterase but is usually resistant to blockade by atropine. The response is therefore possibly mediated by cholinergic and non-cholinergic nerves. A similar atropine resistant contraction is seen in the mammalian bladder and various explanations of the resistance have been considered by Dumsday (1971). It has subsequently been suggested that ATP could be an excitatory transmitter substance in the mammalian bladder (Burnstock, Dumsday and Smythe, 1972). The contraction of the lizard bladder in response to stimulation of the pelvic nerves is reduced by adrenergic neuron blocking agents and adrenoceptor antagonists. In combination with atropine, guanethidine reduced or sometimes blocked the contraction, but usually only when guanethidine treatment preceded the addition of atropine. The dependence of the blocking action on the sequence of addition of the two drugs is puzzling; perhaps the concentration of guanethidine used had a local anaesthetic action with slow onset. A more intriguing puzzle, however, arises when we contrast the blocking actions of antagonists of adrenergic nerves with the observation that exogenously applied adrenaline and noradrenaline invariably caused relaxation of the bladder.

In addition to a contraction, stimulation of the vesical nerves also caused a relaxation of the bladder in 70% of preparations. The inhibition was reduced by adrenergic neuron blocking agents and β-receptor blockers but was abolished only when the tone of the preparation was lowered by the drugs. Thus the inhibition might be adrenergic but the evidence is not good. In fact there is no evidence that the adrenergic fibres seen in the bladder (McLean and Burnstock, 1967b) are present in the vesical nerves.

2. Kidney

While the renal arteries are surrounded by sympathetic adrenergic fibres (Spanner, 1928; Furness and Moore, 1970) nothing is known of the effects of the nerves on kidney function.

3. Vas deferens

The tortoise vas deferens, like the mammalian vas deferens, contains a very high level of noradrenaline (Sjöstrand, 1965). It would be interesting to extend this work to include fields in which there is very detailed knowledge in mammals, e.g. electron microscopy (Richardson, 1962; Merrillees et al., 1963; Furness and Iwayama, 1972), electrophysiology (Burnstock and Holman, 1961; Bennett, 1967; Furness, 1970), pharmacology (Bentley and Sabine, 1963; Birmingham and Wilson, 1963; Ambache et al., 1972) and fluorescence histochemistry (Owman and Sjöstrand, 1965; Bell and McLean, 1967).

4. Penis

Eversion of the lizard hemipenis seems likely to be controlled by somatic nerves, but the process of engorgement with blood is probably controlled by autonomic nerves (Majupuria, 1970). In mammals erection is mediated by pelvic nerves via a non–cholinergic, non–adrenergic mechanism (Dorr and Brody, 1967). Quite possibly erection is mediated in a similar way in reptiles. Pelvic nerves are known to innervate the testudinian penis (Ogushi, 1913a) and are likely to supply the lizard hemipenes. Pelvic preganglionic fibres probably synapse on the multipolar ganglion cells present in the lizard hemipenes (Majupuria, 1969). The origin of these multipolar cells in the lizard hemipenis is unknown, but in turtles Kuntz (1911) has briefly described the formation of genital plexuses from the same cell population which gives rise to the sympathetic nervous system. The adrenergic fibres surrounding penial arteries (Furness and Moore, 1970) might also have an influence on erection.

5. *Summary*

a. Stimulation of sacral parasympathetic nerves causes contraction and relaxation of the lizard bladder. The contraction is enhanced by eserine and reduced by atropine and is therefore probably mediated in part by cholinergic fibres. The excitatory response remaining after atropine treatment is unlikely to be mediated by adrenergic fibres. The relaxation of the bladder caused by stimulation of the pelvic nerves is possibly mediated by adrenergic fibres.

b. Although fluorescent adrenergic fibres are known to innervate the kidney, vas deferens and penis, nothing is known about the physiological actions of the fibres. The functions of the pelvic innervation of the penis are also unknown.

F. ENDOCRINE GLANDS

1. *Thyroid*

The thyroid of Testudines (*Emys*, *Testudo*) is reported to receive branches from the sympathetic and vagus nerves (Naccarati, 1922) while it appears that the thyroid of saurians receives branches only from the inferior laryngeal nerves (Adams, 1939; Oelrich, 1956), although it must be remembered that sympathetic fibres might be present within the vagal branches.

The physiological action of these nerves is completely unknown in reptiles, but it is worth noting that there is strong evidence of a direct sympathetic innervation of the mammalian thyroid parenchyma (Melander *et al.*, 1972).

2. *Pancreas*

Morphological and ultrastructural information is available on the endocrine portion of the reptilian pancreas (see Miller and Lagios, 1970) but as yet the effects of autonomic nerves on pancreatic function have not been studied. Axons containing small agranular vesicles and a few large granular vesicles were seen in close proximity to β-cells in snakes, while no α-cell innervation was seen (Miller and Lagios, 1970). The fibres, then, are probably cholinergic (Watari, 1968), contrary to the claim that such vesicles typify adrenergic fibres (Miller and Lagios, 1970). Exclusive innervation of β-cells suggests that only insulin secretion is neurally controlled in snakes while glucagon secretion is presumably controlled by other means. Cholinergic vagal fibres are known to stimulate insulin secretion in mammals (e.g. Woods, 1972).

3. *Adrenal*

An excellent anatomical and histological account of the reptilian adrenal gland has been published in this series (Gabe, 1970) and discussion here could only be repetitive. It is interesting to note that two distinct populations of cells containing either adrenaline or noradrenaline can be found in the reptilian adrenal. Consequently, it is possible that reptiles could selectively release adrenaline or noradrenaline in response to different stimuli. No matter what causes adrenal release, it is clear from work already presented that circulating catecholamines, if in sufficient concentration, would have profound effects on the cardiovascular system, and on other tissues such as the lung. The adrenal glands could therefore be extremely important in the general physiology of reptiles, and it is extraordinary that they have not attracted the attention of physiologists.

G. Chromatophores

It has long been known that the chromatophores of the integument are variously controlled by hormones, the sympathetic nervous system, or in some animals both these mechanisms (see Parker, 1948, for an excellent historical discussion). Three monographs almost entirely agree about the control of colour change in reptiles (Fingerman, 1963; Waring, 1963; Bagnara and Hadley, 1973). It is agreed that hormones alone regulate the chromatophores in *Anolis* (see also Hadley and Goldman, 1969) and that the sympathetic nervous system provides the sole control of colour change in chameleons. However, there is disagreement over whether, in addition to hormonal control, the sympathetic nervous system is directly involved in colour change in *Phrynosoma*. Both mechanisms were considered to play a role by Fingerman and by Bagnara and Hadley, whereas Waring concluded that the evidence for direct sympathetic participation (Parker, 1938) could be better explained in terms of an hormonal mechanism. Waring considered that sympathetically mediated colour changes resulted from the vaso-constrictor action of the nerves rather than a direct effect on chromatophores. According to this view, as blood-borne melanin dispersing hormone (MDH) is responsible for a dark skin colour, a sufficient reduction of cutaneous blood flow will result in paling of the skin. However, one of Parker's observations is almost impossible to interpret in this way. Parker stimulated the sciatic nerve of four decapitated specimens and observed paling of the stimulated hindlimb. Under these conditions so much blood would have been lost in the time between decapitation and stimulation, that blood flow through the hindlimb would surely have ceased. Consequently even vasoconstriction could not have further reduced the supply of MDH to the melanophores. It is much more likely that sympathetic adrenergic fibres in the sciatic nerve had caused aggregation of melanin and consequent paling of the skin.

Although colour change occurs in many reptiles other than those considered above, virtually nothing is known about the controlling mechanisms involved (see Fingerman, 1963; Waring, 1963). Fine structural studies are available on the chromatophores of *Anolis* (Alexander and Fahrenbach, 1969) and the snake *Natrix* (Miscalencu and Ionescu, 1972).

H. Accessory Structures of the Eye

1. *Iris*

Details of the anatomy and ultrastructure of the iris and nictitating membrane have been discussed by Underwood (1970) and will be mentioned here only as they help to interpret physiological results.

In common with the rest of the gnathostomes, the reptilian iris is innervated by the oculomotor nerve. The pupil constricts in response to ciliary nerve stimulation (Iske, 1929) as well as to illumination with light (Koppanyi and Sun, 1926). It has long been known that the reptilian iris, like the avian, is comprised of striated muscle, so the finding that nicotine constricts the pupil (Koppanyi and Sun, 1926; Iske, 1929) is not surprising. Whether the nicotinic receptors on the iridial muscle resemble those at the autonomic ganglionic synapse, or those at the somatic neuromuscular junction, cannot be decided from the evidence available; Iske (1929) found that curare had no effect on constriction of the pupil whereas Koppanyi and Sun (1926) reported that curare antagonized constrictor responses.

The condition described above of an autonomic nerve supplying fibres to striated muscle is paralleled by the innervation of the vertebrate heart. However, the mediation of muscle responses via nicotinic receptors is unusual for postganglionic cholinergic nerves which usually mediate responses via muscarinic receptors. In fact, there is some evidence that muscarinic receptors might be present in the striated muscle of the iris. Iske (1929) reported that pilocarpine caused contraction of the turtle and alligator iris and that local application of atropine blocked oculomotor mediated contractions of the alligator iris. Iske's evidence points to a membrane excitation system activated by both muscarinic and nicotinic receptor occupation. This unique system receives no support from other physiological studies in which muscarinic agonists and antagonists were reported to have no effect on the iris of turtles or the alligator (Meyer, 1893; Koppanyi and Sun, 1926). Nevertheless, Iske's observations have some anatomical basis in that smooth, myoblast-like muscle cells are found admixed with striated muscle cells in the alligator iris (Reger, 1966). Iske's results suggest that the myoblast-like cells have the pharmacological characteristics of other smooth muscle cells.

So far we have considered only the control of the iridial sphincter, while in most reptiles a dilator muscle is also present. The mammalian dilator is innervated by sympathetic adrenergic fibres, so a sympathetic innervation of the reptilian dilator might be expected. Two early papers on the reptilian heart contained an incidental report that stimulation of the cervical sympathetic trunk caused dilatation of the pupil in turtles (Gaskell and Gadow, 1884; Mills, 1885). Assuming the accuracy of the reports (see Section 2 below), the response was presumably caused by contraction of the striated dilator muscle known to exist in testudines. While such a sympathetic innervation might be expected to be cholinergic in view of the striated muscle of the effector tissue, it should be remembered that the extraocular striated muscles of cats are contracted by adrenaline and by sympathetic stimulation (Eakins and Katz, 1967). In a careful study Iske (1929) found no evidence for a sympathetic innervation of the alligator iris; however, crocodilians lack a dilator muscle. Although a dilator muscle is present in the avian iris the majority of reports find no evidence that the iris is sympathetically innervated (see Bennett, 1974).

Transmission in the ciliary ganglion of birds is partly electrical and partly chemical (e.g. Marwitt et al., 1971). Since the reptiles are the evolutionary precursors of birds a double mode of ganglionic transmission might also occur in the reptilian ciliary ganglion. This possibility is consistent with the observation that the iridial response in the alligator to stimulation of the ciliary ganglion is reduced, but not blocked, by topical application of nicotine to the ganglion (Iske, 1929).

2. Nictitating Membrane

Both Gaskell and Gadow (1884) and Mills (1885) reported that cervical sympathetic stimulation in turtles caused not only dilatation of the pupil, but also retraction of the nictitating membrane. This observation implies that sympathetic fibres innervate a muscle attached to the nictitating membrane. However, according to Underwood's (1970) description, there is no smooth muscle in the reptilian nictitans. Although the findings of Eakins and Katz (1967) suggest that cervical sympathetic stimulation could cause retraction of the membrane; even though it attaches only to striated muscle, there are two further reasons for being cautious of the two early reports. In the first place, the observations were only incidental and, secondly, the fact that sympathetic stimulation was known to cause contraction of the smooth muscle of the mammalian nictitans could have led to the expectation of a similar response in reptiles. For similar reasons the reports that sympathetic stimulation caused pupillodilatation in turtles should also be treated with caution.

The mechanism of protrusion of the nictitating membrane in reptiles and mammals appears to be similar. According to Oelrich (1956, p. 98) the bursalis muscle would function as a pulley to cause the reptilian nictitating membrane to be pulled over the eye, just as contraction of the extraocular muscles moves the membrane over the mammalian eye (see Paton and Thompson, 1970).

3. Glands of the Eye

Under this heading are included the lacrimal and Harderian glands. While anatomical and histological information is available on the glands (West, 1898; Smith and Bellairs, 1947; Bellairs and Boyd, 1950; Underwood, 1970) there is no physiological information available which would enable the control of these glands to be compared with that of similar glands in mammals. Thus we can only presume that glandular secretion is promoted by autonomic fibres in the facial and the glossopharyngeal nerves. The sympathetic fibres distributed in the cranial nerves might also have a direct secretomotor function or they might affect secretion through vasomotor changes.

IV. Central Autonomic Connections

In recent years a large number of studies have begun to elucidate the pathways via which afferent fibres finally project onto the autonomic efferent cell bodies in the CNS of mammals. The studies involve the precise techniques of stereotaxically recording from and stimulating localized regions or centres of the brain. From such work it has become clear that complex neuronal interactions occur between the afferent input and the instructions finally transmitted in the efferent outputs, e.g. see Korner (1971) for a description of the central integration of the cardiovascular controlling system in mammals. Ultimately, it should be possible to obtain information on the electrophysiological and pharmacological properties of CNS synapses with these techniques, but the complexity of the interactions makes this aim difficult.

The reptilian CNS, being anatomically less complex than the mammalian, might provide a simpler model for studying pathways and interactions with the brain. Unfortunately reptiles have yet to be subjected to the sophisticated experiments performed in mammals. The only work available demonstrates that neurons in the anterior hypothalamus of turtles project onto efferent cardiovascular neurons (Rodbard et al., 1950; Heath et al., 1968).

V. Conclusions

The overall picture presented in this chapter can be simply summarized. There is quite a lot known about the autonomic innervation of the heart and lungs of reptiles, there is a reasonable amount of information available on the innervation of the gut and the vascular system, but very little is known about the innervation of the urinogenital system and the endocrine and exocrine glands.

More specifically the ANS has been inadequately studied in the following areas. In the sympathetic nervous system the distribution and physiological actions of the abdominal pathways, and of the cranial and pelvic extensions of the system, have barely been investigated. Although excitatory fibres have been demonstrated in the splanchnic supply to the gut, no attempt has been made to establish whether the fibres are present in the ventral roots, or whether they originate in the dorsal root ganglion as in amphibians. In the parasympathetic nervous system only the vagus nerve has been studied extensively; even so, it is not known how far vagal fibres travel down the gut or where preganglionic fibres form synapses. Some information is available on the physiological actions of the oculomotor nerve, but, even though birds and reptiles both have striated muscle in their iris, the widespread interest in the avian oculomotor nerve has not been extended to include that of reptiles. There is very little known about the origin, distribution and function of pelvic parasympathetic nerves and the physiological actions of the autonomic component of VII and IX have yet to be studied.

Because the ANS of reptiles has attracted so little attention it would be surprising if much could be said about the reflex activation of autonomic nerve fibres. The early collaboration of Carlson and Luckhardt yielded some information on reflexly evoked autonomic responses. In more recent times it has become clear that heating of reptiles evokes vasomotor reflexes (Weathers et al., 1970) and that diving elicits cardiovascular reflex responses (see White 1968, 1969, 1976). However, the field of reflex activation of the ANS is almost untouched and could provide a fruitful area of research.

Acknowledgements

We are indebted to Dr. Graeme Campbell, Dr. Bryan Dumsday, Dr. John

Furness, Dr. David Smith and Mr. Alistair Willis for help with the text, to Ms. Joanne Moore for allowing us to publish some of her material, and to Ms. Jay McKenzie for preparing one of the figures. We are also very grateful to Ms. Gail Liddell and Ms. Marian Rubio for typing the manuscript.

References

Acolat, L. (1955). Note préliminaire sur le pneumogastrique chez les ophidiens. *Annls. Sci. Univ. Besançon. Zool. Phys.* **4**, 17–24.

Adams, W. E. (1939). The cervical region of the Lacertilia. A critical review of certain aspects of its anatomy. *J. Anat.* **74**, 57–71.

Adams, W. E. (1942). Observations on the lacertilian sympathetic system. *J. Anat.* **77**, 6–11.

Akers, T. K. and Peiss, C. N. (1963). Comparative study of effect of epinephrine and norepinephrine on cardiovascular system of turtle, alligator, chicken and opossum. *Proc. Soc. exp. Biol. Med.* **112**, 396–399.

Alanis, J., Benitez, B., Lopez, E. and Martinez-Palomo, A. (1973). Impulse propagation through the cardiac junctional regions of the axolotl and the turtle. *Jap. J. Physiol.* **23**, 149–164.

Alexander, N. J. and Fahrenbach, W. H. (1969). The dermal chromatophores of *Anolis carolinensis* (Reptilia. Iguanidae). *Am. J. Anat.* **126**, 41–56.

Ambache, N., Dunk, L. P., Verney, J. and Zar, M. Aboo (1972). Inhibition of postganglionic motor transmission in vas deferens by indirectly acting sympathomimetic drugs. *J. Physiol., Lond.* **227**, 433–456.

Appelrot, S. and Carlson, A. J. (1930). The influence of the vago-sympathetic nerves on the ventriculo-aortic tonus in the turtle. *Am. J. Physiol.* **95**, 56–63.

Appert, H. and Friedman, M. H. F. (1955). Influence of acetylcholine on turtle auricle and ventricle. *Am. J. Physiol.* **183**, 593–594.

Ashman, R. and Garrey, W. E. (1931). Excitability of the turtle auricle during vagus stimulation. *Am. J. Physiol.* **98**, 109–120.

Azuma, T., Binia, A. and Visscher, M. B. (1965). Adrenergic mechanisms in the bullfrog and turtle. *Am. J. Physiol.* **209**, 1287–1294.

Bagnara, J. T. and Hadley, M. E. (1973). "Chromatophores and Colour Change." Prentice Hall, Englewood Cliffs, New Jersey.

Bell, C. and McLean, J. R. (1967). Localization of norepinephrine and acetylcholinesterase in separate neurons supplying the guinea-pig vas deferens. *J. Pharmac. exp. Ther.* **157**, 69–73.

Bellairs, A. d'A. (1949). Observations on the snout of *Varanus*, and a comparison with that of other lizards and snakes. *J. Anat.* **83**, 116–146.

Bellairs, A. d'A. and Boyd, J. D. (1950). The lachrymal apparatus in lizards and snakes. II. The anterior part of the lachrymal duct and its relationship with the palate and with the vomeronasal organs. *Proc. zool. Soc. Lond.* **120**, 269–310.

Bellairs, A. d'A. and Shute, C. C. D. (1953). Observations on the narial musculature of Crocodilia and its innervation from the sympathetic system. *J. Anat.* **87**, 367–378.

Bennett, M. R. (1966). Rebound excitation of the smooth muscle cells of the guinea-pig taenia coli after stimulation of intramural inhibitory nerves. *J. Physiol., Lond.* **185**, 124–131.

Bennett, M. R. (1967). The effect of cations on the electrical properties of the smooth muscle cells of the guinea-pig vas deferens. *J. Physiol., Lond.* **190**, 465–479.

Bennett, T. (1974). The peripheral and autonomic nervous systems. *In* "Avian Biology". (D. S. Farner and J. R. King, eds). Academic Press, N.Y. **4**, 1–77.

Bentley, G. A. and Sabine, J. R. (1963). The effects of ganglion blocking and postganglionic sympatholytic drugs on preparations of the guinea-pig vas deferens. *Br. J. Pharmac. Chemother* **21**, 190–201.

Bercovitz, Z. and Rogers, F. T. (1921a). The inhibitory effects of vagus stimulation on gastric motility in the turtle. *Am. J. Physiol.* **55**, 310P.

Bercovitz, Z. and Rogers, F. T. (1921b). Contributions to the physiology of the stomach. LV. The influence of the vagi on gastric tonus and motility in the turtle. *Am. J. Physiol.* **55**, 323–338.

Berger, P. J. (1971). The vagal and sympathetic innervation of the heart of the lizard *Tiliqua rugosa*. *Aust. J. exp. Biol. med. Sci.* **49**, 297–304.

Berger, P. J. (1972). The vagal and sympathetic innervation of the isolated pulmonary artery of a lizard and a tortoise. *Comp. gen. Pharmac.* **3**, 113–124.

Berger, P. J. (1973). Autonomic innervation of the visceral and vascular smooth muscle of the lizard lung. *Comp. gen. Pharmac.* **4**, 1–10.

Berger, P. J. (1974). "Pulmonary and Cardiovascular Physiology in Reptiles." Ph.D. Thesis, Univ. of Melbourne, Melbourne, Australia.

Bert, P. (1870). "Leçons sur la Physiologie Comparée de la Respiration Professées au Muséum d'Histoire Naturelle." J.-B. Baillière et Fils. Paris.

Birmingham, A. T. and Wilson, A. B. (1963). Preganglionic and postganglionic stimulation of the guinea-pig isolated vas deferens preparation. *Br. J. Pharmac. Chemother.* **21**, 569–580.

Bishop, G. H. and O'Leary, J. (1938). Pathways through the sympathetic nervous system in the bullfrog. *J. Neurophysiol.* **1**, 442–454.

Blakeley, A. G. H., Brown, G. L. and Ferry, C. B. (1963). Pharmacological experiments on the release of the sympathetic transmitter. *J. Physiol., Lond.* **167**, 505–514.

Bottazzi, F. (1900). Action du vague et du sympathique sur les oreillettes du coeur de l'*Emys europaea*. *Archs ital. Biol.* **34**, 17–35.

Bozler, E. (1943). The initiation of impulses in cardiac muscle. *Am. J. Physiol.* **138**, 273–282.

Brady, A. J. and Dubkin, C. (1964). Coronary circulation in the turtle ventricle. *Comp. Biochem. Physiol.* **13**, 119–128.

Bronkhorst, W. and Dijkstra, C. (1940). Das neuromuskuläre System der Lunge. *Beitr. klin. Tuberk.* **94**, 445–503.

Brown, G. L. and Gillespie, J. S. (1957). The output of sympathetic transmitter from the spleen of the cat. *J. Physiol., Lond.* **138**, 81–102.

Burggren, W. (1977). The pulmonary circulation of the chelonian reptile: morphology haemodynamics and pharmacology. *J. comp. Physiol.* **116**, 303–323.

Burggren, W. (1978). Influence of intermittent breathing on ventricular depolarization patterns in chelonian reptiles. *J. Physiol. Lond.*, **278**, 349–364.

Burnstock, G. (1969). Evolution of the autonomic innervation of visceral and cardiovascular systems in vertebrates. *Pharmac. Rev.* **21**, 247–324.

Burnstock, G. (1972). Purinergic nerves. *Pharmac. Rev.* **24**, 509–581.

Burnstock, G., Campbell, G., Satchell, D. and Smythe, A. (1970). Evidence that adenosine triphosphate or a related nucleotide is the transmitter substance released by nonadrenergic inhibitory nerves in the gut. *Br. J. Pharmac. Chemother.* **40**, 668–688.

Burnstock, G., Dumsday, B. and Smythe, A. (1972). Atropine resistant excitation of the urinary bladder: the possibility of transmission via nerves releasing a purine nucleotide. *Br. J. Pharmac. Chemother.* **44**, 451–461.

Burnstock, G. and Holman, M. E. (1961). The transmission of excitation from autonomic nerve to smooth muscle. *J. Physiol., Lond.* **155**, 115–133.

Burnstock, G., Satchell, D. and Smythe, A. (1972). A comparison of the excitatory and inhibitory effects of non-adrenergic, non-cholinergic nerve stimulation and exogenously applied ATP on a variety of smooth muscle preparations from different vertebrate species. *Br. J. Pharmac. Chemother.* **46**, 234–242.

Burnstock, G. and Wood, M. (1967a). Innervation of the urinary bladder of the sleepy lizard (*Trachysaurus rugosus*). II. Physiology and pharmacology. *Comp. Biochem. Physiol.* **20**, 675–690.

Burnstock, G. and Wood, M. J. (1967b). Innervation of the lungs of the sleepy lizard (*Trachysaurus rugosus*). II. Physiology and Pharmacology. *Comp. Biochem. Physiol.* **22**, 815–831.

Campbell, G. (1966). Nerve mediated excitation of the taenia of the guinea-pig caecum. *J. Physiol., Lond.* **185**, 148–159.

Campbell, G. (1970). Autonomic nervous supply to effector tissues. *In* "Smooth Muscle." (E. Bülbring, A. F. Brading, A. W. Jones and T. Tomita, eds). Edward Arnold, London, 451–495.

Campbell, G. (1971). Autonomic innervation of the lung musculature of a toad (*Bufo marinus*). *Comp. gen. Pharmac.* **2**, 281–286.

Campbell, G. and Burnstock, G. (1968). The comparative physiology of gastrointestinal motility. *In* "Handbook of Physiology." Section 6: Alimentary Canal. American Physiological Society, Washington, D.C. **9**, 2213–2266.

Carlson, A. J. and Luckhardt, A. B. (1920a). Studies on the visceral sensory nervous system. III. Lung automatism and lung reflexes in Reptilia (turtles: *Chrysemys elegans* and *Malacoclemmys lesueurii*; snake: *Eutenia elegans*). *Am. J. Physiol.* **54**, 261–306.

Carlson, A. J. and Luckhardt, A. B. (1920b). Studies on the visceral sensory nervous system. I. Lung automatism and lung reflexes in the frog (*R. pipiens* and *R. catesbeiana*). *Am. J. Physiol.* **54**, 55–95.

Carlson, A. J. and Luckhardt, A. B. (1921). Studies on the visceral sensory nervous system. X. The vagus control of the esophagus. *Am. J. Physiol.* **57**, 299–335.

Cobb, J. L. S. and Santer, R. M. (1972). Excitatory and inhibitory innervation of the heart of the plaice (*Pleuronectes platessa*): anatomical and electrophysiological studies. *J. Physiol., Lond.* **222**, 42–43P.

Cobb, J. L. S. and Santer, R. M. (1973). Electrophysiology of cardiac function in teleosts: cholinergically mediated inhibition and rebound excitation. *J. Physiol., Lond.* **230**, 561–573.

Coburn, R. F. and Tomita, T. (1973). Evidence for non-adrenergic inhibitory nerves in the guinea-pig trachealis muscle. *Am. J. Physiol.* **224**, 1072–1080.

Coombs, H. C. (1920). Some aspects of the neuromuscular respiratory mechanism in chelonians. *Am. J. Physiol.* **50**, 511–519.

Cooper, J. C., Lande, I. S. de la and Tyler, M. J. (1965). The catecholamines in lizard heart. *Aust. J. exp. Biol. med. Sci.* **44**, 205–210.

Couvreur, E. and Duculty, J. (1924). L'innervation cardiaque chez les crocodiliens. *Archs int. Physiol.* **24**, 104–111.

Dearnaley, D. P. and Geffen, L. B. (1966). Effect of nerve stimulation on the noradrenaline content of the spleen. *Proc. R. Soc.* **B166**, 303–315.

Dimond, M. T. (1959). Responses to phenylethylamines and nicotine and histology of turtle atria. *Am. J. Physiol.* **197**, 747–751.

Dogiel, J. and Archangelsky, K. (1907). Die gefässverengernden Nerven der Kranzarterien des Herzens. *Pflügers Arch. ges. Physiol.* **116**, 482–494.

Dorr, L. D. and Brody, M. J. (1967). Hemodynamic mechanisms of erection in the canine penis. *Am. J. Physiol.* 213, 1526–1531.

Drury, A. N. and Smith, F. M. (1924). Observations relating to the nerve supply of the coronary artery of the tortoise. Part I. Direct observations of the artery. *Heart* 11, 71–79.

Drury, A. N. and Sumbal, J. J. (1924). Observations relating to the nerve supply of the coronary arteries of the tortoise. Part II. Perfusion of the artery. *Heart* 11, 267–284.

Dufour, J. J., Hunziker, N. and Posternak, J. (1956). Effets inotropes et chronotropes de l'acetylcholine et de l'adrenaline sur le coeur de la Tortue. *J. Physiol.* Paris 48, 521–524.

Dumsday, B. (1971). Atropine resistance of the urinary bladder innervation. *J. Pharm. Pharmac.* 23, 222–225.

Eakins, K. E. and Katz, R. L. (1967). The effects of sympathetic stimulation and epinephrine on the superior rectus muscle of the cat. *J. Pharmac. exp. Ther.* 157, 524–531.

Edwards, D. J. (1914). A study of the anatomy of the vasomotor phenomena of the sympathetic nervous system in the turtle. *Am. J. Physiol.* 33, 229–252.

Evans, L. T. and Minckler, J. (1938). The ciliary ganglion and associated structures in the gecko, *Gymnodactylus kotschyi*. *J. comp. Neurol.* 69, 303–314.

Falck, B. (1962). Observations on the possibilities of the cellular localization of monoamines by a fluorescence method. *Acta physiol. scand.* 56, Suppl. 197, 1–25.

Falck, B., Mecklenburg, C. von, Myhberg, H. and Persson, H. (1966). Studies on adrenergic and cholinergic receptors in the isolated hearts of *Lampetra fluviatilis* (Cyclostomata) and *Pleuronectes platessa* (Teleostei). *Acta physiol. scand.* 68, 64–71.

Fano, G. and Badano, F. (1900). Sur les causes et sur le signification des oscillations du tonus auriculaire dans le coeur de l'*Emys europaea*. *Archs ital. Biol.* 34, 301–340.

Fano, G. and Fasola, G. (1894). Sur la contractilité pulmonaire. *Archs ital. Biol.* 21, 338.

Fedele, M. (1937). I nervi del tronco arterioso nel quadro della innervazione cardiaca nei rettili e il problema del "depressore" nei Vertebrati. *Mem. R. Acc. Naz. Lincei* Ser. 6, 6, 387–520.

Fillenz, M. (1970). Innervation of the cat spleen. *Proc. R. Soc.* B174, 459–468.

Fingerman, M. (1963). "The Control of Chromatophores." Macmillan, New York.

Fischer, E. (1936). The action of a single vagal volley on the heart of the eel and the turtle. *Am. J. Physiol.* 117, 596–608.

Fischer, J. G. (1852). Die Gehirnnerven der Saurier. *Abh. Naturw. Verein Hamburg* Abt. 2, 109–212.

Fox, A. M. and Musacchia, X. J. (1959). Notes on the pH of the digestive tract of *Chrysemys picta*. *Copeia* 1959(4), 337–339.

François-Franck, Ch.-A. (1908). Études critiques et expérimentales sur la mécanique respiratoire comparée des reptiles. I. Chéloniens (Tortue grecque). *Archs Zool. exp. gén.* 9, 31–187.

François-Franck, Ch.-A. (1909). Études critiques et expérimentales sur la mécanique respiratoire comparée des reptiles. II. Lacertiens fissilingues (Lézard ocellé). *Archs Zool. exp. gén.* 10, 547–615.

Fredericq, H. (1928). Chronaxie. Testing excitability by means of a time factor. *Physiol. Rev.* 8, 501–544.

Fredericq, H. (1951). A propos de l'action cardiaque "diphasique" de l'acetylcholine. *Archs int. Physiol.* 59, 430–433.

Fredericq, H. and Garrey, W. E. (1930). The action of the vagus nerves on the chronaxie of the auricles and the ventricle of the turtle heart; relationship to chronotropic changes. *Am. J. Physiol.* 94, 101–106.

Friedman, A. H. and Bhagat, B. (1962). The concentration of catecholamines in the turtle heart and vagal escape. *J. Pharm. Pharmac.* **14**, 764.

Furness, J. B. (1970). The excitatory input to a single smooth muscle cell. *Pflügers Arch. ges Physiol.* **314**, 1–13.

Furness, J. B. and Costa, M. (1973). The adrenergic innervation of the gastrointestinal tract. *Ergebn. Physiol.* **69**, 1–51.

Furness, J. B. and Iwayama, T. (1972). The arrangement and identification of axons innervating the vas deferens of the guinea-pig. *J. Anat.* **113**, 179–196.

Furness, J. B. and Moore, J. (1970). The adrenergic innervation of the cardio-vascular system of the lizard *Trachysaurus rugosus*. *Z. Zellforsch. mikrosk. Anat.* **108**, 150–176.

Gabe, M. (1970). The adrenal. *In* "Biology of the Reptilia." (C. Gans and T. S. Parsons, eds). Morphology C., Academic Press, London and New York, **3**, 263–318.

Gannon, B. J. (1971). A study of the dual innervation of teleost heart by a field stimulation technique. *Comp. gen. Pharmac.* **2**, 175–183.

Gannon, B. J. and Burnstock, G. (1969). Excitatory adrenergic innervation of the fish heart. *Comp. Biochem. Physiol.* **29**, 765–773.

Garrey, W. E. (1911a). Rhythmicity in the turtle's heart and comparison of action of the two vagus nerves. *Am. J. Physiol.* **28**, 330–351.

Garrey, W. E. (1911b). Dissociation of inhibitory nerve impulses from normal conduction in the heart by means of compression. *Am. J. Physiol.* **28**, 249–256.

Garrey, W. E. (1912). Effects of the vagi upon heart block and ventricular rate. *Am. J. Physiol.* **30**, 451–462.

Garrey, W. E. and Ashman, R. (1931). The excitability of the turtle ventricle during vagus stimulation. *Am. J. Physiol.* **98**, 102–109.

Garrey, W. E. and Chastain, L. L. (1937a). Inotropic and chronotropic effects of acetylcholine upon the chelonian heart. *Am. J. Physiol.* **119**, 315.

Garrey, W. E. and Chastain, L. L. (1937b). Acetylcholine action on the turtle heart. *Am. J. Physiol.* **119**, 314–315.

Gaskell, W. H. (1883). On the innervation of the heart, with especial reference to the heart of the tortoise. *J. Physiol., Lond.* **4**, 43–127.

Gaskell, W. H. (1884). On the augmentor (accelerator) nerves of the heart of cold-blooded animals. *J. Physiol., Lond.* **5**, 46–48.

Gaskell, W. H. (1886). On the structure, distribution and function of the nerves which innervate the visceral and vascular systems. *J. Physiol., Lond.* **7**, 1–80.

Gaskell, W. H. and Gadow, H. (1884). On the anatomy of the cardiac nerves in certain cold-blooded vertebrates. *J. Physiol., Lond.* **5**, 362–372.

Gaupp, E. (1888). Anatomische Untersuchungen über die Nervenversorgung der Mund- und Nasenhöhlendrüsen der Wirbelthiere. *Morph. Jb.* **14**, 436–489.

Gesell, R. (1915). The effects of change in auricular tone and amplitude of auricular systole on ventricular output. *Am. J. Physiol.* **38**, 404–413.

Gilson, A. S. (1932). Vagal depression of the turtle atrium. A study of the integration of effect of nerve impulses. *Am. J. Physiol.* **100**, 457–473.

Goodrich, E. S. (1915). The chorda tympani and middle ear in reptiles, birds and mammals. *Q . Jl. Microsc. Sci.* **61**, 137–160.

Guyénot, E. (1907). Action du pneumogastrique gauche sur le coeur de *Cistudo europae*. Action comparées des deux vagues. *C. r. Séanc. Soc. Biol.* **62**, 1032–1033.

Hadley, M. E. and Goldman, J. M. (1969). Physiological colour change in reptiles. *Am. Zool.* **9**, 489–504.

Hardman, H. F. and Reynolds, R. C. (1965). An effect of pH upon epinephrine inotrophic receptors in the turtle heart. *J. Pharmac. exp. Ther.* **149**, 219–224.

Harris, E. J. and Hutter, O. F. (1956). The action of acetylcholine on the movements of potassium ions in the sinus venosus of the heart. *J. Physiol., Lond.* **133**, 58–59P.

Hartman, F. A., Kilborn, L. G. and Lang, R. S. (1918). Vascular changes produced by adrenaline in vertebrates. *Endocrinology* **2**, 122–142.

Heath, J. E., Gasdorf, E. and Northcutt, R. G. (1968). The effect of thermal stimulation of anterior hypothalamus on blood pressure in the turtle. *Comp. Biochem. Physiol.* **26**, 509–518.

Heinebecker, P. (1931). The effect of fibers of specific types in the vagus and sympathetic nerves on the sinus and atrium of the turtle and frog heart. *Am. J. Physiol.* **98**, 220–229.

Heinekamp, W. J. R. (1919). The action of adrenaline on the heart. *J. Pharmac. exp. Ther.* **14**, 17–24.

Hiatt, E. P. and Garrey, W. E. (1943). Drug actions on the spontaneously beating turtle ventricle indicating lack of innervation. *Am. J. Physiol.* **138**, 758–762.

Hirt, A. (1921). Der Grenzstrang des Sympathicus bei einigen Sauriern. *Z. Anat. Entw-Gesch.* **62**, 536–551.

Hough, T. (1895). On the escape of the heart from vagus inhibition. *J. Physiol., Lond.* **18**, 161–200.

Hutter, O. F. and Trautwein, W. E. (1956). Vagal and sympathetic effects on the pacemaker fibres in the sinus venosus of the heart. *J. gen. Physiol.* **39**, 715–733.

Iijima, T. (1977). A histochemical study of the innervation of cerebral blood vessels in the turtle. *J. comp. Neurol.* **176**, 307–314.

Iijima, T., Wasano, T., Tagawa, T. and Ando, K. (1977). A histochemical study of the innervation of cerebral blood vessels in the snake. *Cell Tiss. Res.* **179**, 143–155.

Iske, M. S. (1929). A study of the iris mechanism of the alligator. *Anat. Rec.* **44**, 57–77.

Jackson, D. E. and Pelz, M. D. (1918). A contribution to the physiology and pharmacology of chelonian lungs. *J. Lab. clin. Med.* **3**, 344–347.

Jones, A. C. (1926). Innervation and nerve terminations of the reptilian lung. *J. comp. Neurol.* **40**, 371–388.

Juhasz-Nagy, A., Szentiványi, M., Szabo, M. and Vámosi, B. (1963). Coronary circulation of the tortoise heart. *Acta physiol. hung.* **23**, 33–48.

Kahle, H. (1913). Histologische Untersuchungen über Veränderungen der Magendrüsenzellen bei der Landschildkröte (*Testudo graeca*) während verschiedener Verdauungsstadien. *Pflügers Arch. ges. Physiol.* **152**, 129–167.

Keeton, R. W., Koch, F. C. and Luckhardt, A. B. (1920). Gastrin studies. III. The response of the stomach mucosa of various animals to gastrin bodies. *Am. J. Physiol.* **51**, 454–468.

Khalil, F. and Malek, S. R. A. (1952a). Studies on the nervous control of the heart of *Uromastyx aegyptia* (Forskål). *Physiologia comp. Oecol.* **2**, 386–390.

Khalil, F. and Malek, S. (1952b). The anatomy of the vago–sympathetic system of *Uromastyx aegyptia* (Forskål) and the significance of its union on the heart beat. *J. comp. Neurol.* **96**, 497–517.

Kirby, S. and Burnstock, G. (1969a). Comparative pharmacological studies of isolated spiral strips of large arteries from lower vertebrates. *Comp. Biochem. Physiol.* **28**, 307–319.

Kirby, S. and Burnstock, G. (1969b). Pharmacological studies of the cardiovascular system in the anaesthetized sleepy lizard (*Tiliqua rugosa*) and toad (*Bufo marinus*). *Comp. Biochem. Physiol.* **28**, 321–331.

Kirkepar, S. M., Prat, J. C., Puig, M. and Wakade, A. R. (1972). Modification of the evoked release of noradrenaline from the perfused cat spleen by various ions and agents. *J. Physiol., Lond.* **221**, 601–615.

Kleitman, N. (1922). Studies on the visceral sensory nervous system. XI. The action of cocaine and aconitine on the pulmonary vagus in the frog and in the turtle. *Am. J. Physiol.* **60**, 203–218.

Knowlton, F. P. (1942). An investigation of inhibition by direct stimulation of the turtle's heart. *Am. J. Physiol.* **135**, 446–451.

Kochva, E. (1978). Oral glands. *In* "Biology of the Reptilia." (C. Gans and K. A. Gans, eds). Physiology B. Academic Press, London and New York, **8**, 43–162.

Koppanyi, T. and Sun, K. H. (1926). Comparative studies on pupillary reaction in tetrapods. *Am. J. Physiol.* **78**, 364–367.

Korner, P. (1971). Integrative neural cardiovascular control. *Physiol. Rev.* **51**, 312–367.

Krogh, A. (1910). On the mechanism of the gas exchange in the lungs of the tortoise. *Skand. Arch. Physiol.* **23**, 200–216.

Kuntz, A. (1911). The development of the sympathetic nervous system in turtles. *Am. J. Anat.* **11**, 279–312.

Kuntz, A. (1953). "The Autonomic Nervous System."4th edn. Lea and Febiger. Philadelphia.

Lande, I. S. de la, Tyler, M. J. and Pridmore, B. J. (1962). Pharmacology of the heart of *Tiliqua* (= *Trachysaurus*) *rugosa* (the sleepy lizard). *Aust. J. exp. Biol. med. Sci.* **40**, 129–137.

Langley, J. N. (1898). On the union of the cranial autonomic (visceral) fibres with the nerve cells of the superior cervical ganglion. *J. Physiol., Lond.* **23**, 241–270.

Langley, J. N. (1921). "The Autonomic Nervous System." Part I. W. Heffer, Cambridge.

Langley, J. N. and Orbeli, L. A. (1911). Observations on the sympathetic and sacral autonomic system of the frog. *J. Physiol., Lond.* **41**, 450–482.

Larsell, O. (1919). Studies on the nervus terminalis: turtle. *J. comp. Neurol.* **30**, 423–443.

Lee, H. M. (1935). Distribution of vagus control of the turtle heart. *Am. J. Physiol.* **112**, 207–213.

Lehnartz, E. (1936). Potassium ions and vagus inhibition. *J. Physiol., Lond.* **86**, 37P.

Lenhossek, M. v. (1912). Das Ciliarganglion der Reptilien. *Arch. mikrosk. Anat. Entw-Mech.* **80**, 89–116.

Lenninger, S. and Ohlin, P. (1971). The flow of juice from the pancreatic gland of the cat in response to vagal stimulation. *J. Physiol., Lond.* **216**, 303–318.

Loomis, A. L., Harvey, E. N. and MacRae, C. (1930). The intrinsic rhythm of the turtle's heart studied with a new type of chronograph, together with the effects of some drugs and hormones. *J. gen. Physiol.* **14**, 105–115.

Luckhardt, A. B. and Carlson, A. J. (1921a). Studies on the visceral sensory nervous system. VIII. On the presence of vasomotor fibres in the vagus nerve to the pulmonary vessels of the amphibian and the reptilian lung. *Am. J. Physiol.* **56**, 72–112.

Luckhardt, A. B. and Carlson, A. J. (1921b). Studies on the visceral sensory nervous system. IV. The action of certain drugs on the lung motor mechanisms of the Reptilia (turtle, snake). *Am. J. Physiol.* **55**, 13–30.

McLean, J. R. and Burnstock, G. (1967a). Innervation of the lungs of the sleepy lizard (*Trachysaurus rugosus*). I. Fluorescent histochemistry of catecholamines. *Comp. Biochem. Physiol.* **22**, 809–813.

McLean, J. R. and Burnstock, G. (1967b). Innervation of the urinary bladder of the sleepy lizard (*Trachysaurus rugosus*). I. Fluorescent histochemical localization of catecholamines. *Comp. Biochem. Physiol.* **20**, 667–673.

Maar, V. (1902). Experimentelle Untersuchungen über den Einfluss des Nervus vagus und des Nervus sympathicus auf den Gaswechsel der Lungen. *Skand. Arch. Physiol.* 13, 269–336.

Majupuria, T.Ch. (1969). The functional anatomy and histophysiology of the copulatory organs of the spiny-tailed lizard, *Uromastyx hardwickii*, Gray. *Zool. Anz.* 183, 155–168.

Majupuria, T. Ch. (1970). The muscles, blood vessels and nerves of the cloaca and copulatory organs of *Uromastyx hardwickii*, Gray; together with the mode of eversion of the hemipenis, the copulation and the sexual dimorphism. *Zool. Anz.* 184, 48–60.

Martinson, J. (1965). Vagal relaxation of the stomach. Experimental reinvestigation of the concept of the transmission mechanism. *Acta physiol. scand.* 64, 453–462.

Marwitt, R., Pilar, G. and Weakly, J. N. (1971). Characterization of two ganglion cell populations in avian ciliary ganglion. *Brain Res.* 25, 317–334.

Meek, W. J. (1927). The question of cardiac tonus. *Physiol. Rev.* 7, 258–287.

Meek, W. J. and Eyster, J. A. E. (1912). The course of the wave of negativity which passes over the tortoise's heart during the normal beat. *Am. J. Physiol.* 31, 31–46.

Meester, W. D., Hardman, H. F. and Barboriak, J. J. (1965). Evaluation of various adrenergic blocking agents in isolated rabbit and turtle hearts. *J. Pharmac. exp. Ther.* 150, 34–40.

Melander, A., Nilsson, E. and Sundler, F. (1972). Sympathetic activation of thyroid secretion in mice. *Endocrinology* 90, 194–199.

Merrillees, N. C. R., Burnstock, G. and Holman, M. E. (1963). Correlation of fine structure and physiology of the innervation of smooth muscle in the guinea-pig vas deferens. *J. Cell Biol.* 19, 529–550.

Meyer, A. B. (1869). "Hemmungsnerven System des Herzens." A. Hirschwald, Berlin.

Meyer, H. (1893). Über einige pharmakologischen Reaktionen der Vogel– und Reptilieniris. *Arch. exp. Path. Pharmak.* 32, 101–123.

Miller, M. R. and Lagios, M. D. (1970). The pancreas. *In* "Biology of the Reptilia." (C. Gans and T. S. Parsons, eds). Morphology C. Academic Press, London and New York, 3, 319–346.

Mills, T. W. (1884). Some observations on the influence of the vagus and accelerators on the heart etc. of the turtle. *J. Physiol., Lond.* 5, 359–361.

Mills, T. W. (1885). The innervation of the heart of the slider terrapin (*Pseudemys rugosa*). *J. Physiol., Lond.* 6, 246–286.

Milsom, W. K., Langille, B. L. and Jones, D. R. (1977). Vagal control of pulmonary vascular resistance in the turtle *Chrysemys scripta. Can. J. Zool.* 55, 359–367.

Miscalencu, D. and Ionescu, M. D. (1972). Fine structure of dermal chromatophores in the *Natrix natrix* (L.) snake. *Anat. Anz.* 131, 470–475.

Morgareidge, K. R. and White, F. N. (1969a). Cutaneous vascular changes during heating and cooling in the Galapagos marine iguana. *Nature, Lond.* 223, 587–591.

Morgareidge, K. R. and White, F. N. (1969b). Nature of heat induced cutaneous vascular response in *Iguana iguana. Physiologist* 12, 306.

Naccarati, S. (1922). Contribution to the morphologic study of the thyroid gland in *Emys europaea. J. Morph.* 36, 279–297.

Noon, L. (1900). Some observations on the nerve cell connections of the efferent vagus fibres in the tortoise. *J. Physiol., Lond.* 26, 5–7P.

Oelrich, T. M. (1956). The anatomy of the head of *Ctenosaura pectinata* (Iguanidae). *Misc. Publ. Mus. Zool. Univ. Mich.* (94), 1–122.

Ogushi, K. (1913a). Anatomische Studien an der japanischen dreikralligen Lippenschildkröte (*Trionyx japonicus*). II. Mitteilung. Muskel und peripheres Nervensystem. *Morph. Jb.* 46, 299–562.

Ogushi, K. (1913b). Zur Anatomie der Hirnnerven und des Kopfsympathicus von *Trionya japonicus* nebst einigen kritischen Bemerkungen. *Morph. Jb.* **45**, 441–480.

Oinuma, S. (1910). Beiträge zur Physiologie der autonom innervierten Muskulatur. III. Über den Einfluss des Vagus und des Sympathicus auf die Tonusschwankungen der Vorhöfe des Schildkrötenherzens. *Pflügers Arch. ges. Physiol.* **133**, 500–518.

Okinaka, S., Nakao, K., Ikeda, M. and Shizume, K. (1951). The cardioaccelerator fibres in the vagus nerve. *Tohoku J. exp. Med.* **54**, 393–398.

Okita, S. (1971). The fine structure of the ventricular muscle cells of the soft-shelled turtle heart (*Amyda*) with special reference to the sarcoplasmic reticulum. *J. Electr. Micr.* **20**, 107–119.

Osawa, G. (1898). Beiträge zur Anatomie der *Hatteria punctata*. *Arch. mikrosk. Anat. EntwMech.* **51**, 481–691.

Ošťádal, B. and Schiebler, T. H. (1971). Die terminale Strombahn im Herzen der Schildkröte (*Testudo hermanni*). *Z. Anat. EntwGesch.* **134**, 111–116.

Owman, Ch. and Sjöstrand, N. O. (1965). Short adrenergic neurons and catecholamine containing cells in vas deferens and accessory male genital glands of different mammals. *Z. Zellforsch. mikrosk. Anat.* **66**, 300–320.

Parker, G. H. (1938). The colour changes in lizards, particularly in *Phrynosoma*. *J. exp. Biol.* **15**, 48–73.

Parker, G. H. (1948). "Animal Colour Changes and their Neurohumours." Cambridge University Press, London and New York.

Paton, W. D. M. and Thompson, J. W. (1970). The roles of striated and smooth muscle in the movement of the cat's nictitating membrane. *J. Physiol., Lond.* **206**. 731–746.

Prevost, J. L. and Saloz, J. (1909). Contribution à l'étude des muscles bronchiques. *Archs int. Physiol.* **8**, 327–355.

Read, J. and Burnstock, G. (1968). Comparative histochemical studies of adrenergic nerves in the enteric plexuses of vertebrate large intestine. *Comp. Biochem. Physiol.* **27**, 505–517.

Read, J. and Burnstock, G. (1969). Adrenergic innervation of the gut musculature in vertebrates. *Histochemie* **17**, 263–272.

Reger, J. F. (1966). The fine structure of the iridial constrictor pupillae muscle of *Alligator mississippiensis*. *Anat. Rec.* **155**, 197–216.

Reibnitz, D. v. (1923). Einiges über die Entwicklung der Fasern in den Rami communicantes des Truncus sympathicus von *Lacerta agilis*. *Z. Anat. EntwGesch.* **69**, 320–328.

Reite, O. B. (1970). The evolution of vascular smooth muscle responses to histamine and 5-hydroxytryptamine. III. Manifestation of dual actions of either amine in reptiles. *Acta physiol. scand.* **78**, 213–231.

Richardson, K. C. (1962). The fine structure of autonomic nerve endings in smooth muscle of the rat vas deferens. *J. Anat.* **96**, 427–442.

Robb, J. S. (1953). Specialized (conducting) tissue in the turtle heart. *Am. J. Physiol.* **172**, 7–13.

Rodbard, S., Samson, F. and Ferguson, D. (1950). Thermo-sensitivity of the turtle brain as manifest by blood pressure changes. *Am. J. Physiol.* **160**, 402–408.

Roddie, I. C. (1962). The transmembrane potential changes associated with smooth muscle activity in turtle arteries and veins. *J. Physiol., Lond.* **163**, 138–150.

Rogers, F. T. and Bercovitz, Z. (1921). A note on the role of the intrinsic plexuses in determining the effects on gastric motility of vagal stimulation. *Am. J. Physiol.* **56**, 257–263.

Rosenzweig, E. (1903). Beiträge zur Kenntniss der Tonusschwankungen des Herzens von *Emys europaea*. *Arch. Physiol.* suppl. 192–208.

Santamaria-Arnaiz, P. (1959). Le ganglion ciliare chez *Chalcides ocellatus. Morph. Jb.* **101**, 263–278.

Schnizer, W., Hoang, N.-D. and Brecht, K. (1968). Transmitter in der Froschlunge. *Pflügers Arch. ges. Physiol.* **304**, 271–283.

Shaner, R. F. (1923). On the smooth muscle in the turtle's heart. *Anat. Rec.* **25**, 71–75.

Shiino, K. (1914). Studien zur Kenntnis des Wirbeltierkopfes. I. Das Chondrocranium von *Crocodilus* mit Berücksichtigung der Gehirnnerven und der Kopfgefässe. *Anat. Hefte* **50**, 253–382.

Sjöstrand, N. O. (1965). High noradrenaline content in the vas deferens of the cock and the tortoise. *Experientia* **21**, 96.

Skoczylas, R. (1970). Salivary and gastric juice secretion in the grass snake *Natrix natrix* L. *Comp. Biochem. Physiol.* **35**, 885–903.

Smit, H. (1968). Gastric secretion in the lower vertebrates and birds. *In* "Handbook of Physiology." Section 6: Alimentary Canal. American Physiological Society, Washington, D.C., **5**, 2791–2805.

Smith, M. and Bellairs, A. d'A. (1947). The head glands of snakes, with remarks upon the evolution of the parotid gland and teeth of the opisthoglypha. *J. Linn. Soc.* (Zool.) **41**, 351–368.

Smith, D. G. and Macintyre, D. H. (1977). The vagal innervation of the visceral and vascular smooth muscle of the lungs of two reptiles: a colubrid snake and a caiman. *Proc. Can. Soc. Zool.* May, 1977.

Sneddon, J. D., Smythe, A., Satchell, D. and Burnstock, G. (1973). An investigation of the identity of the transmitter substance released by non-adrenergic non-cholinergic excitatory nerves supplying the small intestine of some lower vertebrates. *Comp. gen. Pharmac.* **4**, 53–60.

Snyder, C. D. and Light, F. W. Jr. (1928). Initial and recovery heat production in smooth muscle based upon experiments on a urinary bladder-nerve preparation from terrapin. *Am. J. Physiol.* **86**, 399–422.

Soliman, M. A. (1964). Die Kopfnerven der Schildkröten. *Z. wiss. Zool.* **169**, 216–312.

Spanner, R. (1928). Der Bauchsympathicus der Blindschleiche und seine Beziehungen zur Innervation der Niere. *Z. Zellforsch. mikrosk. Anat.* **8**, 740–764.

Spray, D. S. and May, M. L. (1972). Heating and cooling rates in four species of turtles. *Comp. Biochem. Physiol.* **41A**, 507–522.

Staley, F. H. (1925). A study of the gastric glands of *Alligator mississippiensis. J. Morph.* **40**, 169–189.

Stewart, G. N. (1892). The influence of temperature and of endocardiac pressure on the heart and particularly on the action of the vagus and cardiac sympathetic nerves. *J. Physiol., Lond.* **13**, 59–164.

Stewart, G. N. (1909). The influence of the temperature of the heart on the activity of the vagus in the tortoise. *Am. J. Physiol.* **24**, 341–344.

Stiemens, M. J. (1934). Anatomische Untersuchungen über die vago-sympathische Innervation der Baucheingeweide bei den Vertebraten. *Verh. k. Akad. Wet. Amsterdam.* Sect. 2, **33**, (2), 1–356.

Sumbal, J. J. (1924). The action of pituitary extracts, acetylcholine and histamine upon the coronary arteries of the tortoise. *Heart* **11**, 285–297.

Terni, T. (1931). Il simpatico cervicale degli Amnioti (Ricerche di morfologia comparata). *Z. Anat. EntwGesch.* **96**, 289–426.

Tiegs, O. W. (1932). A study by denervation methods of the innervation of the muscles of a lizard (*Egernia*). *J. Anat.* **66**, 300–322.

Underwood, G. (1970). The Eye. *In* "Biology of the Reptilia" (C. Gans and T. S. Parsons, eds). Morphology B. Academic Press, London and New York, **2**, 1–97.

Van Harn, G. L., Emaus, T. L. and Meester, W. D. (1973). Adrenergic receptors in turtle ventricle myocardium. *Europ. J. Pharmac.* **24**, 145–150.

Veach, H. O. (1925). Studies on the innervation of smooth muscle. I. Vagus effects on the lower end of the oesophagus, cardia and stomach of the cat, and the stomach and lung of the turtle in relation to Wedensky inhibition. *Am. J. Physiol.* **71**, 229–264.

Waring, H. (1963). "Colour Change Mechanisms of Cold-blooded Vertebrates." Academic Press, London and New York.

Watari, N. (1968). Fine structure of nervous elements in the pancreas of some vertebrates. *Z. Zellforsch. mikrosk. Anat.* **85**, 291–314.

Watkinson, G. B. (1906). The cranial nerves of *Varanus bivittatus. Morph. Jb.* **35**, 450–472.

Weathers, W. W., Baker, L. A. and White, F. N. (1970). Regional redistribution of blood flow in lizards during heating. *Physiologist.* **13**, 336.

Weathers, W. W. and Morgareidge, K. R. (1971). Cutaneous vascular responses to temperature change in the spiny-tailed iguana *Ctenosaura hemilopha. Copeia* **1971**(3), 548–551.

Weathers, W. W. and White, F. N. (1971). Physiological thermoregulation in turtles. *Am. J. Physiol.* **221**, 704–710.

Weiss, G. K. and Priola, D. V. (1972). Brainstem sites for activation of vagal cardioaccelerator fibres in the dog. *Am. J. Physiol.* **223**, 300–304.

West, G. S. (1898). The histology of the salivary, buccal and Harderian glands of the Colubridae, with notes on their tooth succession. *J. Linn. Soc. (Zool.)* **26**, 517–526.

White, F. N. (1968). Functional anatomy of the heart of reptiles. *Am. Zool.* **8**, 211–219.

White, F. N. (1969). Redistribution of cardiac output in the diving alligator. *Copeia* **1969** (3), 567–570.

White, F. N. (1976). Circulation. *In* "Biology of the Reptilia." (C. Gans and W. R. Dawson, eds). Physiology A. Academic Press, London and New York, **5**, 275–334.

White, F. N. and Ross, G. (1966). Circulatory changes during experimental diving in the turtle. *Am. J. Physiol.* **211**, 15–18.

Widdicombe, J. G. (1963). Regulation of tracheobronchial smooth muscle. *Physiol. Rev.* **43**, 1–37.

Willard, W. A. (1915). The cranial nerves of *Anolis carolinensis. Bull. Mus. comp. Zool. Harv.* **49**, 15–116.

Woods, S. C. (1972). Conditioned hypoglycemia: effect of vagotomy and pharmacological blockade. *Am. J. Physiol.* **223**, 1424–1427.

Wright, R. D., Florey, H. W. and Sanders, A. G. (1957). Observations on the gastric mucosa of Reptilia. *Q . Jl exp. Physiol.* **42**, 1–14.

Yamauchi, A. (1969). Innervation of the vertebrate heart as studied with the electron microscope. *Arch. histol. japon.* **31**, 83–117.

Yamauchi, A. and Chiba, T. (1973). Adrenergic and cholinergic innervation of the turtle heart ventricle. *Z. Zellforsch. mikrosk. Anat.* **143**, 485–493.

CHAPTER 2

Intrinsic Organization of the Spinal Cord

A. KUSUMA, H. J. ten DONKELAAR and R. NIEUWENHUYS

Department of Anatomy and Embryology,
University of Nijmegen,
Nijmegen, The Netherlands

I. Introduction

The organizations of the spinal cord and brainstem of reptiles are reviewed in this and the following two chapters. The present chapter emphasizes the gross anatomy and intrinsic organization of the spinal cord. The gross morphology of the cord is considered, followed by a discussion of the organization of the gray matter and a survey of our current knowledge of the terminations of dorsal root fibers, descending systems from the brainstem and propriospinal systems. Differences in spinal organization among reptiles with different locomotor patterns are emphasized and the spinal cords of reptiles are compared with those of other amniotes. Chapter 3 deals more extensively with the organization of systems which descend from the brainstem to the spinal cord. Information available on lizards is stressed because species of this group have been the most extensively studied. Chapter 4 includes a discussion of systems which originate in the spinal cord and terminate in the brainstem.

We still lack a systematic comparative analysis of the cell and fiber patterns of reptilian spinal cords; some remarks on this topic occur in Ariëns Kappers *et al.* (1936), and in a review on comparative aspects of the spinal cord (Nieuwenhuys, 1964).

The material studied includes transversely sectioned series of the spinal cords of a lizard, *Tupinambis nigropunctatus* (suborder: Sauria; order: Squamata), a turtle, *Testudo hermanni* (order: Testudines) and a snake, *Python reticulatus* (suborder: Serpentes, order: Squamata). One or more series of each of the three species studied were stained with cresylechtviolet for the analysis of cell patterns. The fibers were studied in series stained according to Häggqvist's (1936) modification of the Alzeheimer Mann methyl blue–eosin stain. This technique stains axons blue and the myelin sheaths of the individual fibers red. In Häggqvist material many bundles and tracts are clearly set off against their environment by their characteristic fiber pattern (*see* van Beusekom, 1955; van den Akker, 1970; Verhaart, 1970; ten Donkelaar and Nieuwenhuys, Chapter 4 of this volume). For instance, the descending fiber systems to the cord are conspicuous in the brainstem as well as the spinal cord because of their numerous coarse fibers. In addition, material stained according to Klüver and Barrera (1953) has been used.

II. Gross Morphology

A. GENERAL

Reptiles differ profoundly in the shape and development of their trunks, tails and extremities, and the gross structure of the spinal cord clearly reflect this (Fig. 1). In forms that lack extremities, as do snakes and limbless lizards, the cord lacks cervical and lumbar enlargements. However, such enlargements are obvious in crocodilians, turtles, and other lizards; thus, the spinal cord shows cervical and lumbar intumescences related to the development of limbs. *Tupinambis nigropunctatus*, and other reptiles with strongly developed posterior extremities, show lumbar enlargements. It is interesting to note that the volume of lumbar intumescence of some dinosaurs with large posterior extremities exceeded the volume of the endocranial cavity.

The spinal cord extends throughout the entire length of the vertebral canal in reptiles, nearly reaching the end of the tail (Ariëns Kappers *et al.*, 1936; Nieuwenhuys, 1964; Kuhlenbeck, 1975). The relative length of the spinal cord may correlate with the retention of metameres in reptilian tails (Kuhlenbeck, 1975).

B. REGIONAL VARIATIONS

There are no standardized subdivisions of the reptilian spinal cord similar to those in mammals. This may reflect the greater morphological uniformity of reptilian vertebrae. The following comments on the reptilian vertebral column are based largely on the discussion of Hoffstetter and Gasc (1969).

Turtles generally have 18 presacral vertebrae. Despite the lack of a sternum, it is easy to distinguish a cervical region consisting of eight movable elements, as well as a trunk region. Some turtles may show nine cervical vertebrae as individual variation. The ten dorsal vertebral bodies of the trunk are ankylosed and their rib remnants are connected to the dermal carapace. There are two sacral vertebrae and about 16 caudals.

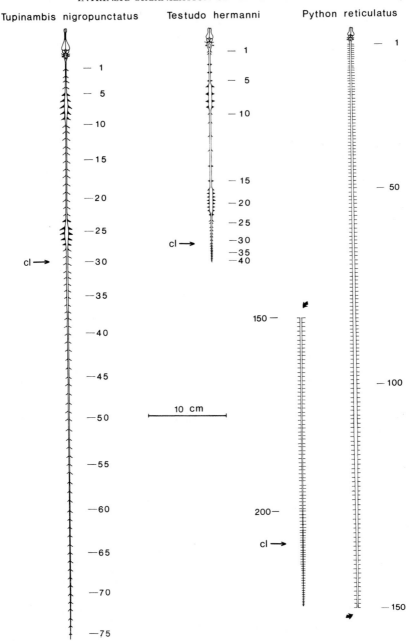

F<small>IG</small>. 1. Schematic representation of the central nervous system in *Tupinambis nigropunctatus*, *Testudo hermanni* and *Python reticulatus*, showing, in particular, the number and distribution of spinal segments. cl, Level of cloaca.

In lizards, the number of presacral (or precloacal) vertebrae varies widely. Only two families, which contain species frequently used in neuroanatomical research, are mentioned here: the Iguanidae (e.g. *Iguana iguana*) and the Teiidae (e.g. *Tupinambis nigropunctatus*). In iguanids, the number of presacral vertebrae varies from 22–28 (with 24 as modal value). In teiids, 24–27 (with 26 as modal value) precloacal vertebrae are present. Since Cuvier, and especially after the work of Stannius (1849), cervical vertebrae have been defined as those preceding that bearing the first rib united to the sternum. All other definitions offer too many exceptions or contradictions to be adopted (Hoffstetter and Gasc, 1969). Teiids have but one true lumbar vertebra, i.e. a caudal presacral vertebra which lacks ribs, as well as two sacral vertebrae that support the pelvis. *Tupinambis nigropunctatus* has some 50 caudal vertebrae.

The precloacal region of snakes is relatively uniform. The absence of a pectoral girdle makes it impossible to define a sharp boundary between the cervical and trunk regions. Snakes have high numbers of vertebrae. Total numbers range from 160 to 400, and 120 to 320 of these are precloacal. *Python reticulatus*, here discussed, has 200 to 220 precloacal and about 30 caudal vertebrae.

Given these variations in the number and composition of vertebrae, a nomenclature for the segments of the spinal cord, as is customary in mammals, seems inappropriate at this time. Therefore, we have numbered the spinal segments sequentially from the first cervical. In *Tupinambis nigropunctatus*, the roots of the 6th to 9th segments enter the brachial plexus, whereas the roots of the 24th to 28th segments enter the lumbosacral plexus. The brachial plexus of the turtle *Testudo hermanni* is made up of spinal roots arising from the 7th to 10th segments; spinal roots of the 19th to 22nd segments enter the lumbosacral plexus.

III. Organization of the Spinal Gray

A. GENERAL

Several longitudinal furrows are seen on the surface of the cord (Fig. 2). A deep, anterior median fissure and a shallow posterior median sulcus are obvious on the spinal cords of all the reptiles studied. Anterolateral and posterolateral grooves are not obvious. Especially in the lizard *Tupinambis nigropunctatus* and in the snake *Python reticulatus*, a shallow groove is present on the lateral surface of the cord in the area where the so-called marginal nuclei (Fig. 2 and Section IIIC) are situated. The spinal cord is closely attached to its meninges at this region.

A cross-section of the cord shows a central, four-horned area of gray matter surrounded by a much larger area of white matter. The boundary between gray and white matter, although more distinct than in fish, is less definite than in birds and mammals (Nieuwenhuys, 1964). The gray matter of the reptilian cord shows a clear division into ventral and dorsal horns. The dorsal horns separate off a portion of the white matter, the so-called dorsal funiculus. The remainder of the white matter can be subdivided into lateral and ventral funiculi, using the intraspinal trajectory of the ventral root fibers as a landmark. As reptilian spinal gray lacks an intermediate lateral wall, it is inappropriate to use the mammalian categories of postero-lateral and anterolateral regions for the lateral funiculus.

B. Frontal Accumulation

Figure 2 illustrates diagrammatic transverse sections through representative segments of the spinal cord, specifically through the cervical and lumbosacral enlargements. These are supplemented by a midthoracic section, a high cervical section, and a section on the caudal level for the lizard *Tupinambis nigropunctatus* and the turtle *Testudo hermanni*. For the snake *Python reticulatus*, the 12th, the 56th, the 110th (about the middle of this animal), the 170th and the 223rd spinal segments are illustrated. The size and shape of the spinal cord and the relative proportion of the gray and white matter vary greatly. Several factors appear to be responsible for these differences (Ranson and Clark, 1959). The variation in size of the nerve roots at the various levels of the spinal cord may be significant. At levels where great numbers of nerve fibers enter the spinal cord, particularly in the intumescences, they cause a clear increase in the size of the cord. All levels of the spinal cord are connected to the brainstem by bundles of long ascending as well as descending fibers. The long ascending fibers increase in number rostrally and, therefore, might cause an increase in the cross-sectional area of the white matter. This phenomenon is known as *frontal accumulation* (Ariëns Kappers *et al.*, 1936). A third factor responsible for differences in size of the spinal cord might be the influence of propriospinal fibers. The descending pathways conceivably behave in a comparable way by showing a gradual decrease in the rostrocaudal direction. However, recent physiological experiments reveal that axons of the vestibulospinal (Abzug *et al.*, 1973, 1974), reticulospinal (Peterson *et al.*, 1975) and corticospinal tracts (Shinoda *et al.*, 1976) show a considerable *branching* during their spinal course in cats. In reptiles, there is no direct evidence for collateral branching of descending fibers. However, the observation (ten Donkelaar, 1976a) that

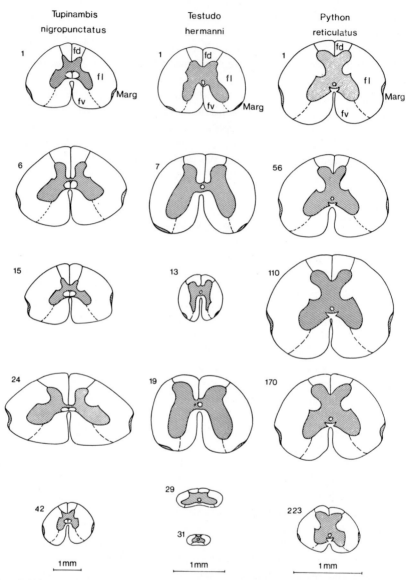

FIG. 2. Diagrammatic representation of transverse sections through representative levels of the spinal cord of *Tupinambis nigropunctatus*, *Testudo hermanni* and *Python reticulatus* showing the variations in the size of the cord. fd, Dorsal funiculus; fl, lateral funiculus; fv, ventral funiculus; Marg, marginal nucleus. The numbers refer to the postcranial vertebrae corresponding to the section.

retrograde cell changes in the brainstem reticular formation can be observed following cervical lesions, whereas such cell changes are lacking following lumbar lesions, renders it likely that collateral branching of descending pathways also occurs in reptiles.

In order to obtain more precise information on frontal accumulation in reptiles, the technique used in the ostrich *Struthio camelus* (Streeter, 1904), and in various mammals (the opossum *Didelphis virginiana*, Voris, 1928; man, Donaldson and Davis, 1903), has been employed. Two sections were selected from the middle of each segment in the three reptiles studied. Outline drawings of the sections were prepared with a Bausch and Lomb microprojector, and the gray matter, the dorsal funiculus, the ventral funiculus and the lateral funiculus indicated. The cross-sectional areas of the entire section, the gray matter and the dorsal, ventral and lateral funiculi were determined planimetrically. The areas of the ventral and lateral funiculi were combined. Data from two sections were then averaged and plotted for *Tupinambis nigropunctatus* (Fig. 3a), *Python reticulatus* (Fig. 3b) and *Testudo hermanni* (Fig. 4).

The following conclusions can be drawn:

1. Variations in size of the spinal cord are mainly due to changes in the ventral and lateral funiculi. These funiculi form by far the greatest area at all levels.

2. The curves which represent the cross-sectional areas of the gray matter and the dorsal funiculi are very similar although the former shows a greater increase in the enlargements.

3. In *Tupinambis* and *Testudo* the area of the gray matter is remarkably constant between the intumescences.

4. In both the cervical and lumbosacral enlargements of *Tupinambis* and *Testudo*, the increase in area of the ventral and lateral funiculi is greater than that of the gray matter and dorsal funiculus. This is undoubtedly due to the large number of propriospinal fibers in the intumescences.

5. The dorsal funiculi are the least variable. The dorsal funiculus curve shows an abrupt rise near the entrance of the large dorsal roots from the extremities. These data suggest that the course of the dorsal root fibers is a short one and that only a small proportion of these fibers reaches the brainstem via the dorsal funiculus.

6. *Testudo* definitely shows frontal accumulation in the dorsal funiculus (Fig. 4). However, frontal accumulation could not be demonstrated in the other reptiles studied (Fig. 3). Goldby and Robinson (1962) were also unable to show frontal accumulation in the lizard *Lacerta viridis*. They supposed that variations in the number of the propriospinal

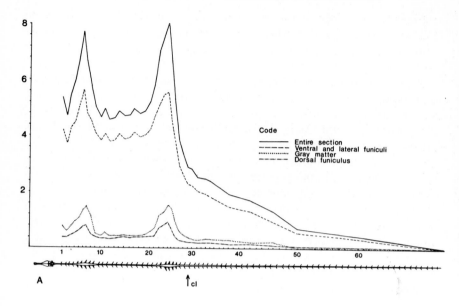

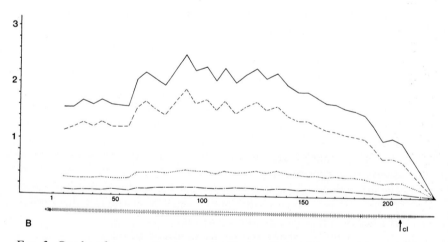

Fig. 3. Graphs of cross-sectional areas in *Tupinambis nigropunctatus* (A) and *Python reticulatus* (B). The spinal segments are marked to scale on the abscissa, whereas the cross-sectional areas are represented on the ordinates in square millimeters. cl, level of cloaca.

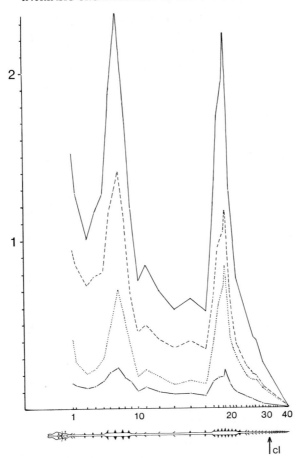

FIG. 4. Graphic chart showing the cross-sectional areas in *Testudo hermanni*. For code see Fig. 3. cl, level of cloaca.

fibers present at different levels mask the effects of additions of a few, long ascending fibers from each segment.

7. An even more pronounced frontal accumulation occurs in the remainder of the white matter in *Testudo*. It seems likely that frontal accumulation is due to long ascending and descending fibers.

8. *Python* (Fig. 3b) shows an enlargement of the spinal cord, which is related to the well-developed main part of its trunk. This intumescence may be designated as the *intumescentia trunci*. It is most pronounced in the curve of the ventral and lateral funiculi, but the gray

matter also shows a clear increase in cross-sectional area. The curves are flat in the "neck" area. Therefore, the trunk enlargement of *Python* is not due to an increase in pathways connecting the spinal cord with the brainstem, but to a profuse development of propriospinal fibers.

Finally, the relative cross-sectional area of ventral and lateral funiculi have been plotted along the length of the animal (Fig. 5). The changes here

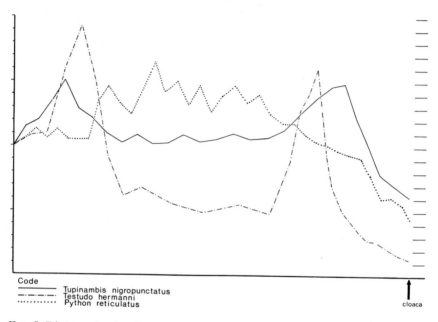

Code
——————— Tupinambis nigropunctatus
—·—·—·— Testudo hermanni
············ Python reticulatus

cloaca

FIG. 5. Diagram showing the cross-sectional areas of the ventral and lateral funiculi in *Tupinambis nigropunctatus, Testudo hermanni* and *Python reticulatus*. The intumescentia trunci in *Python reticulatus* is situated between the enlargements in the other reptiles studied. The body lengths have been standardized for purposes of comparison.

seen reflect those of the cross-sectional area of the cord as a whole. The graph documents that the trunk intumescence of *Python reticulatus* falls between the enlargements associated with extremities in other reptiles.

C. LAMINAR ORGANIZATION OF GRAY MATTER

1. *General*

The gray matter of the reptilian cord shows a clear division into dorsal and ventral horns. The dorsal horn has a dorsal root input; the ventral horn contains the motoneurons. A large intermediate zone remains between dorsal and ventral horns; it consists mainly of interneurons.

Subdivisions of the reptilian spinal gray have been provisional so far (Ariëns Kappers et al., 1936; Nieuwenhuys, 1964; ten Donkelaar, 1976b). A more detailed analysis of the gray matter is necessary for experimental neuroanatomical and physiological studies of the reptilian spinal cord. The most widely adopted scheme for subdivision of the spinal gray stems from extensive cytoarchitectonic studies in cat (Rexed, 1952, 1954, 1964). Figure 6 shows the classical subdivision of the gray matter as well as Rexed's

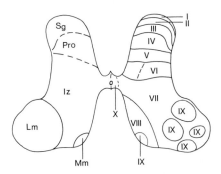

FIG. 6. Diagram showing the classical subdivision of the gray matter at the left as well as Rexed's parcellation of the cat spinal gray into ten laminae at the right. Iz, intermediate zone; Lm, lateral column of motoneurons; Mm, medial column of motoneurons; Pro, nucleus proprius; Sg, substantia gelatinosa. (Redrawn from Rexed, 1954.)

parcellation of the spinal gray into ten laminae. The same principles of *laminar organization* are considered to apply to the spinal cord of "lower" (e.g. opossum: Martin and Fischer, 1968) and "higher" mammals (Rexed, 1964). Recently, Rexed's subdivision has also been applied to the cords of nonmammalian vertebrates, namely to the pigeon *Columba livia* (Leonard and Cohen, 1975a) and the lizard *Tupinambis nigropunctatus* (Cruce, 1975, Chapter 3 of this volume).

The subdivision presented here clearly reflects the influence of Rexed's laminar approach, especially as regards the dorsal horn. The neutral term "area" has been used, as not all cell groups are distinguishable as laminae. We have followed Rexed's approach and numbering convention as closely as possible to facilitate comparison with Rexed's parcellation and to avoid confusion by introducing a different subdivision for the reptilian spinal gray. The delineation of cell groups has been performed with the help of the usual cytoarchitectonic criteria (Cruce and Nieuwenhuys, 1974): (1) the size and shape of the somata, (2) the disposition of the Nissl substance, and (3) the density and the pattern of the cell arrangement. The cells in the spinal cord of the three reptiles studied show considerable differences in size, ranging from 4 to 60 μm. For convenience of description we have subdivided these cells into three categories: large (15 to 60 μm), medium-sized (10 to 15 μm) and small (4 to 10 μm). The following description is based primarily on Nissl-stained serial sections (Fig. 7), but some Klüver and Barrera (1953) material was available. The various areas of the spinal gray will now be reviewed for *Tupinambis nigropunctatus*. Unless indicated otherwise, the description also applies to *Testudo hermanni* and *Python reticulatus*. In order to elucidate the description, diagrams of the gray matter of representative levels of the spinal cord of the three reptiles studied are presented in Figs 8 and 9.

2. Description of Laminae

In the dorsal horn of *Tupinambis* (Fig. 8) and *Python* (Figs 7, 9), four more or less distinct cellular areas can be recognized. The first three show a distinct laminar arrangement. In *Testudo*, the subdivision of the dorsal horn is less clear than in the other reptiles studied.

Area I consists of a single layer of cells which caps the dorsal horn. This area extends ventrally along the medial and lateral aspects of the dorsal horn, without, however, reaching the base. Most of the neurons of this area are small and round or fusiform in shape. They have relatively large, clear nuclei with indistinct nucleoli. Their cytoplasm is restricted to a narrow perinuclear region with the Nissl substance concentrated close to the nuclear membrane. This area cannot be delineated in *Testudo*.

Area II is situated directly ventral to area I and follows its contours. It consists of small, rather loosely arranged cells. Most are spindle shaped with round, clear nuclei. Their Nissl substance is sparse and surrounds the large clear nucleus. In *Testudo*, areas I and II are not distinguished as separate entities, and therefore have been taken together. Areas I–II contain medium-sized cells in this turtle; in other reptiles studied, areas I and II are occupied by small cells.

Area III is an almost cell-free zone, lying ventral to area II in all reptiles studied.

Area IV constitutes the main part of the dorsal horn. Its ventral boundary is quite distinct as the cells of areas V–VI show a characteristic arrangement which will be described below. Area IV is a zone of very tightly packed, spindleshaped, medium-sized cells. The neurons have round clear nuclei with dark nucleoli. In most rostral (2nd upwards) and caudal (28th downwards) segments, area IV extends across the midline dorsal to area X. In *Python*, area IV extends across the midline at all levels of the spinal cord and constitutes the wide dorsal gray commissure, characteristic for the

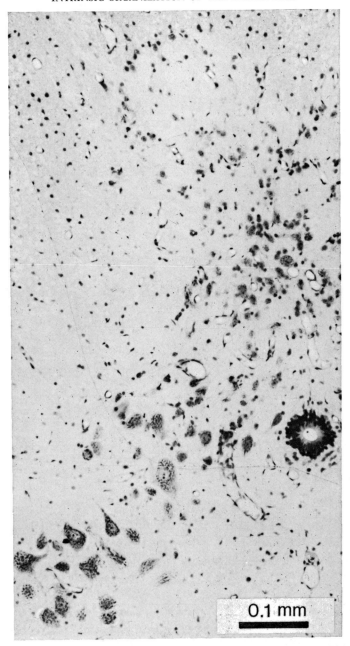

FIG. 7. Transverse section showing the arrangement of the spinal gray in the 56th segment of the snake *Python reticulatus*. Nissl stain.

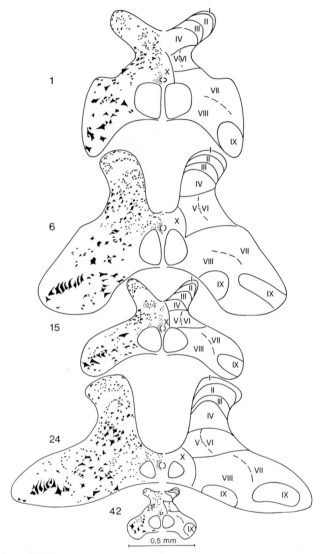

Fig. 8. Camera lucida drawings representing transverse sections through the spinal gray of *Tupinambis nigropunctatus*. At the left the cell picture, at the right the cytoarchitectonic regions outlined.

cord in this animal. In *Testudo*, the border between areas IV and V–VI is rather indistinct. Cell size and packing density gradually change here.

The remaining part of the spinal gray, the base of dorsal horn, the intermediate gray zone and the motoneurons in the ventral horn, do not show a clear laminar arrangement. The motoneuron groups (area IX) and a central

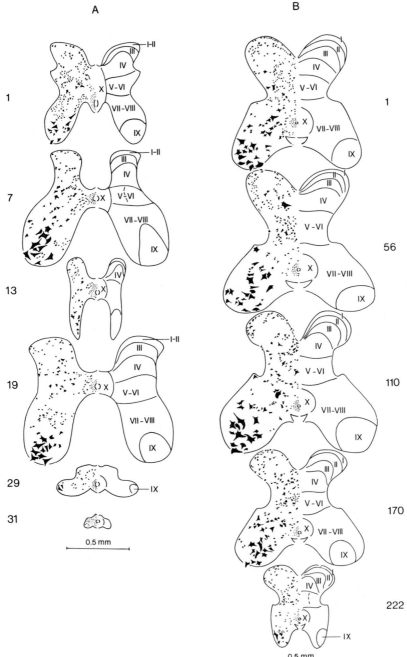

FIG. 9. Camera lucida drawings representing transverse sections through the spinal gray of *Testudo hermanni* (A) and *Python reticulatus* (B). At the left the cell picture, at the right the cytoarchitectonic regions outlined.

zone (area X) form distinct areas. The large, remaining region can be subdivided into dorsal and ventral zones. The dorsal part consists of the base of the dorsal horn and the adjacent part of the intermediate zone. The ventral zone contains the main part of the intermediate zone. Rexed has subdivided this large region into four laminae (V–VIII). Comparison with mammals renders it likely that the dorsal part of the reptilian spinal gray mentioned above corresponds to Rexed's laminae V and VI, whereas the so-called ventral zone resembles Rexed's laminae VII and VIII. Therefore these two regions have been designated as areas V–VI and areas VII–VIII in the present study. Motoneurons are absent in the thoracic region of *Testudo* due to the lack of trunk musculature. Therefore, the ventral horns are extremely narrow. The cells occurring in the ventral horn represent commissural cells, various interneurons, and possibly, cells of origin for preganglionic fibers (Ariëns Kappers *et al.*, 1936).

Areas V–VI form a relatively wide zone which can be clearly distinguished from area IV due to distinct differences in cytoarchitecture and fiber pattern. This region is bounded on the medial side by the central area X, and ventrally by areas VII–VIII. Areas V–VI can be divided into lateral and medial zones. The lateral zone contains large polygonal cells (15–30 µm) with round to spindleshaped nuclei and clear, deeply stained nucleoli. They possess abundant Nissl substance scattered throughout the cytoplasm. The lateral zone is traversed by bundles of entering dorsal root fibers which create a reticulated appearance. The medial zone contains scattered, small lightly staining cells (6–10 µm). Their Nissl substance has a rough granular aspect, spreading throughout the cytoplasm without any characteristic arrangement. In *Python*, areas V–VI may be subdivided into lateral and medial zones at most levels. In *Testudo*, however, these two zones can only be recognized in the cervical intumescence.

Areas VII–VIII contain numerous large polygonal cells (20–30 µm) with round and distinct nucleoli. These large neurons are found particularly in the medial ventral horn. The Nissl substance is fine granular, and evenly scattered throughout the cytoplasm. Round to oval, small cells with round nuclei and distinct nucleoli occur. Their Nissl substance is situated at the periphery of the cytoplasm. In *Tupinambis*, at least in the enlargements, the area in question can be divided into a dorsolateral (area VII) and a ventromedial (area VIII) zone. This distinction is based on the heterogeneous cell population in the ventromedial part of area VII–VIII, which ranges from small cells to cells as large as motoneurons (Cruce, 1975, Chapter 3 of this volume). The lateral border of area VIII with area VII is indistinct. In *Python* and *Testudo*, as in the tegu, areas VII–VIII cannot be subdivided.

Area IX, i.e. the motoneuron area, consists of two longitudinal columns, a medial and a lateral one, in *Tupinambis*. The medial column, which is present throughout the cord, is related to the innervation of neck, trunk and tail musculature. The lateral column is present only in the cervical and lumbosacral enlargements and is related to the innervation of the extremity muscles (Ariëns Kappers *et al.*, 1936; Nieuwenhuys, 1964). Motoneurons are large (30–60 μm), darkly staining cells, which are multipolar in shape with large, round nuclei and clear, deeply staining nucleoli. They possess abundant Nissl substance scattered throughout their cytoplasm. In *Tupinambis*, the cells of the lateral column show a palisadelike arrangement. In *Testudo*, motoneurons occur throughout the spinal cord, except for the thoracic region. There are two groups; more medial motoneurons innervate neck and tail musculature, while more lateral motoneurons occur only in the enlargements. The motoneurons of *Python* form a single continuous column, which is particularly large in the intumescentia trunci and probably comparable to the medial group of limbed reptiles.

Area X, which surrounds the central canal, can be distinguished throughout the spinal cord. This area, also called substantia grisea centralis, is composed of very small (4–6 μm) round cells with round nuclei and indistinct nucleoli. These cells have a very narrow rim of cytoplasm which does not contain discrete Nissl substance.

In summary, the present findings suggest that the spinal gray of the reptiles *Tupinambis nigropunctatus*, *Testudo hermanni* and *Python reticulatus* can be divided into a number of areas on a cytoarchitectonic basis. However, while some layers are clear, others are less so, and their delineation is somewhat arbitrary; a fact which has also been emphasized by other workers (e.g. Rexed, 1952; Leonard and Cohen, 1975a). In general, most boundaries between areas in the dorsal horn are distinct, whereas the cellular elements of the more ventral areas are more diffusely arranged. Figure 10 illustrates the subdivision of the spinal gray in the three reptiles studied here. A comparable parcellation of the spinal gray can be made for all species studied. The spinal gray is least differentiated in *Testudo*, among the reptiles studied. Cruce (1975, and Chapter 3 of this volume) has also described the laminar organization of the spinal gray in *Tupinambis* (Fig. 10). Our data differ substantially from his, particularly in the subdivision of the dorsal horn. The present parcellation apparently corresponds to subdivisions made in other amniotes.

3. Neuronal Types

a. *Funicular cells and commissural cells.* Among the funicular and commissural neurons there are large, elongate elements which send numerous dendrites into the white matter, but the dendritic trees of others are much more restricted and confined to the gray substance (Banchi, 1903). Many of

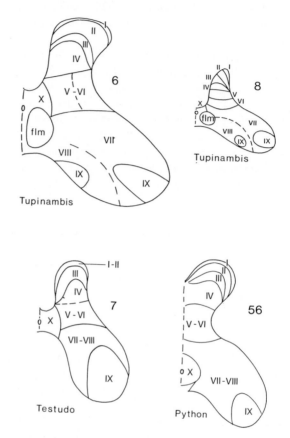

FIG. 10. Diagrams summarizing the subdivisions of the reptilian spinal gray made in the present study. A diagram of the subdivision of the gray matter in *Tupinambis* (Cruce, 1975, and Chapter 3 of this volume) is also included, flm, medial longitudinal fasciculus.

the secondary neurons in the reptilian spinal cord send one of their dendrites across the midline via a commissure situated dorsal to the central canal. This, the dorsal gray commissure, contains a number of spindleshaped neurons, the so-called dorsal median cells (Ramón y Cajal, 1891; Banchi, 1903). Cruce (Chapter 3 of this volume) described cells with dendrites confined to his laminae V to VII (Fig. 10) which send their axons into the ipsilateral white matter or through a commissure central to the central canal to the contralateral side. These elements possibly represent the cells of origin of long ascending pathways. Such cells have been localized in mammals with the horseradish peroxidase technique. Their shapes can be studied with the newly developed intracellular staining techniques (Kater and Nicholson, 1973; Jankowska, 1975).

b. *Interneurons.* The reptilian dorsal horn contains, besides elements with long axons, true internuncial cells of Golgi's type II (Banchi, 1903). They are provided with a rather restricted, but richly ramifying dendritic tree, and their axons branch ventral to the cell body in the basal part of the dorsal horn.

c. *Cells with ascending connections.* A column of Clarke, giving rise to the dorsal spinocerebellar tract as in mammals, could not be convincingly demonstrated in reptiles. In birds (van den Akker, 1970; Leonard and Cohen, 1975a), a column of large cells is present in layer V (Leonard and Cohen, 1975a), which extends beyond thoracic and upper lumbar segments. Moreover, van den Akker (1970) considers the dorsal position of the above-mentioned column as further cause for reservation, as Rexed (1952) asserts that Clarke's column always lies in lamina VII. For several reasons, however, Leonard and Cohen (1975a, b) consider the dorsal magnocellular column in lamina V in the pigeon as the avian homologue of Clarke's column in mammals. The large-celled lateral part of the reptilian area V may be a candidate for a reptilian equivalent of the above mentioned longitudinal structure of the pigeon.

It must be emphasized that experimental data on the cells of origin of the various pathways ascending to the brainstem and diencephalon thus far are only available for mammals. In these, the precise anatomical locations of the cells giving rise to these ascending pathways have been demonstrated with the horseradish peroxidase (HRP) technique as well as by means of antidromic stimulation. The cells of origin of spinothalamic (Trevino et al., 1973; Albé-Fessard et al., 1974, 1975; Tevino and Carstens, 1975; Giesler et al., 1976), spinoreticular (Fields et al., 1977), spinocerebellar (Matsushita and Ikeda, 1975; Cummings and Petras, 1977; Petras and Cummings, 1977; Petras, 1977; R. L. Snyder, 1977) and spinocervical (Bryan et al., 1973, 1974) tracts have been analysed in this way. The morphology of such neurons can be studied by intracellular staining techniques such as Procion yellow (Stretton and Kravitz, 1968; Jankowska and Lindström, 1973; Llinás, 1973; Brown et al., 1976). The recently developed technique of intracellular injection of HRP (Jankowska et al., 1976; Snow et al., 1976; Brown, 1977) has several advantages over Procion yellow. HRP lets one visualize not only the soma and dendrites of the cells (also possible with Procion yellow) but also the trajectory of their axons, even to the terminals when cells are well-stained (Cullheim and Kellerth, 1976; Snow et al., 1976). Thus far, this promising technique has been used mainly for study of axonal projections of spinocervical tract neurons (Jankowska et al., 1976; Brown, 1977) and of spinal interneurons (Czarkowska et al., 1976).

d. *Preganglionic neurons.* Preganglionic cells are undoubtedly present, but they are not arranged into a lateral horn, as in mammals. It seems reasonable to assume that these cells must occupy a fairly central position in the thoracic part of the spinal cord of turtles, since only the central portions of the gray substance are preserved in the thoracic region.

e. *Motoneurons.* Motoneurons possess an extensive dendritic plexus. The medial group of motoneurons tends to elaborate its dendrites within area VIII (Cruce, Chapter 3 of this volume). The dendrites of the lateral column of motoneurons extend from the gray matter into the ventral and lateral funiculi. Two prominent dendrites are present (Banchi, 1903; Cruce, this volume), one extending medially and ventrally, the other extending dorsally along the medial border of the lateral funiculus. The latter sends numerous branches radially into the lateral funiculus. The terminal ramification of these radial dendrites constitute a dense subpial plexus.

No γ-motoneurons are present in the reptilian spinal cord. The motor innervation of muscle spindles is derived from collaterals of axons which innervate extrafusal muscle fibers (Crowe and Ragab, 1970; Cliff and Ridge, 1973; Proske and Ridge, 1974; Ichiki *et al.*, 1976).

f. *Marginal nuclei.* A peculiarity of the reptilian spinal cord is the accumulation of nerve cells just beneath the pial surface and dorsal to the ventral roots. These clusters, the marginal nuclei (Fig. 2), were first described by Gaskell (1885) in the alligator, and have been demonstrated in a wide variety of reptiles (cf. Ariëns Kappers *et al.*, 1936). The marginal nuclei, also called the nuclei of Gaskell or nuclei of Hofmann-von Kölliker, form a column extending throughout the spinal cord (Fig. 2). They constitute easily recognizable clusters in *Tupinambis nigropunctatus* and *Python reticulatus*. However, in *Testudo hermanni*, only a few cells are scattered at the periphery. In all reptiles, the marginal cells are ovoid to multipolar, have relatively large nuclei, clear nucleoli and distinct Nissl substance. Besides these marginal nuclei, cells of diverse shape and size are scattered over the lateral funiculus.

4. *Comparison to Other Amniotes*

Some comparative notes will be made on the laminar organization of the spinal gray in terrestrial vertebrates. Figure 11 shows diagrams of the parcellation of the spinal gray in a frog, *Rana catesbeiana* (Ebbesson, 1967), a lizard, *Tupinambis nigropunctatus* (the present study), the pigeon *Columba livia* (Leonard and Cohen, 1975a) and the opossum *Didelphis virginiana* (Martin and Fischer, 1968). There is a strong resemblance in the organization of the spinal gray in these forms. In frogs, the cell groups in the spinal cord show a poor differentiation. Therefore, the frog spinal gray has been subdivided by Ebbesson (1976) into a number of fields, coinciding with

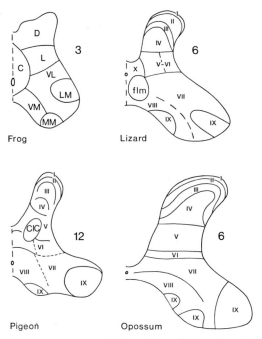

Fig. 11. Diagrams indicating the parcellation of the spinal gray in a frog *Rana catesbeiana* (based on Ebbesson, 1976), a lizard *Tupinambis nigropunctatus* (the present study), the pigeon *Columba livia* (after Leonard and Cohen, 1975a) and the opossum *Didelphis virginiana* (after Martin and Fisher, 1968). C, central field; ClC, Clarke's column; D, dorsal field; flm, medial longitudinal fasciculus; L, lateral field; LM, lateral motor field; MM, medial motor field; VL, ventrolateral field; VM, ventromedial field.

afferent fiber systems, rather than into laminae. It appears, however, that Rexed's parcellation of the spinal gray can be applied to all amniotes.

The following section presents connectional data and compares the laminar organization of the reptilian spinal cord in more detail with that of anurans, birds, and mammals.

IV. Terminations of Fiber Systems

A. Dorsal Root Projections

1. *Reptiles*

It has been reported that in reptiles, as in mammals, each dorsal root can be divided into a large-fibered medial, and a thin-fibered, lateral bundle (Ariëns Kappers *et al.*, 1936). The large diameter dorsal root fibers bifurcate and send ascending and descending branches into the dorsal funiculus.

Smaller diameter fibers contribute to the dorsolateral fascicle, known as Lissauer's tract. However, since Lissauer's 1885 description of small myelinated axons from the dorsal root entering the dorsolateral fascicle, the organization of the dorsal rootlets into medial and lateral divisions has been the subject of considerable controversy (R. Snyder, 1977). Snyder's results indicate that the dorsal root is laterally divided in the monkey, but not in the cat. In addition to dorsal root fibers of small caliber, the tract of Lissauer receives axons from dorsal horn neurons (LaMotte, 1977).

Some variation has been reported in relation to the course of the dorsal root fibers after their entrance into the cord in reptiles. In turtles (Banchi, 1903; de Lange, 1917) and in snakes (Ramón y Cajal, 1891; Retzius, 1894, 1898; van Gehuchten, 1897; de Lange, 1917), a projection of dorsal root fibers to the lateral funiculus has been claimed.

Our Klüver-Barrera material (Fig. 12) shows that in *Tupinambis nigropunctatus* each dorsal root enters the spinal cord over a broad zone, whereas in *Testudo hermanni* and *Python reticulatus* the dorsal root splits up into a dorsal and a ventral bundle, the latter passing through the lateral funiculus. In *Testudo*, the ventral bundle enters the spinal gray via the tract of Lissauer,

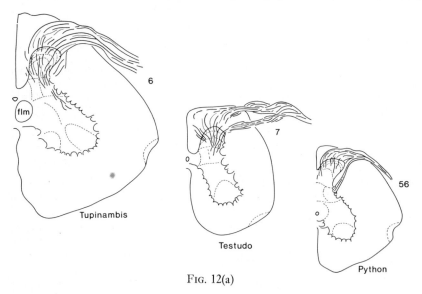

FIG. 12(a)

FIG. 12. The pattern of fiber entry into the dorsal horn in *Tupinambis nigropunctatus*, *Testudo hermanni* and *Python reticulatus* based on Klüver-Barrera material. (a) Diagrammatic representation of the distribution of dorsal root fibers into the spinal cord (see text for further details). (b) Photomicrographs of the spinal cord in *Tupinambis*, *Testudo* and *Python* in Klüver-Barrera material. (A) Low power view of the cord in *Tupinambis*. (B) The dorsal horn in *Tupinambis* at a higher magnification. (C) The dorsal horn in *Testudo*. (D) The dorsal horn in *Python*.

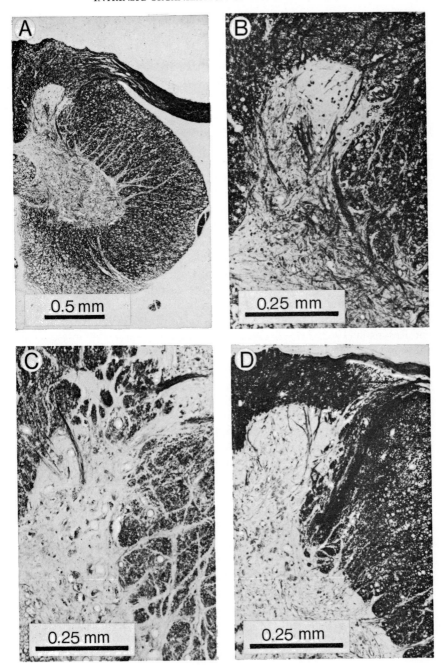

Fig. 12(b)

whereas in *Python* this distinct bundle of medium-sized fibers (cf. Section IVB1 for definition of small, medium-sized and coarse fibers) courses through the dorsal part of the lateral funiculus to the lateral border of areas V–VI. The distinction between medium-sized and small fibers, as mentioned in the earlier literature (Ariëns Kappers *et al.*, 1936), is only ill-defined, and the various types of fibers are mostly intermingled. Dorsal root fibers pass not only to the spinal gray, but some enter the dorsal funiculus.

The distribution of primary afferent fibers within the gray matter of the reptilian spinal cord has been examined with experimental anatomical techniques by Goldby and Robinson (1962, *Lacerta viridis*), Joseph and Whitlock (1968, *Caiman crocodilus*, and two lizards: *Ctenosaura hemilopha* and *Iguana iguana*), van der Sloot (1968, *Testudo hermanni*), and Cruce (Chapter 3 of this volume, *Tupinambis nigropunctatus*). The distribution of sensory input is restricted to the dorsal and adjacent intermediate gray matter of turtle and caiman spinal cord. In *Ctenosaura* and *Iguana*, Joseph and Whitlock (1968) observed a different relationship. Primary afferent fibers could be traced along the lateral margin of the ventral horn in both lizards, and in several instances appeared to cascade down along the dorsal dendrites to a point very close to the somata of the motoneurons. A similar dorsal root projection into the ventral horn has been described by Goldby and Robinson (1962, *Lacerta viridis*) and Cruce (Chapter 3 of this volume, *Tupinambis nigropunctatus*).

A preliminary analysis of dorsal root transections made by the present authors in *Testudo hermanni*, *Tupinambis nigropunctatus* and *Python reticulatus* is presented in Fig. 13. There is no clear segregation of medium-sized fibers medially and smaller fibers laterally at the dorsal root entry zone. The subdivision into medial and lateral divisions is further obscured by the well-developed lateral bundle of medium-sized fibers, which passes through the lateral funiculus. Medium-sized fibers entering the dorsal funiculus bifurcate and send rostral branches as far as the medulla oblongata and caudal branches downward for a variable number of segments. The ascending dorsal column fibers are discussed in Chapter 4. The smaller "lateral division" fibers enter the dorsolateral fasciculus directly and branch to ascend and descend for a few segments. The lateral bundle, which traverses the lateral funiculus (Figs 12, 13), can be traced to the lateral side of the spinal gray, where it enters the lateral part of area V–VI.

Degenerated fibers are distributed ipsilaterally following a dorsal root transection. Single dorsal roots project over two to five segments. The most limited projections, namely two segments rostral as well as caudal, are observed in *Python* and *Testudo* (cf. also Rosenberg, 1974). Within the rhizotomized spinal segment, degenerated fibers and their endings are dense in area III–IV, less dense in area I and very sparse in area II. In the

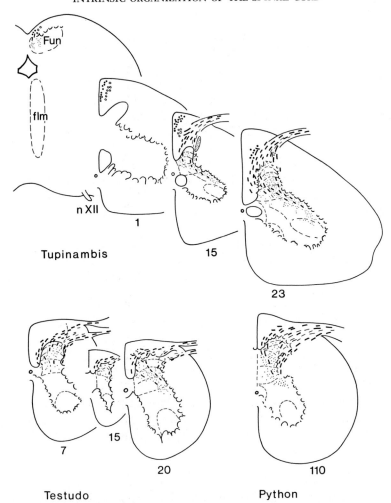

Fig. 13. Schematic drawing of the distribution of degeneration after dorsal root transections in *Tupinambis nigropunctatus*, *Testudo hermanni* and *Python reticulatus*. Broken lines and coarse dots indicate, respectively, longitudinally and transversally cut degenerating fibers (in *Tupinambis* circles have also been used to indicate the long ascending projection to the brainstem after the dorsal root transection at segment 15). Small dots represent evidence of terminal degeneration. flm, medial longitudinal fasciculus; Fun, nucleus dorsal funiculi; nXII, hypoglossal nerve.

thoracic cord (*Tupinambis*, *Testudo*), a concentration of degeneration is found in the medial parts of areas IV–VI. This restricted zone may correspond to Clarke's column in mammals. No such limited area of gray matter receiving a primary afferent projection has been found so far in *Python*.

The lateral bundle of medium-sized fibers, passing via the dorsal part of the lateral funiculus, enters the spinal gray at the lateral side of area IV–VI in *Tupinambis* and *Python*. Together with fibers from the "medial division" of the dorsal root coursing through the dorsal horn, this lateral bundle distributes to the dorsolateral part of areas VII–VIII in *Tupinambis* and other lizards (Joseph and Whitlock, 1968). In *Tupinambis nigropunctatus* (cf. also Cruce, Chapter 3 of this volume), *Ctenosaura hemilopha* and *Iguana iguana* (Joseph and Whitlock, 1968), a few degenerated fibers can be traced to the dorsal part of the lateral column of motoneurons. In *Testudo* and *Python* (Fig. 13), as well as in *Caiman crocodilus* (Joseph and Whitlock, 1968), almost no fibers extend into the ventral horn. This considerable variation in dorsal root distribution has been correlated with the gross hindlimb structure of the reptiles studied (Joseph and Whitlock, 1968). The caiman limb has no appreciable capacity for fine prehensile movements, whereas the lizards mentioned above possess long, multijointed digits which give their limbs a marked prehensile character. Joseph and Whitlock claim that a closer potential coupling between the primary input and output systems of the spinal cord accompanies this adaptive increase. It has already been noted that in reptiles the motoneurons have extensive dendritic trees which invade the dorsal horn (cf. Banchi, 1903; Joseph and Whitlock, 1968; Petras, 1976). It seems likely that the primary afferent fibers of turtles, caimans and snakes, establish synaptic contacts with distal parts of the motoneuronal dendritic tree, whereas those of lizards reach more proximal parts. Unfortunately, few physiological data on afferent–efferent segment relationships are available in reptiles. The work of Rosenberg (1972, 1974), however, does indicate that *Testudo graeca* has monosynaptic connections between primary afferents and ventral horn cells, and thus supports the Joseph–Whitlock hypothesis.

2. *Comparisons with Other Vertebrates*

There is a tremendous variation in the dorsal root projections of various terrestrial vertebrates (Joseph and Whitlock, 1968; Ebbesson, 1976). In frogs, for example, the dorsal root distribution is practically restricted to the dorsal horn. Physiological studies have shown the presence of monosynaptic activation of motoneurons by primary afferents in frog lumbar cord (Cruce, 1974; Székely and Czéh, 1976), but not in the thoracic cord (Carlsen and Mendell, 1977). In pigeons (van den Akker, 1970; Leonard and Cohen, 1975b), the course, extent and pattern of distribution of dorsal root fibers is very similar to that of mammals. In mammals, such as the opossum (Culberson and Kimmel, 1975), such fibers not only reach the ventral horn, but the contralateral side as well.

It is likely that primary afferent fibers contact distal parts of the dendritic

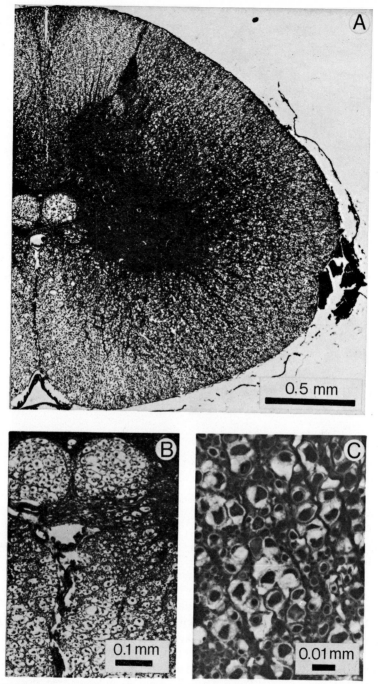

FIG. 14. Photomicrographs of Häggqvist sections of the spinal cord of *Tupinambis nigro-punctatus*. (A) The 6th segment. (B) Detail of the ventral funiculus (6th segment). (C) Detail of the ventral funiculus to show the axon and myelin sheath of individual fibers (6th segment).

A

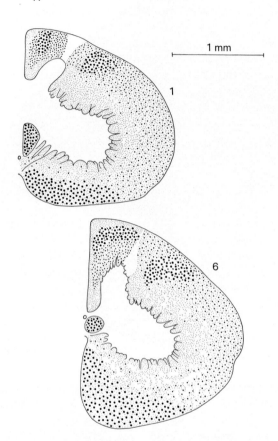

FIG. 15 (A) and (B). Diagrammatic representations of transverse sections through representative levels of the spinal cord in the lizard *Tupinambis nigropunctatus*, showing the fiber pattern, based on Häggqvist material. Dots of three different sizes are employed to indicate small (0 to 3 μm), medium-sized (3 to 6 μm), and coarse (6 to 12 μm in axon diameter) fibers. In order to avoid crowding, fibers less than 1 μm in diameter have not been indicated in these diagrams.

trees of spinal motoneurons in frogs and in turtles, caimans and snakes. In lizards and in pigeons, more proximal parts of the motoneuron dendrites are reached, whereas in mammals axosomatic synaptic contacts have also been found. This further ventral extent of dorsal root fibers is accompanied by a "retraction" of the motoneuronal dendritic trees (Joseph and Whitlock, 1968; Ebbesson, 1976). These findings seem to indicate that dorsal root fibers occupy places where dendrites once extended (Ebbesson, 1976).

B

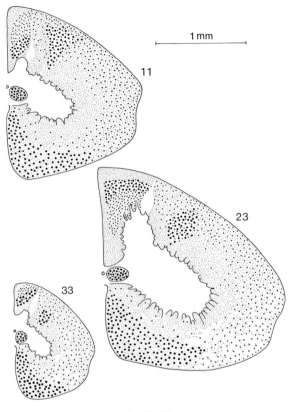

FIG. 15 (B)

Finally, it should be noted that primary afferents form only a small percentage of synaptic input to motoneurons in all vertebrates (Conradi, 1969; McLaughlin, 1972; Bodian, 1975). The majority of their synaptic input is derived from interneurons (Gelfan et al., 1974).

B. DESCENDING PATHWAYS

1. General

In Häggqvist material (Figs 14–17), two major zones can be distinguished in the lateral as well as in the ventral funiculus: (a) a *superficial zone* is composed of mainly coarse fibers in the ventral funiculus but contains all types of fibers (small, medium-sized and coarse) in the lateral funiculus; (b) an *inner zone*, surrounds the spinal gray and consists only of small fibers. As will be detailed below, this zone contains propriospinal fibers.

To describe the fiber patterns of the various systems in the spinal cord (Fig. 14), the general terms small, medium-sized and coarse fibers are used. These terms are not strictly defined, but in general it may be said that the axon diameter of the small fibers ranges from 0 to 3 μm, of the medium-sized from 3–6 μm, and of the coarse fibers from 6 to 12 μm. The largest sizes only occur in *Tupinambis nigropunctatus*. In *Testudo hermanni* and *Python reticulatus*, the axon diameters of the coarse fibers do not extend beyond 7 μm. It must be emphasized that the positions of the different tracts, as well as the sizes of the areas they occupy, may change during their course through the spinal cord. Therefore, the structure of the cord at various levels may differ considerably. It is obvious that the cord cannot be studied without taking these changes into consideration and thus, the white matter has to be examined throughout the whole extent of the cord.

The fiber systems descending in the ventral and lateral funiculus will now be discussed. Their origins are discussed in the following two chapters.

2. *The Rubrospinal Path*

In the reptiles studied, the superficial zone of the lateral funiculus is composed of intermingled, medium-sized and small fibers (Figs 14–17). In *Tupinambis nigropunctatus*, the most dorsal part of the lateral funiculus contains, in addition, a conspicuous zone of closely packed, medium-sized and coarse fibers (4–8 μm). This zone has been shown experimentally to represent the crossed rubrospinal tract (ten Donkelaar, 1976a, b; ten Donkelaar and Nieuwenhuys, Chapter 4 of this volume). A rubrospinal pathway has also been demonstrated in *Lacerta viridis* (Robinson, 1969) and in *Testudo hermanni* (ten Donkelaar, 1976a, b). In Häggqvist material of this turtle, rubrospinal fibers could not be identified as a separate pathway. It is important to note that no evidence for the presence of a rubrospinal tract has been found in *Python reticulatus* (cf. ten Donkelaar, 1976a, b) with experimental techniques. Other descending fibers in the lateral funiculus originate in the inferior reticular nucleus and in the inferior nucleus of the raphé (Robinson, 1969; ten Donkelaar, 1976a, b; Cruce, 1975, and Chapter 3 of this volume). The terminations of the rubrospinal tract are discussed in Chapter 4.

The large remainder of the superficial zone of the lateral funiculus consists mainly of long ascending fibers projecting to the brain stem and diencephalon. Their terminations are discussed below (ten Donkelaar and Nieuwenhuys, Chapter 4 of this volume).

3. Vestibulospinal and Reticulospinal Paths

The superficial zone of the ventral funiculus contains the bulk of the descending fibers from the brainstem to the spinal cord (ten Donkelaar and Nieuwenhuys, Chapter 4 of this volume). It is characterized by the presence of many coarse fibers (6–10 μm axon diameter) intermingled with

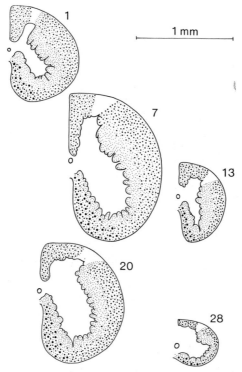

FIG. 16. Diagrammatic representations of transverse sections through representative levels of the spinal cord in the turtle *Testudo hermanni*, showing the fiber pattern based on Häggqvist material. Dots of three different sizes are employed to indicate small (0 to 3 μm), medium (3 to 6 μm), and coarse (6 to 12 μm in axon diameter) fibers. In order to avoid crowding, fibers less than 1 μm in diameter are omitted from the diagrams.

some smaller fibers. In *Tupinambis nigropunctatus* (Fig. 15), a number of very coarse fibers (8–12 μm axon diameter) are separated from the main part of the ventral funiculus by an accessory commissure. The part of the ventral funiculus lying dorsal to that commissure contains interstitiospinal fibers (ten Donkelaar, 1976b) which originate in the nucleus interstitialis of the medial longitudinal fasciculus. As an accessory commissure is indistinct in *Testudo hermanni* and *Python reticulatus*, a zone of interstitiospinal fibers cannot be distinguished in Häggqvist material of these species. The main part of the superficial zone of the ventral funiculus is composed of reticulospinal and vestibulospinal fibers (Robinson, 1969; ten Donkelaar, 1976a, b; Cruce, 1975, and Chapter 3 of this volume; ten Donkelaar and

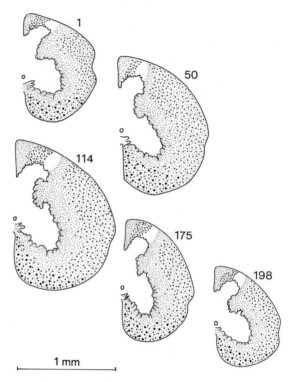

Fig. 17. Diagrammatic representations of transverse sections through representative levels of the spinal cord in the snake *Python reticulatus*, showing the fiber pattern based on Häggqvist material. For code, see Fig. 16.

Nieuwenhuys, Chapter 4 of this volume), but there is no clear distinction between these two fiber contingents in normal material (Figs 15–17). With anterograde degeneration techniques, however, it has been shown that vestibulospinal fibers constitute the most peripheral rim (Fig. 18), and the reticulospinal fibers lie laterally (ten Donkelaar, 1976b).

Reticulospinal fibers (present in the ventral as well as in the lateral funiculus) probably constitute the bulk of the descending fibers to the spinal cord in reptiles. Reticulospinal fibers in the lateral funiculus arise in the inferior reticular nucleus and in the inferior nucleus of the raphé, whereas reticulospinal fibers in the ventral funiculus originate in the medial, superior and isthmus reticular nuclei (Robinson, 1969; ten Donkelaar, 1976a). These reticulospinal pathways might be qualified as a supraspinal "final common path" by way of which the forebrain and the brainstem influence

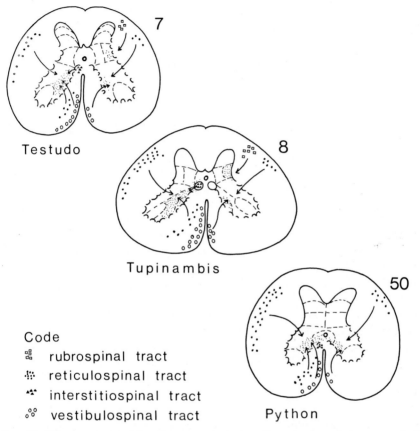

Testudo

Tupinambis

50

Code

⊡ rubrospinal tract

⦂⦂ reticulospinal tract

⁑ interstitiospinal tract

∘∘ vestibulospinal tract   Python

FIG. 18. Diagram summarizing the course and site of termination of the supraspinal descending pathways, represented in approximately comparable transverse sections, namely, the cervical intumescence in *Testudo hermanni* and *Tupinambis nigropunctatus*, and the 50th segment in *Python reticulatus*. Small dots represent evidence of (pre) terminal degeneration. (Modified after ten Donkelaar, 1976b.)

spinal motoneurons. A direct projection from the telencephalon, comparable to the mammalian corticospinal tract, is not present in reptiles (Lohman and van Woerden-Verkley, 1976; Hoogland, 1977). The prosencephalon probably acts indirectly on the spinal cord via the mesencephalic reticular formation, which in its turn projects to the magnocellular rhombencephalic reticular formation. The mesencephalic tectum, which does not project beyond the first spinal segment, can influence the spinal motor centers by way of the tectobulbar tracts, which impinge upon the rhombencephalic reticular formation.

The interstitiospinal, vestibulospinal and reticulospinal tracts in *Tupinambis nigropunctatus*, *Testudo hermanni* and *Python reticulatus* all terminate in the medial part of the ventral horn, namely in the medial part of areas VII–VIII and the adjacent part of area X (Fig. 18). *Tupinambis* and *Testudo* have a distinct rubrospinal tract, which terminates in the later part of areas V–VI, and in *Tupinambis* overlaps into area IV. The experimental techniques applied to *Python* (ten Donkelaar, 1976a, b) show quantitative variations in the reticulospinal (more development than in turtles and lizards) and in the vestibulospinal (less development than in other reptiles) tracts. Most remarkably, a rubrospinal tract is missing.

Grillner (1976) considered it likely that fast-conducting pathways serve to produce locomotor behavior. Findings in fish (Rovainen, 1967; Kashin *et al.*, 1974) and mammals (Grillner and Shik, 1973; Grillner, 1976; Shik and Orlovsky, 1976; Wetzel and Stuart, 1976) suggest that these may be reticulospinal pathways. Stein (1976) and Lennard and Stein (1977) did produce evidence supporting the hypothesis that fast-conducting pathways exist in the turtles *Chrysemys picta marginata* and *C. scripta elegans*, which serve to produce locomotion; swimming movements of the hindlimbs could be produced in response to electrical stimulation of the dorsal part of the lateral funiculus. These movements can be elicited in turtles in which the thoracic cord has been transsected, as well as in those with an intact CNS. Several lines of evidence (Lennard and Stein, 1977) support the hypothesis that the stimulating electrode is, in fact, eliciting swimming movements by activating reticulospinal pathways. Monosynaptic connections of reticulospinal fibers to lumbar lateral motoneurons in turtles have been demonstrated by Shapovalov (1975).

4. Monoaminergic Paths

In mammals, much work (Forssberg and Grillner, 1973; Grillner and Shik, 1973; Shik and Orlovsky, 1976; Wetzel and Stuart, 1976) has centered around the hypothesis that there are slow-conducting, monoaminergic pathways which serve to activate locomotion. Grillner and Shik (1973) have suggested that stimulation of the mesencephalic locomotor region, described by Shik *et al.* (1966), leads to the activation of descending noradrenergic fibers and subsequent release of spinal mechanisms for locomotion in the cat. Steeves *et al.* (1975) have presented evidence that direct activation of catecholamine-containing neurons in the locus coeruleus occurs during stimulation of the mesencephalic locomotor region, and experimental neuroanatomical data suggest that locus coeruleus neurons in the cat (Kuypers and Maisky, 1975), as well as in other mammals (Fougerousse and Hancock, 1976; Nygren and Olson, 1977), project to the spinal cord. Consequently, various mammals have a noradrenergic coeruleospinal pathway. Reptiles (Parent and Poitras, 1974; ten Donkelaar and Nieuwen-huys, Chapter 4 of this volume; Parent, Chapter 6 of this volume), and other nonmammalian vertebrates (Tohyama, 1976) have a locus coeruleus. The locus coeruleus has been found to project to the spinal cord (ten Donkelaar and de Boer-van Huizen, 1978; *Lacerta*).

5. *Other Paths*

Recently, with the HRP-technique the presence of cerebellospinal and hypothalamospinal pathways has been demonstrated (ten Donkelaar and de Boer-van Huizen, 1978; *Lacerta*). In the cat, a fastigiospinal pathway has been recently demonstrated with the aid of the HRP and antidromic stimula-tion techniques (Fukushina *et al.*, 1977). This projection from the deep cerebellar fastigial nucleus terminates primarily in the upper cervical cord. In the opossum, a few degenerated fibers are present at cervical levels, terminating in lamina VII and VIII after fastigial lesions (Martin *et al.*, 1975). A hypothalamospinal pathway has been demonstrated in various mam-mals with the HRP technique (e.g. Kuypers and Maisky, 1975; Hancock, 1976; Saper *et al.*, 1976; Castiglioni *et al.*, 1977). The course and termination of the hypothalamospinal pathway in the rat, cat and two primate species (*Saimiri sciureus* and *Macaca fascicularis*) has been shown by the anterograde transport of radioactively labeled amino acids (Saper *et al.*, 1976). The hypothalamospinal pathway passes via the lateral funiculus and terminates in the intermediolateral cell column at thoracic levels. This area occupies, in mammals, the preganglionic nuclei of the sympathetic nervous system.

6. *Comparison to Other Amniotes*

It appears that two sites of termination for descending supraspinal fiber systems have been demonstrated in the reptilian cord. The rubrospinal tract terminates in the lateral part of areas V–VI, whereas interstitiospinal, retriculospinal and vestibulospinal fibers terminate in the medial part of areas VII–VIII. Details of the significance of this pattern are considered in the following chapter. The above classification makes it likely that the lack of a lateral focus of termination, as well as a rubrospinal tract, in *Python reticulatus* is correlated with limblessness.

Some general notes compare the pattern of descending pathways to the spinal cord in terrestrial vertebrates. Figure 19 offers a schematic repre-sentation of experimental data concerning these pathways in amphibians (toad and bullfrog), a reptile (tegu lizard), the pigeon and the opossum.

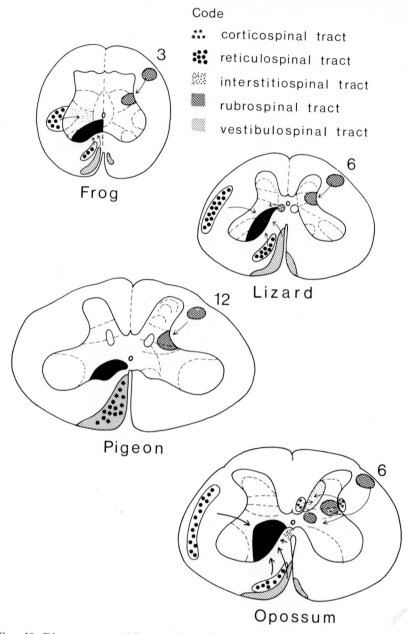

Code

::: corticospinal tract
::: reticulospinal tract
::: interstitiospinal tract
▓ rubrospinal tract
▧ vestibulospinal tract

Frog

Lizard

Pigeon

Opossum

FIG. 19. Diagram summarizing experimental data concerning supraspinal descending fiber systems in the frog (after Ebbesson, 1976), in the tegu lizard (after ten Donkelaar, 1976a, b; Cruce, 1975, and Chapter 3 of this volume), in the pigeon (based on van den Akker, 1969, 1970) and in the opossum (after Martin *et al.*, 1975). Comparable fiber systems and their site of termination are indicated with the same code in sections through the cervical intumescence. Small dots also indicate sites of termination.

A vestibulospinal tract, projecting bilaterally to the spinal cord, has experimentally been demonstrated in the toad (Corvaja and Grofová, 1972; Corvaja et al., 1973) and in the bullfrog (Fuller, 1974). In the toad (Corvaja and Grofová, 1972), two other pathways have been shown. Following a high hemisection of the spinal cord, these authors noted a dorsolateral tract, terminating in an area between the dorsal and the ventral horn (i.e. the lateral field as distinguished by Ebbesson, 1976), and a ventrolateral pathway ending in a part of the ventral horn (Ebbesson's ventrolateral field). The dorsolateral tract possibly represents a rubrospinal tract, whereas the ventrolateral pathway consists of reticulospinal fibers (Mensah, 1974). Monosynaptic connections of these reticulospinal fibers in the lateral funiculus to the lateral column of motoneurons have been demonstrated in the lumbar cord of Rana catesbeiana (Cruce, 1974). The lateral funiculus in frogs also contains descending fibers from the inferior raphé nucleus (Soller, 1977). Reticulospinal fibers, in addition, pass via the ventral funiculus (Mensah, 1974).

In the pigeon, a rubrospinal tract has been experimentally demonstrated by Zecha (1961) and van den Akker (1969, 1970). This tract terminates in the lateral part of area 4 of van den Akker (i.e. laminae V and VI of Leonard and Cohen, 1975a). Following a high hemisection of the spinal cord (van den Akker, 1969), a large ventral descending bundle, consisting of vestibulospinal (Groebbels, 1927, Marchi technique) and reticulospinal (Janzik and Glees, 1967, retrograde degeneration technique) fibers appears in the ventral funiculus.

In the pigeon, experimental studies have produced evidence of two long fiber systems from the forebrain extending as far as the upper segments of the spinal cord. Zecha (1962) and Zeier and Karten (1971) traced degenerated fibers originating from caudal forebrain regions (the archistriatum) into the posterolateral funiculus. Karten et al. (1973) also demonstrated a projection from the anterior part of the Wulst to the upper segments of the cord (for discussion of the avian forebrain see Nauta and Karten, 1970; Karten and Dubbeldam, 1973). Recently, telencephalic efferents have been shown to extend as far as the upper cervical spinal cord in the tiger salamander, Ambystoma t. tigrinum (Kokoros and Northcutt, 1977). However, a true pyramidal system, bringing motor activity under the direct control of the cerebral cortex occurs only in mammals (Nieuwenhuys, 1964), and large variations have been observed (Verhaart, 1970). The corticospinal tract descends via the dorsal funiculus in opossums (Marrin and Fisher, 1968; Martin et al., 1975) and some other mammals (the rat: Brown, 1971), and terminates in the dorsal horn adjacent to substantia gelatinosa. The tract apparently is more concerned with the modulation of incoming afferent information than with motor control (Martin and Fisher, 1968; Martin *et al.*, 1975), a relation further exemplified by the relatively small motor deficit after removal of the neocortex (Martin *et al.*, 1975).

It has been suggested that the rubrospinal system is capable of motor control in species which lack a functional corticospinal system (Massion, 1967). In the opossum, the rubrospinal tract, in contrast to the corticospinal tract, extends the entire length of the spinal cord (Martin and Dom, 1970); indeed the rubrospinal tract may play an important role in the supraseg-mental control over lower motor neuron activity. The motor area of the neocortex does not directly influence such activity within the lumbosacral cord, but is potentially capable of doing so indirectly by way of its projection to the red nucleus (Martin, 1969).

In summary, there are remarkable similarities in the descending pathways from the brainstem to the spinal cord. All of the groups depicted have rubro-spinal, reticulospinal and vestibulospinal tracts, terminating in comparable areas of the spinal gray matter.

C. PROPRIOSPINAL PROJECTIONS

1. *Reptiles*

The inner zone of the lateral and ventral funiculi is composed of small-sized fibers (Figs 15–17). These parts of the funiculi bordering the gray matter contain mainly propriospinal fibers, arising from interneurons. The connections of these interneurons with the motoneurons are especially important, as spinal motoneurons receive only slight direct imput from by fibers conducting nerve impulses from the periphery or from the brain. Most influences on motoneurons are exerted via spinal interneurons (Gelfan *et al.*, 1974). Short propriospinal fibers lie in the deepest parts of the funiculi, whereas long propriospinal fibers lie more peripherally (van Beusekom, 1955, cat).

Relatively little is known as regards propriospinal connections in reptiles. Physiological studies (Shimamura, 1973) in various vertebrates including reptiles (snake, alligator, iguana and turtle) show that descending proprio-spinal reflexes from forelimb to hindlimb can be elicited in all reptiles studied, except understandably snakes. Ascending interlimb reflexes from hindlimb to forelimb have been observed in mammals, birds, turtles, frogs and toads. The turtle *Chrysemys scripta elegans* exhibits a strong crossed interlimb reflex. Ascending interlimb reflexes are not altered by spinal transection at the C_1 level. These findings imply that the ascending interlimb reflex may involve only propriospinal mechanisms in the turtle. In the yellow rat snake, *Elaphe obsoleta quadrivittata*, a single shock to any dorsal root studied elicits local intersegmental reflexes in a rostral direction for three to four segments, whereas the caudal extension of the reflex was limited to only one or two segments (Shimamura, 1973).

A few notes on the various anatomical techniques available for analyzing propriospinal connections may be appropriate here:

i. Anterograde degeneration and transport techniques. Anterograde degeneration techniques (Nauta and Gygax, 1954; Fink and Heimer, 1967) are especially useful in studying the course and site of termination of ascending propriospinal fibers. The descending propriospinal systems need a more complicated approach: one has to take advantage of the so-called successive hemisection technique (Giovanelli Barilari and Kuypers, 1969) in order to eliminate degenerated fibers produced by descending supraspinal systems. Placement of small lesions in the funiculi allows study of the differential distribution of the propriospinal fibers from different parts of the ventral and lateral funiculi to the spinal gray, especially the motoneuronal area. The dense degeneration which occurs in the lateral motoneuronal column following such lesions, for example, in the cat (Sterling and Kuypers, 1968; Rustioni et al., 1971) must represent mainly short propriospinal elements. Silver impregnation studies have shown that in the cat, the bulk of the fibers of the descending supraspinal pathways (Nyberg-Hansen, 1966) as well as long propriospinal fibers (Giovanelli Barilari and Kuypers, 1969; McLaughlin, 1972; Matsushita and Ikeda, 1973) avoid the lateral moto-neuronal area.

The recently developed technique applying anterograde transport of radioactively labeled amino acids (Cowan et al., 1972; Cowan and Cuénod, 1975) offers new ways to study the propriospinal connections.

ii. Retrograde degeneration and transport techniques. The differential location of the cells of origin of fibers in different parts of the ventral and lateral funiculi can be determined by comparing the distribution of chro-matolytic cells in the spinal gray of animals in which small lesions have been made in different parts of these funiculi (Sterling and Kuypers, 1968; Molenaar et al., 1974) or by retrograde transport of the enzyme HRP (Molenaar and Kuypers, 1975; Skinner, 1977).

The combination of data obtained in these two types of experiments makes it possible to determine the differential location of cells in the spinal intermediate zone which project to different groups of motoneurons.

The various techniques mentioned above are used by the present authors to analyze the propriospinal connections in the reptiles studied. Some preliminary results will be presented here. Short as well as long propriospinal fibers have been found in *Testudo hermanni* and *Tupinambis nigropunctatus*. In *Python reticulatus*, only short propriospinal fibers have been found.

In Fig. 20, the course and site of termination of ascending fibers following a lumbar hemisection (segment 23) in the lizard *Tupinambis nigropunctatus* have been indicated. Propriospinal as well as long spinal fibers ascending to the brainstem are shown. Short propriospinal fibers ascending to segment 22 directly border the gray substance, whereas fibers ascending to segment 21 are somewhat more peripherally located (Fig. 20). Long propriospinal fibers are still more peripherally situated and even reach the cervical enlargement, passing via the ventral as well as via the lateral funiculus. The short

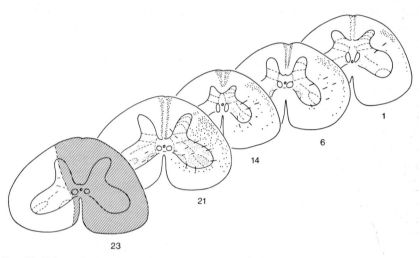

FIG. 20. Schematic drawing of the rostral distribution of degeneration following a lumbar (segment 23) hemisection in the lizard *Tupinambis nigropunctatus*. Hatching indicates the extent of the lesion; coarse dots and broken lines indicate, respectively, transversally and longitudinally cut degenerating fibers; small dots represent evidence of preterminal degeneration.

propriospinal fibers terminate in the entire ventral horn, including the lateral motoneuronal area, predominantly ipsilaterally. Long propriospinal fibers terminate in area VIII. The long spinal fibers ascending to the brainstem are situated in the medial part of the dorsal funiculus and in the dorsal part of the lateral funiculus. No ascending spinal fibers reach the brainstem by way of the ventral funiculus. Comparable results were obtained in *Testudo hermanni*.

Lesions directly caudal to the cervical intumescence in *Tupinambis* and *Testudo* suggest that long propriospinal fibers descend to the lumbosacral enlargement. Successive hemisections carried out in *Testudo* (Kusuma and ten Donkelaar, in preparation) confirm them. The descending supraspinal pathways were first interrupted by a hemisection at the second spinal segment. After 11 months, debris of the degenerated supraspinal fibers could no longer be demonstrated in the spinal gray and white matter by means of Nauta-Gygax (1954) and Fink-Heimer (1967) techniques. Consequently the distribution of descending propriospinal fibers could be determined by studying the fiber degeneration in the cord resulting from a hemisection just caudal to the cervical intumescence.

In *Python reticulatus*, only short propriospinal fibers have been observed following spinal cord hemisections, confirming the results of Shimamura (1973) for the yellow rat snake. The course and site of termination of the long ascending spinal fibers passing to the brainstem agree with Ebbesson's (1969) findings.

Thus, quadrupedal reptiles, such as lizards and turtles, which move their limbs in diagonal patterns (R. C. Snyder, 1952; Bellairs, 1970; Guibé, 1970), have long propriospinal fibers connecting the intumescences. Forms without extremities, such as *Python reticulatus*, lack these connections. It has been proposed (Miller and van der Burg, 1973; Halbertsma *et al.*, 1976; cf. also Wetzel and Stuart, 1976) that long propriospinal pathways may represent intrinsic links between the spinal "motor centers" controlling the hindlimb and forelimb. As a working hypothesis, it is suggested that the long ascending propriospinal pathways facilitate the flexors of the forelimb once the ipsilateral hindlimb has begun the first extension leading to its placement on the ground. The influence of long descending propriospinal fibers is less clear (cf. Miller and van der Burg, 1973; Jankowska *et al.*, 1974). Apparently, the several locomotor patterns seen in snakes (Gans, 1966; Bellairs, 1970; Guibé, 1970) involve short propriospinal fibers, as no longer intraspinal pathways could be demonstrated.

2. *Comparisons with Other Amniotes*

Findings in the cat suggest that propriospinal connections follow the same organizational principles as those governing the descending brainstem pathways (Kuypers, 1973). The bulk of the propriospinal fibers is short and terminates in nearby segments. However, fibers in the ventral funiculus which are distributed to the ventromedial portion of the intermediate zone (lamina VIII) travel over much longer distances, some of them interconnecting the enlargements. It seems probable that the propriospinal neurons connected primarily to the lateral descending systems, as well as the propriospinal neurons connected to the medial ones, form relatively specialized pathways for the transmission of signals to the motoneurons (Kuypers, 1973; Kostyuk, 1975, 1976). The former system projects mainly to motoneurons innervating the distal extremity and the intrinsic extremity flexors; propriospinal neurons connected to the medial descending system project especially to motoneurons innervating axial and proximal limb muscles.

V. Summary and Concluding Remarks

The basic features of reptilian spinal cords are summarized in this final section. Some variations in the organization of the reptilian spinal cord related to different locomotion patterns will be indicated, and certain major trends in the organization of the spinal cord in terrestrial vertebrates will be mentioned.

i. Gross structure. Reptiles differ profoundly in the shape and development of the trunk, tail and extremities, and these differences are clearly reflected in the gross structure of their spinal cord. In forms without extremities, such as snakes, the cord lacks cervical or lumbar enlargements, but such swellings are well marked in turtles, crocodilians, and lizards. The occurrence of cervical and lumbar enlargements thus correlates with the presence of limbs. The snake *Python reticulatus* shows an *intumescentia trunci* or enlargement of the spinal cord, definitely related to the well-developed main part of its trunk.

ii. Frontal accumulation. Frontal accumulation is an increase in the cross-sectional area of the white matter in the rostral part of the cord due to an increase in the number of long ascending fibers. Such accumulation has been observed in the turtle *Testudo hermanni*, but not in *Tupinambis nigropunctatus* and *Python reticulatus*. Its absence probably reflects variation in the number of propriospinal fibers at different levels.

iii. Cytoarchitectonics. The cytoarchitectonic subdivision of the reptilian spinal cord, particularly its dorsal horn, presented in this survey clearly reflects Rexed's laminar approach. The spinal gray has been subdivided and the neutral term "area" has been used for these subdivisions as some cell groups are indistinguishable as laminae. It must again be stressed that the delineation of areas is somewhat arbibrary as they differ in definition. In general, most boundaries are distinct in the dorsal horn, whereas cellular elements are more diffuse in the ventral areas. Terrestrial vertebrates show a strong resemblance in the organization of their spinal gray; Rexed's parcellation may be applied to all amniotes discussed in the present survey.

iv. The distribution of dorsal root fibers into the cord. No clear segregation, with large fibers of the dorsal root entering medially and smaller fibers laterally, has been observed at their site of entrance. Reptiles characteristically show a lateral bundle of primary afferent fibers that traverses the dorsal part of the lateral funiculus and enters the spinal gray at the lateral side of the dorsal horn.

The dorsal root distribution of reptiles shows notable variation. Almost no fibers extend into the ventral horn in *Testudo hermanni*, *Python reticulatus* and *Caiman crocodilus* (Joseph and Whitlock, 1968). However, lizards show a distinct projection into the ventral horn.

The mode of termination of dorsal root fibers has been reviewed for various terrestrial vertebrates. It seems likely (Joseph and Whitlock, 1968; Ebbesson, 1976) that the primary afferent fibers terminate on different parts of the dendritic trees of motoneurons; in frogs and in such reptiles as turtles, crocodilians and snakes, primary afferent fibers terminate on distal parts of the dendritic trees. In lizards and the pigeon, more proximal parts of the motoneuronal dendrites are reached; in mammals, one also sees axosomatic synaptic contacts.

v. Pathways descending to the spinal cord. Reptiles show interstitiospinal, vestibulospinal and reticulospinal tracts. A crossed rubrospinal tract occurs in *Testudo hermanni* and *Typinambis nigropunctatus*, but apparently not in *Python reticulatus*. Two sites of termination occur in the spinal gray, mainly a lateral zone (lateral part of areas V–VI) for the rubrospinal tract, and the medial part of areas VII–VIII for the interstitiospinal, reticulospinal and vestibulospinal fibers.

In reptiles, as in mammals, the retibulospinal pathways are important in the activation of locomotor movements.

A comparison of experimental data concerning the systems descending from the brainstem to the spinal cord in amphibians, reptiles, birds and mammals suggests that origin, course and termination of these systems share a common pattern.

vi. Propriospinal pathways. Short and long propriospinal fibers have been shown in *Testudo hermanni* and *Tupinambis nigropunctatus*. *Python reticulatus* has only short propriospinal fibers. The long propriospinal fibers which interconnect the intumescences in quadrupedal reptiles, such as *Testudo hermanni* and *Tupinambis nigropunctatus*, are very important in coordination of forelimb and hindlimb movements. The locomotion of snakes probably involves short propriospinal fibers.

vii. Layer by layer comparison of the spinal gray in terrestrial vertebrates. Detailed comparison of the laminar organization of the reptilian spinal cord with that of anurans, birds and mammals permits the following remarks:

The pattern of distribution of the dorsal roots allows a rough lamina by lamina comparison of the dorsal horn in reptiles, birds and mammals.

The pathways descending from the brainstem to the spinal cord terminate in comparable areas of the spinal gray; however, these sites of termination are not completely restricted to particular areas.

As no information as regards the cells of origin of non-primary ascending pathways and propriospinal systems is available in non-mammalian vertebrates, a detailed layer by layer comparison as indicated above must await further connectional data.

viii. Concluding statement. It must be stressed that neurobiological research in reptiles and other non-mammalian vertebrates is still in its infancy. Recently developed tracer techniques (retrograde transport of the enzyme HRP, anterograde transport of radioactively labeled amino acids), such physiological techniques as antidromic stimulation, as well as intercellular staining techniques, will be of great help in solving the many remaining problems in the organization of the reptilian spinal cord.

Acknowledgements

The authors wish to express their gratitude to Miss Annelies Pellegrino, Mrs. Carla de Vocht-Poort and Miss Nellie Verijdt for preparing the many histological preparations, to Mr. Joop Russon for the drawing, to Mr. Ad Reynen for the photomicrographs, and to Miss Wanda de Haan and Mrs. Trudy van Son-Verstraeten for their secretarial assistance.

The present study was supported in part by a grant from the Foundation for Medical Research FUNGO, which is subsidized by the Netherlands Organization for the Advancement of Pure Research (ZWO).

References

Abzug, C., Maeda, M., Peterson, B. W. and Wilson, V. J. (1973). Branching of individual lateral vestibulospinal axons at different spinal cord levels. *Brain Res.* 56, 327–330.

Abzug, C., Maeda, M., Peterson, B. W. and Wilson, V. J. (1974). Cervical branching of lumbar vestibulospinal axons. With an appendix by C. P. Bean. *J. Physiol., Lond.* 243, 499–522.

Albé-Fessard, D., Boivie, J., Grant, G. and Levante, A. (1975). Labeling of cells in the medulla oblongata and the spinal cord of the monkey after injections of horseradish peroxidase in the thalamus. *Neurosci. Lett.* 1, 75–80.

Albé-Fessard, D., Levante, A. and Lamour, Y. (1974). Origin of spinothalamic tract in monkeys. *Brain Res.* 65, 503–509.

Ariëns Kappers, C. U., Huber, G. C. and Crosby, E. C. (1936). "The Comparative Anatomy of the Nervous system of Vertebrates, Including Man." Macmillan, New York.

Banchi, A. (1903). La minuta struttura della midollo spinale dei Chelonii (*Emys europaea*). *Arch. ital. Anat. Embriol.* 2, 291–307.

Bellairs, A. d'A. (1970). "The life of Reptiles." Universe Books, New York.

Bodian, D. (1975). Origin of specific synaptic types in the motoneuron neuropil of the monkey. *J. comp. Neurol.* 159, 225–244.

Brown, A. G. (1977). Cutaneous axons and sensory neurones in the spinal cord. *Br. med. Bull.* 33, 109–112.

Brown, A. G., House, C. R., Rose, P. K. and Snow, P. J. (1976). The morphology of spinocervical tract neurones in the cat. *J. Physiol., Lond.* 260, 719–738.

Brown, L. T. (1971). Projections and termination of the corticospinal tract in rodents. *Expl. Brain Res.* 13, 432–450.

Bryan, R. N., Coulter, J. D. and Willis, W. D. (1974). Cells of origin of the spinocervical tract in the monkey. *Expl. Neurol.* 42, 574–586.

Bryan, R. N., Trevino, D. L., Coulter, J. D. and Willis, W. D. (1973). Location and somatotopical organization of the cells of origin of the spinocervical tract. *Expl. Brain Res.* 17, 177–189.

Carlsen, R. C. and Mendell, L. M. (1977). A comparison of the reflex organization of thoracic and lumbar segments in the frog spinal cord. *Brain Res.* 124, 415–426.

Castiglioni, A. J., Gallaway, M. C. and Coulter, J. D. (1977). Origins of brainstem projections to spinal cord in monkey. *Anat. Rec.* 187, 547.

Cliff, G. S. and Ridge, R. M. A. P. (1973). Innervation of extrafusal and intrafusal fibres in snake muscle. *J. Physiol., Lond.* 233, 1–18.

Conradi, S. (1969). Ultrastructure of dorsal root boutons on lumbosacral motoneurons of the adult cat, as revealed by dorsal root section. *Acta physiol. scand.* suppl. 332, 85–115.

Corvaja, N. and Grofová, I. (1972). Vestibulospinal projections in the toad. *Prog. Brain Res.* 37, 297–307.

Corvaja, N., Grofová, I. and Pompeiano, O. (1973). The origin, course and termination of vestibulospinal fibers in the toad. *Brain, Behav. Evol.* 7, 401–423.

Cowan, W. M., and Cuénod, M. (eds) (1975). "The Use of Axonal Transport for Studies of Neuronal Connectivity." Elsevier, Amsterdam.

Cowan, W. M., Gottlieb, D. I., Henrickson, A. E., Price, J. L. and Woolsey, T. A. (1972). The autoradiographic demonstration of axonal connections in the central nervous system. *Brain Res.* 37, 21–51.

Crowe, A. and Ragab, A. H. M. F. (1970). The structure, distribution and innervation of spindles in the extensor digitorum brevis I muscle of the tortoise *Testudo graeca*. *J. Anat.* 106, 521–538.

Cruce, W. L. R. (1974). A supraspinal monosynaptic input to hindlimb motoneurons in lumbar spinal cord of the frog, *Rana catesbeiana*. *J. Neurophysiol.* 37, 691–704.

Cruce, W. L. R. (1975). Termination of supraspinal descending pathways in the spinal cord of the tegu lizard (*Tupinambis nigropunctatus*). *Brain, Behav. Evol.* 12, 247–269.

Cruce, W. L. R. and Nieuwenhuys, R. (1974). The cell masses in the brainstem of the turtle *Testudo hermanni*; a topographical and topological analysis. *J. comp. Neurol.* 156, 277–306.

Culberson, J. L. and Kimmel, D. L. (1975). Primary afferent fiber distribution at brachial and lumbosacral spinal cord levels in the opossum (*Didelphis marsupialis virginiana*). *Brain, Behav. Evol.* 12, 229–246.

Cullheim, S. and Kellerth, J. O. (1976). Combined light and electron microscopical tracing of neurons, including axons and synaptic terminals, after intracellular injection of horseradish peroxidase. *Neurosci. Lett.* 2, 307–313.

Cummings, J. F. and Petras, J. M. (1977). The origin of spinocerebellar pathways. I. The nucleus cervicalis centralis of the cranial cervical spinal cord. *J. comp. Neurol.* 173, 655–692.

Czarkowska, J., Jankowska, E. and Sybirska, E. (1976). Axonal projections of spinal interneurons excited by group I afferents in the cat, revealed by intracellular staining with horseradish peroxidase. *Brain Res.* 118, 115–118.

de Lange, S. J. (1917). Das Hinterhirn, das Nachhirn und das Rückenmark der Reptilien. *Fol. Neurobiol.* 10, 385–423.

Donaldson, H. H. and Davis, D. J. (1903). Description of charts showing areas of the cross-sections of the human spinal cord at the level of each nerve. *J. comp. Neurol.* 13, 19–40.

Ebbesson, S. O. E. (1969). Brainstem afferents from the spinal cord in a sample of reptilian and amphibian species. *Ann. N.Y. Acad. Sci.* 167, 80–102.

Ebbesson, S. O. E. (1976). Morphology of the spinal cord. *In* "Frog Neurobiology." (R. Llinás and W. Precht, eds). Springer Verlag, Berlin, pp. 679–706.

Fields, H. L., Clanton, C. H. and Anderson, S. D. (1977). Somatosensory properties of spinoreticular neurons in the cat. *Brain Res.* **120**, 49–66.

Fink, R. P. and Heimer, L. (1967). Two methods for selective impregnation of degenerating axons and their synaptic endings in the central nervous system. *Brain Res.* **4**, 369–374.

Forssberg, H. and Grillner, S. (1973). The locomotion of the acute spinal cat injected with clonidine i.v. *Brain Res.* **50**, 184–186.

Fougerousse, C. L. and Hancock, M. B. (1976). Retrograde transport of horseradish peroxidase from the spinal cord to cells in the dorsolateral pontine tegmentum in the rat, cat and monkey. *Anat. Rec.* **184**, 405.

Fukushima, K., Peterson, B. W., Uchino, Y., Coulter, J. D. and Wilson, V. J. (1977). Direct fastigiospinal fibers in the cat. *Brain Res.* **126**, 538–542.

Fuller, P. M. (1974). Projections of the vestibular nuclear complex in the bullfrog (*Rana catesbeiana*). *Brain, Behav. Evol.* **10**, 157–169.

Gans, C. (1966). Locomotion without limbs. *Nat. Hist. N.Y.* **75**, 10–17, 36–41.

Gaskell, W. H. (1885). On a segmental group of ganglion cells in the spinal cord of the alligator. *J. Physiol., Lond.* **7**, Proc. p. 19.

Gelfan, S., Field, T. H. and Pappas, G. D. (1974). The receptive surface and axonal terminals in severely denervated neurons within the lumbosacral cord of the dog. *Expl. Neurol.* **43**, 162–191.

Giesler, G. J. Jr., Menétrey, D., Guilbaud, G. and Besson, J.-M. (1976). Lumbar cord neurons at the origin of the spinothalamic tract in the rat. *Brain Res.* **118**, 320–324.

Giovanelli Barilari, M. and Kuypers, H. G. J. M. (1969). Propriospinal fibers interconnecting the spinal enlargements in the cat. *Brain Res.* **14**, 321–330.

Goldby, F. and Robinson, L. R. (1962). The central connections of dorsal spinal nerve roots and the ascending tracts in the spinal cord of *Lacerta viridis*. *J. Anat., Lond.* **96**, 153–170.

Grillner, S. (1976). Some aspects on the descending control of the spinal circuits generating locomotor movements. *In* "Neural Control of Locomotion." (R. M. Herman, S. Grillner, P. S. G. Stein and D. G. Stuart, eds). Plenum, New York, pp. 351–376.

Grillner, S. and Shik, M. L. (1973). On the descending control of the lumbosacral spinal cord from the "mesencephalic locomotor region." *Acta physiol. scand.* **87**, 320–333.

Groebbels, F. (1927). Die Lage und Bewegungsreflexe der Vögel. VII. Die Lage und Bewegungsreflexe der Haustaube nach Läsionen des Rückenmarks und der Oblongata. *Pflügers Arch. ges. Physiol.* **218**, 198–208.

Guibé, J. (1970). La locomotion. *In* "Traité de Zoologie." (P.-P. Grassé, ed.). Masson, Paris, **14**, 181–193.

Häggqvist, G. (1936). Analyse der Faserverteilung in einem Rückenmarkquerschnitt (Th. 3). *Z. mikr.-anat. Forsch.* **39**, 1–34.

Halbertsma, J., Miller, S. and van der Meché, F. G. A. (1976). Basic programs for the phasing of flexion and extension movements of the limbs during locomotion. *In* "Neural Control of Locomotion." (R. M. Herman, S. Grillner, P. S. G. Stein and D. G. Stuart, eds). Plenum, New York, pp. 489–517.

Hancock, M. B. (1976). Cells of origin of hypothalamospinal projections in the rat. *Neurosci. Lett.* **3**, 179–184.

Hoffstetter, R. and Gasc, J.-P. (1969). Vertebrae and ribs of modern reptiles. *In* "Biology of the Reptilia." (C. Gans, A. d'A. Bellairs and T. S. Parsons, eds). Academic Press, New York, **1**, 201–310.

Hoogland, P. V. (1977). Efferent connections of the striatum in *Tupinambis nigropunctatus*. *J. Morph.* **152**, 229–246.

Ichiki, M., Nakagaki, I., Konishi, A. and Fukami, Y. (1976). The innervation of muscle spindles in the snake, *Elaphe quadrivirgata*. *J. Anat.* 122, 141–167.

Jankowska, E. (1975). Identification of interneurons interposed in different spinal reflex pathways. In "Golgi Centennial Symposium." (M. Santini, ed.). Raven Press, New York, pp. 235–246.

Jankowska, E. and Lindström, S. (1973). Procion Yellow staining of functionally identified interneurones in the spinal cord of the cat. In "Intracellular Staining in Neurobiology." (S. B. Kater and C. Nicholson, eds). Springer Verlag, Heidelberg, pp. 199–209.

Jankowska, E., Lundberg, A., Roberts, W. J. and Stuart, D. (1974). A long propriospinal system with direct effect on motoneurons and on interneurons in the cat lumbosacral cord. *Expl. Brain Res.* 21, 169–194.

Jankowska, E. Rastad, J. and Westman, J. (1976). Intracellular applications of horseradish peroxidase and its light and electron microscopical appearance in spinocervical tract cells. *Brain Res.* 105, 557–562.

Janzik, H. H. and Glees, P. (1967). The origin of the spinal ventromedial tract in the chick. *J. Hirnforsch.* 9, 91–97.

Joseph, B. S. and Whitlock, D. G. (1968). The morphology of spinal afferent–efferent relationships in vertebrates. *Brain, Behav. Evol.* 1, 2–18.

Karten, H. J. and Dubbeldam, J. L. (1973). The organization and projections of the paleostriatal complex in the pigeon (*Columba livia*). *J. comp. Neurol.* 148, 61–90.

Karten, H. J., Hodos, W., Nauta, W. J. H. and Revzin, A. M. (1973). Neural connections of the "visual Wulst" of the avian telencephalon. Experimental studies in the pigeon (*Columba livia*) and owl (*Speotyto cunicularia*). *J. comp. Neurol.* 150, 253–278.

Kashin, S. M., Feldman, A. G. and Orlovsky, G. N. (1974). Locomotion of fish evoked by electrical stimulation of the brain. *Brain Res.* 82, 41–47.

Kater, S. B. and Nicholson, C., eds. (1973). "Intracellular Staining in Neurobiology." Springer Verlag, Heidelberg.

Klüver, H. and Barrera, E. (1953). A method for the combined staining of cells and fibers in the central nervous system. *J. Neuropath. expl Neurol.* 12, 400–403.

Kokoros, J. J. and Northcutt, R. G. (1977). Telencephalic efferents of the tiger salamander *Ambystoma tigrinum tigrinum* (Green). *J. comp. Neurol.* 173, 613–628.

Kostyuk, P. G. (1975). Interneuronal mechanisms of interactions between descending and afferent signals in the spinal cord. In "Golgi Centennial Symposium: Perspectives in Neurobiology." (M. Santini, ed.). Raven Press, New York, pp. 247–259.

Kostyuk, P. G. (1976). Supraspinal mechanisms on a spinal level. In "The Motor System: Neurophysiology and Muscle Mechanisms." (M. Shahani, ed.). Elsevier, Amsterdam, pp. 211–259.

Kuhlenbeck, H. (1975). "The Central Nervous System of Vertebrates." Karger, Basel, Vol. 4.

Kusuma, A. and ten Donkelaar, H. J. (1979). Propriospinal fibers interconnecting the spinal enlargements in reptiles. In press.

Kuypers, H. G. J. M. (1973). The anatomical organization of the descending pathways and their contributions to motor control especially in primates. In "New Developments in Electromyography and Clinical Neurophysiology." (J. E. Desmedt, ed.). Karger, Basel, 3, 38–68.

Kuypers, H. G. J. M. and Maisky, V. A. (1975). Retrograde axonal transport of horse-radish peroxidase from spinal cord to brainstem cell groups in the cat. *Neurosci. Lett.* 1, 9–14.

LaMotte, C. (1977). Distribution of the tract of Lissauer and the dorsal root fibers in the primate spinal cord. *J. comp. Neurol.* 172, 529–562.

Lennard, P. R. and Stein, P. S. G. (1977). Swimming movements elicited by electrical stimulation of turtle spinal cord. I. Low spinal and intact preparations. *J. Neurophysiol.* 40, 768–778.

Leonard, R. B. and Cohen, D. H. (1975a). A cytoarchitectonic analysis of the spinal cord of the pigeon (*Columba livia*). *J. comp. Neurol.* 163, 159–180.

Leonard, R. B. and Cohen, D. H. (1975b). Spinal terminal fields of dorsal root fibers in the pigeon (*Columba livia*). *J. comp. Neurol.* 163, 181–192.

Lissauer, H. (1885). Beitrag zum pathologischen Anatomie der Tabes dorsalis und zum Faserverlauf im menschlichen Rückenmark. *Neurol. Cbl.* 4, 245–246.

Llinás, R. (1973). Procion yellow as a tool for the study of structure–function relationships in vertebrate central nervous systems. In "Intracellular Staining in Neurobiology." (S. B. Kater and C. Nicholson, eds). Springer Verlag, Heidelberg, pp. 211–226.

Lohman, A. H. M. and van Woerden-Verkley, I. (1976). Further studies on the cortical connections of the Tegu lizard. *Brain Res.* 103, 9–28.

Martin, G. F. (1969). The pattern of neocortical projections to the mesencephalon of the opossum, *Didelphis virginiana*. *Brain Res.* 11, 593–610.

Martin, G. F., Beattie, M. S., Bresnahan, J. C., Henkel, C. K. and Hughes, H. C. (1975). Cortical and brainstem projections to the spinal cord of the American opossum (*Didelphis marsupialis virginiana*). *Brain, Behav. Evol.* 12, 270–310.

Martin, G. F. and Dom, R. (1970). The rubrospinal tract of the opossum (*Didelphis virginiana*). *J. comp. Neurol.* 138, 19–30.

Martin, G. F. and Fisher, A. M. (1968). A further evaluation of the origin, the course and the termination of the opossum corticospinal tract. *J. Neurol. Sci.* 7, 177–188.

Matsushita, M. and Ikeda, M. (1973). Propriospinal fiber connections of the cervical motor nuclei in the cat: a light and electron microscope study. *J. comp. Neurol.* 150, 1–32.

Matsushita, M. and Ikeda, M. (1975). The central cervical nucleus as cell origin of a spinocerebellar tract arising from the cervical cord: a study in the cat using horseradish peroxidase. *Brain Res.* 100, 412–417.

Massion, J. (1967). The mammalian red nucleus. *Phys. Rev.* 47, 383–436.

McLaughlin, B. J. (1972). Propriospinal and supraspinal projections to the motor nuclei in the cat spinal cord. *J. comp. Neurol.* 144, 475–500.

Mensah, P. L. (1974). "The Course and Distribution of the Descending Fibers of the Lateral Funiculus of the Amphibian Spinal Cord." Thesis Univ. California, Irvine.

Miller, S. and van der Burg, J. (1973). The function of long propriospinal pathways in the coordination of quadrupedal stepping in the cat. In "The Control of Posture and Locomotion." (R. B. Stein, ed.). Plenum, New York, pp. 561–577.

Molenaar, I. and Kuypers, H. G. J. M. (1975). Identification of cells of origin of long fiber connections in the cat's spinal cord by means of the retrograde axonal horseradish peroxidase technique. *Neurosci. Lett.* 1, 193–197.

Molenaar, I., Rustioni, A. and Kuypers, H. G. J. M. (1974). The location of cells of origin of the fibers in the ventral and the lateral funiculus of the cat's lumbosacral cord. *Brain Res.* 78, 239–254.

Nauta, W. J. H. and Gygax, P. A. (1954). Silver impregnation of degenerating axons in the central nervous system: a modified technique. *Stain Technol.* 29, 91–93.

Nauta, W. J. H. and Karten, H. J. (1970). A general profile of the vertebrate brain, with sidelights on the ancestry of cerebral cortex. In "The Neurosciences, Second Study Program." (F. O. Schmidt, ed.). Rockefeller University Press, New York, pp. 7–26.

Nieuwenhuys, R. (1964). Comparative anatomy of the spinal cord. *Prog. Brain Res.* 11, 1–57.

Nyberg-Hansen, R. (1966). Functional organization of descending supraspinal fiber systems to the spinal cord. Anatomical observations and physiological correlations. *Ergebn. Anat. EntwGesch.* **39**, 1–48.

Nygren, L.-G. and Olson, L. (1977). A new major projection from locus coeruleus: the main source of noradrenergic nerve terminals in the ventral and dorsal columns of the spinal cord. *Brain Res.* **132**, 85–93.

Parent, A. and Poitras, D. (1974). Projection of catecholamine neurons of the lower brainstem to the cerebral cortex in the turtle (*Chrysemys picta*). *Anat. Rec.* **178**, 435.

Peterson, B. W., Maunz, R. A., Pitts, N. G. and Mackel, R. G. (1975). Patterns of projection and branching of reticulospinal neurons. *Expl. Brain Res.* **23**, 333–351.

Petras, J. M. (1976). Comparative anatomy of the tetrapod spinal cord: dorsal root connections. *In* "Evolution of Brain and Behaviour in Vertebrates." (R. B. Masterton, M. E. Bitterman, C. B. G. Campbell and N. Hotton, eds). L. Erlbaum, Hillsdale, pp. 345–381.

Petras, J. M. (1977). Spinocerebellar neurons in the rhesus monkey. *Brain Res.* **130**, 146–151.

Petras, J. M. and Cummings, J. F. (1977). The origin of spinocerebellar pathways. II. The nucleus centrobasalis of the cervical enlargements and the nucleus dorsalis of the thoracolumbar spinal cord. *J. comp. Neurol.* **173**, 693–716.

Proske, U. and Ridge, R. M. A. P. (1974). Extrafusal muscle and muscle spindles in reptiles. *Prog. Neurobiol.* **3**, 1–29.

Ramón y Cajal, S. (1891). "La Médulla Espinal de los Reptiles. Pequenas Contribuciones al Conociniento del Sistema Nervioso." Barcelona.

Ranson, S. W. and Clark, S. L. (1959). "The Anatomy of the Nervous System." Saunders, Philadelphia.

Retzius, G. (1894). Die embryonale Entwicklung der Rückenmarkselemente bei den Ophidiern. *Biol. Unters.* **6**, 41.

Retzius, G. (1898). Weiteres über die embryonale Entwicklung der Rückenmarkselemente der Ophidiern. *Biol. Unters.* **8**, 105–108.

Rexed, B. (1952). The cytoarchitectonic organization of the spinal cord in the cat. *J. comp. Neurol.* **96**, 415–496.

Rexed, B. (1954). A cytoarchitectonic atlas of the spinal cord in the cat. *J. comp. Neurol.* **100**, 297–379.

Rexed, B. (1964). Some aspects of the cytoarchitectonics and synaptology of the spinal cord. *Prog. Brain Res.* **11**, 58–92.

Robinson, L. R. (1969). Bulbospinal fibres and their nuclei of origin in *Lacerta viridis* demonstrated by axonal degeneration and chromatolysis respectively. *J. Anat.* **105**, 59–88.

Rosenberg, M. E. (1972). Excitation and inhibition of motoneurons in the tortoise. *J. Physiol., Lond.* **221**, 715–730.

Rosenberg, M. E. (1974). The distribution of the sensory input in the dorsal spinal cord of the tortoise. *J. comp. Neurol.* **156**, 29–38.

Rovainen, C. M. (1967). Physiological and anatomical studies on large neurons of the central nervous system of the sea lamprey (*Petromyzon marinus*). I. Müller and Mauthner cells. *J. Neurophysiol.* **30**, 1000–1023.

Rustioni, A., Kuypers, H. G. J. M. and Holstege, G. (1971). Propriospinal projections from the ventral and lateral funiculi to the motoneurons in the lumbosacral cord of the cat. *Brain Res.* **34**, 255–275.

Saper, C. B., Loewy, A. D., Swanson, L. W. and Cowan, W. M. (1976). Direct hypothalamo-autonomic connections. *Brain Res*, **117**, 305–312.

Shapovalov, A. I. (1975). Neuronal organization and synaptic mechanisms of supraspinal motor control in vertebrates. *Rev. Physiol. Biochem. Pharmacol.* **72**, 1–54.

Shik, M. L. and Orlovsky, G. N. (1976). Neurophysiology of locomotor automatism. *Physiol. Rev.* **56**, 465–502.

Shik, M. L., Severin, F. V. and Orlovsky, G. N. (1966). Control of walking and running by means of electrical stimulation of the midbrain. *Biophysics* **11**, 756–765.

Shimamura, M. (1973). Spino-bulbo-spinal and propriospinal reflexes in various vertebrates. *Brain Res.* **64**, 141–165.

Shinoda, Y., Arnold, A. P. and Asanuma, H. (1976). Spinal branching of corticospinal axons in the cat. *Expl. Brain Res.* **26**, 215–234.

Skinner, R. D. (1977). Cells of origin of the long ascending and descending propriospinal tracts. *Anat. Rec.* **187**, 715.

Snow, P. J., Rose, P. K. and Brown, A. (1976). Tracing axons and axon collaterals of spinal neurones using intracellular injection of horseradish peroxidase. *Science, N.Y.* **191**, 312–313.

Snyder, R. (1977). The organization of the dorsal root entry zone in cats and monkeys. *J. comp. Neurol.* **174**, 47–70.

Snyder, R. C. (1952). Quadrupedal and bipedal locomotion in lizards. *Copeia* **1952**(2), 64–70.

Snyder, R. L. (1977). A comparative study of the neurons of origin of cerebellar afferents in the rat, cat and squirrel monkey based on the horseradish peroxidase retrograde tracer technique: The spinal afferents. *Anat. Rec.* **187**, 719.

Soller, R. W. (1977). Monoaminergic inputs to frog motoneurons: an anatomical study using fluorescence histochemical and silver impregnation techniques. *Brain Res.* **122**, 445–458.

Stannius, H. (1849). "Nouveau Manuel d'Anatomie Comparée." Roret, Paris, Vol. 2.

Steeves, J. D., Jordan, L. M. and Lake, N. (1975). The close proximity of catecholamine-containing cells to the "mesencephalic locomotor region" (MLR). *Brain Res.* **100**, 663–670.

Stein, P. S. G. (1976). Mechanisms of interlimb phase control. *In* "Neural Control of Locomotion." (R. M. Herman, S. Grillner, P. S. G. Stein and D. G. Stuart, eds). Plenum, New York, pp. 465–487.

Sterling, P. and Kuypers, H. G. J. M. (1968). Anatomical organization of the brachial spinal cord. III. The propriospinal connections. *Brain Res.* **7**, 419–443.

Streeter, G. L. (1904). The structure of the spinal cord of the ostrich. *Am. J. Anat.* **3**, 1–27.

Stretton, O. W. and Kravitz, E. A. (1968). Neuronal geometry: determination with a technique of intracellular dye injection. *Science, N.Y.* **162**, 132–134.

Székely, G. and Czéh, G. (1976). Organization of locomotion. *In* "Frog Neurobiology." (R. Llinás and W. Precht, eds). Springer, Berlin, pp. 765–792.

ten Donkelaar, H. J. (1976a). Descending pathways from the brainstem to the spinal cord in some reptiles. I. Origin. *J. comp. Neurol.* **167**, 421–442.

ten Donkelaar, H. J. (1976b). Descending pathways from the brainstem to the spinal cord in some reptiles. II. Course and site of termination. *J. comp. Neurol.* **167**, 443–463.

ten Donkelaar, H. J. and de Boer-van Huizen, R. (1978). Cells of origin of pathways descending to the spinal cord in a lizard (*Lacerta galloti*). *Neurosci. Lett.* **9**, 123–128.

Tohyama, M. (1976). Comparative anatomy of cerebellar catecholamine innervation from teleosts to mammals. *J. Hirnforsch.* **17**, 43–60.

Trevino, D. L. and Carstens, E. (1975). Confirmation of the location of spinothalamic neurons in the cat and monkey by the retrograde transport of horseradish peroxidase. *Brain Res.* 98, 177–182.

Trevino, D. L., Coulter, J. D. and Willis, W. D. (1973). Location of cells of origin of spinothalamic tract in lumbar enlargement of the monkey. *J. Neurophysiol.* 36, 750–761.

van den Akker, L. M. (1969). The termination of three long descending systems in the cord of the pigeon. *Psychiat. Neurol. Neurochir.* 72, 11–16.

van den Akker, L. M. (1970). "An Anatomical Outline of the Spinal Cord in the Pigeon." Thesis, University of Leiden, Van Gorcum, Assen.

van Beusekom, G. T. (1955). "Fibre Analysis of the Anterior and Lateral Funiculi of the Cord of the Cat." Thesis, University of Leiden. Eduard, Ydo, Leiden.

van Gehuchten, A. (1897). Contribution à l'étude de la moelle épinière chez les vertébrés (*Tropidonotus natrix*). *Cellule* 12, 113–165.

van der Sloot, C. J. (1968). De eindiging van de vezels van de dorsale wortel in het ruggemerg van de schildpad (*Testudo hermanni*). *Ned. Tijdschr. v. Geneesk.* 112, 430.

Verhaart, W. J. C. (1970). "Comparative Anatomical Aspects of the Mammalian Brainstem and the Cord." Van Gorcum, Assen.

Voris, H. C. (1928). The morphology of the spinal cord of the Virginian opossum (*Didelphis virginiana*). *J. comp. Neurol.* 46, 407–459.

Wetzel, M. C. and Stuart, D. G. (1976). Ensemble characteristics of cat locomotion and its neurol control. *Prog. Neurobiol.* 7, 1–98.

Zecha, A. (1961). Bezit een vogel een fasciculus rubro-bulbo-spinalis? *Ned. Tijdschr. v. Geneesk.* 105, 2373.

Zecha, A. (1962). The "pyramidal tract" and other telencephalic efferents in birds. *Acta Morphol. Neerl.-Scand.* 5, 194.

Zeier, H. and Karten, H. J. (1971). The archistriatum of the pigeon: organization of afferent and efferent connections. *Brain Res.* 31, 313–326.

CHAPTER 3

Spinal Cord in Lizards

WILLIAM L. R. CRUCE

Neurobiology Department,
Northeastern Ohio Universities
College of Medicine,
Rootstown, Ohio, U.S.A.

I. Introduction

The relationship between the brain and spinal cord has been most extensively studied in lizards. The overall pattern of spinal cord organization is,
therefore, best known for members of this group of reptiles and can serve
as a paradigm within which to discuss the spinal cords of species in other
taxa or with particular locomotory adaptations. This chapter summarizes
our current understanding of spinal cord anatomy in lizards, emphasizing
particularly the tegu lizard, *Tupinambis nigropunctatus*. It discusses, in
turn, the organization of the gray matter, ascending pathways and descending pathways, and concludes with a brief statement of the overall organization
of spinal systems in lizards. The following chapter contains a general discussion of reptilian brainstems, including those cellular groups which
participate in projections to the spinal cord. More detailed treatments of
the intrinsic organization of the spinal cords of members of other groups
are contained in the preceding chapter.

II. Organization of the Spinal Gray

A. GENERAL

The spinal cord is divided into an exterior mantle of white matter, composed of fibers, and an interior core of gray matter, composed of cells. The
gray matter can be subdivided into dorsal and ventral horns, as in mammals.
The gray matter of the tegu lizard spinal cord is divisible into ten transverse
regions (Cruce, 1974b, 1975, 1978), similar to the "laminae" described by
Rexed (1952, 1954, 1964) for the cat (Fig. 1). They have the same numbers

used in that analysis. The precise definition of these laminae is important as a basis for studying the termination sites of descending systems. The following description of the laminae is based primarily on Nissl-stained material (cresyl violet or thionin stains) and fiber-stained material (Heidenhain's stain), except where it is specifically mentioned that Golgi-impregnated material was used.

B. Laminar Organization of Gray Matter

Lamina I (Figs 2, 3) is composed of large, spindle shaped cells with lightly stained cytoplasm. They are very sparse, often numbering one per 100 μm section. This lamina is one cell thick in a composite drawing made from several adjacent sections. It is present only at the lateral border of the dorsal horn. The long axes of the cells are parallel to the borders of gray and white matter. Occasionally, similar spindle shaped cells are found in the adjacent white matter between bundles of fibers; thus the exact border of this lamina with the white matter is indistinct.

Lamina II (Figs 2, 3) is composed of tightly packed, small cells which possess sparse cytoplasmic rims. They are located just beneath and central to lamina I.

Lamina III (Figs 2, 3) is composed of cells similar in appearance to those found in lamina II, but it differs from the latter in that its cells are loosely packed. Occasional large cells are seen, but they probably belong to lamina IV (see below).

The area comprised by laminae I, II and III is pale in silver stains for nerve fibers. It lacks large caliber fibers, except dorsal root fibers which pass through this region in small bundles. It therefore probably corresponds to the substantia gelantinosa described for reptiles by Keenan (1929).

Lamina IV (Figs 2, 3) is distinguished by large, lightly staining cells which contain clumps of Nissl material. It also contains small cells which resemble those of lamina III, although they are more closely packed. In the brachial and lumbar enlargements, this lamina is capped on its dorsal, lateral and medial aspects by lamina III, into which it occasionally protrudes (see above). In thoracic and caudal segments, lamina IV extends across the midline dorsal to lamina V.

Lamina V (Figs 2, 3, 4) is distinguished at its lateral border by a reticulated appearance. It is composed of two zones. The lateral zone contains a few large, dark, triangular or polygonal cells and is penetrated by longitudinal fiber bundles which create the reticulated appearance. The medial zone contains scattered, small-to-medium sized cells which are lightly stained. The medial part of the border between lamina V and lamina VI is quite distinct, while the lateral part is indistinct.

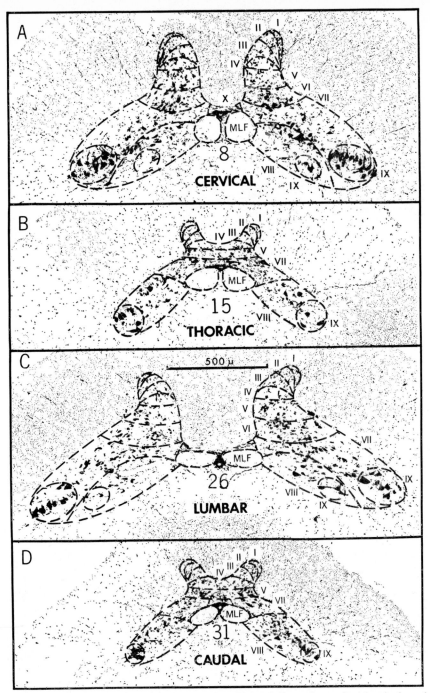

Fig. 1. High contrast photographs of 30 μm thick sections of tegu lizard spinal cord stained by the Nissl method. Boundaries of different cellular regions are indicated by dashed lines. These were determined by using the criteria of Rexed and studying the sections under high magnification. Roman numerals indicate the different cellular regions, or "laminae." Representative sections shown are: (A) middle of brachial enlargement; (B) thoracic level; (C) middle of lumbar enlargement; (D) caudal level. The medial longitudinal fasciculus (MLF) is a spinal continuation of the brainstem pathway of that same name. (After Cruce, 1975.)

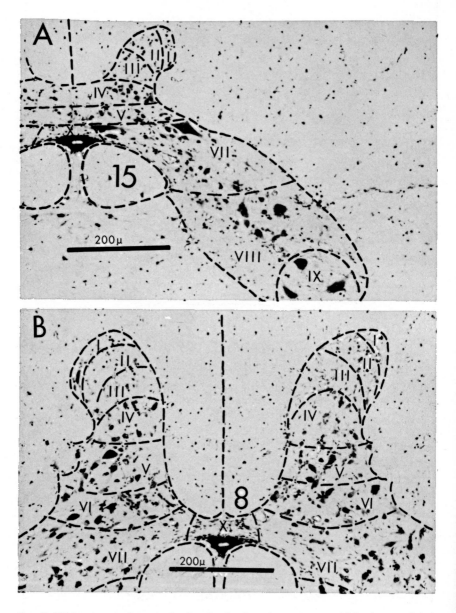

FIG. 2. High contrast photographs showing laminae (roman numerals) in the tegu lizard spinal gray. (A) A 30 μm section through segment 15 (thoracic). (B) A 30 μm section through segment 8 (cervical).

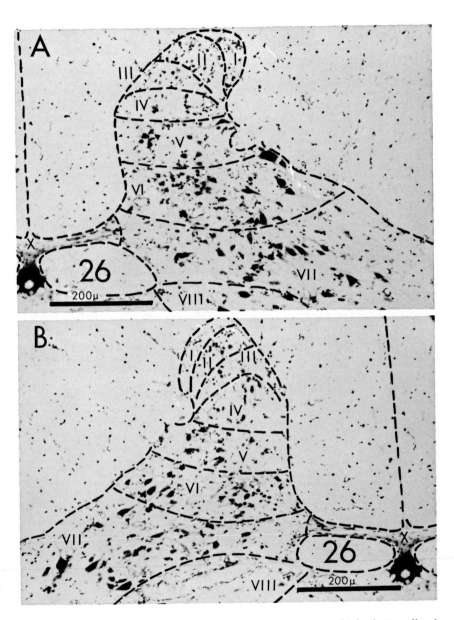

Fig. 3. High contrast photographs showing laminae (roman numerals) in the tegu lizard spinal gray. (A) A 30 μm section through segment 26 (lumbar). (B) A 30 μm section through the contralateral side of the same segment.

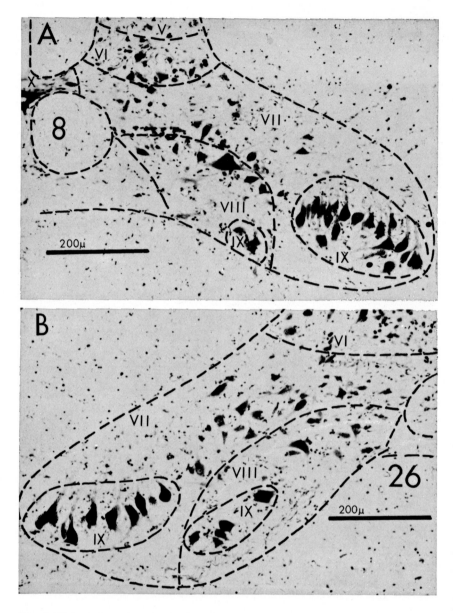

FIG. 4. High contrast photographs showing laminae (roman numerals) in the tegu lizard spinal gray. (A) A 30 μm section through segment 8 (cervical). (B) A 30 μm section through segment 26 (lumbar).

Lamina VI (Figs 2, 3, 4) is characterized by a medial zone of very tightly packed triangular or polygonal, medium-to-large sized cells. Its lateral zone contains the same cell types, although the large cells are more evident and all the cells are more loosely packed. Lamina VI exists only in the brachial and lumbosacral enlargements.

Lamina VII (Figs 2, 3, 4) is composed of a homogeneous group of scattered, medium-sized, lightly staining cells. There are a few cells which are either very small or very large. No lateral horn is evident. Although preganglionic sympathetic fibers are thought to exit through the ventral roots (Ariëns Kappers *et al.*, 1936), their cells of origin have never been described. No group of large cells which might be homologous to Clarke's column is seen anywhere in the cord. At thoracic and caudal levels, this lamina is much reduced and does not extend deep into the ventral horn.

In Golgi-impregnated material, cells in lamina VII generally fall into three classes: (a) those with dendrites and axons confined to lamina VII and the lateral lamina IX group, which is embedded within it; (b) those with dendrites and axons ramifying in the lateral white matter amongst the dendrites of lateral motoneurons and the lateral marginal plexus; and (c) those with dendrites confined to laminae V, VI and VII, which send their axons into the ipsilateral white matter or through the ventral accessory commissure to the contralateral side. The first two classes of cells are presumably interneurons which connect with other cells in lamina VII and in lateral lamina IX (see below). The third class of cells are candidates for neurons which give rise to the dorsal and ventral spinocerebellar pathways (Jacobs, 1968; Joseph and Whitlock, 1968b) or the spinoreticular, spinotectal and spinothalamic pathways (Goldby and Robinson, 1962; Ebbesson, 1967, 1969).

Lamina VIII (Figs 2, 4) is distinguished from lamina VII by its heterogeneous cell population, which ranges in size from the smallest cells found in the dorsal horn, to cells as large as motoneurons. Cells are mostly triangular or polygonal, but along the medial border with the white matter there are spindle-shaped cells which lie parallel to each other and to the border. The lateral border of lamina VIII with lamina VII is never very sharp.

In Golgi-impregnated material, cells in lamina VIII generally fall into two classes: (a) those with dendrites and axons the ramifications of which are entirely confined to the lamina; and (b) those with dendrites which ramify widely throughout lamina VIII, the ventromedial white matter and occasionally into lateral areas of gray and white. The axons of the latter cells frequently pass through the ventral accessory commissure to the contralateral side. The first class of cells are probably interneurons which connect with other cells in lamina VIII and in medial lamina IX (see below). The second class of cells are probably commissural cells particularly involved in connecting lamina VIII and medial lamina IX with their contralateral counterparts.

Lamina IX (Figs 2, 4) is composed of large, darkly staining cells possessing abundant Nissl substance and is not at all laminar in formation. Rather, it consists of two longitudinal columns, one (present throughout the spinal cord) in a medial position and the other (present only in enlargements) in a lateral position. The medial group is presumably composed of motoneurons which innervate axial or trunk musculature; the lateral group of motoneurons innervates the limbs (Ariëns Kappers *et al.*, 1936; Nieuwenhuys, 1964; Romanes, 1964; Cruce, 1974a).

In Golgi-stained material, the motoneurons of the two lamina IX groups present contrasting dendritic arborizations (Fig. 5). The medial group of motoneurons tends to elaborate its dendrites within lamina VIII and in a somewhat radial pattern. On the other hand, each lateral motoneuron has two prominent dendrites; one extends into the ventral parts of lamina VIII and medial lamina IX before arborizing, and the other extends along the dorsolateral border of lamina VII to send branches radially into the lateral funiculus and into the subpial dendritic plexus. Although the longitudinal organization of lizard motoneurons has not yet been thoroughly analyzed, some preliminary observations have been made on horizontal and sagittal sections of Golgi-impregnated material. Motoneuronal dendrites run in the rostrocaudal axis through the column of motoneurons. Dendritic bundles, or thickets, such as are seen in the spinal cords of mammals (Scheibel and Scheibel, 1970; Matthews *et al.*, 1971) and amphibians (Stensaas and Stensaas, 1971) have not been recognized, but further analysis is necessary.

Lamina X (Figs 2, 3, 4) is a compact region of small cells dorsal to the central canal and the *medial longitudinal fasciculus* (MLF). It also contains decussating fibers of some descending pathways (Cruce, 1975, 1978, and discussion below).

The Golgi picture of the organization of axons and dendrites of neurons intrinsic to the tegu lizard spinal cord is similar to that seen by Ramón y Cajal (1891, 1909–11) in the lizard *Lacerta* and by Banchi (1903) in the turtle *Emys*. In some respects it is also similar to that seen in mammals (e.g. Matsushita, 1970a, b); i.e. neurons of lamina VII are related ventrally and laterally to neurons of lateral lamina IX and the lateral funiculus, while neurons of lamina VIII are related ventrally and medially to medial lamina IX, the ventral funiculus and the commissures. Since it is probable that lateral lamina IX contains motoneurons innervating the limbs, and medial lamina IX contains those innervating the trunk (Cruce, 1974a), it may be suggested that laminae VII and VIII are involved in the integration of limb and trunk movement respectively, as has been proposed to be the case in mammals (Sterling and Kuypers, 1968).

A notable difference between reptilian and mammalian spinal organization is also revealed by analysis of Golgi-impregnated material. Whereas mam-

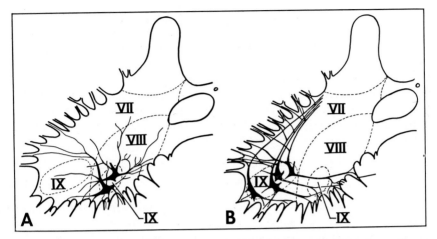

FIG. 5. Camera lucida drawing prepared from Golgi-impregnated sections of tegu lizard spinal cord. Different cellular regions of the ventral horn as determined in Nissl-stained sections are indicated by dashed lines. (A) Motoneurons of the medial lamina IX group; note that motoneuronal dendrites are confined primarily to the medial lamina IX area and lamina VIII. (B) Motoneurons of the lateral lamina IX group; note the extensive ramification of motoneuron dendrites into laminae VII, VIII, and the medial lamina IX region. (After Cruce, 1975.)

malian spinal motoneurons exhibit a uniform multipolar dendritic pattern (Testa, 1964), tegu lizard lateral motoneurons usually possess two primary dendrites—a medial one and a lateral one. This dendritic configuration is reminiscent of the structure of the goldfish Mauthner cell (Bodian, 1937) and raises the intriguing possibility that different types of synaptic input might be confined to either the medial or the lateral dendrite.

C. FIBER SYSTEMS RELATED TO THE GRAY MATTER

There are neither neurons nor commissural fibers immediately beneath the central canal in lizards. Instead, this region is occupied by a bundle of extremely large, predominantly myelinated axons. This bundle, which lies on each side of the midline, is a direct caudal continuation of the medial longitudinal fasciculus of the brainstem (Goldby and Robinson, 1961; Nieuwenhuys, 1964). Terni (1921) thought this region contained ascending fibers, short propriospinal fibers and fibers from ventral horn cells. Beccari (1921), Leghissa (1954), Robinson (1969), Cruce (1975) and ten Donkelaar (1976a, b) have shown that the medial longitudinal fasciculus contains descending fibers from the brainstem (see below).

Immediately beneath the medial longitudinal fasciculus is the ventral accessory commissure of Mauthner (Ariëns Kappers *et al.*, 1936) which contains decussating axons of spinal neurons (especially from lamina VIII), decussating axons of some descending pathways, and dendrites of various cells in the ventral horn. This commissure serves as a boundary between the medial longitudinal fasciculus and the rest of the ventral funiculus in lizards. It does not exist in snakes and turtles; instead, fibers decussate immediately beneath the central canal and the medial longitudinal fasciculus is blended with the rest of the ventral funiculus, as in mammals. The significance of this difference is unknown.

D. MARGINAL NUCLEI

Cell groups located outside the gray matter and just beneath the pial surface have been described in several reptiles as the *marginal nuclei* (or nuclei of Gaskell). It has sometimes been claimed that they are found throughout the extent of the spinal cord (Ariëns Kappers *et al.*, 1936). In the tegu lizard, such cells occupy a dorsolateral position, immediately below the pia, in the first few segments of cervical spinal cord, but nowhere else. Their functional significance is unknown.

III. Ascending Spinal Pathways

A. DORSAL ROOT PROJECTIONS

Large diameter dorsal root fibers bifurcate as they enter the spinal cord and send ascending and descending branches into the dorsal funiculus. Small diameter fibers contribute to a dorsolateral tract, known as Lissauer's tract (Fig. 6). This tract, associated with processing noxious stimuli in mammals, is especially prominent in axonal silver stains (Nauta, 1957; Ebbesson, 1970; Heimer, 1970), where the fine fiber bundle contrasts sharply with the surrounding groups of large diameter fibers.

After ascending or descending for variable distances, fibers in the dorsal funiculus may send a branch into the spinal gray of the dorsal horn (Goldby and Robinson, 1962; Joseph and Whitlock, 1968b). Terminal arborizations of these fibers are primarily localized in the medial two-thirds of laminae IV and V in *Tupinambis* (Fig. 6; W. L. R. Cruce, unpublished data). Fibers in the substantia gelatinosa (laminae I–III) are grouped in tight bundles which terminate more ventrally. Dorsal root afferents do not cross the midline (Joseph and Whitlock, 1968b; W. L. R. Cruce, unpublished data). The contrary results of Goldby and Robinson (1962) may have been due to damage to descending fibers in the dorsolateral funiculus, which do send projections contralaterally (see below).

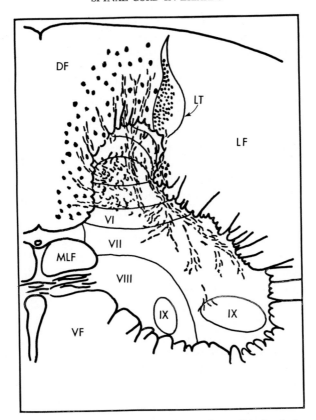

Fig. 6. A plot of axonal degeneration in segment 9 of tegu lizard spinal cord following complete transection of the ipsilateral 9th dorsal root. Axon terminals are not distinguished from preterminal debris and axons-of-passage. DF, dorsal funiculus; LF, lateral funiculus; LT, Lissauer's tract; MLF, medial longitudinal fasciculus; VF, ventral funiculus. Laminae are indicated by roman numerals. (From W. L. R. Cruce, unpublished data).

Fibers ascending in the dorsal funiculus transmit touch and vibratory sensations in mammals. They are somatotopically arranged in lizards, such that fibers originating caudally are located medially and those originating rostrally are found laterally (Fig. 6; Goldby and Robinson, 1962; Ebbesson, 1967, 1969). Although there is no septum separating them, these two groups of fibers form simple gracile and cuneate funiculi. Somatotopy is maintained in the terminations of dorsal column fibers in the dorsal column nuclei of the caudal medulla (Kruger and Witkovsky, 1961; Joseph and Whitlock, 1968b). Fibers from this region decussate and form medial lemnisci which reach the thalamus (Ariëns Kappers et al., 1936; Ebbesson, 1976).

In lizards, a small number of large diameter dorsal root fibers take up a lateral position in the reticulated substance of lamina V (Fig. 6; W. L. R. Cruce, unpublished data; Goldby and Robinson, 1962). This "lateral bundle" is much larger in snakes and turtles than in lizards (Nieuwenhuys, 1964). Its large size in snakes may partially account for the reduction in size of the dorsal columns in these forms. Thus the lateral bundle might represent a displaced dorsal column. In experimental degeneration studies (Fig. 6; W. L. R. Cruce, unpublished data; Goldby and Robinson, 1962), fibers from the lateral bundle appear to enter the spinal gray and, along with fibers passing from the dorsal funiculus, to terminate in the lateral parts of ventral horn laminae VI and VII. In *Tupinambis*, a few of these laterally placed dorsal root fibers reach the vicinity of the cell bodies of lateral lamina IX (Fig. 6; W. L. R. Cruce, unpublished data). In *Iguana*, dorsal root fibers reach down the entire lateral border of lamina VII, as in *Tupinambis*, but they do not quite reach the motoneuronal perikarya. In *Ctenosaura*, the fibers reach no farther than the dorsolateral part of lamina VII. In *Caiman* they appear not to reach into the ventral horn at all (Joseph and Whitlock, 1968b). These differences may be related to differing degrees of segmental control over motoneurons and to evolving dexterity of digital use (Joseph and Whitlock, 1968a). The connections have not yet been studied physiologically in crocodilians and lizards, but they probably establish synaptic contacts on motoneurons. Physiological techniques have shown that dorsal root fibers make monosynaptic connections with ventral horn motoneurons in a turtle (Rosenberg, 1972).

B. SECOND ORDER PATHWAYS

Cells in the spinal gray which receive afferents from the dorsal roots give rise to axons which ascend in the lateral funiculus to the reticular formation, vestibular nuclei, cerebellum, tectum and thalamus, as well as various other brainstem areas (Goldby and Robinson, 1962; Jacobs, 1968; Ebbesson, 1967, 1969). Details of these projections are considered in the following chapter. Although dorsal and ventral spinocerebellar tracts can be distinguished in experimental studies (Jacobs, 1968; Ebbesson, 1967, 1969), a distinct Clarke's nucleus (giving rise to the dorsal tract) has not been identified in either normal or experimental material. No chromatolytic cells were seen in the spinal gray following high spinal hemisection (Cruce, 1975). Similarly, a crossed spinal pathway carrying noxious cutaneous information can also be demonstrated on the basis of behavioural deficits following high spinal hemisection, but the location of the cells giving rise to this pathway remains unknown (Cruce, 1975, 1978).

IV. Supraspinal Descending Pathways

A. GENERAL

Reptiles are believed to possess the same supraspinal descending pathways as do mammals (Ariëns Kappers et al., 1936; Nieuwenhuys, 1964; Robinson, 1969; Cruce and Nieuwenhuys, 1974; Cruce, 1975, 1978; Cruce et al., 1976; ten Donkelaar, 1976a, b; W. L. R. Cruce and D. B. Newman, unpublished observations; W. L. R. Cruce, unpublished observations), with the notable exception of the corticospinal pathway (Goldby, 1937; Goldby and Gamble, 1957; Kruger and Berkowitz, 1960; Cruce, 1975; ten Donkelaar, 1976a; W. L. R. Cruce and D. B. Newman, unpublished observations). Experimental studies of anterograde fiber degeneration in lizards following lesions of the spinal white matter (Robinson, 1969; Cruce, 1975; ten Donkelaar, 1976b; W. L. R. Cruce, unpublished observations) have shown that there are major descending bundles of fibers in the medial longitudinal fasciculus (MLF), the dorsolateral funiculus (DLF), and the ventromedial funiculus (VMF). Descending fibers in the ventrolateral funiculus (VLF) are fewer in number and are scattered (Fig. 7). Following a complete cord hemisection at high cervical levels (Cruce, 1975), descending fiber terminal fields are absent in the dorsal horn (laminae I–IV), sparse, bilaterally, in laminae V–VII, and intense, bilaterally, in lamina VIII and medial lamina IX (Fig. 7).

B. DORSOLATERAL FUNICULUS

Smaller lesions of the spinal white matter demonstrate that fibers in the dorsolateral funiculus give rise to the sparse terminals in ipsilateral laminae V–VII and also cross in the dorsal commissure to terminate contralaterally in the medial parts of these laminae (Cruce et al., 1976; W. L. R. Cruce, unpublished observations; Fig. 8). Using retrograde chromatolysis (Robinson, 1969; Cruce et al., 1976, W. L. R. Cruce and D. B. Newman, unpublished observations), it has been shown that fibers in the dorsolateral funiculus originate in the contralateral red nucleus, solitary nucleus, dorsal motor nucleus of the vagus, inferior reticular nucleus, ventral part (Fig. 9). Fibers also originate in the ipsilateral dorsolateral metencephalic (subcoeruleus) nucleus, inferior reticular nucleus, dorsal part, and ventrolateral reticular nucleus. It has been hypothesized (e.g. Lawrence and Kuypers, 1968a, b) that fibers in the dorsolateral funiculus exert a descending control on limb musculature, both through direct contact with lateral motoneurons, which innervate limb musculature, and, more importantly, through synapses on

124 WILLIAM L. R. CRUCE

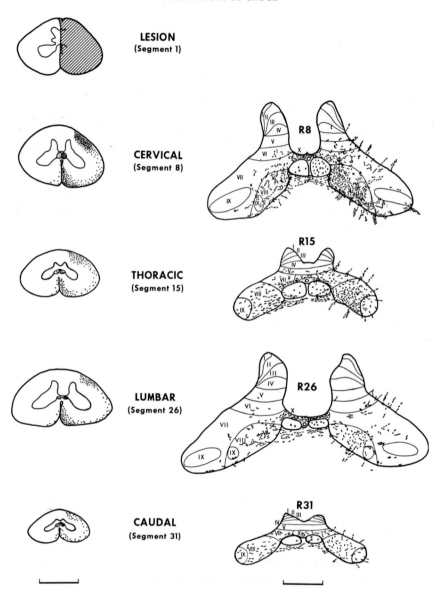

FIG. 7. A plot of axonal degeneration of representative levels of the lizard spinal cord following a complete hemisection at the first cord segment. Small drawings to the left show transversely cut axonal degeneration in the white matter. The large drawings to the right depict degeneration in the gray matter. Axon terminals are not distinguished from preterminal debris and axons-of-passage. (After Cruce, 1975.)

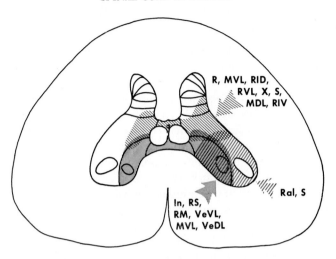

FIG. 8. A summary of spinal terminal fields of supraspinal descending fibers in the tegu lizard as revealed by axonal degeneration following experimental lesions. R, red nucleus; MVL, ventrolateral metencephalic nucleus; RID, inferior reticular nucleus, dorsal part; RVL, ventrolateral reticular nucleus; X, dorsal motor nucleus of vagus; S, nucleus of the solitary tract; MDL, dorsolateral metencephalic nucleus; RIV, inferior reticular nucleus, ventral part; RaI, inferior raphé nucleus; In, interstitial nucleus; RS, superior reticular nucleus; RM, middle reticular nucleus; VeVL, ventrolateral vestibular nucleus; VeDL, dorsolateral vestibular nucleus. (From W. L. R. Cruce, unpublished observations).

interneurons in laminae V–VIII, which are involved in integrating the activity in lateral motoneurons.

The sparse termination of dorsolateral funiculus fibers in the spinal gray of lizards correlates well with the minimal effects which lesions of this pathway have on coordinated limb movement (Cruce, 1975, 1978). It seems likely that descending control of the limbs is not well organized except in those animals, e.g. mammals, where the corticospinal and cortico-rubrospinal pathways have become highly developed. Since fibers of the dorsolateral funiculus pathway (Fig. 7) terminate in a region which overlaps with part of the terminal field of dorsal root afferents (Fig. 6), dorsolateral funiculus fibers possibly exert brainstem control over incoming sensory activity at spinal levels, either through presynaptic inhibition or some other mechanism.

C. VENTRAL FUNICULUS

The ventrolateral funiculus contains fibers descending from the ipsilateral solitary nucleus and inferior raphé bilaterally (Cruce et al., 1976; Fig. 9). These fibers distribute primarily to lamina VII, lamina VIII and medial lamina IX (Fig. 8).

The ventromedial funiculus contains fibers from the ipsilateral superior reticular nucleus and the ventrolateral vestibular nucleus (Deiters nucleus) (Cruce et al., 1976; Fig. 9). Many ventromedial funiculus fibers decussate at the level of their termination, so that there is a dense bilateral distribution to lamina VIII and medial lamina IX (Cruce et al., 1976; Fig. 8). These fiber terminals are located in the region containing interneurons and motoneurons which control axial musculature. Their high density correlates well with the observation that spinal lesions which involve the VMF result in dramatic abnormalities in the use of axial musculature. A major role of descending pathways in lizards may be to control trunk movements (Cruce, 1975, 1978).

The medial ventromedial funiculus and medial longitudinal funiculus contain fibers originating in the interstitial nucleus, middle reticular nucleus, ventrolateral metencephalic nucleus and dorsolateral vestibular nucleus. (Fig. 9). The terminal field of medial longitudinal funiculus fibers in the spinal cord is limited to lamina VIII and medial lamina IX. There is strong experimental evidence that the medial longitudinal funiculus carries fibers mediating rhythmic, respiratory movements of thoracic musculature (Ebbesson, 1967; Cruce, 1975). The medial longitudinal funiculus also continues as a large bundle below thoracic levels, but the function of these fibers is unknown.

D. FUNCTIONAL STUDIES

The behavioral effects of spinal hemisection in lizards are most dramatic in the trunk musculature, which is innervated by medial motoneurons. The marked, contralateral flexion observed in hemisected animals suggests that the net action of the descending pathways, acting reciprocally on agonistic and antagonistic muscle groups, is to facilitate ipsilateral trunk flexion. Such a pattern of descending synaptic activity might mediate a horizontal wave of flexion in the trunk, such as that observed during normal locomotion (Snyder, 1952; Bellairs, 1969).

High cervical cord hemisection has little effect on limb movements. Some of the effects which do appear, such as inability to support body weight, are probably due to weakness in shoulder and hip musculature, which is more related to deficits in axial musculature. Other effects, such as passive dragging of the limbs, might be due to sensory losses caused by interruption of the ascending sensory pathways (Cruce, 1975). The lack of supraspinal effect on limb movements in lizards correlates well with the lack of direct projections to the lateral motoneuron column and the sparseness of projections to interneuron regions (lateral laminae V, VI and VII) which influence lateral motoneurons. The lateral motoneurons still may come under supra-

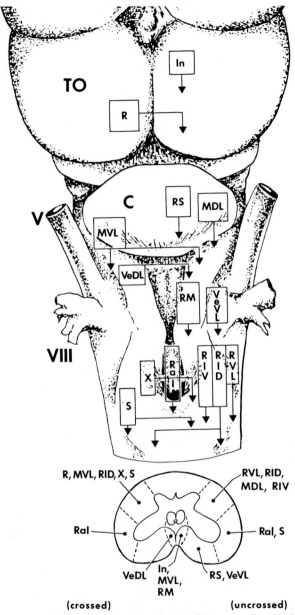

FIG. 9. A summary of the brainstem origins of and pathways in the spinal white matter of descending fiber tracts in tegu lizards as revealed by retrograde chromatolysis following experimental lesions. TO, optic tectum; C, cerebellum; V, trigeminal nerve; VIII, vestibulo-cochlear nerve, and as in Fig. 8. Pathways which descend in the dorsolateral funiculus (R. MVL, MDL, RID, RVL, RIV, X, S) terminate in laminae V, VI and VII (Fig. 8) and influence limb musculature, though weakly. Pathways descending in the ventrolateral and ventromedial funiculi (RaI, S, RS, VeVL, In, MVL, RM, VeDL) terminate in laminae VII, VIII and medial IX (Fig. 8) and influence axial musculature. (From W. L. R. Cruce and D. B. Newman, unpublished observations.)

spinal influence of the medial descending pathways via the medial moto-neuronal dendrites which extend into lamina VIII. It is also possible that lateral pathways may influence the lateral motoneurons directly via synapses on their lateral dendrites, though these would probably be sparse. The lateral dendrite is much more likely to be influenced by dorsal root fibers, which have profuse terminations in the lateral parts of laminae V, VI and VII, exactly where the dendrite is located (Figs 5 and 6; Joseph and Whitlock, 1968b).

Shapovalov (1975) has reported that, in turtles, stimulation of the medullary reticular formation generates EPSPs in lumbar lateral motoneurons, whereas stimulation of the red nucleus fails to generate even polysynaptic EPSPs. This physiological evidence may not apply to lizards, since it is from a turtle which lacks both trunk musculature and any significant number of medial motoneurons (Ariëns Kappers et al., 1936; Nieuwenhuys, 1964). However, it does corroborate the anatomical evidence that the medullary reticulospinal pathways in lizards could terminate on the medial dendrites of lateral motoneurons, whereas it is far less likely that the rubrospinal pathway can influence lateral motoneurons to any great extent, due both to the sparse and inappropriate location of its terminal field.

V. Conclusion

The organization of spinal systems in lizards, especially the tegu lizard, have now been studied using several normal and experimental neuroanatomical techniques. In addition, there have been a few studies of the behavioral deficits induced by spinal cord lesions. These studies suggest that two general, supraspinal systems exist in lizards, comparable to those described by Kuypers (1973) in mammals. These systems are diagrammed in Fig. 9. Neurons in the red nucleus (R), solitary nucleus (S), several reticular nuclei (MDL, MVL, RID, RIV, RVL) and the dorsal motor nucleus of the vagus have axons which descend in the dorsolateral funiculus and terminate on interneurons in laminae V–VII. These interneurons, in turn, influence the lateral motoneurons through propriospinal systems. The lateral motoneurons innervate appendicular musculature. These projections are relatively sparse, and lesions of this pathway produce minimal effects on limb movements. Dorsal root fiber projections overlap the terminal field of the dorsolateral descending pathway and may have a greater effect on the function of limb movement than supraspinal fibers.

The second pathway involves neurons in the ipsilateral solitary nucleus (S), inferior raphé nucleus (RaI), interstitial nucleus (In), vestibular nuclei (VeVL, VeDL) and several reticular nuclei (RS, RM, MVL). Their axons descend in the ventromedial and ventrolateral funiculi, often decussating.

They terminate in laminae VII and VIII and in medial lamina IX. Laminae VII and especially VIII contain interneurons which influence motoneurons in medial lamina IX via propriospinal systems. Medial motoneurons innervate axial musculature. These projections are dense, and lesions of this pathway produce drastic abnormalities in the use of axial musculature.

In the future it would be interesting to study the connections of these spinal pathways in reptiles with different proportions of limb and axial musculature. For example, snakes, which lack limb musculature, have been shown to lack a rubrospinal pathway (Donkelaar, 1976a, b). A study of this pathway in limbless lizards and amphisbaenids would be interesting.

Acknowledgements

I wish to thank Dr. J. A. Finkelstein and Dr. D. B. Newman for their criticisms of this manuscript, and Ms. B. Alexander, Mr. T. Nevin and Mr. S. Stefl for technical assistance. Portions of the author's work reported here were performed in the Department of Anatomy, Howard University, Washington, D.C. and the Department of Neurobiology, Armed Forces Radiobiology Research Institute, Bethesda, Md. Supported in part by GRS grant 5-S01-RR-05351-14, NSF grant BMS75-09643, and NIH grant 1 R01 NS14346.

References

Ariëns Kappers, C. U., Huber, G. C. and Crosby, E. C. (1936). "The Comparative Anatomy of the Nervous System of Vertebrates including Man." Macmillan, New York. (Hafner, New York, 1967.)

Banchi, A. (1903). La minuta struttura della midolla spinale dei Chelonii. *Emys europae. Archs. ital. Anat. Embriol.* 2, 291–307.

Beccari, N. (1921). Studi comparitivi sulla structura del rombencefalo. II. Centri tegmentali del rombencefalo. *Archs. ital. Anat. Embriol.* 19, 216–291.

Bellairs, A. d'A. (1969). "The Life of Reptiles." Weidenfeld and Nicolson, London.

Bodian, D. (1937). The structure of the vertebrate synapse. A study of the axon endings on Mauthner's cell and neighbouring centers in the goldfish. *J. comp. Neurol.* 68, 117–159.

Cruce, W. L. R. (1974a). The anatomical organization of hindlimb motoneurons in the lumbar spinal cord of the frog, *Rana catesbeiana. J. comp. Neurol.* 153, 59–76.

Cruce, W. L. R. (1974b). Supraspinal projections to the spinal cord of the Tegu lizard (*Tupinambis nigropunctatus*). *Anat. Rec.* 178, 337.

Cruce, W. L. R. (1975). Termination of supraspinal descending pathways in the spinal cord of the Tegu lizard (*Tupinambis nigropunctatus*). *Brain, Behav. Evol.* 12, 247–269.

Cruce, W. L. R. (1978). The organization of descending pathways in the Tegu lizard and some comments on the evolution of motor systems. *In* "Behavior and Neurology of Lizards." (N. Greenberg and P. D. MacLean, eds). NIMH, Rockville, Md., pp. 105–120.

Cruce, W. L. R. and Nieuwenhuys, R. (1974). The cell masses in the brainstem of the turtle, *Testudo hermani*: A topographical and topological analysis. *J. comp. Neurol.* 156, 277–306.

Cruce, W. L. R., Newman, D. B. and Stefl, S. (1976). Brainstem origins of supraspinal pathways in a reptile (*Tupinambis nigropunctatus*). *Anat. Rec.* 184, 385.

Ebbesson, S. O. E. (1967). Ascending axon degeneration following hemisection of the spinal cord in the Tegu lizard (*Tupinambis nigropunctatus*). *Brain Res.* 5, 178–206.

Ebbesson, S. O. E. (1969). Brainstem afferents from the spinal cord in a sample of reptilian and amphibian species. *Ann. N. Y. Acad. Sci.* 167, 80–101.

Ebbesson, S. O. E. (1970). The selective silver impregnation of degenerating axons and their synaptic endings in nonmammalian species. *In* "Contemporary Research Methods in Neuroanatomy." (W. J. H. Nauta and S. O. E. Ebbesson, eds). Springer Verlag, New York, pp. 132–161.

Ebbesson, S. O. E. (1976). The somatosensory thalamus in reptiles. *Anat. Rec.* 184, 395–396.

Goldby, F. (1937). An experimental investigation of the cerebral hemispheres of *Lacerta viridis*. *J. Anat.* 71, 332–354.

Goldby, F. and Gamble, H. J. (1957). The reptilian cerebral hemispheres. *Biol. Rev.* 32, 383–420.

Goldby, F. and Robinson, L. R. (1961). Experimental degeneration in the ventral longitudinal bundles of the spinal cord of *Lacerta viridis*. *Proc. Anat. Soc. Gt Britain and Ireland*, pp. 41–44.

Goldby, F. and Robinson, L. R. (1962). The central connexions of dorsal spinal nerve roots and the ascending tracts in the spinal cord of *Lacerta viridis*. *J. Anat.* 96, 153–170.

Heimer, L. (1970). Selective silver impregnation of degenerating axoplasm. *In* "Contemporary Research Methods in Neuroanatomy." (W. J. H. Nauta and S. O. E. Ebbesson, eds). Springer Verlag, New York, pp. 106–131.

Jacobs, V. L. (1968). An experimental study of the course and termination of the spino-cerebellar systems in a lizard (*Lacerta viridis*). *Brain Res.* 11, 154–176.

Joseph, B. S. and Whitlock, D. G. (1968a). The morphology of spinal afferent–efferent relationships in vertebrates. *Brain, Behav. Evol.* 1, 2–18.

Joseph, B. S. and Whitlock, D. G. (1968b). Central projections of brachial and lumbar dorsal roots in reptiles. *J. comp. Neurol.* 132, 469–484.

Keenan, E. (1929). The phylogenetic development of the substantia gelatinosa Rolandi. *Proc. Kon. Akad. Wet.* (*Amsterdam*) 32, 299–310.

Kruger, L. and Berkowitz, E. C. (1960). The main afferent connections of the reptilian telencephalon as determined by degeneration and electrophysiological methods. *J. comp. Neurol.* 115, 125–141.

Kruger, L. and Witkovsky, P. (1961). A functional analysis of neurons in the dorsal column nuclei and spinal nucleus of the trigeminal in the reptile (*Alligator mississipiensis*). *J. comp. Neurol.* 117, 97–105.

Kuypers, H. G. J. M. (1973). The anatomical organization of the descending pathways and their contributions to motor control especially in primates. *In* "New Developments in Electromyography and Clinical Neurophysiology." (J. E. Desmedt, ed.). Karger, Basel, 3, 38–68.

Lawrence, D. C. and Kuypers, H. G. J. M. (1968a). The functional organization of the motor system in the monkey. I. The effects of bilateral pyramidal lesions. *Brain* 91, 1–14.

Lawrence, D. C. and Kuypers, H. G. J. M. (1968b). The functional organization of the motor system in the monkey. II. The effects of lesions on the descending brainstem pathways. *Brain* 91, 15–36.

Leghissa, S. (1954). Richerche anatomo-comparative sul sistemo longitudinale mediale nelle serie dei vertebrati. *Comment. Pont. Acad. Sci.* 16, 197–239.

Matsushita, M. (1970a). The axonal pathways of spinal neurons in the cat. *J. comp. Neurol.* 138, 391–418.

Matsushita, M. (1970b). Dendritic organization of the ventral spinal gray matter in the cat. *Acta anat.* 76, 263–288.

Matthews, M. A., Willis, W. D. and Williams, V. (1971). Dendrite bundles in lamina IX of cat spinal cord: a possible source for electrical interaction between motoneurons? *Anat. Rec.* 171, 313–328.

Nauta, W. J. H. (1957). Silver impregnation of degenerating axons. *In* "New Research Techniques of Neuroanatomy." (W. F. Windle, ed.). Thomas, Springfield, pp. 17–26.

Nieuwenhuys, R. (1964). Comparative anatomy of the spinal cord. *Prog. Brain Res.* 11, 1–57.

Ramón y Cajal, S. (1891). Estructura de la medulla espinal de los reptiles. *In* "Pequeñas Contribuciones al Conocimiento del Sistema Nervioso." Barcelona.

Ramón y Cajal, S. (1908–11). "Histologie du Système Nerveux de l'Homme et des Vértébrés." Maloine, Paris. Reprinted Consejo Superior de Investigaciones Cientificas, Madrid, 1972.

Rexed, B. (1952). The cytoarchitectonic organization of the spinal cord in the cat. *J. comp. Neurol.* 96, 415–495.

Rexed, B. (1954). A cytoarchitectonic atlas of the spinal cord in the cat. *J. comp. Neurol.* 100, 297–379.

Rexed, B. (1964). Some aspects of the cytoarchitectonics and synaptology of the spinal cord. *Prog. Brain Res.* 11, 58–92.

Robinson, L. R. (1969). Bulbospinal fibers and their nuclei of origin in *Lacerta viridis* demonstrated by axonal degeneration and chromatolysis, respectively. *J. Anat.* 105, 59–88.

Romanes, G. J. (1964). The motor pools of the spinal cord. *Prog. Brain Res.* 11, 93–119.

Rosenberg, M. E. (1972). Excitation and inhibition of motoneurons in the tortoise. *J. Physiol., Lond.* 221, 715–730.

Scheibel, M. E. and Scheibel, A. B. (1970). Organization of spinal motoneuron dendrites in bundles. *Expl Neurol.* 28, 106–112.

Shapovalov, A. I. (1975). Neuronal organization and synaptic mechanisms of supraspinal motor control in vertebrates. *Rev. Physiol. Biochem. Pharmacol.* 72, 1–54.

Snyder, R. C. (1952). Quadrupedal and bipedal locomotion of lizards. *Copeia* 1952, 64–70.

Stensaas, L. J. and Stensaas, S. S. (1971). Light and electron microscopy of motoneurons and neuropile in the amphibian spinal cord. *Brain Res.* 31, 67–84.

Sterling, P. and Kuypers, H. G. J. M. (1968). Anatomical organization of the brachial spinal cord of the cat. III. The propriospinal connections. *Brain Res.* 7, 419–443.

ten Donkelaar, H. J. (1976a). Descending pathways from the brainstem to the spinal cord in some reptiles. I. Origin. *J. comp. Neurol.* 167, 421–442.

ten Donkelaar, H. J. (1976b). Descending pathways from the brainstem to the spinal cord in some reptiles. II. Course and site of termination. *J. comp. Neurol.* 167, 443–464.

Terni, T. (1921). Richerche istologiche sul midollo spinale dei rettili, con particolare reguardo ai componenti spinali del fasicolo longitudinale mediale. (Osservazionai in *Gongylus ocellatus* Wagl.). *Arch. ital. Anat. Embriol.* 18, 16–61.

Testa, C. (1964). Functional implications of the morphology of the spinal ventral horn neurons of the cat. *J. comp. Neurol.* 123, 425–444.

CHAPTER 4

The Brainstem

H. J. ten DONKELAAR and R. NIEUWENHUYS

Department of Anatomy and Embryology,
University of Nijmegen,
Nijmegen, The Netherlands

I. Introduction

The brainstem as defined here comprises the mesencephalon and the rhombencephalon. Figures 1 and 2 show that the reptilian rhombencephalon is rather strongly curved. The cerebellum is generally treated as a separate section of the central nervous system; however, it should be remembered that ontogenetically the cerebellum represents a dorsal outgrowth of the rhombencephalon. The cerebella of the various groups of reptiles show considerable differences in both size and shape (cf. Nieuwenhuys, 1967), but the gross structure of the brainstem *sensu strictuori* is basically similar among all reptilian groups (Figs 1, 2). The most rostral parts of the cerebellum and of the rhombencephalic wall constitute a narrowed part of the brainstem, which is known as the isthmus. The mesencephalon constitutes the most rostral part of the brainstem. It consists of the ventral mesencephalic tegmentum and the dorsal mesencephalic tectum. The brainstem is bounded rostrally by the diencephalon and caudally it passes over into the spinal cord. The interest of this "intermediate" part of the reptilian central nervous system derives from the fact that here originate or terminate ten of the twelve cranial nerves (II through X, XII). The brainstem of reptiles also contains a well-developed reticular formation and numerous sensory and motor relay nuclei with their associated ascending and descending connections. This chapter surveys the present knowledge of the micro-structure of the reptilian brainstem, based on personal investigations, as well as a review of the literature.

The material studied includes transversely sectioned series of the brains of the following four species: a turtle, *Testudo hermanni* (order: Testudines), a lizard, *Tupinambis nigropunctatus* (suborder: Sauria; order: Squamata), a snake, *Python reticulatus* (suborder: Serpentes; order: Squamata) and a

134   H. J. TEN DONKELAAR AND R. NIEUWENHUYS

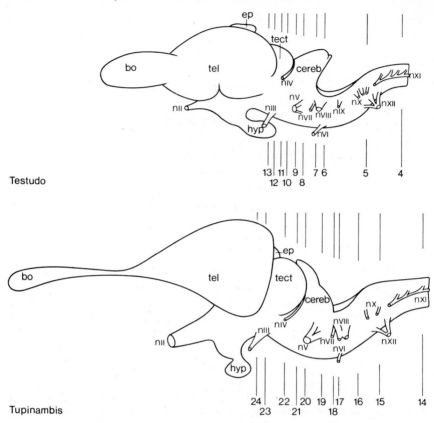

Testudo

Tupinambis

FIG. 1. Lateral view of the brains of the turtle *Testudo hermanni* and the lizard *Tupinambis nigropunctatus*. The levels of the transverse sections through the first spinal segment and through the brain stem, shown in Figs 4–24, have been indicated. bo, Olfactory bulb; cereb, cerebellum; ep, epiphysis; hyp, hypophysis; nII, optic nerve; nIII, oculomotor nerve; nIV, trochlear nerve; nV, trigeminal nerve; nVI, abducens nerve; nVII, facial nerve; nVIII, eighth nerve; nIX, glossopharyngeal nerve; nX, vagus nerve; nXI, accessory nerve; nXII, hypoglossal nerve; tect, mesencephalic tectum; tel, telencephalon.

caiman, *Caiman crocodilus* (order: Crocodilia). No material was available of *Sphenodon punctatus*, the only living representative of the order Rhynchocephalia. However, as far as can be judged from the study of Christensen (1927), the brainstem of this species does not differ markedly from that of the Squamata.

For the analysis of the cell masses, one or more series of each of the four species was stained with cresylecht violet. The fibers were studied in series stained according to Häggqvist's (1936) modification of the Alzheimer

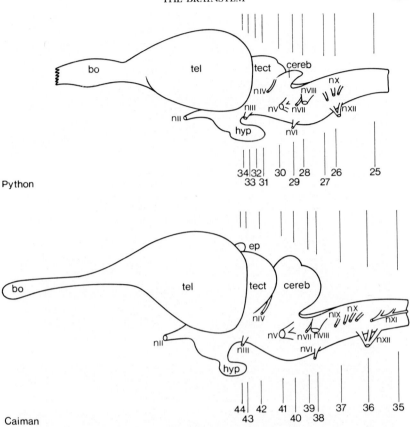

FIG. 2. Lateral view of the brains of the snake *Python reticulatus* and the caiman *Caiman crocodilus*. The levels of the transverse sections through the first spinal segment and through the brain stem, shown in Figs 25–44, have been indicated. bo, Olfactory bulb; cereb, cerebellum; ep, epiphysis; hyp, hypophysis; nII, optic nerve; nIII, oculomotor nerve; nIV, trochlear nerve; nV, trigeminal nerve; nVI, abducens nerve; nVII, facial nerve; nVIII, eighth nerve; nIX, glossopharyngeal nerve; nX, vagus nerve; nXI, accessory nerve; nXII, hypoglossal nerve; tect, mesencephalic tectum; tel, telencephalon.

Mann methyl blue–eosin stain. This technique stains the axons blue and the myelin sheaths of the individual fibers red. In Häggqvist material many bundles and tracts can be clearly distinguished from their environment on account of their characteristic fiber pattern (cf. Fig. 3), i.e. by the relative diameters of the constituent fibers (Busch, 1961; Verhaart, 1970). The general terms, small, medium-sized, and coarse are applied to the fibers of the various systems. These terms are not strictly defined, but the small

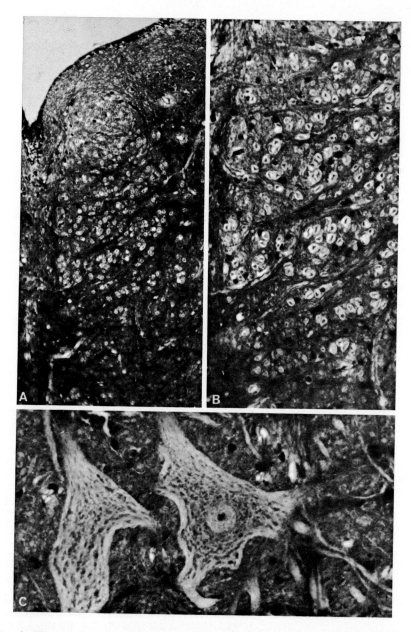

FIG. 3. Photomicrographs of Häggqvist-stained transverse sections through the brain stem of the snake *Python reticulatus* at the level of the abducens nucleus: (a) the f.l.m. and predorsal bundle, × 130; (b) detail of predorsal bundle, × 250; (c) detail of medial reticular nucleus, × 400.

fibers generally range from 0 to 3 μm, the medium-sized ones from 3 to 6 μm, and the coarse fibers from 6 to 12 μm in diameter.

The topographical relationships of the various cell masses and fiber systems are illustrated in cross-sections through the first segment of the spinal cord and through consecutive levels of the brainstem of the four species studied (Figs 4–44). Each figure shows the cell bodies at the left and the fiber systems at the right. Dots of three different sizes correspond to the three fiber categories indicated above. The levels of these cross-sections are indicated in outline drawings of the brains of the species studied (Figs 1, 2).

In treating the works of other authors this review emphasizes evidence gathered with experimental techniques. No attempt is made to cover the vast, older literature on the structure of the reptilian brainstem, as it has comprehensively been dealt with in the encyclopedic work of Ariëns Kappers et al. (1936). The present survey attempts to discuss the microstructure of the reptilian brainstem in terms of functional systems; wherever possible the cell masses will be treated in the framework of their interconnecting fiber paths. The discussion of the various functional systems is followed by a consideration of the structural variation in reptilian brainstems. The final section of this chapter offers some comments on the similarities and differences between the reptilian and the mammalian brainstem.

II. Dorsal Column Nuclei and their Afferent and Efferent Connections

Dorsal column nuclei have been identified in all reptilian groups, and separate medial (gracile) and lateral (cuneate) nuclei have been distinguished in several lizards and crocodilians (Zeehandelaar, 1921; Huber and Crosby, 1926, *Alligator*; Shanklin, 1930, *Chamaeleo*). Ebbesson (1967) found a small nucleus of Bischoff in the lizard *Tupinambis nigropunctatus*, and the same author also presented evidence for the existence of an external cuneate nucleus (Ebbesson, 1967, 1969). Nissl material of the snake *Python reticulatus* (Fig. 26) and the turtle *Testudo hermanni* (Fig. 5) shows only a single, small-celled dorsal column nucleus, the nucleus of the dorsal funiculus. This nucleus can be divided into a lateral and a medial part in the lizard and caiman studied (Figs 15, 36, 37). In *Tupinambis* and *Python* the nucleus of Bischoff is a small, mediocaudal extension of the nucleus of the dorsal funiculus. An external cuneate nucleus appears to be absent in all of the species studied.

It is known that each dorsal root can be divided into a coarse-fibered medial and a thin-fibered lateral bundle in reptiles, as in mammals (Ariëns Kappers et al., 1936). A certain proportion of the primary afferent fibers

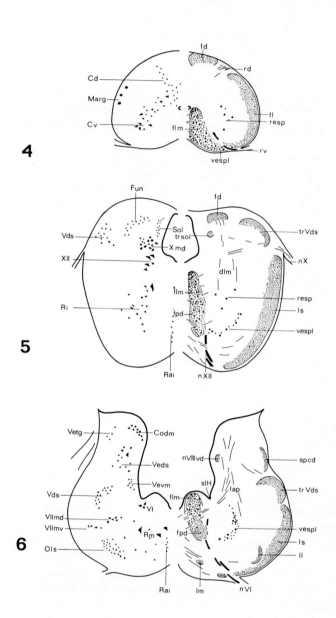

Figs 4–6. Transverse sections through the first segment of the spinal cord and through the caudal part of the rhombencephalon in the turtle *Testudo hermanni*. At the left the cell picture, based on a Nissl-stained series; at the right the fiber systems based on Häggqvist preparations. Cd, Dorsal horn; Codm, dorsal magnocellular nucleus; Cv, ventral horn; dlm, decussation of the medial lemniscus; Fun, nucleus of the dorsal funiculus; fap, deep arcuate fibers; fd, dorsal funiculus; fl, lateral funiculus; flm, medial longitudinal fasciculus; fpd, predorsal bundle; ll, lateral lemniscus; lm, medial lemniscus; ls, spinal lemniscus; Marg, marginal nucleus; nVI, abducens nerve; nX, vagus nerve; nXII, hypoglossal nerve; Ols, superior olive; Rai, inferior nucleus of the raphé; Ri, inferior reticuler nucleus; Rm, medial reticular nucleus; rd, dorsal root; resp, reticulospinal fibers; rv, ventral root; Sol, nucleus of the solitary fasciculus; spcd, dorsal spinocerebellar tract; trsol, solitary fasciculus; trVds, spinal tract of the trigeminal nerve; Veds, descending vestibular nucleus; Vetg, tangential nucleus; Vevm, ventromedial vestibular nucleus; vespl, lateral vestibulospinal tract; Vds, nucleus of the spinal tract of the trigeminal nerve; VI, abducens nucleus; VIImd, motor nucleus of the facial nerve, dorsal part; VIImv, motor nucleus of the facial nerve, ventral part; Xmd, dorsal motor nucleus of the vagus nerve; XII, hypoglossal nucleus.

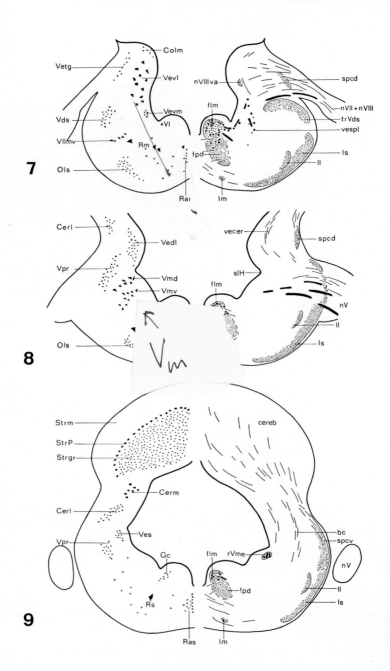

Figs 7–9. Transverse sections through the rostral part of the rhombencephalon in the turtle *Testudo hermanni*. bc, Brachium conjunctivum; Cerl, lateral cerebellar nucleus; Cerm, medial cerebellar nucleus; Colm, nucleus laminaris; cereb, cerebellum; flm, medial longitudinal fasciculus; fpd, predorsal bundle; Gc, central gray; ll, lateral lemniscus; lm, medial lemniscus; ls, spinal lemniscus; nV, trigeminal nerve; nVII, facial nerve; nVIII, eighth nerve; nVIIIva, eighth nerve, ascending vestibular root; Ols, superior olive; Rai, inferior nucleus of the raphé; Ras, superior nucleus of the raphé; Rm, medial reticular nucleus; Rs, superior reticular nucleus; rVme, mesencephalic root of the trigeminal nerve; Strgr, granular layer of the cerebellum; Strm, molecular layer of the cerebellum; StrP, Purkinje layer of the cerebellum; slH, sulcus limitans (His); spcd, dorsal spinocerebellar tract; spcv, ventral spinocerebellar tract; trVds, spinal tract of the trigeminal nerve; Vedl, dorsolateral vestibular nucleus; Ves, superior vestibular nucleus; Vetg, tangential nucleus; Vevl, ventrolateral vestibular nucleus; Vevm, ventromedia; vestibular nucleus; vecer, vestibulocerebellar fibers; vespl, lateral vestibulospinal tractl Vd, spinal nucleus of the trigeminal nerve; Vmd, motor nucleus of the trigeminal nerve, dorsal part; Vmv, motor nucleus of the trigeminal nerve, ventral part; Vpr, principal nucleus of the trigeminal nerve; VI, abducens nucleus; VII mv, motor nucleus of the facial nerve, ventral part.

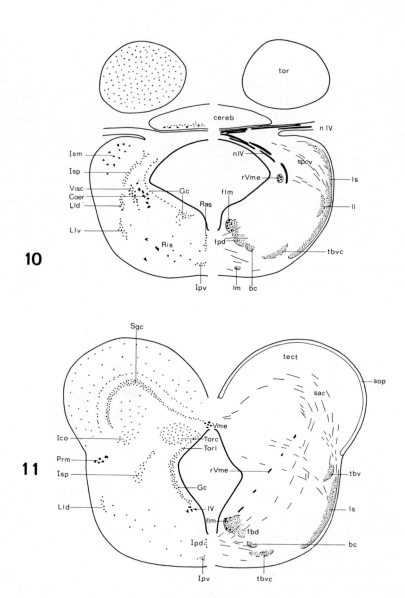

FIGS 10 and 11. Transverse sections through the isthmus region and through the caudal part of the mesencephalon in the turtle *Testudo hermanni*. bc, Brachium conjunctivum; Coer, locus coeruleus; cereb, cerebellum; flm, medial longitudinal fasciculus; fpd, predorsal bundle; Gc, central gray; Ico, intercollicular nucleus; Ipd, interpeduncular nucleus, dorsal part; Ipv, interpeduncular nucleus, ventral part; Ism, nucleus isthmi, magnocellular part; Isp, nucleus isthmi, parvocellular part; Lld, nucleus of the lateral lemniscus, dorsal part; Llv, nucleus of the lateral lemniscus, ventral part; ll, lateral lemniscus; lm, medial lemniscus; ls, spinal lemniscus; nIV, trochlear nerve; Prm, nucleus profundus mesencephali; Ras, superior nucleus of the raphé; Ris, reticular nucleus of the isthmus; rVme, mesencephalic root of the trigeminal nerve; Sgc, stratum griseum centrale; sac, stratum album centrale; sop, stratum opticum; spcv, ventral spinocerebellar tract; Torc, central nucleus of the torus semicircularis; Torl, laminar nucleus of the torus semicircularis; tbd, dorsal tectobulbar tract; tbv, ventral tectobulbar tract; tbvc, ventral cruciate tectobulbar tract; tect, mesencephalic tectum; tor, torus semicircularis; Visc, secondary visceral nucleus; IV, trochlear nucleus; Vme, mesencephalic nucleus of the trigeminal nerve.

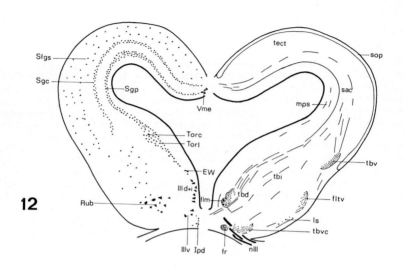

12

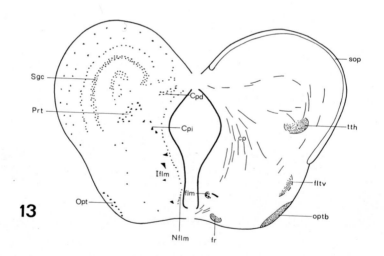

13

Figs 12 and 13. Transverse sections through the middle and rostral parts of the mesencephalon in the turtle *Testudo hermanni*. bc, Brachium conjunctivum; Cpd, dorsal nucleus of the posterior commissure; Cpi, interstitial nucleus of the posterior commissure; cp, posterior commissure; EW, nucleus of Edinger-Westphal; flm, medial longitudinal fasciculus; fr, fasciculus retroflexus; fitv, ventral peduncle of the lateral forebrain bundle; Iflm, interstitial nucleus of the flm; Ipd, interpeduncular nucleus, dorsal part; ls, spinal lemniscus; mps, mesencephalic periventricular system (Huber and Crosby); Nflm, nucleus of the flm; nIII, oculomotor nerve; Opt, nucleus opticus tegmenti; optb, basal optic tract; Prt, pretectal nucleus; Rub, red nucleus; Sfgs, stratum fibrosum et griseum superficiale; Sgc, stratum griseum centrale; Sgp, stratum griseum periventriculare; sac, stratum album centrale; sfp, stratum fibrosum periventriculare; sop, stratum opticum; Torc, central nucleus of the torus semicircularis; Torl, laminar nucleus of the torus semicircularis; tbd, dorsal tectobulbar tract; tbi, intermediate tectobulbar tract; tbv, ventral tectobulbar tract; tbvc, ventral cruciate tectobulbar tract; tect, mesencephalic tectum; tth, tectothalamic tract; IIId, oculomotor nucleus, dorsal part; IIIi, oculomotor nucleus, intermediate part; IIIv, oculomotor nucleus, ventral part; Vme, mesencephalic nucleus of the trigeminal nerve.

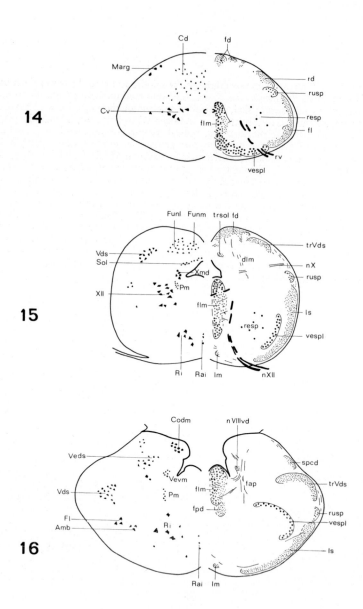

Figs 14–16. Transverse sections through the first spinal segment and through the caudal part of the rhombencephalon in the lizard *Tupinambis nigropunctatus*. The levels of these sections as well as those of Figs 17–24 have been indicated in Fig. 1. Amb, Nucleus ambiguus; Cd, dorsal horn; Codm, dorsal magnocellular nucleus; Cv, ventral horn; dlm, decussation of the medial lemniscus; Fl, nucleus of the lateral funiculus; Funl, nucleus of the dorsal funiculus, lateral part; Funm, nucleus of the dorsal funiculus, medial part; fap, deep arcuate fibers; fd, dorsal funiculus; fl, lateral funiculus; flm, medial longitudinal fasciculus; fpd, predorsal bundle; lm, medial lemniscus; ls, spinal lemniscus; Marg, marginal nucleus; nVIIIvd, descending root of the eighth nerve; nX, vagus nerve; nXII, hypoglossal nerve; Pm, medial parvocellular nucleus; Rai, inferior nucleus of the raphé; Ri, inferior reticular nucleus; rd, dorsal root; resp, reticulospinal fibers; rusp, rubrospinal tract; rv, ventral root; Sol, nucleus of the solitary fasciculus; spcd, dorsal spinocerebellar tract; trsol, solitary fasciculus; trVds, spinal tract of the trigeminal nerve; Veds, descending vestibular nucleus; Vevm, ventromedial vestibular nucleus; vespl, lateral vestibulospinal tract; Vds, spinal nucleus of the trigeminal nerve; Xmd, dorsal motor nucleus of the vagus nerve; XII, hypoglossal nucleus.

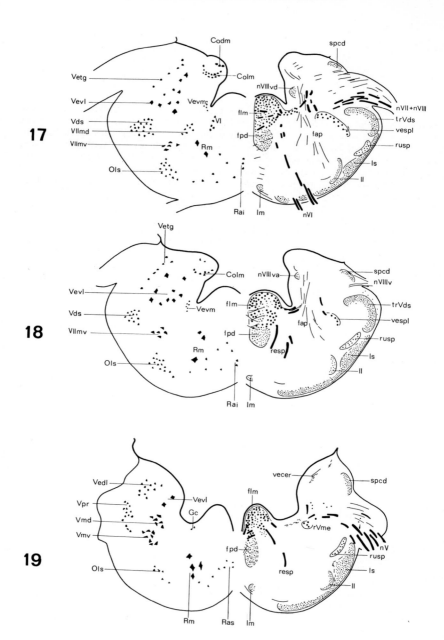

Figs 17–19. Transverse sections through the middle part of the rhombencephalon in the lizard *Tupinambis nigropunctatus*. bc, Brachium conjunctivum; Codm, dorsal magnocellular nucleus; Colm, nucleus laminaris; fap, deep arcuate fibers; flm, medial longitudinal fasciculus; fpd, predorsal bundle; Gc, central gray; ll, lateral lemniscus; lm, medial lemniscus; ls, spinal lemniscus; nV, trigeminal nerve; nVI, abducens nerve; nVII, facial nerve; nVIII, eighth nerve; nVIIIv, vestibular root of the eighth nerve; nVIIIva, ascending vestibular root of the eighth nerve; nVIIIvd, descending vestibular root of the eighth nerve; Ols, superior olive; Rai, inferior nucleus of the raphé; Ras, superior nucleus of the raphé; Rm, medial reticular nucleus; resp, reticulospinal fibers; rusp, rubrospinal tract; rVme, mesencephalic root of the trigeminal nerve; spcd, dorsal spinocerebellar tract; trVds, spinal tract of the trigeminal nerve; Vedl, dorsolateral vestibular nucleus; Vetg, tangential nucleus; Vevl, ventrolateral vestibular nucleus; Vevm, ventromedial vestibular nucleus; vecer, vestibulocerebellar fibers; vespl. lateral vestibulospinal tract; Vds, spinal nucleus of the trigeminal nerve; Vmd, motor nucleus of the trigeminal nerve, dorsal part; Vmv, motor nucleus of the trigeminal nerve, ventral part; Vpr, principal nucleus of the trigeminal nerve; VI, abducens nucleus; VIImd, motor nucleus of the facial nerve, dorsal part; VIImv, motor nucleus of the facial nerve, ventral part.

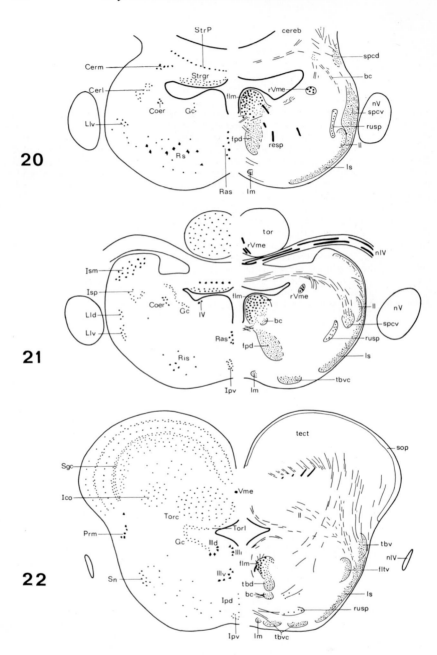

Figs 20–22. Transverse sections through the rostral part of the rhombencephalon, the isthmus region and the caudal part of the mesencephalon in the lizard *Tupinambis nigropunctatus*. bc, Brachium conjunctivum; Cerl, lateral cerebellar nucleus; Cerm, medial cerebellar nucleus; Coer, locus coeruleus; cereb, cerebellum; flm, medial longitudinal fasciculus; fpd, predorsal bundle; fltv, ventral peduncle of the lateral forebrain bundle; Gc, central gray; Ico, intercollicular nucleus; Ipd, interpeduncular nucleus, dorsal part; Ipv, interpeduncular nucleus, ventral part; Ism, nucleus isthmi, magnocellular part; Isp, nucleus isthmi, parvocellular part; Lld, nucleus of the lateral lemniscus, dorsal part; Llv, nucleus of the lateral lemniscus, ventral part; ll, lateral lemniscus; lm, medial lemniscus; ls, spinal lemniscus; nIV, trochlear nerve; nV, trigeminal nerve; Prm, nucleus profundus mesencephali; Ras, superior nucleus of the raphé; Ris, reticular nucleus of the isthmus; Rs, superior reticular nucleus; resp, reticulospinal fibers; rusp, rubrospinal tract; rVme, mesencephalic root of the trigeminal nerve; Sgc, stratum griseum centrale; Sn, substantia nigra; Strgr, granular layer of the cerebellum; StrP, Purkinje layer of the cerebellum; sop, stratum opticum; spcd. dorsal spinocerebellar tract; spcv, ventral spinocerebellar tract; Torc, central nucleus of the torus semicircularis; Torl, laminar nucleus of the torus semicircularis; tbd, dorsal tectobulbar tract; tbv, ventral tectobulbar tract; tbvc, ventral cruciate tectobulbar tract; tect, mesencephalic tectum; tor, torus semicircularis; IIId, oculomotor nucleus, dorsal part; IIIi, oculomotor nucleus, intermediate part; IIIv, oculomotor nucleus, ventral part; IV, trochlear nucleus; Vme, mesencephalic nucleus of the trigeminal nerve.

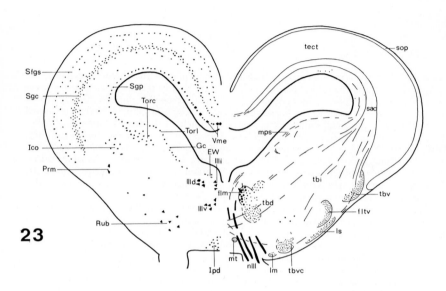

23

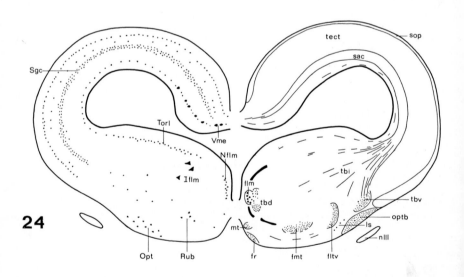

24

FIGS 23 and 24. Transverse sections through the middle and rostral parts of the mesencephalon of the lizard *Tupinambis nigropunctatus*. EW, Nucleus of Edinger-Westphal; flm, medial longitudinal fasciculus; fltv, ventral peduncle of the lateral forebrain bundle; fmt, medial forebrain bundle; fr, fasciculus retroflexus; Gc, central gray; Ico, intercollicular nucleus; Iflm, interstitial nucleus of the flm; Ipd, interpeduncular nucleus, dorsal part; lm, medial lemniscus; ls, spinal lemniscus; mps, mesencephalic periventricular system; mt, mamillotegmental tract; Nflm, nucleus of the flm; nIII, oculomotor nerve; Opt, nucleus opticus tegmenti; optb, basal optic tract; Prm, nucleus profundus mesencephali Rub, red nucleus; Sfgs, stratum fibrosum et griseum superficiale; Sgc, stratum griseum centrale; Sgp, stratum griseum periventriculare; sac, stratum album centrale; sfp, stratum fibrosum periventriculare; sop, stratum opticum; Torc, central nucleus of the torus semicircularis; Torl, laminar nucleus of the torus semicircularis; tbd, dorsal tectobulbar tract; tbi, intermediate tectobulbar tract; tbv, ventral tectobulbar tract; tbvc, ventral cruciate tectobulbar tract; tect, mesencephalic tectum; IIId, oculomotor nucleus, dorsal part; IIIi, oculomotor nucleus, intermediate part; IIIv, oculomotor nucleus, ventral part; Vme, mesencephalic nucleus of the trigeminal nerve.

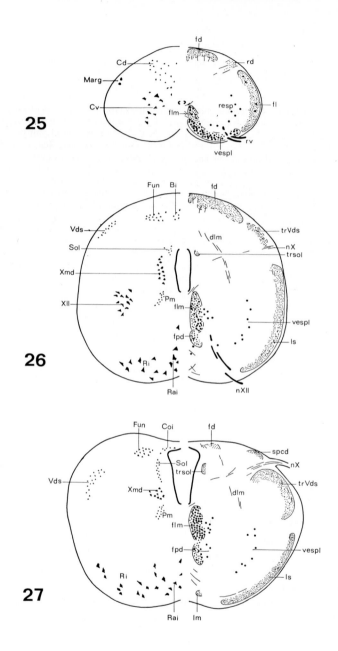

FIGS 25–27. Transverse sections through the first spinal segment and through the caudal part of the rhombencephalon in the snake *Python reticulatus*. The levels of these sections as well as those in Figs 28–34 have been indicated in Fig. 2. Bi, Nucleus of Bischoff; Cd, dorsal horn; Coi, nucleus commissurae infimae; Cv, ventral horn; dlm, decussation of the medial lemniscus; Fun, nucleus of the dorsal funiculus; fd, dorsal funiculus; fl, lateral funiculus; flm, medial longitudinal fasciculus; fpd, predorsal bundle; lm, medial lemniscus; ls, spinal lemniscus; Marg, marginal nucleus; nX, vagus nerve; nXII, hypoglossal nerve; Pm, nucleus parvocellularis medialis; Rai, inferior nucleus of the raphé; Ri, inferior reticular nucleus; rd, dorsal root; resp, reticulospinal fibers; rv, ventral root; Sol, nucleus of the solitary fasciculus; trVds, spinal tract of the trigeminal nerve; vespl, lateral vestibulospinal tract; Vds, spinal nucleus of the trigeminal nerve; Xmd, dorsal motor nucleus of the vagus nerve.

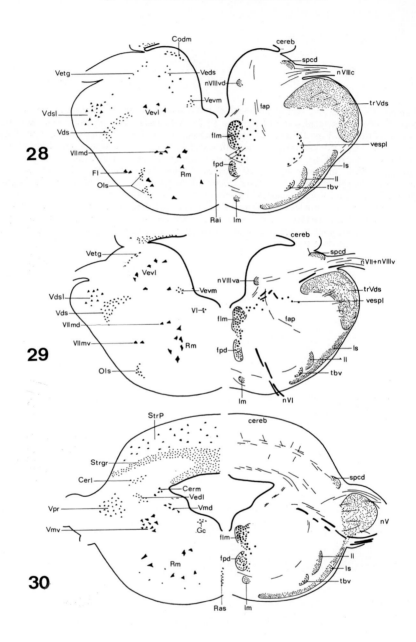

FIGS 28–30. Transverse sections through the rostral part of the rhombencephalon in the snake *Python reticulatus*. Cerl, Lateral cerebellar nucleus; Cerm, medial cerebellar nucleus; Codm, dorsal magnocellular nucleus; cereb, cerebellum; Fl, nucleus of the lateral funiculus; fap, deep arcuate fibers; flm, medial longitudinal fasciculus; fpd, predorsal bundle; Gc, central gray; ll, lateral lemniscus; lm, medial lemniscus; ls, spinal lemniscus; nV, trigeminal nerve; nVI, abducens nerve; nVII, facial nerve; nVIIIc, cochlear root of the eighth nerve; nVIIIv, vestibular root of the eighth nerve; nVIIIva, ascending vestibular root of the eighth nerve; nVIIIvd, descending vestibular root of the eighth nerve; Ols, superior olive; Rai, inferior nucleus of the raphe; Ras, superior nucleus of the raphé; Rm, medial reticular nucleus; Strgr, granular layer of the cerebellum; StrP, Purkinje layer of the cerebellum; spcd, dorsal spinocerebellar tract; tbv, ventral tectobulbar tract; trVds, spinal tract of the trigeminal nerve; Vedl, dorsolateral vestibular nucleus; Veds, descending vestibular nucleus; Vetg, tangential nucleus; Vevl, ventrolateral vestibular nucleus; Vevm, ventromedial vestibular nucleus; Vespl, lateral vestibulospinal tract; Vds, nucleus of the spinal tract of the trigeminal nerve; Vdsl, lateral spinal nucleus of the trigeminal nerve; Vmd, motor nucleus of the trigeminal nerve, dorsal part; Vmv, motor nucleus of the trigeminal nerve, ventral part; Vpr, principal nucleus of the trigeminal nerve; VI, abducens nucleus; VIImd, motor nucleus of the facial nerve, dorsal part; VIImv, motor nucleus of the facial nerve, ventral part.

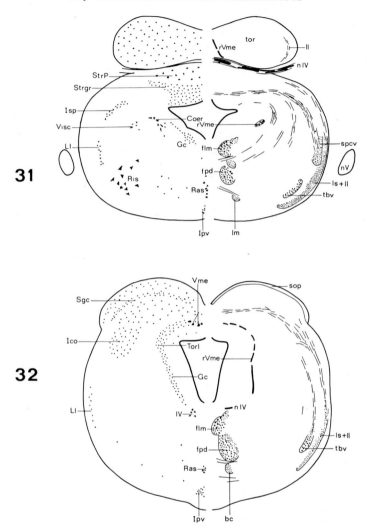

FIGS 31 and 32. Transverse sections through the isthmus region and through the caudal part of the mesencephalon in the snake *Python reticulatus*. bc, Brachium conjunctivum; Coer, locus coeruleus; flm, medial longitudinal fasciculus; fpd, predorsal bundle; Gc, central gray; Ico, intercollicular nucleus; Ipv, interpeduncular nucleus, ventral part; Isp, nucleus isthmi pars parvocellularis; Ll, nucleus of the lateral lemniscus; ll, lateral lemniscus; lm, medial lemniscus; ls, spinal lemniscus; nIV, trochlear nerve; nV, trigeminal nerve; Ras, superior nucleus of the raphé; Ris, reticular nucleus of the isthmus; rVme, mesencephalic root of the trigeminal nerve; Sgc, stratum griseum centrale; Strgr, granular layer of the cerebellum; StrP, Purkinje layer of the cerebellum; sop, stratum opticum; spcv, ventral spinocerebellar tract; Torl, laminar nucleus of the torus semicircularis; tbv, ventral tectobulbar tract; tor, torus semicircularis; Visc, secondary visceral nucleus; IV, trochlear nucleus; Vme, mesencephalic nucleus of the trigeminal nerve.

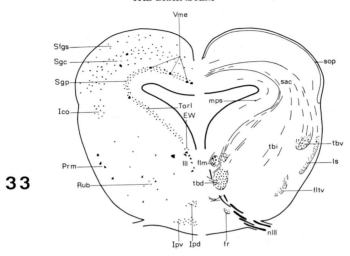

33

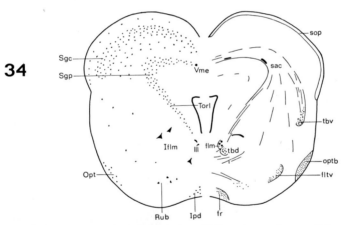

34

FIGS 33 and 34. Transverse sections through the middle and rostral parts of the mesencephalon in the snake *Python reticulatus*. EW, Nucleus of Edinger-Westphal; flm, medial
longitudinal fasciculus; fltv, ventral peduncle of the lateral forebrain bundle; fr, fasciculus
retroflexus; Ico, intercollicular nucleus; Iflm, interstitial nucleus of the flm; Ipd, interpeduncular nucleus, dorsal part; Ipv, interpeduncular nucleus, ventral part; ls, spinal
lemniscus; mps, mesencephalic periventricular system (Huber and Crosby); nIII,
oculomotor nerve; Opt, nucleus opticus tegmenti; optb, basal optic tract; Prm, nucleus
profundus mesencephali; Rub, red nucleus; Sfgs, stratum fibrosum et griseum superficiale; Sgc, stratum griseum centrale; Sgp, stratum griseum periventriculare; sac,
stratum album centrale; sfp, stratum fibrosum periventriculare; sop, stratum opticum;
Torl, laminar nucleus of the torus semicircularis; tbd, dorsal tectobulbar tract; tbi,
intermediate tectobulbar tract; tbv, ventral tectobulbar tract; III, oculomotor nucleus.

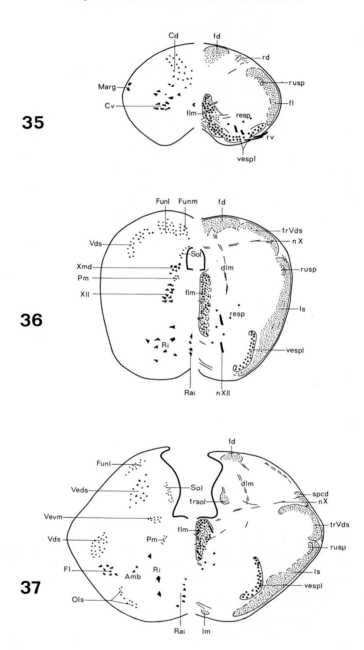

Figs 35–37. Transverse sections through the first spinal segment and the caudal part of the rhombencephalon in the caiman *Caiman crocodilus*. The levels of these sections as well as those in Figs 38–44 have been indicated in Fig. 2. Amb, Nucleus ambiguus; Cd, dorsal horn; Cv, ventral horn; dlm, decussation of the medial lemniscus; Fl, nucleus of the lateral funiculus; Funl, nucleus of the dorsal funiculus, lateral part; Funm, nucleus of the dorsal funiculus, medial part; fd, dorsal funiculus; fl, lateral funiculus; flm, medial longitudinal fasciculus; lm, medial lemniscus; ls, spinal lemniscus; Marg, marginal nucleus; nX, vagus nerve; nXII, hypoglossal nerve; Ols, superior olive; Pm, nucleus parvocellularis medialis; Rai, inferior nucleus of the raphé; Ri, inferior reticular nucleus; rd, dorsal root; resp, reticulospinal fibers; rusp, rubrospinal tract; rv, ventral root; Sol, nucleus of the solitary fasciculus; trVds, spinal tract of the trigeminal nerve; Veds, descending vestibular nucleus; Vevm, ventromedial vestibular nucleus; vespl, lateral vestibulospinal tract; Xmd, dorsal motor nucleus of the vagus nerve; XII, hypoglossal nucleus.

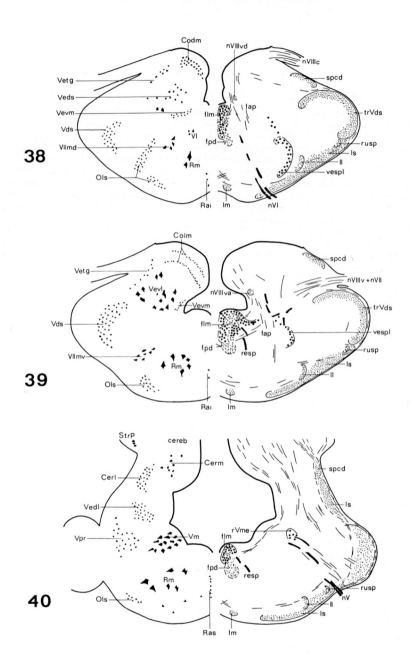

FIGS 38–40. Transverse sections through the rostral part of the rhombencephalon in the caiman *Caiman crocodilus*. Cerl, Lateral cerebellar nucleus; Cerm, medial cerebellar nucleus; Codm, dorsal magnocellular nucleus; Colm, nucleus laminaris; cereb, cerebellum; fap, deep arcuate fibers; flm, medial longitudinal fasciculus; fpd, predorsal bundle; ll, lateral lemniscus; lm, medial lemniscus; ls, spinal lemniscus; nV, trigeminal nerve; nVI, abducens nerve; nVII, facial nerve; nVIIIc, cochlear root of the eighth nerve; nVIIIv, vestibular root of the eighth nerve; nVIIIva, ascending vestibular root of the eighth nerve; nVIIIvd, descending vestibular root of the eighth nerve; Ols, superior olive; Rai, inferior nucleus of the raphé; Ras, superior nucleus of the raphé; Ri, inferior reticular nucleus; Rm, medial reticular nucleus; resp, reticulospinal fibers; rusp, rubrospinal tract; rVme, mesencephalic root of the trigeminal nerve; StrP, Purkinje layer of the cerebellum; spcd, dorsal spinocerebellar tract; trVds, spinal tract of the trigeminal nerve; Vedl, dorsolateral vestibular nucleus; Veds, descending vestibular nucleus; Vetg, tangential nucleus; Vevl, ventrolateral vestibular nucleus; Vevm, ventromedial vestibular nucleus; vespl, lateral vestibulospinal tract; Vds, spinal trigeminal nucleus; Vm, motor nucleus of the trigeminal nerve; Vpr, principal nucleus of the trigeminal nerve; VIImd, facial motor nucleus, dorsal part; VIImv, facial motor nucleus, ventral part.

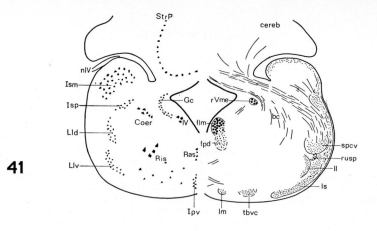

41

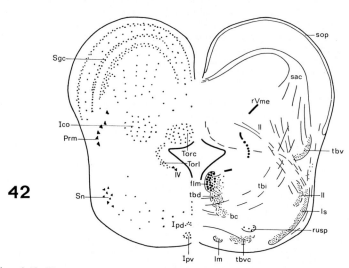

42

FIGS 41 and 42. Transverse sections through the isthmus region and through the caudal part of the mesencephalon in the caiman *Caiman crocodilus*. bc, Brachium conjunctivum, Coer, locus coeruleus; cereb, cerebellum; flm, medial longitudinal fasciculus; fpd, predorsal bundle; Gc, central gray; Ico, intercollicular nucleus; Ipd, interpeduncula-nucleus, dorsal part; Ipv, interpeduncular nucleus, ventral part; Ism, nucleus isthmi, magnocellular part; Isp, nucleus isthmi, parvocellular part; Lld, nucleus of the lateral lemniscus, dorsal part; Llv, nucleus of the lateral lemniscus, ventral part; ll, lateral lemniscus; lm, medial lemniscus; ls, spinal lemniscus; nIV, trochlear nerve; Prm, nucleus profundus mesencephali; Ras, superior nucleus of the raphé; Ris, reticular nucleus of the isthmus; rusp, rubrospinal tract; rVme, mesencephalic root of the trigeminal nerve; Sgc, stratum griseum centrale; StrP, Purkinje layer of the cerebellum; sac, stratum album centrale; sop, stratum opticum; spcv, ventral spinocerebellar tract; Torc, central nucleus of the torus semicircularis; Torl, laminar nucleus of the torus semicircularis; tbd, dorsal tectobulbar tract; tbi, intermediate tectobulbar tract; tbv, ventral tectobulbar tract; IV, trochlear nucleus.

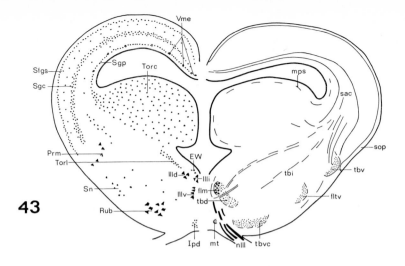

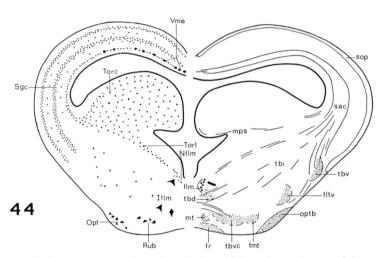

Figs 43 and 44. Transverse sections through the middle and rostral parts of the mesencephalon in the caiman *Caiman crocodilus*. EW, Nucleus of Edinger-Westphal; flm, medial longitudinal fasciculus; fltv, ventral peduncle of the lateral forebrain bundle; fmt, medial forebrain bundle; fr, fasciculus retroflexus; Iflm, interstitial nucleus of the flm; Ipd, interpeduncular nucleus, dorsal part; mps, mesencephalic periventricular system (Huber and Crosby); mt, mamillotegmental tract; Nflm, nucleus of the flm; nIII, oculomotor nerve; Opt, nucleus opticus tegmenti; optb, basal optic tract; Prm, nucleus profundus mesencephali; Rub, nucleus ruber; rusp, rubrospinal tract; Sfgs, stratum fibrosum et griseum superficiale; Sgc, stratum griseum centrale; Sgp, stratum griseum periventriculare; Sn, substantia nigra; sac, stratum album centrale; sfp, stratum fibrosum periventriculare; sop, stratum opticum; Torc, central nucleus of the torus semicircularis; Torl, laminar nucleus of the torus semicircularis; tbd, dorsal tectobulbar tract; tbi, intermediate tectobulbar tract; tbv, ventral tectobulbar tract; tbvc, ventral tectobulbar tract; IIId, oculomotor nucleus, dorsal part; IIIi, oculomotor nucleus, intermediate part; IIIv, oculomotor nucleus, ventral part.

of the former bundle enter the dorsal funiculus and then pass rostrally to reach the nuclei of the dorsal funiculus. These long ascending fibers are somatotopically arranged in such a fashion that fibers of caudal origin are most medial and those joining at more rostral levels are situated more laterally (Kruger and Witkovsky, 1961; Goldby and Robinson, 1962; Ebbesson 1967, 1969; Joseph and Whitlock, 1968; Kusuma *et al.*, Chapter 2 of this volume). Transection of the dorsal funiculus at various levels of the spinal cord documents a somatotopical projection upon the dorsal funicular nuclei. The most medial and consequently the most caudal fibers appear to terminate in the nucleus of Bischoff, which therefore has been considered as concerned with the reception of primary afferent fibers from the tail. Fibers from a more rostral origin terminate in the medial part of the nucleus of the dorsal funiculus, and still more rostrally arising fibers in the lateral part of the nucleus (Ebbesson, 1967).

After experimental transection of the dorsal funiculus most of the long ascending dorsal funicular fibers appear to terminate in the nucleus of the dorsal funiculus. However, a small bundle bypasses this nucleus and travels rostrally into the cerebellum (Ebbesson, 1967, 1969; Pedersen, 1973). On their way rostralward some fibers of this small bundle terminate in a nucleus of the vestibular area, the ventrolateral vestibular nucleus (Jacobs, 1967; Ebbesson, 1967, 1969; Pedersen, 1973).

An input from cerebral centers to the dorsal column nuclei, which occurs in the opossum (Martin and West, 1967) and many other mammals, has not been demonstrated in reptiles.

A decussating, ascending system has been claimed by many authors to represent the efferent connections of the nucleus of the dorsal funiculus (Christensen, 1927, *Sphenodon*; Huber and Crosby, 1926, *Alligator*; Papez, 1929, *Nerodia*; Shanklin, 1930, *Chamaeleo*). This system has been termed the medial lemniscus. In the Häggqvist material of all the species studied, this system is represented as a small, but distinct thin-fibered bundle, lying ventrally close to the median plane throughout the brainstem. However, this system is no longer obvious at the mesencephalic level; e.g. in *Tupinambis* at the level of the red nucleus (cf. Fig. 23). Recently, the presence of a medial lemniscus has been definitely shown experimentally in the monitor lizard (Ebbesson, 1976). The medial lemniscus in this reptile appears to terminate in the contralateral ventrolateral thalamic area.

III. Fiber Systems Ascending in the Lateral Funiculus

A. GENERAL

The superficial zone of the lateral funiculus of the spinal cord consists chiefly of thin fibers which ascend to the brainstem. Investigators working with normal material have described spinocerebellar, spinobulbar and spino-tectal components (cf. Ariëns Kappers *et al.*, 1936). The latter two components have been designated by Ebbesson (1967) as the spinal lemniscus, a term that was introduced by Herrick (1914, 1930, 1948) in his extensive descriptions of the brain of urodeles. In the caudal part of the brainstem the spinal lemniscus and the spinocerebellar tracts become indistinguishable. Hence in our drawings of sections through this region, the spinal lemniscus includes the spinocerebellar tracts, which will be described under the heading of the cerebellar connections.

Degeneration studies following hemicordotomies have revealed that the spinal lemniscus can be divided into spinorhombencephalic, spinomesence-phalic and spinothalamic projections. These components will now be discussed.

B. Spinorhombencephalic Projections

The experimental work of Ebbesson (1967, 1969) in the lizard *Tupinambis nigropunctatus*, the turtle *Pseudemys scripta elegans* and the snake *Boa constrictor* has shown that many of the fibers of the spinal lemniscus pass dorsomedially and terminate in the ipsilateral reticular formation. Most of these spinoreticular fibers terminate in the inferior reticular nucleus and the caudal part of the medial reticular nucleus. A much less dense projection was demonstrated to the rostral part of the latter nucleus and to the superior reticular nucleus. Only a few fibers were found to terminate in the contra-lateral reticular formation.

Under the heading "spinonuclear" projections, certain fiber contingents terminating in more circumscript rhombencephalic nuclei will be discussed. The spinal lemniscus projects rather diffusely to a nucleus termed provision-ally the medial parvocellular nucleus (Ebbesson, 1967, 1969). This nucleus, situated between the medial longitudinal fasciculus and the hypoglossal nucleus (Figs 15, 16, 26, 27, 36 and 37) could not be identified in the turtle *Testudo hermanni*. Two other spinonuclear projections pass via the lateral funiculus to the ventral part of the facial motor nucleus and to the dorsal motor nucleus of the vagus (Ebbesson, 1967, 1969; Pedersen, 1973). A spinovestibular component of the spinal lemniscus has also been traced to three vestibular nuclei, namely the descending vestibular nucleus, the ventrolateral vestibular nucleus and the ventromedial vestibular nucleus.

C. Spinomesencephalic Projections

The older literature mentions a projection from the spinal cord to the mesencephalon, more particularly to the mesencephalic tectum (Edinger,

1908; Huber and Crosby, 1926). This tract supposedly terminates in the stratum griseum centrale of the caudal tectum near the cells of origin of the tectothalamic tract, which has been assumed to terminate in the nucleus rotundus (Ariëns Kappers et al., 1936). Transections of the lateral funiculus showed projections to three mesencephalic structures: the central gray, the laminar nucleus of the torus and the intercollicular nucleus (Ebbesson, 1967, 1969). The latter nucleus, which receives a comparatively large number of fibers, lies between the mesencephalic tectum and the torus semicircularis (Figs 11, 22, 32 and 42). In contrast to reports in the older literature, neither Ebbesson (1967, 1969) nor Pedersen (1973) could confirm the existence of a clear termination in the deeper layers of the mesencephalic tectum. The only spinomesencephalic projection detectable in our Häggqvist material is represented by a few fibers from the spinal lemniscus into the intercollicular nucleus (cf. Figs 11, 22, 32 and 42).

D. Spinothalamic Projections

It has been suggested that there is a spinal projection to the dorsal thalamus, and more particularly to nucleus rotundus (Ariëns Kappers et al., 1936). Our normal material does not permit tracing of the spinal lemniscus beyond mesencephalic levels. However, experimental work (Ebbesson, 1967, 1969; Pedersen, 1973) has demonstrated the existence of a direct spinothalamic projection, terminating in the dorsal intermediate nucleus of the thalamus. This nucleus (Ebbesson, 1967) lies between the dorsolateral anterior nucleus and the ventral lateral geniculate nucleus. For a more detailed description of the thalamus we refer to the works of Papez (1935, *Chelonia*), Senn (1968, *Lacerta*), Butler and Northcutt (1973, *Iguana*) and Cruce (1974, *Tupinambis*).

IV. Organization and Connections of the Sensory Trigeminal Nuclei

The sensory part of the trigeminal nuclear complex comprises three nuclei: the spinal nucleus, the principal nucleus and the mesencephalic nucleus. In two families of snakes (Crotalidae and Boidae) in addition to the usual descending nucleus a separate, lateral descending nucleus can be distinguished (Molenaar, 1974). The descending and principal nuclei constitute a column of gray which extends from the entrance of the trigeminal nerve into the rostral part of the spinal cord, where it is continuous with the peripheral part of the dorsal horn.

The major portion of the sensory trigeminal root constitutes the thin-fibered spinal tract. This tract probably receives additional afferents from the vagus nerve, as demonstrated in amphibians (Friedman et al., 1972).

During its course caudalward the spinal trigeminal tract discharges its fibers to the spinal nucleus which lies directly medial to the tract. Reference to Figs 28 and 29 shows that this nucleus is particularly well developed in *Python reticulatus*. In favourable Häggqvist sections of this snake (family: Boidae) a separate lateral bundle could be distinguished as described by Molenaar (1974) and Schroeder and Loop (1976). This bundle is related to the lateral descending nucleus (Figs 28 and 29) which is present in the Crotalidae and Boidae and is probably related to the specialized pit organs of these snakes (Molenaar, 1974; Schroeder and Loop, 1976). These pit organs function as infrared receptors (Harris and Gamow, 1971; Gamow and Harris, 1973), allowing the animal to recognize and locate warm-blooded prey.

The principal trigeminal nucleus (Figs 8, 9, 19, 30 and 40) constitutes the rostral enlargement of the trigeminal gray column. It lies at the level of the entrance of the sensory part of V, from which it receives a direct component.

Woodburne (1936, *Anolis*) suggested on the basis of normal material that fibers from the nuclei of the trigeminal gray column terminate in the cerebellum, in the tectum and in the motor nucleus of the trigeminal nerve. We are unable to confirm the existence of these connections in our Häggqvist material.

The fibers of the mesencephalic root of V pass peripherally together with the motor fibers of the same nerve. After entering the brainstem the first-mentioned fibers ascend rostrodorsalward between the principal sensory and motor nuclei of V towards the mesencephalon, where they originate in the large cells of the mesencephalic nucleus. Experimental studies by Desole *et al.* (1970) have demonstrated that these fibers mediate proprioceptive impulses from the muscles of mastication. The mesencephalic nucleus includes a compact median group, which constitutes a continuous strip extending throughout the rostrocaudal extent of the tectum, and a diffuse lateral group (Weinberg, 1928). This lateral group is particularly well developed in *Python*. Goldstein and Jacobs (1969, *Lacerta*) made small tectal lesions in the region of the mesencephalic nucleus of V and studied the ensuing degeneration. From their experiments they concluded that efferents from the mesencephalic nucleus terminate in the motor nuclei of V, VII and X, as well as in the spinal nucleus of V and the cervical spinal cord.

V. Solitary Fasciculus and Related Nuclei

The reptilian solitary fasciculus (Figs 5, 15, 26, 27 and 37) is a circumscript, thin-fibered bundle that receives fibers from the VIIth, IXth and Xth cranial nerves. Its fibers terminate in the nucleus of the solitary fasciculus

(Figs 5, 15, 26, 27, 36 and 37) and in its mediocaudal extension, the nucleus commissurae infimae (Fig. 27). The nucleus of the solitary tract is at times poorly separated from some adjacent nuclei, such as the spinal nucleus of V, the nucleus of the dorsal funiculus and the descending vestibular nucleus. The solitary tract of reptiles and its termination have not yet been studied with experimental techniques. In the Anura, however, Friedman *et al.* (1972) demonstrated a projection from the vagal nerve, passing via the solitary tract to the nucleus of this tract and the nucleus of the commissurae infimae. Fuller and Ebbesson (1973) showed that in anurans the solitary tract also receives a projection from the trigeminal nerve. The only afferent system to the nucleus of solitary fasciculus and the nucleus commissurae infimae, which so far has been demonstrated experimentally in reptiles, is a small projection from the lateral funiculus of the spinal cord (Ebbesson, 1967, 1969).

Efferents from the nuclei in question have not been traced experimentally. In the older literature, based on normal material, a connection has been suggested to the secondary visceral nucleus located in the rostral part of the rhombencephalon (Shanklin, 1930; Barnard, 1936). This nucleus lies just ventromedial to the nucleus isthmi. A probable equivalent of the secondary visceral nucleus could be delimited by us in *Testudo* and in *Python* (Figs 10 and 31), but not in *Tupinambis* and *Caiman*. Since no projection has been established experimentally to this nucleus from the nucleus of the solitary tract, its visceral nature is still to be proved. It should be noted, however, that recently Norgren and Leonard (1971, 1973) have shown that in the rat the dorsomedial part of the parabrachial nucleus (a cell mass situated in the most rostral part of the rhombencephalon) receives a projection from the anterior part of the nucleus of the solitary fasciculus and represents a taste center. This center may well correspond to the secondary visceral nucleus of Shanklin (1930), Barnard (1936) and of the present survey.

VI. Vestibular System

In reptiles the VIIIth nerve has been divided by most authors into dorsal and ventral roots, the dorsal root considered to be cochlear, the ventral vestibular. A detailed description of the pattern of termination of the vestibular root, based on normal material, is given by Weston (1936) and Landmann (1971). According to these authors the vestibular root divides, after passing fibers to the tangential nucleus, into ascending and descending roots. The ascending root (Figs 7, 18, 29 and 39) sends its fibers to the dorsolateral and superior vestibular nuclei. The descending root (Figs 6, 16, 27, 28 and 38) discharges its fibers into the ventrolateral and descending vestibular nuclei.

Recently the primary afferent projections of the VIIIth cranial nerve have been studied with experimental techniques in *Caiman crocodilus* (Leake, 1974) and in *Tupinambis nigropunctatus* (DeFina and Webster, 1974). Degenerated fibers were traced to the six ipsilateral vestibular nuclei as distinguished by Weston (1936). In addition, direct fibers were noted from the vestibular root to the granular layer of the cerebellum.

The vestibular nuclei in reptiles have been extensively studied by Weston (1936), who distinguished six vestibular nuclei: ventrolateral, tangential, ventromedial, descending, dorsolateral and superior. This subdivision of the vestibular nuclear complex appears also to the applicable to the reptiles studied here.

The ventrolateral vestibular nucleus (Figs 7, 17, 18, 28, 29 and 39) consists of very large cells (in *Testudo* they have an average diameter of 44 μm, Cruce and Nieuwenhuys, 1974), among which small elements are scattered. The nucleus, which is generally considered as the equivalent of the mammalian nucleus of Deiters, is particularly well developed in lizards and caiman.

The tangential vestibular nucleus (Figs 6, 7, 17, 18, 28, 29, 38 and 39) consists of a collection of medium-sized cells, intercalated among the entering fibers of the vestibular root. It lies directly lateral to the ventrolateral vestibular nucleus. Weston (1936) and later Stefanelli (1944a, b) have suggested that the degree of development of the tangential nucleus is correlated with the relative development of the trunk musculature.

The ventromedial vestibular nucleus (Figs 6, 7, 17, 18, 28, 29, 37–39) is a rather ill-defined cell mass, consisting of medium-sized cells. It is situated in the ventrolateral angle of the fourth ventricle and extends along the whole length of the vestibular region.

The descending vestibular nucleus (Figs 6, 16, 28, 37 and 38), which can be considered as the more diffuse, caudal continuation of the ventrolateral vestibular nucleus, has also been termed the inferior nucleus (Beccari, 1911; Stefanelli, 1944a). It consists of medium-sized and small cells. Its most caudal part merges with the dorsal funicular nucleus.

The dorsolateral vestibular nucleus (Figs 8, 19, 30 and 40) has also been called the superior nucleus by various authors (Beccari, 1911; Larsell, 1926; Papez, 1929; Stefanelli, 1944a). It lies between the ventrolateral vestibular nucleus and the deep cerebellar nuclei. The boundaries of this rather diffuse nucleus are ill defined.

The superior vestibular nucleus has been considered by Stefanelli (1944a) as a direct rostral continuation of the medial part of the dorsolateral vestibular nucleus. It lies between the lateral cerebellar nucleus and the principal nucleus of the trigeminal nerve, from which it is very poorly delimited. So far this cell mass has only been distinguished in the turtle *Testudo hermanni* (Fig. 9).

Stefanelli (1944a, b) noted, and we have been able to confirm, the considerable differences in the development of the vestibular nuclei and their connections. The ventrolateral and dorsolateral vestibular nuclei are strongly developed in those reptiles with a wholly or partly quadrupedal locomotion, whereas the tangential nucleus is particularly large in species with serpentine modes of movement.

Apart from afferents entering via the vestibular nerve, fibers to the vestibular nuclear complex enter from the spinal cord, the cerebellum and some cranial nerve nuclei. Spinovestibular connections passing via the dorsal funiculus and the spinal lemniscus have already been mentioned in the sections on the spinal ascending systems. Cerebellar projections have been experimentally demonstrated in *Caiman crocodilus* to terminate in the dorsolateral, ventrolateral and tangential vestibular nuclei (Senn and Goodman, 1969). Weston (1936) also suggested that there are afferents from cochlear, trigeminal and vagal centers to the ventromedial vestibular nucleus.

Efferent connections from the vestibular nuclear complex consist of projections to the cerebellum, the brain stem and the spinal cord. Secondary vestibulocerebellar fibers running into the granular layer of the cerebellum first mentioned by Weston (1936), have recently been demonstrated in *Testudo hermanni* and *Python reticulatus* (ten Donkelaar, 1975, 1976b).

Connections of the vestibular nuclear complex with other areas of the brainstem, in particular with the nuclei which supply the external eye muscles (III, IV and VI), were described by Beccari (1911), Weston (1936) and Stefanelli (1944a, b). These fibers were supposed to pass via the medial longitudinal fasciculus (f.l.m.), which will be discussed in the section on the reticular formation. Such a vestibulomesencephalic connection, passing via the f.l.m. is strongly suggested in the Häggqvist material. Moreover, the presence of this projection has been recently confirmed with anterograde degeneration techniques (ten Donkelaar, 1975, 1976b). Lesions in the vestibular area of *Testudo hermanni, Tupinambis nigropunctatus* and *Python reticulatus*, reveal a bilateral (mainly ipsilateral) projection via the f.l.m. to the nuclei supplying the external eye muscles.

In our Häggqvist material the vestibulospinal fibers constitute two different bundles, the lateral vestibulospinal and the medial vestibulospinal tracts. The fibers of the latter enter the f.l.m. The lateral vestibulospinal tract, already described by Beccari (1911), arises from the ventrolateral vestibular nucleus. It can be traced as a bundle of coarse fibers descending through the lower brainstem. As it passes caudally, it gradually shifts ventromedialward, finally attaining a superficial position just lateral to the f.l.m. and its caudal continuation (cf. Figs 14–17). The lateral vestibulospinal tract is particularly well developed in *Tupinambis* and *Caiman*, but rather small in *Python*. The existence of a direct bilateral projection from the ventrolateral vestibular nucleus to the spinal cord has been demonstrated with retrograde (Robinson, 1969, *Lacerta*; ten Donkelaar, 1975, 1976a, *Testudo, Tupinambis, Python*) as well as anterograde techniques (ten Donkelaar, 1975, 1976b). Recently, spinal projections from the descending and ventromedial vestibular nuclei have been demonstrated (ten Donkelaar and de Bour-van Huizen, 1978, *Lacerta*).

VII. Acoustic System

The cochlear root of the VIIIth nerve sends its fibers to the cochlear nuclei. In reptiles these include the dorsal magnocellular nucleus and nucleus laminaris, both of which lie in the most dorsal part of the rhombencephalic alar plate. We could not confirm the presence of a nucleus angularis as described by Ariëns Kappers *et al.* (1936) and Miller (1975). Recently, Foster (1974, *Iguana*) and Leake (1974, *Caiman*) confirmed with experimental techniques the projection of the cochlear root to these cochlear nuclei.

The dorsal magnocellular nucleus (Figs 6, 16, 28 and 38) is composed of closely packed, medium-sized cells and is considered homologous to the mammalian ventral cochlear nucleus.

Nucleus laminaris (Figs 7, 17, 39) consists of a row of small cells, and lies immediately rostral to the dorsal magnocellular nucleus. In the caiman the nucleus in question is differentiated into two laminae.

The efferent connections of the cochlear nuclei have been studied by Foster (1974) in the lizard *Iguana iguana*. Following discrete lesions placed in the two main cochlear nuclei, most degenerating fibers decussate (deep arcuate fibers) and, after having passed through or along the superior olive, arch rostrally to form the lateral lemniscus (cf. Figs 6, 16–18, 28, 29, 38 and 39).

The superior olive (Figs 6–8, 17–19, 28, 29, 37–40) also receives a projection from the cochlear nuclei and is particularly well developed in *Caiman crocodilus*. It probably is the homologue of the mammalian superior olivary complex and trapezoid body. The designation superior olive remains tentative, however, since its fiber connections are only imperfectly known in reptiles. Recently, a projection to the superior olive has been demonstrated from the mesencephalic tectum (ten Donkelaar, 1975, 1976b). A similar observation has been made in *Rana pipiens* (Rubinson, 1968). This projection from the tectum to the superior olive suggests that the superior olive has some visual functions. A similar suggestion has also been made (Harrison and Irving, 1966) on the basis of comparative studies in diurnal and nocturnal mammals. In diurnal mammals the medial superior olive is particularly large, whereas in nocturnal forms this nucleus is reduced or absent.

The lateral lemniscus, arising from the deep arcuate fibers, passes rostrally in a superficial position at the ventrolateral border of the brainstem. In the isthmic region a nucleus of the lateral lemniscus can be distinguished which, as its name implies, is closely related to the lateral lemniscus. It consists of small cells and can be divided into dorsal and ventral parts in all species studied (Figs 10, 11, 20, 21 and 41), except for *Python* (Figs 31 and 32). The lateral lemniscus terminates in the central nucleus of the torus semicircularis (Foster, 1974, *Iguana*). In the Häggqvist material it can be traced into the torus, bending medially from its superficial position (Figs 11, 22, 32).

The torus semicircularis of reptiles is generally considered to be comparable to the mammalian inferior colliculus. The torus is wholly or partly covered by the tectum. In *Caiman crocodilus* very large tori protrude into the ventricle (Figs 43, 44). Two nuclei, the central nucleus and the laminar nucleus, can be distinguished in the reptilian torus semicircularis. The laminar nucleus of the torus forms part of the compact periventricular cell layer that extends throughout the mesencephalon. Dense degeneration occurs in this nucleus following lesions of the lateral funiculus of the spinal cord (Ebbesson, 1967, 1969). Electrophysiological experiments (Hartline 1971; Kennedy, 1975) indicate that the toral nuclei can be activated by sound stimuli. An acoustic projection has been demonstrated by Foster (1974) in the lizard *Iguana iguana*.

The toral nuclei (Foster, 1974, *Iguana*; Pritz, 1974a, *Caiman*) project to the nucleus reuniens of the thalamus. The latter nucleus, in turn, projects to the medial parts of the telencephalic structure which Crosby (1917) designated as dorsolateral and intermediolateral areas (Pritz, 1974b; Foster and Peele, 1975). This projection reaches the telencephalon by way of the dorsal peduncle of the lateral forebrain bundle.

VIII. Visual System

The reptilian mesencephalic tectum receives the bulk of the fibers of the optic nerve. This projection from the retina upon the tectum is probably the most intensively studied pathway in reptiles. It will be dealt with in other chapters, hence, its discussion is kept short. The retinal projections are bilateral in lizards, snakes and caiman, but apparently not consistently so in turtles. Upon entering the optic chiasm the optic nerve divides in *Caiman crocodilus* (Burns and Goodman, 1967) into four components, namely an uncrossed part and three decussating tracts: the main or marginal tract, the axillary tract and the basal optic root. The uncrossed fibers appear to terminate in the upper layers (the stratum opticum and stratum fibrosum et griseum superficiale) of the lateral portion of the ipsilateral tectum. At the rostral border of the tectum the main optic tract divides into medial and lateral fascicles, with the medial fascicle distributing to medial and rostral parts of the tectum, and the lateral to lateral and dorsal parts. This tract also projects to the lateral geniculate nucleus and certain pretectal nuclei. The small axillary tract rejoins the main optic tract after discharging some fibers to the lateral geniculate nucleus. It has been found only in caiman (Burns and Goodman, 1967). The fourth component, the basal optic root, terminates in the nucleus opticus tegmenti, which will be dealt with later in this section.

In addition to a visual input, the mesencephalic tectum receives fibers from several other sources, i.e. from the thalamus, the lateral lemniscus, the trigeminal centers and the spinal cord. Thus far there is only experimental evidence for a spinal projection. The statements in the older literature (cf. Ariëns Kappers et al., 1936) that the spinal lemniscus sends fibers to the superficial layers of the tectum, has not received experimental support (Ebbesson, 1967, 1969). As already mentioned, the mesencephalic component of the spinal lemniscus terminates in the nucleus intercollicularis and the laminar nucleus of the torus.

The mesencephalic tectum has been divided into fourteen layers by Ramón (1896, Chamaeleo). Huber and Crosby (1926, 1933) were of the opinion that several of the layers described by Ramón can be considered substrata of one and the same zone (cf. Table I). Thus they arrived at a subdivision into the following six layers: (1) the stratum opticum, the outer layer, receiving the fibers from the optic tract; (2) the stratum fibrosum et griseum superficiale, considered as a receptive and correlative layer; (3) the central gray layer, the stratum griseum centrale, consisting of neurons, the axons of

TABLE I

Comparison of nomenclatures for the layers of the mesencephalic tectum

Huber and Crosby (1926, 1933, *Alligator, Varanus, Pseudemys, Python*) ten Donkelaar and Nieuwenhuys (the present survey)	Ramón (1896, *Chamaeleo*) Senn (1968, *Lacerta*) Butler and Northcutt, (1971, *Iguana*) Butler and Ebbesson (1975, *Tupinambis*)
(1) Stratum opticum	Zone 14
(2) Stratum fibrosum et griseum superficiale	Zone 8 to 13
(3) Stratum griseum centrale	Zone 7
(4) Stratum album centrale	Zone 6
(5) Stratum griseum periventriculare	Zone 3 to 5
(6) Stratum fibrosum periventriculare	Zone 2
ependyma	Zone 1

which constitute a most important part of the efferent system of the tectum; (4) the *stratum album centrale*, in which many of the axons of the previous layer descend; (5) the *stratum griseum periventriculare*, containing neurons with short dendrites which extend toward the ventricle and establish relations with entering fibers of the diencephalic and mesencephalic periventricular system; (6) the periventricular fibers, which are considered a dorsoventral correlation system (Huber and Crosby, 1926, 1933), constitute the innermost layer of the tectum, i.e. the *stratum fibrosum periventriculare*.

The subdivision into six layers just reviewed is employed by many present-day workers. In the material at our disposal they could be clearly distinguished, except in *Python*, in which a more diffuse arrangement was found.

The efferent connections of the mesencephalic tectum can be divided into an ascending and a descending projection. Several previous workers claimed that the ascending system involved a tectothalamic tract, which was considered to terminate mainly in the nucleus rotundus, and to discharge some of its fibers into the lateral geniculate nucleus and certain pretectal nuclei (Huber and Crosby, 1926, 1933; Papez, 1935; Curwen and Miller, 1939). Recent experimental studies (Ebbesson, 1970; Hall and Ebner, 1970a; Belekhova and Kosareva, 1971; Butler and Northcutt, 1971; Braford, 1973; Foster and Hall, 1975; ten Donkelaar, 1975, 1976b; Ulinski, 1973) have confirmed the reality of these projections. The nucleus rotundus in its turn sends fibers to certain telencephalic structures (Hall and Ebner, 1970a, b; Pritz, 1975). On the basis of its afferent and efferent connections the nucleus rotundus has been considered the homologue of the mammalian lateral posterior nucleus (Hall and Ebner, 1970a, b).

The descending projections of the mesencephalic tectum have been divided into dorsal, intermediate and ventral (or lateral) tectobulbar tracts (de Lange, 1910, 1913). These tracts, which consist of medium-sized fibers, are rather easily recognized in our Häggqvist material and have been illustrated in the sections through the mesencephalon. The dorsal tract crosses the midline just ventral to the f.l.m. (cf. Figs 12, 23, 33 and 43) and continues caudalward as the predorsal bundle. This bundle extends throughout the rhombencephalon, where it is situated immediately ventral to the f.l.m. A tectospinal component could not be demonstrated in the Häggqvist material. The intermediate tract terminates chiefly in the ipsilateral mesencephalic tegmentum. In *Python reticulatus* the ventral tectobulbar tract can be traced as far caudal as the vestibular region. In the other reptiles studied, however, this fiber system fades out at the isthmic level. The subdivision of the tectobulbar system just outlined has received experimental support from degeneration studies by Foster and Hall (1975, *Iguana*) and ten Donkelaar (1975, 1976b, *Testudo, Tupinambis* and *Python*). Moreover, the above experimental studies have shown that the predorsal bundle discharges fibers along its course at approximately right angles, these fibers terminate in the medial part of the reticular formation. The ipsilateral, ventral tectobulbar pathway projects to the nucleus isthmi. Descending along the ventrolateral wall of the brainstem, the bundle in question also sends fibers into the more lateral parts of the medial reticular formation. Only after lesions which are extended to the periventricular layers can one note an appreciable amount of degeneration in this ipsilateral tract. These degeneration experiments demonstrate that both descending pathways reach the lowest levels of the brainstem, but do not extend into the spinal cord. It seems evident that the tectum only indirectly influences the spinal motor centers, the connection being by way of the reticular formation.

The nucleus opticus tegmenti (Figs 13, 24, 34 and 44), or ganglion ectomammillare of other authors (Edinger, 1899; Beccari, 1923), forms the end station of the entirely crossed basal optic root. It consists of a rather diffuse zone of small cells along the ventrolateral border of the mesencephalic tegmentum. Shanklin (1933) described efferent connections from this nucleus to the oculomotor nucleus and certain thalamic nuclei on the basis of normal material, however, these connections still require experimental confirmation.

IX. Projections to the Brainstem from Higher Levels

Input from higher centers to the brainstem reaches the mesencephalic tegmentum via the habenulo-interpeduncular tract, the lateral forebrain bundle and the medial forebrain bundle.

As its name implies, the habenulo-interpeduncular tract, or fasciculus retroflexus, originates in the habenular nuclei. These nuclei receive a projection from several telencephalic centers by way of the stria medullaris. Experimental work in various reptiles has shown that the stria medullaris contains many secondary olfactory fibers, which after decussating in the habenular commissure terminate in certain telencephalic structures (Gamble, 1956; Heimer, 1969; Scalia et al., 1969; Northcutt, 1970). Thus this commissure constitutes at least partly a telencephalic commissure. The efferent connection of the habenular nuclei, the fasciculus retroflexus, can be traced in the Häggqvist material to the interpeduncular nucleus. This nucleus, situated between the oculomotor nerves, can be divided into a dorsal and a ventral part (Figs 10–12, 21–23, 31–34, 41–43). The interpeduncular nucleus receives in addition the mamillotegmental tract (Figs 23, 24, 43, 44), which is reported to arise in the mamillary bodies (de Lange, 1913; Frederikse, 1931; Tuge, 1932).

The main efferent paths of the telencephalon are the lateral and medial forebrain bundles. The medial forebrain bundle is a diffusely arranged fiber system which extends from the septum, via the lateral hypothalamic area, to the mesencephalic tegmentum. Experimental work in *Pseudemys* (Hall, 1971; Hall and Ebner, 1974) revealed that the so-called general cortex sends fibers by way of the medial forebrain bundle that spread diffusely in the mesencephalic tegmentum. The septum also contributes fibers to the medial forebrain bundle, but these do not extend beyond the hypothalamus (Lohman *et al.*, 1973, *Tupinambis*). The most caudal termination appeared to be the mamillary body.

The lateral forebrain bundle can be divided into a dorsal and a ventral peduncle. The dorsal peduncle ascends from the thalamus to the cerebral hemisphere. The ventral peduncle, on the other hand, consists mainly of fibers which descend from the telencephalon to the diencephalic entopeduncular nuclei and to the mesencephalic tegmentum. Experimental work in *Tupinambis* demonstrates that the ventral part of the striatum contributes an appreciable number of fibers to the ventral peduncle of the lateral forebrain bundle. Part of these reach the mesencephalic tegmentum, specifically the neuropil ventral to the red nucleus and a more circumscribed area termed the substantia nigra (Lohman *et al.*, 1973; Hoogland, 1977). Moreover, some fibers could be traced to the lateral cerebellar nucleus.

The substantia nigra has already been labeled as such in the older literature (Beccari, 1923; Huber and Crosby, 1933; Papez, 1935). In the material at our disposal a possible substantia nigra could only be distinguished as a cell cluster in the lateral part of the mesencephalic tegmentum in *Tupinambis* and *Caiman* (Figs 22, 42 and 43). The reptilian substantia nigra has also been localized with histochemical techniques (Baker-Cohen, 1968) and by using fluorescence microscopy (Parent and Poirier, 1971, *Chrysemys picta*). The latter technique disclosed a rather diffuse catecholamine-containing cell mass at the level of the oculomotor nucleus and extending from the ventromedial to the dorsolateral portion of the midbrain tegmentum. From this cell mass Parent and Poitras (1973) were able to trace a catecholamine-containing projection to what they termed the basal strio-amygdaloid complex. They suggest that this projection shows a striking resemblance to the nigrostriatal dopaminergic system of the mammalian brain (cf. Andén *et al.*, 1964, 1965).

X. Cerebellum and its Connections

The normal anatomy of the reptilian cerebellum has recently been reviewed extensively by Larsell (1967) and Nieuwenhuys (1967), and will be described in a separate chapter of this series. The present section offers only a brief discussion of the afferents and efferents of the cerebellum.

The afferents of the cerebellum consist of projections from the spinal cord, certain rhombencephalic nuclei and the mesencephalic tectum. Small projections pass from the ventral striatum (Hoogland, 1977, *Tupinambis*), as well as from the red nucleus (ten Donkelaar, 1975, 1976b, *Tupinambis*) to the lateral cerebellar nucleus.

The spinocerebellar projection has been divided into dorsal and ventral spinocerebellar tracts (Ariëns Kappers *et al.*, 1936; Larsell, 1967; Nieuwenhuys, 1967). Both ascend via the lateral funiculus. The Häggqvist material confirms this division for the reptiles studied. These spinocerebellar tracts cannot be delimitated at caudal sections of the brainstem, where they are still included in the spinal lemniscus. At more rostral rhombencephalic levels the spinocerebellar tracts arise from the spinal lemniscus. The ventral tract extends more rostrally than the dorsal one, and partly decussates in the anterior medullary velum. Experimental work (Jacobs, 1968; Ebbesson, 1967, 1969; Pedersen, 1973) reveals that spinal afferents to the cerebellum terminate largely in the ipsilateral part of the cerebellum. Only some fibers end in the contralateral part. Spinocerebellar fibers reach the cerebellum mainly by way of the lateral funiculus. Ebbesson (1967, 1969) and Pedersen 1936). Primary (DeFina and Webster, 1974; Leake, 1974) as well as secondary (ten Donkelaar, 1975, 1976b) vestibulocerebellar fibers occur in reptiles. interpretation, Ebbesson and Pedersen consider the ventral spinocerebellar tract to consist of all of the spinocerebellar fibers passing by way of the lateral funiculus.

Afferents to the cerebellum from rhombencephalic centers have been reported from trigeminal and vestibular nuclei (Weston, 1936; Woodburne, 1936). Primary (DeFina and Webster, 1974; Leake, 1974) as well as secondary (ten Donkelaar, 1975, 1976b), vestibulocerebellar fibers occur in reptiles. The lower brainstem of mammals shows two nuclei, i.e. the external cuneate nucleus and the nucleus of the lateral funiculus, both of which send fibers to the cerebellum. An equivalent of the former nucleus has been described by Ebbesson (1967, 1969). The nucleus of the lateral funiculus (Figs 16, 28 and 37) or lateral reticular nucleus (Ariëns Kappers *et al.*, 1936) has been recognized in *Tupinambis*, *Python*, and *Caiman*, but not in *Testudo*. We lack experimental evidence that the external cuneate nucleus and the nucleus of the lateral funiculus do project to the cerebellum.

A tectocerebellar projection suggested in the older literature (Shanklin, 1930; Weston, 1936) and experimentally demonstrated in birds (Zecha, 1964) has not been confirmed in reptiles by tectal ablations.

The projections comprising the reptilian efferent cerebellar pathways originate in part from the Purkinje cell layer and in part from the deep cerebellar nuclei, which occupy a periventricular position, close to the cerebellotegmental junction. The deep cerebellar nuclei can be divided into a lateral and a medial nucleus. The lateral cerebellar nucleus (Figs 8, 9, 20, 30 and 40) consists of small and medium-sized, diffusely scattered cells.

The medial cerebellar nucleus (Figs 9, 20, 30 and 40) is chiefly composed of medium-sized elements and is rather indistinctly set off as compared to the lateral cerebellar nucleus. Experimental data on the corticonuclear projection are scanty. Senn and Goodman (1969) reported that in *Caiman* these fibers arise chiefly from the middle lobe of the three cerebellar lobes.

The efferent connections of the cerebellum, from the cerebellar cortex and from the deep cerebellar nuclei, include the cerebellovestibular tract, the cerebellomotor and cerebellotegmental tracts and the brachium conjunctivum. The cerebellovestibular tract arises chiefly from the medial cerebellar nucleus and projects to the dorsolateral and ventrolateral vestibular nuclei (Weston, 1936). Superficial lesions in the cerebellar cortex, sparing the deep nuclei (Senn and Goodman, 1969), also produce degeneration in the dorsolateral, the ventrolateral and the tangential vestibular nuclei. Both deep cerebellar nuclei project to the spinal cord (ten Donkelaar and de Boer-van Huizen, 1978; *Lacerta*).

The brachium conjunctivum originates from the lateral cerebellar nucleus and terminates in the contralateral red nucleus (Shanklin, 1930; Larsell, 1932). This tract can be distinguished in the Häggqvist material as a thin-fibered system (e.g. Figs 21, 22), which decussates just caudal to the red nucleus (Figs 11, 22). In reptiles an extension of the brachium conjunctivum to thalamic levels is not known, and pertinent experimental data are entirely lacking.

The red nucleus (Figs 12, 23, 24, 33, 34, 43 and 44) is rather well developed in most reptiles, consisting of medium-sized and large cells. However, it can hardly be distinguished in *Python* (Figs 33, 34). With regard to the efferents of the red nucleus, a rubrospinal tract has been described by previous workers (de Lange, 1912; Papez, 1929, 1935). In the Häggqvist material of *Tupinambis* and caiman this system appears as a bundle of medium-sized fibers lying ventromedial to the spinal tract of V (Figs 15–18), thus occupying a position comparable to that in the pigeon (Zecha, 1961; van den Akker, 1970) and in the opossum (Martin and Dom, 1970). Experimental studies of the reptilian red nucleus (ten Donkelaar, 1975, 1976a, b) reveal a crossed rubrospinal tract coursing through the brain stem in *Tupinambis nigropunctatus* and *Testudo hermanni* (Figs 14–18). In *Tupinambis* the red nucleus projects to various parts of the trigeminal nuclei, to the facial motor nucleus, to the lateral (parvocellular) part of the reticular formation and to the lateral cerebellar nucleus. The rubrospinal tract descends in the most dorsal part of the lateral funiculus of the spinal cord and terminates in the so-called intermediate zone of the spinal gray matter (cf. ten Donkelaar, 1975, 1976b). Neither the retrograde nor anterograde studies reveal a rubrospinal tract in *Python reticulatus*, the absence of which is probably related to the absence of limbs (cf. ten Donkelaar, 1975, 1976b).

XI. Reticular Formation

Our knowledge of the reticular formation of the reptilian brainstem is largely based on the work of van Hoevell (1911), Beccari (1922), Tuge (1932) and Stefanelli (1941a, 1944a). The findings of these authors are readily comparable, but, unfortunately, their nomenclatures are rather divergent. Ariëns Kappers *et al.* (1936) introduced a number of simple and clear terms, based on the observations of van Hoevell (1911), which will be adopted in this review.

The reticular formation of reptiles shows an evident resemblance to that of mammals. However, detailed comparisons between the reticular centers of these two groups cannot be made as yet, mainly because fiber connections are only imperfectly known in reptiles. Golgi studies by Newman (1974, 1975, *Pseudemys*, *Chrysemys*) indicate that the reptilian reticular formation is composed of isodendritic neurons (cf. Ramón-Moliner and Nauta, 1966). These are similar to the isodendritic neurons of the mammalian reticular formation, characterized by long, poorly ramified dendrites. These neurons are considered to represent a pool of pluripotential neurons which have remained relatively undifferentiated in the course of phylogeny (Ramón-Moliner and Nauta, 1966).

Brodal (1957, cat), Petrovicky (1966, pigeon) and Cruce and Nieuwenhuys (1974, turtle) subdivided the reticular formation into three longitudinal zones, median, medial and lateral. Since this subdivision appears to be applicable to the reptiles studied, it will be followed in the present account. The median zone is confined to the rhombencephalon and consists of cells situated in or near the raphé. The medial column contains the magno-cellular reticular nuclei and, in addition, certain mesencephalic centers. The lateral reticular zone, which consists of small cells, lies directly medial to the descending nucleus of V.

Apart from scattered elements, the median zone comprises two condensations, the inferior nucleus of the raphé and the superior nucleus of the raphe. The inferior nucleus of the raphé (Figs 5–7, 15–18, 26–28, 36–39) corresponds to the caudal part of the column a of van Hoevell (1911), to the pars inferior nuclei raphes of Tuge (1932) and to the nucleo mielencefalico del rafe of Beccari (1922) and Stefanelli (1941a, 1944a). The nucleus in question extends from the level of the nucleus of VI to the spinobulbar junction. Its most rostral and caudal ends consist entirely of small cells, whereas its intermediate part contains, in addition, numerous large elements. This large-celled part, which is particularly strongly developed in snakes, cannot be sharply delimited from the inferior reticular nucleus, as van Hoevell (1911) and Tuge (1932) have already pointed out. The superior nucleus of the raphé (Figs 8–10, 19–21, 30–32, 40–41) corresponds to the nucleus parvocellularis raphes of Tuge (1932) and to the nucleo metencefalico del rafe of Beccari (1922) and Stefanelli (1941a, 1944a). It is a compact mass of medium-sized cells, which occasionally constitutes bilateral vertical rows, adjacent to the median plane.

The nuclei of the medial reticular zone jointly constitute a continuous chain, which extends throughout the brainstem. The rhombencephalic part of this zone comprises the column b of van Hoevell (1911), and the nucleus motorius tegmenti of Tuge (1932). Ariëns Kappers et al. (1936) indicated the principal magnocellular rhombencephalic centers of this zone as the inferior, medial and superior reticular nuclei. These terms will be adopted in the present survey. The most rostral part of the rhombencephalic reticular formation is constituted by a somewhat ill-defined cellular mass, the nucleus reticularis isthmi of Stefanelli (1941a, 1944a). Rostral to this cell mass lies the mesencephalic reticular formation. There is no unanimity of opinion regarding those centers in the reptilian mesencephalic tegmentum that should be considered as reticular. In the present survey the interstitial nucleus of the medial longitudinal fasciculus will be considered as such. The inferior reticular nucleus (Figs 5, 6, 15, 16, 26, 27, 36, 37) is composed of medium-sized and very large cells, the latter being confined to the more caudal parts of the nucleus. The inferior reticular nucleus corresponds to the pars inferior nuclei motorii tegmenti of Tuge (1932) and to the nucleo mielencefalico principale mediale of Beccari (1922) and Stefanelli (1941a, 1944a). The medial reticular nucleus (Figs 6–8, 17–19, 28–30, 38–40) corresponds to the caudal part of the pars superior nuclei motorii tegmenti of Tuge (1932) and to the nucleo metencefalico principale of Beccari (1922) and Stefanelli (1941a, 1944a). Just like the inferior reticular nucleus, this nucleus consists of medium-sized and very large cells. The superior reticular nucleus (Figs 9, 20) lies in front of the trigeminal motor nucleus, as was already pointed out by Ariëns Kappers et al. (1936). The superior reticular nucleus can be delimited from the medial reticular nucleus by the presence of a short, but distinct gap in the column of very large cells, as shown by Cruce and Nieuwenhuys in the turtle Testudo (1974). As far as the medium-sized cells are concerned, however, the two nuclei are directly continuous. The reticular nucleus of the isthmus (Figs 10, 21, 31, 41), or nucleus reticularis diffusus of Tuge (1932) and presumably both the nucleo del isthmo and the nucleo metencefalico superiore laterale of Stefanelli (1941a, 1944a), is a large cell mass consisting of scattered small and medium-sized elements. In Python and Caiman, however, some rather large cells are present as well. The most central part of the gray substance of the mesencephalic tegmentum is occupied by a rather compact zone of which the motor nuclei of III and the nucleus of the f.l.m. (Figs 13, 24, 44) form part. The latter nucleus could not be delimited in Python. Peripheral to this compact zone and just rostral to the red nucleus, lie scattered large cells, which Beccari (1923) and Tuge (1932) termed the nucleus interstitialis of the f.l.m. (Figs 13, 24, 34, 44). The latter author subdivided this nucleus into groups A, B and C, but the subdivision could not be confirmed for the material studied by the present authors. Beccari (1923) considered the interstitial nucleus the "starting point" of the medial longitudinal fascicle.

In mammals the lateral reticular zone comprises (Brodal, 1957) the so-called lateral reticular formation, which consists of small cells and lies directly medial to the descending tract and nucleus of V, as well as the lateral reticular nucleus, already discussed in the preceding section. In the lower part of the rhombencephalon of *Caiman* van Hoevell (1911) observed two laterally situated cell groups labeled provisionally as L1 and L2 and later called nucleus reticularis lateralis and the pars lateralis nuclei motorii tegmenti by Tuge (1932). Van Hoevell (1911) stated that they belonged to the reticular formation, but did not find equivalent cell masses in the turtle *Chelonia*. Tuge (1932) in contrast did detect two cell masses in the brainstem of *Chrysemys*, and noted that they probably correspond to the nuclei L1 and L2. In their analysis of the brainstem in *Testudo*, Cruce and Nieuwenhuys (1974; Figs 3–5) illustrated a large, diffuse area, extending from the medial reticular zone to the spinal nucleus of V. They considered it quite possible that the cells of this area were generally homologous to the "lateral reticular formation" of mammals; yet a further subdivision of it on a cytoarchitectonic basis appeared to be impossible.

It has already been stated that the fiber connections of the reptilian reticular formation are still imperfectly known. Afferents to the reticular formation have been experimentally demonstrated from the spinal cord (Ebbesson, 1967, 1969; Pedersen, 1973), and from the mesencephalic tectum (Foster and Hall, 1975; ten Donkelaar, 1975, 1976b). Spinoreticular fibers constitute the main part of the spinal lemniscus. The experimental work of Ebbesson (1967, 1969) has shown that these fibers terminate predominantly in the ipsilateral reticular formation, more particularly in the inferior reticular nucleus and in the caudal part of the medial reticular nucleus. A much less dense projection was demonstrated to the rostral part of the latter nucleus and to the superior reticular nucleus. Only a few fibers were found to terminate in the contralateral reticular formation. The projection from the mesencephalic tectum reaches the reticular formation by way of the crossed predorsal bundle as well as via the ipsilateral ventral tectobulbar tract. Along its course the predorsal bundle discharges fibers to the medial part of the medial reticular zone, whereas the ipsilateral tectobulbar tract supplies the more lateral parts of the same zone.

Many efferent fibers of the reptilian reticular formation appear to enter the medial longitudinal fasciculus. This is a rather complex bundle which received much attention in the older literature (Ramón, 1897; Edinger, 1899; Beccari, 1923; Tuge, 1932; Stefanelli, 1941a, 1944a; Leghissa, 1954). It extends from the interstitial nucleus of the f.l.m. throughout the brainstem and continues caudally in the ventral funiculus of the spinal cord as the sulcomarginal fasciculus. In the brainstem the f.l.m. is situated just lateral to the median plane. It is closely related to the somatic motor nuclei. In the Häggqvist material the f.l.m. stands out as composed of predominantly coarse fibers. The bulk of its constituent fibers arise from the vestibular nuclear area and from the median and medial reticular zones. The ascending and descending fibers from the vestibular area passing via the f.l.m. have already been discussed (Section VI). The magnocellular reticular nuclei send fibers to the spinal cord by way of this bundle. In favorable Häggqvist sections, axons of reticular cells can be traced over considerable distances in the f.l.m. (e.g. Figs 18, 19). At the level of the medial reticular nucleus these fibers constitute a separate lateral bundle which enters the f.l.m. at a more caudal level. Because of the many entering reticulospinal fibers the f.l.m. increases in size caudalward. Apart from reticulospinal fibers passing by way of the f.l.m., some direct reticulospinal fibers, arising predominantly in the inferior reticular nucleus, could be distinguished in the Häggqvist material (cf. Figs 4, 5, 14, 15, 25, 35 and 36).

A few notes on the problems in studying the reticulospinal pathways are appropriate here. The diffuse arrangement of cells in the reticular formation poses special problems for its analysis. Electrolytic lesions within the reticular formation destroy fibers from many different sources. Traditionally the most reliable anatomical approach for determining the origin of reticulospinal fibers is based on retrograde cell changes following lesions of the spinal cord. Recently, the horseradish peroxidase technique has become available. If injected into the central nervous system, the enzyme horseradish peroxidase (HRP) is transported in significant amounts in the retrograde direction by axons which terminate near the site of injection.

Both techniques just mentioned have been used to study the descending pathways from the brainstem to the spinal cord in *Testudo hermanni*, *Python reticulatus* and *Tupinambis nigropunctatus* (ten Donkelaar, 1975, 1976b). The reticular formation projects to the spinal cord in all reptiles studied. In *Python* and *Tupinambis* the magnocellular rhombencephalic reticular formation is divided into two parts. The caudal part comprises the inferior reticular nucleus and projects bilaterally to the cord via the lateral funiculus. The rostral part consists of the medial reticular nucleus, superior reticular nucleus, and nucleus of the isthmus, and projects to the spinal cord predominantly ipsilaterally by way of the ventral funiculus. In addition, the inferior nucleus of the raphé and the interstitial nucleus of the f.l.m. have been found to project to the cord. These experiments confirm the results obtained by Robinson (1969) in *Lacerta viridis*.

Very little is known about the ascending reticular efferents of reptiles. Such fibers passing via the f.l.m., were described by Ramón (1897) and Tuge (1932), but the exact site of termination was not determined. No fibers comparable to the ascending reticular system of mammals have thus far been described for reptiles. However, it might be interesting to note in this context that recently Hall and Ebner (1970b, *Pseudemys*) demonstrated by hemisections at midbrain levels projections from the midbrain tegmentum to what they termed "basal telencephalic nuclei". They considered this system comparable to a similar pathway in mammals, where it arises in the rostral midbrain tegmentum, which terminates in the globus pallidus, the putamen and the head of the caudate nucleus (Bucher and Burgi, 1953; Nauta and Kuypers, 1958).

XII. Cranial Nerve Motor Nuclei

A. Visceral Efferent Nuclei

Reptiles have only two delimitable visceral efferent nuclei, the dorsal motor nucleus of the vagus and the nucleus of Edinger–Westphal. The dorsal motor nucleus of the vagus (Figs 5, 15, 26, 27, 36) is a distinct, compact cell mass consisting of medium-sized cells. It shows diffuse degeneration following lesions of the lateral funiculus of the spinal cord (Ebbesson, 1967, 1969). A nucleus of Edinger–Westphal (Figs 12, 23, 33, 43), also called the accessory oculomotor nucleus (de Lange, 1913), could be distinguished in all reptiles studied by the present authors. This nucleus is composed of small and medium-sized cells, forms part of the central layer of the mesencephalic tegmentum (cf. Senn, 1970) and caps the dorsal part of the oculomotor nucleus. In the Häggqvist material some small fibers of the oculomotor nerve issue from the Edinger–Westphal nucleus (Figs 12, 23, 33, 43). Both the Edinger–Westphal nucleus and the dorsal motor nucleus of the vagus project to the spinal cord (ten Donkelaar and de Boer-van Huizen, 1978; *Lacerta*).

B. Branchiomotor Nuclei

In all reptiles studied the branchiomotor nuclei, the nucleus ambiguus and the efferent nuclei of VII and V, constitute an almost continuous column in the lateral part of the rhombencephalic basal plate.

The nucleus ambiguus, consisting of rather large cells, could be clearly distinguished in *Tupinambis* and *Caiman* (Figs 16, 37), but not in *Python* and *Testudo* (in contrast see Cruce and Nieuwenhuys, 1974). Our interpretation agrees with those of Black (1920) and Gillaspy (1954), who described the nucleus ambiguus as a caudal continuation of the ventral part of the motor nucleus of VII. Gillaspy (1954) found retrograde cell changes following section of the branchiomotor nerves IX, X and XI.

A separate reptilian glossopharyngeal motor nucleus has thus far only been observed by Addens (1933) and Stefanelli (1944a). Most students of the brainstem in reptiles concluded that the motor root of IX takes origin in the caudal part of a nucleus common to it and the motor root of VII. We agree with the latter observations.

The motor nucleus of the facial nerve which consists of large cells, can be divided into dorsal and ventral parts (Figs 6, 7, 17, 18, 28, 29, 38, 39).

Just as the previous nucleus, the motor nucleus of the trigeminal contains large cells and can also be divided into a dorsal and a ventral part (Figs 8, 19, 30). In *Caiman crocodilus* (Fig. 40) this subdivision into two parts is not distinct.

C. Somatic Motor Nuclei

The somatic efferent column comprises the nucleus of the hypoglossal nerve and the centers which supply the external ocular muscles, namely the abducens, trochlear and oculomotor nuclei. All of these nuclei are situated close to the median plane and show a distinct relation to the f.l.m. The hypoglossal and abducens nuclei lie lateral to the f.l.m., whereas the trochlear and oculomotor nuclei are situated dorsomedial to that bundle.

The hypoglossal nucleus is well developed in reptiles and consists mainly of large cells (Figs 5, 15, 26 and 36). Previous workers have already pointed out that its caudal limit cannot be exactly identified, since there is a continuity with the motor column of the spinal cord (Black, 1920; Tuge, 1932). A quantitative analysis of the hypoglossal of *Boa constrictor* (Ulinski, 1973) notes that there are 942 ± 162 neurons on each side.

The abducens nucleus (Figs 6, 7, 17, 29, 38) consists of medium-sized cells, which are somewhat diffusely arranged. We remained unable to confirm the existence of an accessory abducens nucleus, which has been reported by Terni (1922), Addens (1933) and Stefanelli (1941b).

The trochlear nucleus (Figs 11, 22, 32, 41, 42) is clearly separated from the caudal end of the oculomotor nucleus in *Testudo* and *Python*. In *Tupinambis* and *Caiman*, however, it gradually passes over into the dorsal part of the oculomotor nucleus.

In *Tupinambis* and *Caiman* (Figs 22, 23, 43) the oculomotor nucleus can be divided into three parts: the pars dorsalis, the pars intermedia and the pars ventralis. In *Testudo* (Fig. 12) the boundaries between the dorsal and intermediate parts are rather ill-defined, whereas *Python* (Figs 33, 34) discloses no subdivision at all of the oculomotor nucleus.

XIII. Four Centers in the Isthmus Region and in the Mesencephalic Tegmentum

Under this heading the following cell masses will be briefly considered: the nucleus isthmi, the locus coeruleus, the central gray and the nucleus profundus mesencephali.

The nucleus isthmi (Figs 10, 11, 21, 31 and 41) is highly developed in reptiles, forming a protuberance at the level of the anterior medullary velum. In all reptiles studied, except for *Python*, it can be divided into magnocellular and parvocellular parts. The homology and the functional significance of the reptilian isthmic nucleus are still to be clarified. Some previous authors held that it should be linked with the auditory system (Joustra, 1918; Shanklin, 1930; Le Gros Clark, 1933). However, experimental anatomical studies in birds (Karten, 1967; Boord, 1968, 1969) have shown that the nucleus isthmi is not related to the auditory system. As the nucleus in question is particularly well developed in *Chamaeleo* (Shanklin, 1930), this cell mass may be related to the visual system. In this context it is interesting to note that a strong tectoisthmic projection has been demonstrated in various reptiles (Foster and Hall, 1975; *Iguana*; ten Donkelaar, 1975, 1976b, *Testudo, Tupinambis, Python*).

The locus coeruleus (Figs 10, 20, 21, 31 and 41) is a group of scattered, medium-sized cells, which corresponds in position to a nucleus-labeled nucleus loci coerulei by van Hoevell (1911, 1916). Ebbesson (1967) found diffuse degeneration in this area following lesions of the lateral funiculus of the spinal cord. The use of the term locus coeruleus for this nucleus is strongly supported by the evidence of Parent and Poitras (1974) in the turtle *Chrysemys picta*. Fluorescence microscopy reveals a striking resemblance between a catecholamine-containing pathway from the locus coeruleus to the forebrain in *Chrysemys picta* and the "dorsal noradrenergic bundle" of the mammalian brain. The locus coeruleus in *Lacerta galloti* projects to the spinal cord (ten Donkelaar and de Boer-van Huizen, 1978).

The central gray (Figs 8–11, 19–23, 30–32, 41) constitutes a compact zone of periventricular cells, which extends from the level of the motor nucleus of V to the level of the oculomotor nucleus. In the mesencephalic tegmentum the central gray passes over into the laminar nucleus of the torus semicircularis and into the periventricular cell layer of the tectum. Ebbesson (1967, 1969) demonstrated some degeneration in the mesencephalic part of the central gray, following spinal cord lesions.

The nucleus profundus mesencephali (Figs 11, 22, 23, 33, 42 and 43), also termed the nucleus lateralis profundus mesencephali (Beccari, 1923; Senn, 1968), lies in the stream of descending fibers of the ventral tectobulbar tract. It consists of medium-sized and large cells. Its functional significance is still obscure.

XIV. Summary and Conclusion

A. GENERAL

Beyond summarizing the main results it appears useful to make some comparisons with the relations in birds and mammals.

In terms of cellular structure the reptilian brainstem is readily comparable to the brainstems of birds (cf. Karten and Hodos, 1967, pigeon) and of primitive mammals, such as the opossum (cf. Voris and Hoerr, 1932; Oswaldo-Cruz and Rocha-Miranda, 1968). However, reptiles apparently lack an inferior olive and pontine nuclei.

B. SUMMARY OF SPECIFIC SYSTEMS

1. *The Dorsal Column Nuclei and their Afferent and Efferent Connections* (Figs 45, 46)

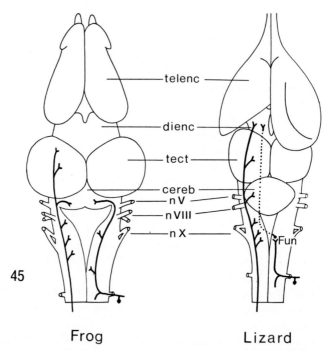

FIGS 45 and 46. Semidiagrammatic representation of the primary (at the right) and non-primary (at the left) long ascending spinal pathways demonstrated in the frog (Hayle, 1973), in lizards, in the pigeon (Karten, 1963) and in the opossum (Hazlett *et al.*, 1972). cereb, Cerebellum; Ci, colliculus inferior; Cs, colliculus superior; dienc, diencephalon; Fun, nucleus funiculi dorsalis; nV, nervus trigeminus; nVIII, nervus octavus; nX, nervus vagus; tect, tectum mesencephali; telenc, telencephalon; Vb, ventrobasal nuclear complex.

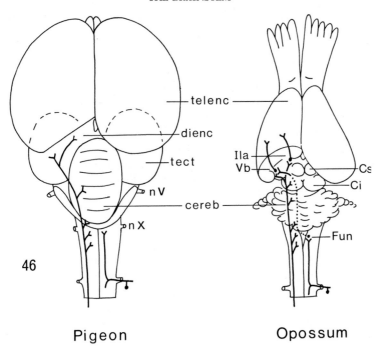

Pigeon   Opossum

FIG. 46

Transection of the dorsal funiculus at various levels of the spinal cord has revealed the existence of a somatotopical projection upon the dorsal funicular nuclei.

So far the reptilian medial lemniscus has been demonstrated experimentally only in the monitor lizard (Ebbesson, 1976). The medial lemniscus appears to terminate in the contralateral ventrolateral thalamic area.

Surveying experimental data in lizards (Fig. 45), the pigeon and the opossum (Fig. 46) it should be noted that the presence of a medial lemniscus has been definitely shown so far only in mammals (cf. e.g. Hazlett *et al.*, 1972) and in the above-mentioned lizard (Ebbesson, 1976).

2. *Fiber Systems Ascending in the Lateral Funiculus* (Figs 45, 46)

At the level of the spinobulbar junction the fibers, which ascend towards the brainstem via the lateral funiculus constitute a continuous superficial fiber zone termed the spinal lemniscus. This system comprises: (a) a large spinoreticular component which terminates mainly in the caudal part of the ipsilateral reticular formation; (b) spinocerebellar fibers which at caudal sections of the brainstem cannot be separated from the spinal lemniscus, but more rostrally can be delimited as distinct tracts (see Section X); and (c) a small spinothalamic component which terminates in the dorsal intermediate nucleus of the thalamus.

Spinothalamic fibers have been demonstrated also in the pigeon (Karten, 1963) and in the opossum (Hazlett et al., 1972). In the opossum the spinothalamic component of the spinal lemniscus projects to the ventrobasal nuclear complex. Although the dorsal intermediate nucleus thalami of reptiles and the mammalian ventrobasal nuclear complex both receive a projection from the spinal cord, equivalence of these two nuclei is still uncertain. This results from the considerable difference in relative position, and also from our ignorance concerning the efferents of the dorsal intermediate nucleus thalami in reptiles.

3. Organization and Connections of the Sensory Trigeminal Nuclei

The sensory part of the trigeminal nuclear complex is well developed in reptiles, more particularly in *Python* and *Caiman*. It comprises three nuclei: the spinal nucleus, the principal nucleus and the mesencephalic nucleus. We lack experimental evidence about the central connections of these nuclei. Normal material shows trigeminocerebellar fibers, a trigeminal lemniscus (to the mesencephalic tectum) and a small quintofrontal tract arising in the chief sensory nucleus and passing to the striatum. The presence of a quintofrontal tract of Wallenberg has been experimentally demonstrated in the pigeon by Zeigler and Karten (1973). This pathway passes from the chief sensory nucleus of V to a telencephalic structure called the nucleus basalis. Behavioral studies suggest that the quintofrontal tract and its related nuclei are afferent components of a network of structures controlling feeding behavior in the pigeon.

4. Solitary Fasciculus and its Related Nuclei

Normal material suggests that the nucleus of the solitary fasciculus, the end station of the solitary tract, projects to the secondary visceral nuclei lying in the isthmal area. Recently, Norgren and Leonard (1971, 1973) have shown that the dorsomedial part of the parabrachial nucleus in the rat (a cell mass situated in the most rostral part of the rhombencephalon) receives a projection from the anterior part of the solitary nucleus and represents a taste center. This center may well correspond to the secondary visceralis nucleus of Shanklin (1930), Barnard (1936) and of the present survey.

5. Vestibular System

The vestibular nuclear complex is well differentiated in reptiles; it comprises six different cell masses. Some of these show a considerable variation in development. The ventrolateral vestibular nucleus and its efferent tract, the lateral vestibulospinal tract, are strongly developed in those reptiles that are wholly or partly quadrupedal (turtles, some lizards, and crocodilians), whereas limbless species (other lizards, snakes) have a particularly large tangential vestibular nucleus (Stefanelli, 1944a, 1944b). The locus coeruleus in *Lacerta galloti* projects to the spinal cord (ten Donkelaar and de Boer-van Huizen, 1978).

6. *Acoustic System*

The reptilian cochlear nuclei include the dorsal magnocellular nucleus and the nucleus laminaris. The central connections of the cochlear nuclei are rather well known in reptiles from the recent experimental work of Foster (1974), Foster and Peele (1975) and Pritz (1974a, b). The efferent tract of the cochlear nuclei, the lateral lemniscus, could be traced to the torus semicircularis (Foster, 1974). It has also been demonstrated that the torus projects to the nucleus reuniens of the thalamus (Foster, 1974; Pritz, 1974a). The latter nucleus, in turn, projects to telencephalic area, designated by Crosby (1917) as rostral and intermediolateral areas (Pritz, 1974b; Foster and Peele, 1975). This projection reaches the telencephalon by way of the dorsal peduncle of the lateral forebrain bundle. It is worth noting that Karten (1967, 1968) and Boord (1968, 1969) have experimentally demonstrated that the acoustic projection of the pigeon also reaches the telencephalon via mesencephalic and diencephalic relay nuclei (from the nucleus mesencephali lateralis pars dorsalis to the nucleus ovoidalis thalami and from the latter via the l.f.b. to the mediocaudal neostriatum and the field L of Rose).

7. *Mesencephalic Tectum*

The reptilian efferent projections of the mesencephalic tectum prove by ablation experiments to be comparable to those of primitive mammals (Martin, 1969, opossum; Rafols and Matzke, 1970, opossum; Hall and Ebner, 1970a, hedgehog). The ascending projection is the tectothalamic tract which sends most of its fibers to the nucleus rotundus of the dorsal thalamus. Hall and Ebner (1970a, b) discussed some interesting parallels between the tectothalamic and thalamotelencephalic projections of the turtle *Pseudemys scripta* and the hedgehog, *Paraechinus hypomelas*. On the basis of its afferent and efferent connections they considered the nucleus rotundus homologous to the mammalian nucleus lateralis posterior. The descending projection of the tectum has two pathways, namely the crossed predorsal bundle and the ipsilateral tectobulbar tract. The predorsal bundle discharges fibers to the medial part of the reticular formation along its course, whereas the ipsilateral tract projects to the nucleus isthmi and supplies the more lateral parts of the reticular formation. Both descending pathways reach the lowest levels of the brainstem, but do not extend into the spinal cord. Evidently the tectum only indirectly influences the spinal motor centers by way of the reticular formation.

8. Projections from Higher Centers to the Brainstem

Fibers descending from the prosencephalon enter the brainstem by way of the fasciculus retroflexus and the lateral and medial forebrain bundles. So far, experimental work has revealed that only a very small component extends beyond the mesencephalic tegmentum, namely a projection from the ventral striatum to the lateral cerebellar nucleus (Hoogland, 1977).

9. Cerebellar Connections

It has been experimentally shown that most spinocerebellar fibers reach the cerebellum by way of the lateral funiculus. Some fibers, however, pass via the dorsal funiculus. It is well known that, apart from direct spino-cerebellar tracts, mammals also have a number of so-called indirect spinocerebellar projections. These systems are synaptically interrupted in the rhombencephalon. Two of these spinocerebellar relay centers, namely the nucleus of the lateral funiculus and the external cuneate nucleus have also been reported in reptiles. However, the cerebellar connections of these two nuclei remain to be demonstrated. Birds and mammals have an inferior olive and pontine nuclei that project to the cerebellum. Reptiles lack an inferior olive and pontine nuclei.

The efferent connections of the cerebellum may be divided into three systems: (a) the cerebellovestibular tract, arising chiefly in the medial cerebellar nucleus and terminating in various nuclei of the vestibular complex; (b) the cerebellomotor and cerebellotegmental tracts, which reportedly connect the cerebellum with the motor and reticular nuclei of the rhombencephalon; and (c) the brachium conjunctivum. The latter takes its origin from the lateral cerebellum nucleus and terminates in the red nucleus. In reptiles no cerebellothalamic component has thus far been shown.

The reptilian red nucleus is rather well developed except in *Python* in which it can hardly be distinguished. The course and termination of the reptilian rubrospinal tract corresponds to that in the pigeon (Zecha, 1961; van den Akker, 1970) and in the opossum (Martin and Dom, 1970). A rubrospinal tract could not be demonstrated in *Python* (ten Donkelaar, 1975, 1976a, b). It has been argued by the latter author that the absence of a rubrospinal pathway is correlated with the absence of limbs.

10. Reticular Formation

The reticular formation of reptiles shows an evident resemblance to that of mammals. However, the reticular centers of these two groups cannot as yet be compared in detail, as their fiber connections are only imperfectly known in reptiles. The four magnocellular reticular nuclei, namely the superior, medial, and inferior reticular nuclei, as well as the inferior nucleus of the raphé vary considerably in the reptiles studied. These centers are particularly large in *Python*, which led Stefanelli (1941a) to the conclusion that the nuclei in question are functionally related to the control of the trunk musculature. The magnocellular reticular nuclei exert their influence on the spinal cord by way of the reticulospinal fibers, which mainly descend via the f.l.m.

It is safe to assume that the reticulospinal fibers constitute the bulk of the descending fibers to the spinal cord. They might be qualified as a "final common path" by way of which supraspinal influences reach the spinal motor neurons. The prosencephalon probably acts indirectly on the spinal cord via the mesencephalic reticular formation, whereas the mesencephalic tectum influences the spinal motor centers by way of the tectobulbar tracts, which impinge upon the rhombencephalic reticular formation.

In addition to reticulospinal pathways, reptiles have vestibulospinal and rubrospinal (except for *Python*) pathways. Experimental data in amphibians (cf. Corvaja and Grofová, 1972), reptiles, the pigeon (van den Akker, 1970) and mammals show remarkable similarities in these descending systems. All of these groups possess rubrospinal, reticulospinal and vestibulospinal pathways which terminate in comparable areas of the spinal gray matter. Homologies of the corticobulbar and corticospinal tract have not been demonstrated in reptiles.

11. *Cranial Nerve Motor Nuclei*

Reptiles have only two delimitable visceral efferent nuclei, namely the dorsal motor nucleus of the vagus and the nucleus of Edinger–Westphal.

The nuclei of the branchiomotor column, namely the nucleus ambiguus and the efferent nuclei of VII and V, constitute an almost continuous column in the lateral part of the rhombencephalic alar plate. A separate glossopharyngeal motor nucleus could not be confirmed in the present survey. It is probably represented by the caudal part of the motor nucleus of VII.

The reptilian somatic efferent column is rather well developed. It comprises the nucleus of the hypoglossal nerve and the centers which supply the external ocular muscles, i.e. the abducens, trochlear and oculomotor nuclei.

12. *Nuclei of the Isthmus Region and the Mesencephalic Tegmentum*

In the older literature, the conspicuous nucleus isthmi has been linked

194 H. J. DONKELAAR AND R. NIEUWENHUYS

with the auditory system, but experimental anatomical work (Foster, 1974; Pritz, 1974a) has shown this to represent an error. The projection from the tectum to this nucleus, by way of the ipsilateral tectobulbar tract, suggests a relation to the visual system. The nucleus profundus mesencephali has also been considered related to the auditory system; however, its functional significance is still obscure.

Acknowledgements

The authors wish to express their gratitude to Mrs. Irene Vos-Artz, Mrs. Carla de Vocht-Poort, Mrs. Coby Staleman-Hilgeholt and Mrs. Annelies Hoogland-Pellegrino for preparing the histological preparations, to Mr. C. P. Nicolasen and Mr. E. Noyons for the drawing, to Mr. A. Reynen for the photomicrographs and to Mrs. Trudy van Son-Verstraeten for her secretarial assistance.

The present study was supported in part by a grant from the Foundation for Medical Research FUNGO which is subsidized by the Netherlands Organization for the Advancement of Pure Research (Z.W.O.).

References

Addens, J. L. (1933). The motor nuclei and roots of the cranial and first spinal nerves of vertebrates. Z. Anat. EntwGesch. 101, 307–410.
Andén, N.-E., Carlsson, A., Dahlström, A., Fuxe, K. and Hillarp, N.-A. (1964). Demonstration and mapping out of nigrostriatal dopamine neurons. Life Sci. 3, 523–530.
Andén, N.-E., Dahlström, A., Fuxe, K. and Larsson, K. (1965). Further evidence for the presence of nigroneostriatal dopamine neurons. Am. J. Anat. 116, 329–333.
Ariëns Kappers, C. U., Huber, G. C. and Crosby, E. C. (1936). "The Comparative Anatomy of the Nervous System of Vertebrates, including Man." Macmillan, New York.
Baker-Cohen, K. F. (1968). Comparative enzyme histochemical observations on submammalian brains. Ergebn. Anat. EntwGesch. 40, 1–70.
Barnard, J. W. (1936). A phylogenetic study of the visceral afferent areas associated with the facial, glossopharyngeal, and vagus nerves, and their fiber connections. The efferent facial nucleus. J. comp. Neurol. 65, 503–602.
Beccari, N. (1911). La costituzione, i nuclei terminali, e le vie di connessione del nervo acustico nella Lacerta muralis, Merr. Archo. ital. Anat. Embriol. 10, 646–698.
Beccari, N. (1922). Studi comparativi sulla struttura del rombencefalo. II. Centri tegmentali del rombencefalo. Archo. ital. Anat. Embriol. 19, 216–291.
Beccari, N. (1923). Il centro tegmentale e interstiziale ed altre formazioni poco note nel mesencefalo e nel diencefalo di un rettile. Archo. ital. Anat. Embriol. 20, 560–619.
Belekhova, M. G. and Kosareva, A. A. (1971). Organization of the turtle thalamus: visual, somatic and tectal zones. Brain Behav. Evol. 4, 337–375.
Black, D. (1920). The motor nuclei of the cerebral nerves in phylogeny—a study of the phenomena of neurobiotaxis. III. Reptiles. J. comp. Neurol. 32, 61–98.
Boord, R. L. (1968). Ascending projections of the primary cochlear nuclei and nucleus laminaris in the pigeon. J. comp. Neurol. 133, 523–542.

Boord, R. L. (1969). The anatomy of the avian auditory system. *Ann. N.Y. Acad. Sci.* 167, 186–198.

Braford, Jr., M. R. (1972). Ascending efferent tectal projections in the South American spectacled Caiman. *Anat. Rec.* 172, 275–276.

Brodal, A. (1957). "The Reticular Formation of the Brain Stem. Anatomical Aspects and Functional Correlations." The Henderson Trust Lecture. Oliver and Boyd, Edinburgh.

Bucher, V. M. and Burgi, S. M. (1953). Some observations on the fiber connections of the di- and mesencephalon in the cat. 4. The ansa lenticularis, pars ascendens mesencephalica, with observations on other systems ascending from the descending to the mesencephalon. *J. comp. Neurol.* 99, 415–435.

Burns, A. H. and Goodman, D. C. (1967). Retinofugal projections of *Caiman sklerops*. *Expl Neurol.* 18, 105–115.

Busch, H. F. M. (1961). "An Anatomical Analysis of the White Matter in the Brain Stem of the Cat." Thesis, Univ. of Leiden.

Butler, A. B. and Ebbesson, S. O. E. (1975). A Golgi study of the optic tectum of the tegu lizard, *Tupinambis nigropunctatus. J. Morph.* 146, 215–228.

Butler, A. B. and Northcutt, R. G. (1971). Ascending tectal efferent projections in the lizard *Iguana iguana. Brain Res.* 35, 597–602.

Butler, A. B. and Northcutt, R. G. (1973). Architectonic studies of the diencephalon of *Iguana iguana* (Linnaeus). *J. comp. Neurol.* 149, 439–462.

Christensen, K. (1927). The morphology of the brain of *Sphenodon. Univ. Iowa Stud. Nat. Hist.* 12, 1–29.

Corvaja, N. and Grofová, I. (1972). Vestibulospinal projections in the toad. *Prog. Brain Res.* 37, 297–307.

Crosby, E. C. (1917). The forebrain of *Alligator mississippiensis. J. comp. Neurol.* 27, 325–402.

Cruce, J. A. F. (1974). A cytoarchitectonic study of the diencephalon of the tegu lizard, *Tupinambis nigropunctatus. J. comp. Neurol.* 153, 215–238.

Cruce, W. L. R. and Nieuwenhuys, R. (1974). The cell mass in the brain stem of the turtle *Testudo hermanni*; a topographical and topological analysis. *J. comp. Neurol.* 156, 277–306.

Curwen, A. O. and Miller, R. N. (1939). The pretectal region of the turtle, *Pseudemys scripta troostii. J. comp. Neurol.* 71, 99–120.

DeFina, A. V. and Webster, D. B. (1974). Projections of the intraotic ganglion to the medullary nuclei in the tegu lizard, *Tupinambis nigropunctatus. Brain, Behav. Evol.* 10, 197–211.

de Lange, S. J. (1910). The descending tracts of the corpora quadrigemina. *Fol. neurobiol.* 3, 633–657.

de Lange, S. J. (1912). The red nucleus in reptiles. *Proc. Acad. Sci. Amst.* 14, 1082–1090.

de Lange, S. J. (1913). Das Zwischenhirn und das Mittelhirn der Reptilien. *Fol. neurobiol.* 7, 67–138.

Desole, C., Palmieri, G. and Veggetti, A. (1970). Mesencephalic trigeminal nucleus and jaw muscle proprioception in reptiles. *Arch. ital. Biol.* 108, 121–130.

Ebbesson, S. O. E. (1967). Ascending axon degeneration following hemisection of the spinal cord in the tegu lizard (*Tupinambis nigropunctatus*). *Brain Res.* 5, 178–206.

Ebbesson, S. O. E. (1969). Brain stem afferents from the spinal cord in a sample of reptilian and amphibian species. *Ann. N.Y. Acad. Sci.* 167, 80–102.

Ebbesson, S. O. E. (1970). On the organization of central visual pathways in vertebrates. *Brain, Behav. Evol.* 3, 178–194.

Ebbesson, S. O. E. (1976). The somatosensory thalamus in reptiles. *Anat. Rec.* 184, 395–396.

Edinger, L. (1899). Untersuchungen über die vergleichende Anatomie des Gehirns. IV. Studien über das Zwischenhirn der Reptilien. *Abh. Senckenb. naturf. Ges.* 20, 160–202.

Edinger, L. (1908). "Vorlesungen über den Bau der nervösen Zentralorgane des Menschen und der Tiere." Vogel Verl., Leipzig, Vol. 2.

Foster, R. E. (1974). The ascending brainstem auditory pathways in a reptile, *Iguana iguana*. *Anat. Rec.* 178, 357.

Foster, R. E. and Hall, W. C. (1975). The connections and laminar organization of the optic tectum in a reptile (*Iguana iguana*). *J. Comp. Neurol.* 163, 397–426.

Foster, R. E. and Peele, T. L. (1975). Thalamotelencephalic auditory pathways in the lizard (*Iguana iguana*). *Anat. Rec.* 181, 530.

Frederikse, A. (1931). "The Lizard's Brain." Thesis, Univ. of Amsterdam.

Friedman, B. E., Rubinson, K. and Colman, D. R. (1972). Vagus nerve projections in anurans. *Anat. Rec.* 172, 312.

Fuller, P. M. and Ebbesson, S. O. E. (1973). Central projections of the trigeminal nerve in the bull frog (*Rana catesbeiana*). *J. comp. Neurol.* 152, 193–200.

Gamble, H. J. (1956). An experimental study of the secondary olfactory connexions in *Testudo graeca*. *J. Anat.* 90, 15–29.

Gamow, R. I. and Harris, J. F. (1973). The infrared receptors of snakes. *Scient. Am.* 228, 94–100.

Gillaspy, C. C. (1954). Experimental study of the cranial motor nuclei in Reptilia. *J. comp. Neurol.* 100, 481–510.

Goldby, F. and Robinson, L. R. (1962). The central connections of dorsal spinal nerve roots and the ascending tracts in the spinal cord of *Lacerta viridis*. *J. Anat.* 96, 153–170.

Goldstein, M. H. and Jacobs, V. L. (1969). The central projection of the mesencephalic root of the trigeminus in a lizard (*Lacerta viridis*). *Brain Res.* 14, 307–320.

Häggqvist, G. (1936). Analyse der Faserverteilung in einem Rückenmarkquerschnitt (Th. 3). *Z. mikrosk- anat. Forsch.* 39, 1–34.

Hall, J. A. (1971). "The Efferent Connections of General Cortex in the Turtle, *Pseudemys scripta*." Thesis, Brown Univ.

Hall, J. A. and Ebner, F. F. (1974). The efferent projections of general cortex to the brain stem in the turtle, *Pseudemys scripta*. *Anat. Rec.* 178, 513.

Hall, W. C. and Ebner, F. F. (1970a). Parallels in the visual afferent projections of the thalamus in the hedgehog (*Paraechinus hypomelas*) and the turtle (*Pseudemys scripta*). *Brain Behav. Evol.* 3, 135–154.

Hall, W. C. and Ebner, F. F. (1970b). Thalamotelencephalic projections in the turtle (*Pseudemys scripta*). *J. comp. Neurol.* 140, 101–122.

Harris, J. F. and Gamow, R. I. (1971). Snake infrared receptors: thermal or photo-chemical mechanism? *Science, N.Y.* 172, 1252–1253.

Harrison, T. M. and Irving, R. (1966). Visual and non-visual auditory systems in mammals. *Science, N.Y.* 154, 738–743.

Hartline, P. H. (1971). Midbrain responses of the auditory and somatic vibration systems in snakes. *J. exp. Biol.* 54, 373–391.

Hayle, T. H. (1973). A comparative study of spinal projections to the brain (except cerebellum) in three classes of poikilothermic vertebrates. *J. comp. Neurol.* 149, 463–476.

Hazlett, J. C., Dom, R. and Martin, G. F. (1972). Spinobulbar, spinothalamic and medial lemniscal connections in the American opossum, *Didelphis marsupialis virginiana*. *J. comp. Neurol.* **146**, 95–118.

Heimer, L. (1969). The secondary olfactory connections in mammals, reptiles and sharks. *Ann. N.Y. Acad. Sci.* **167**, 129–146.

Herrick, C. J. (1914). The medulla oblongata of larval *Amblystoma*. *J. comp. Neurol.* **24**, 343–427.

Herrick, C. J. (1930). The medulla oblongata of *Necturus*. *J. comp. Neurol.* **50**, 1–96.

Herrick, C. J. (1948). "The Brain of the Tiger Salamander, *Amblystoma tigrinum*." Univ. of Chicago Press, Chicago.

Hoogland, P. V. J. M. (1977). Efferent connections of the striatum in *Tupinambis nigropunctatus*. *J. Morph.* **152**, 229–246.

Huber, G. C. and Crosby, E. C. (1926). On thalamic and tectal nuclei and fiber paths in the brain of the American alligator. *J. comp. Neurol.* **40**, 97–227.

Huber, G. C. and Crosby, E. C. (1933). The reptilian optic tectum. *J. comp. Neurol.* **57**, 57–163.

Jacobs, V. L. (1967). A spinovestibular component of the dorsal funiculus in a lizard (*Lacerta viridis*). *Anat. Rec.* **157**, 264–265.

Jacobs, V. L. (1968). An experimental study of the course and termination of the spinocerebellar systems in a lizard (*Lacerta viridis*). *Brain Res.* **11**, 154–176.

Joseph, B. S. and Whitlock, D. G. (1968). Central projections of brachial and lumbar dorsal roots in reptiles. *J. comp. Neurol.* **132**, 469–484.

Joustra, N. (1918). Over de homologie van het ganglion isthmi. *Psychiat. Neurol.* Bl. **22**: Feestbundel, Winkler, Amsterdam, pp. 361–416.

Karten, H. J. (1963). Ascending pathways from the spinal cord in the pigeon (*Columba livia*). *Proc. 16th Int. Congr. Zool.* **2**, 23.

Karten, H. J. (1967). The organization of the ascending auditory pathway in the pigeon (*Columba livia*). I. Diencephalic projections of the inferior colliculus (nucleus mesencephalicus lateralis, pars dorsalis). *Brain Res.* **6**, 409–427.

Karten, H. J. (1968). The ascending auditory pathway in the pigeon (*Columba livia*). II. Telencephalic projections of the nucleus ovoidalis thalami. *Brain Res.* **11**, 134–153.

Karten, H. J. and Hodos, W. (1967). "A Stereotaxic Atlas of the Brain of the Pigeon (*Columba livia*)." Johns Hopkins Univ., Baltimore.

Kennedy, M. C. (1975). Vocalization elicited in a lizard by electrical stimulation of the midbrain. *Brain Res.* **91**, 321–325.

Kruger, L. and Witkovsky, P. (1961). A functional analysis of neurons in the dorsal column nuclei and spinal nucleus of the trigeminal in the reptile (*Alligator mississippiensis*). *J. comp. Neurol.* **117**, 97–105.

Landmann, L. (1971). "Bau und Ontogenese des vestibulären Systems bei *Lacerta sicula*." Thesis. Birkhäuser A.G., Basel.

Larsell, O. (1926). The cerebellum of reptiles: lizards and snake. *J. comp. Neurol.* **41**, 59–94.

Larsell, O. (1932). The cerebellum of reptiles: chelonians and alligator. *J. comp. Neurol.* **56**, 299–345.

Larsell, O. (1967). "The Comparative Anatomy and Histology of the Cerebellum from Myxinoids through Birds." Univ. of Minnesota Press, Minneapolis.

Leake, P. A. (1974). Central projections of the statoacoustic nerve in *Caiman crocodilus*. *Brain Behav. Evol.* **10**, 170–196.

Le Gros Clark, W. E. (1933). The medial geniculate body and the nucleus isthmi. *J. Anat.* **67**, 536–548.

Leghissa, S. (1954). Ricerche anatomocomparative sul sistema longitudinale mediale nella serie dei vertebrati. *Commentat. pontif. Acad. Scient.* **16**, 197–239.

Lohman, A. H. M., Hoogland, P. V. J. M. and van Woerden-Verkley, I. (1973). Experimental studies of the efferent telencephalic connections in the tegu lizard. *Anat. Rec.* **175**, 374–375.

Martin, G. F. (1969). Efferent tectal pathways of the opossum (*Didelphis virginiana*). *J. comp. Neurol.* **135**, 209–224.

Martin, G. F. and Dom, R. (1970). The rubrospinal tract of the opossum (*Didelphis virginiana*). *J. comp. Neurol.* **138**, 19–30.

Martin, G. F. and West, H. J. (1967). Efferent neocortical projections to sensory nuclei in the brain stem of the opossum (*Didelphis virginiana*). *J. neurol. Sci.* **5**, 287–302.

Miller, M. R. (1975). The cochlear nuclei of lizards. *J. comp. Neurol.* **159**, 375–406.

Molenaar, G. J. (1974). An additional trigeminal system in certain snakes possessing infrared receptors. *Brain Res.* **78**, 340–344.

Nauta, W. J. H. and Kuypers, H. G. J. M. (1958). Some ascending pathways in the brain stem reticular formation. *In* "Reticular Formation of the Brain." (H. H. Jasper, ed.). Little, Brown, Boston, pp. 3–30.

Newman, D. (1974). Organization of reticular formation in reptiles. *Anat. Rec.* **178**, 426–427.

Newman, D. (1975). Cytoarchitecture of the metencephalic reticular formation in the turtles *Pseudemys* and *Chrysemys*. *Anat. Rec.* **181**, 435–436.

Nieuwenhuys, R. (1967). Comparative anatomy of the cerebellum. *Prog. Brain Res.* **25**, 1–93.

Norgren, R. and Leonard, C. M. (1971). Taste pathways in rat brain stem. *Science, N.Y.* **173**, 1136–1139.

Norgren, R. and Leonard, C. M. (1973). Ascending central gustatory pathways in the rat. *J. comp. Neurol.* **150**, 217–238.

Northcutt, R. G. (1970). The telencephalon of the western painted turtle (*Chrysemys picta belli*). *Illinois Biol. Monogr.* (43), 1–113.

Oswaldo-Cruz, E. and Rocha-Miranda, C. E. (1968). "The Brain of the Opossum (*Didelphis marsupialis*)." Instituto de Biofisica, Universidade Federal de Rio de Janeiro, Rio de Janeiro.

Papez, J. W. (1929). "Comparative Neurology." Thomas Y. Crowell, New York.

Papez, J. W. (1935). Thalamus of turtles and thalamic evolution. *J. comp. Neurol.* **61**, 433–476.

Parent, A. and Poirier, L. J. (1971). Occurrence and distribution of monoamine-containing neurons in the brain of the painted turtle. *Chrysemys picta.* *J. Anat.* **110**, 81–90.

Parent, A. and Poitras, D. (1973). Telencephalic projection of rostral midbrain catecholamine-containing neurons in the turtle (*Chrysemys picta*). *Anat. Rec.* **175**, 407.

Parent, A. and Poitras, D. (1974). Projection of catecholamine neurons of the lower brain stem to the cerebral cortex in the turtle (*Chrysemys picta*). *Anat. Rec.* **178**, 435.

Pedersen, R. (1973). Ascending spinal projections in three species of side-necked turtle: *Podocnemis unifilis, Pelusios subniger,* and *Pelomedusa subrufa. Anat. Rec.* **175**, 409.

Petrovicky, P. (1966). Reticular formation of the pigeon. *Folia Morphol.* **14**, 334–345.

Pritz, M. B. (1974a). Ascending connections of a midbrain auditory area in a crocodile, *Caiman crocodilus. J. comp. Neurol.* **153**, 179–198.

Pritz, M. B. (1974b). Ascending connections of a thalamic auditory area in a crocodile, *Caiman crocodilus. J. comp. Neurol.* **153**, 199–214.

Pritz, M. B. (1975). Anatomical identification of a telencephalic visual area in crocodiles: ascending connections of nucleus rotundus in *Caiman crocodilus. J. comp. Neurol.* **164**, 323–338.

Rafols, J. A. and Matzke, H. A. (1970). Efferent projections of the superior colliculus in the opossum. *J. comp. Neurol.* 138, 147–160.

Ramón, P. (1896). El structura del encéfalo del Cameléon. *Rev. trimest. micrograf.* 1, 46–82.

Ramón, P. (1897). El fasciculo longitudinal posterior en los reptiles. *Rev. trimest. micrograf* 2, 153–162.

Ramón-Moliner, E. and Nauta, W. J. H. (1966). The isodendritic core of the brain stem. *J. comp. Neurol.* 126, 311–336.

Robinson, L. R. (1969). Bulbospinal fibres and their nuclei of origin in *Lacerta viridis* demonstrated by axonal degeneration and chromatolysis respectively. *J. Anat.* 105, 59–88.

Rubinson, K. (1968). Projections of the tectum opticum of the frog. *Brain, Behav. Evol.* 1, 529–561.

Scalia, F., Halpern, M. and Riss, W. (1969). Olfactory bulb projections in the South American caiman. *Brain, Behav. Evol.* 2, 238–262.

Schroeder, D. M. and Loop, M. S. (1976). Trigeminal projections in snakes possessing infrared sensitivity. *J. comp. Neurol.* 169, 1–14.

Senn, D. G. (1968). Bau und Ontogenese von Zwischen- und Mittelhirn bei *Lacerta sicula* (Rafinesque). *Acta anat.*, Suppl. 55 = 1 ad Vol. 71, 1–150.

Senn, D. G. (1970). The stratification in the reptilian central nervous system. *Acta anat.*, 75, 521–552.

Senn, D. G. and Goodman, D. C. (1969). Patterns of localization in the cerebellar corticofugal projections of the alligator (*Caiman sclerops*). *In* "Neurobiology of Cerebellar Evolution and Development." (R. Llinás, ed.). Proc. 1st Int. Symp. Inst. Biomed. Res., A.M.A., pp. 475–479.

Shanklin, W. M. (1930). The central nervous system of *Chameleon vulgaris*. *Acta zool.* 11, 425–491.

Shanklin, W. M. (1933). The comparative neurology of the nucleus opticus tegmenti with special reference to *Chameleon vulgaris*. *Acta zool.* 14, 163–184.

Stefanelli, A. (1941a). Ricerche comparative sui centri tegmentali dei Rettili in rapporto alla loro locomozione. *Arch. zool. ital.* 29, 159–199.

Stefanelli, A. (1941b). I centri motori dell'occhio e le loro connessioni nel *Chameleon vulgaris*, con riferimenti comparativi in altri rettili. *Arch. ital. Anat. Embriol.* 45, 360–412.

Stefanelli, A. (1944a). I centri statici e della coordinazione motoria dei rettili. *Commentat. pontif. Acad. Scient.* 8, 147–293.

Stefanelli, A. (1944b). La fisiologia dei centri statici alla luce delle ricerche di morfologia ecologica nei rettili. *Archo Fisiol.* 44, 49–77.

ten Donkelaar, H. J. (1975). "Descending Pathways from the Brain Stem to the Spinal Cord in Some Reptiles." Thesis, Univ. of Nijmegen.

ten Donkelaar, H. J. (1976a). Descending pathways from the brain stem to the spinal cord in some reptiles. I. Origin. *J. comp. Neurol.*, 167, 421–442.

ten Donkelaar, H. J. (1976b). Descending pathways from the brain stem to the spinal cord in some reptiles. II. Course and site of termination. *J. comp. Neurol.*, 167, 443–463.

ten Donkelaar, H. J. and de Boer-van Huizen, R. (1978). Cells of origin of pathways descending to the spinal cord in a lizard ((*Lacerta galloti*). *Neurosci. Lett.* 9, 123–128.

Terni, T. (1922). Ricerche sul nervo abducente e in special modo intorno al significato del suo nucleo accessorio d'origine. *Fol. neurobiol.* 12, 277–327.

Tuge, H. (1932). Somatic motor mechanisms in the midbrain and medulla oblongata of *Chrysemys elegans* (Wied). *J. comp. Neurol.* 55, 185–271.

200   H. J. TEN DONKELAAR AND R. NIEUWENHUYS

Ulinski, P. S. (1973). Quantitative studies on motoneurons: Hypoglossal neurons in the boa constrictor, *Constrictor constrictor. Anat. Rec.* 175, 127–139.

Ulinski, P. S. (1977) .Tectal efferents in the banded water snake, *Natrix sipedon. J. comp. Neurol.* 173, 251–274.

Van den Akker, L. M. (1970). "An Anatomical Outline of the Spinal Cord of the Pigeon." Thesis, Univ. of Leiden, v. Gorcum, Assen.

van Hoevell, J. J. L. D. (1911). Remarks on the reticular cells of the oblongata in different vertebrates. *Proc. Acad. Sci. Amst.* 13, 1047–1065.

van Hoevell, J. J. L. D. (1916). De kernen der kleine hersenen. *Proc. Acad. Sci. Amst.* 24, 1485–1498.

Verhaart, W. J. C. (1970). "Comparative Anatomical Aspects of the Mammalian Brain Stem and the Cord." Van Gorcum N.V., Assen, 2 vols.

Voris, H. C. and Hoerr, N. L. (1932). The hindbrain of the opossum, *Didelphis virginiana. J. comp. Neurol.* 54, 277–356.

Weinberg, E. (1928). The mesencephalic root of the fifth nerve. *J. comp. Neurol.* 46, 249–406.

Weston, J. K. (1936). The reptilian vestibular and cerebellar gray with fiber connections. *J. comp. Neurol.* 65. 93–200.

Woodburne, R. T. (1936). A phylogenetic consideration of the primary and secondary centers and connections of the trigeminal complex in a series of vertebrates. *J. comp. Neurol.* 65, 403–502.

Zecha, A. (1961). Bezit een vogel een fasciculus rubro-bulbo-spinalis? *Ned. T. Geneesk.* 105, 2373.

Zecha, A. (1964). Efferent systems of the avian tectum. Proc. 72nd Meeting Anat. Assoc., Leiden. *Acta Morphol. Neerl.-scand.* 4, 282.

Zeehandelaar, I. (1921). Ontogenese und Phylogenese der Hinterstrangkerne in Verband mit der Sensibilität. *Fol. neurobiol.* 12, 1–133.

Zeigler, H. P. and Karten, H. J. (1973). Brain mechanisms and feeding behavior in the pigeon (*Columba livia*). I. Quinto-frontal structures. *J. comp. Neurol.* 152, 59–82.

CHAPTER 5

Variation in the Rhombencephalon

MARTIN ERNST SCHWAB

Institute of Zoology,
University of Basel,
Basel, Switzerland*

I. Introduction

The rhombencephalon of reptiles comprises approximately one-third of the total length of the brain. It arises embryonically from both the anterior and posterior vesicles of von Kupffer (1906) and is homologous to the pons (metencephalic floor) and medulla oblongata (myelencephalon) of mammals. The rostral border is marked by the motor cells of the medial longitudinal fasciculus (Fig. 1). The caudal border is not as distinct as the rostral one, as the somatic motor neurons of the last cranial nerve (XII) grade into the somatic motor column of the spinal cord.

The definition of the rhombencephalon includes the floor of the mesencephalon due to its similarities with cell populations and fiber systems of the more caudal myelencephalon. The mesencephalon is clearly a transitional brain region, as the organization of its roof areas is most similar to that of the prosencephalon (Von Kupffer, 1906; Senn, 1966, 1968; Schwab, 1973), whereas its floor is most similar to that of the metencephalon.

The rhombencephalon contains the motor neurons innervating the head muscles, as well as the primary sensory nuclei of most of the sensory cranial nerves. In fact, the rhombencephalon can be defined as that portion of the brain innervating the myotomal and branchiomeric portions of the vertebrate head (Starck, 1963, 1965); this explains the phylogenetic constancy of the rhombencephalon. The organization of the reptilian rhombencephalon shows less variation than does that of the prosencephalon, and the sensory areas of the rhombencephalon account for most of the variation.

The rhombencephalon has been divided segmentally (von Kupffer, 1906; Bergquist, 1952) and longitudinally (His, 1888; Herrick, 1899; Johnston, 1902, 1905), depending on the phylogenetic theory being proposed. In this account, the rhombencephalon will be divided into "systems", based on

* Present address: Max Planck Institute for Psychiatry, Munich, Federal Republic of Germany.

MARTIN ERNST SCHWAB

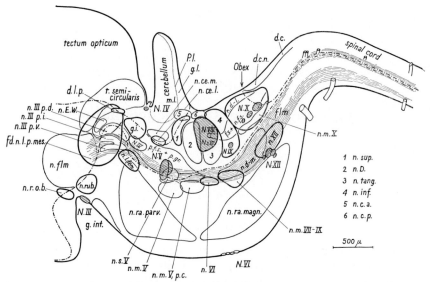

FIG. 1. Midsagittal reconstruction of the rhombencephalic nuclei of the lizard *Lacerta sicula*. d.c., Dorsal column (dorsal funiculus) of the spinal cord; d.c.n., dorsal column nuclei; d.l.p., dorsolateral part of nucleus lateralis profundus mesencephali; f.s., fasciculus solitarius; fd.n.l.p.mes., field of nucleus lateralis profundus mesencephali; flm, fasciculus longitudinalis medialis; g.i., ganglion isthmi; g.int., ganglion interpedunculare; g.l., granular layer; m.l., molecular layer; n.c.a., nucleus cochlearis anterior; n.c.p., nucleus cochlearis posterior; n.ce.l., lateral cerebellar nucleus; n.ce.m., medial cerebellar nucleus; n.D., nucleus Deiters; n.d.-l., nucleus dorsolateralis; n.d.-m., nucleus dorsomedialis; n.E.W., nucleus Edinger-Westphal; n.f.s., nucleus of the fasciculus solitarius; n.flm., nuclei of the fasciculus longitudinalis medialis; n.l.lem. nucleus of the lateral lemniscus; n.m.V, nucleus motorius of the trigeminal; n.m.V,p.c., caudal part of the motor trigeminal nucleus; n.m. VII-IX, motor nucleus of the facial and glossopharyngeal nerves; n.m.X, motor nucleus of the vagal nerve; n.r.o.b., nucleus of the radix optica basalis; n.ra.magn., nucleus raphé magnocellularis; n.ra.par., nucleus raphé parvocellularis; n.rub., nucleus ruber; n.s.V, nucleus sensibilis principalis of the trigeminal; N.s.VII, sensory facial nerve; n.inf., nucleus vestibularis inferior; n. sup., nucleus vestibularis superior; n. tang., nucleus tangentialis; n.III p.d., nucleus oculomotorius pars dorsalis; n.III p.i., nucleus oculomotorius pars intermedia; n.III p.v., nucleus oculomotorius pars ventralis; N.III, nervus oculomotorius; n.IV, nucleus trochlearis; N.IV, nervus trochlearis; N.V, nervus trigeminis; n.VI, nucleus abducens; N.VI, nervus abducens; N.VIII, nervus statoacousticus; N.IX, glossopharyngeal nerve; N.X. vagal nerve; n.XII, nucleus of the hypoglossal nerve; N.XII, nervus hypoglossus; p.f.s., periventricular fiber system; p.gr., periventricular gray; P.l., Purkinje layer of the cerebellum.

similarities in sensory or motor functions as well as topographical proximity. This description of the reptilian rhombencephalon and its variation is based on an examination of the brains of species listed in Table I. The brains were cut in the three standard anatomical planes stained by the Bodian, Luxol fast blue, or Golgi–Cox method, and counterstained with cresyl violet.

TABLE I

Species examined

CROCODILIA
  Caiman crocodilus
TESTUDINES
  Chelydra serpentina
  Phrynops nasutus
  Platemys spixii
  Chrysemys picta
  Chrysemys scripta elegans
  Sternotherus minor
  Sternotherus odoratus
  Pelomedusa subrufa
  Podocnemis unifilis
  Gopherus polyphemus
  Geochelone denticulata
  Testudo hermanni
  Trionyx ferox
  Trionyx triunguis
RHYNCHOCEPHALIA
  Sphenodon punctatus
SAURIA
  Agama mutabilis
  Agama stellio
  Uromastyx sp.
  Anguis fragilis
  Gerrhonotus multicarinatus
  Anniella pulchra
  Chamaeleo chamaeleon
  Cordylus cordylus
  Gerrhosaurus nigrolineatus
  Gerrhosaurus validus
  Platysaurus guttatus
  Gekko gecko
  Ptyodactylus hasselquistii
  Tarentola mauritanica
  Heloderma suspectum
  Varanus indicus
  Anolis carolinensis
  Basiliscus sp.
  Dipsosaurus dorsalis
  Iguana iguana
  Lacerta galloti
  Lacerta sicula
  Lacerta viridis
  Chalcides ocellatus
  Cnemidophorus tigris
  Tupinambis nigropunctatus

TABLE I—*continued*

AMPHISBAENIA
Amphisbaena caeca
Bipes biporus
Rhineura floridana
Diplometopon zarudnyi
Trogonophis wiegmanni
SERPENTES
Cylindrophis rufus
Leptotyphlops humilis
Leptotyphlops scutifrons
Typhlops vermicularis
Teretrurus rhodogaster
Xenopeltis unicolor
Acrochordus javanicus
Boa constrictor
Python reticulatus
Natrix natrix
Nerodia sipedon
Elaphe longissima
Bungarus fasciatus
Walterinnesia aegyptia
Atractaspis sp.
Echis carinatus
Vipera aspis
Vipera russelli
Bothrops atrox

II. Dorsal Column Nuclei

Some of the spinal nerve sensory root fibers do not terminate within the spinal segment of their entry but enter the dorsal funiculus of the spinal cord and ascend to the obex region of the medulla. Here they terminate in the dorsal column nuclei on cells giving rise to fibers of the medial lemniscus, which ascends to higher brain centers.

Older descriptions of the dorsal column nuclei in reptiles (Huber and Crosby, 1926) agree closely with more recent reports based on experimental data (Kruger and Witkovsky, 1961; Ebbesson, 1967, 1969).

The dorsal column nuclei are closely related topographically to the most caudal sensory fields of the medulla, namely the nucleus dorsolateralis and nucleus of the descending trigeminal tract (Figs 1–5). The cells of the dorsal column nuclei are scattered among the endings of the dorsal funicular fibers. Three nuclei can be distinguished in the best-developed cases: a medially placed, small nucleus of Bischoff, and two lateral, paired nuclei, the gracile nucleus and the cuneate nucleus. Bischoff's nucleus is not readily identified in most forms, nor are the gracile and cuneate nuclei clearly distinguishable in turtles and many small lizards. In snakes, the entire dorsal column system is poorly developed, presumably due to the loss of the limbs (Ebbesson, 1969).

In mammals, the cuneate nucleus is related to ascending sensory information from the anterior trunk and limbs, whereas the gracile nucleus is related to that from the posterior trunk and limbs. A similar somatotopic organization characterizes the dorsal column nuclei of *Alligator* (Kruger and Witkovsky, 1961) and *Lacerta* (Goldby and Robinson, 1962). The hindlimb and tail are represented medially, whereas the forelimb is represented laterally. The distal parts of the limbs are represented dorsally and the thorax ventrally.

The information relayed by the dorsal column nuclei originates mainly from mechanoreceptors in the skin and joints. In mammals the dorsal column nuclei give rise to a crossed tract, the medial lemniscus, which ascends to thalamic levels. The existence, exact origin and termination of this pathway in reptiles are still unresolved (de Lange, 1916; Huber and Crosby, 1926; Kruger and Witkovsky, 1961; Ebbesson, 1967, 1969).

III. Hypoglossal and Accessory Nerves and Nuclei

A. HYPOGLOSSAL NERVE AND NUCLEUS

A variable number of fine nerve rootlets exit the rhombencephalon just rostral to the first spinal nerves. These rootlets possess no sensory components but anastomose and form several rami of the hypoglossal cranial nerve (XII), which innervates the hypobranchial muscles of the head and tongue. The number of rootlets and their rami vary among different reptiles. However, in most reptiles at least ten rootlets and two or three rami leave the neurocranium.

In most anamniotes a separate hypoglossal nucleus cannot be identified and the hypoglossal nerve roots exit the rostralmost part of the ventral horn of the spinal cord. By contrast, reptiles have well-defined hypoglossal nuclei, although a caudal contact with the more dorsal part of the spinal motor column is present cytoarchitectonically. Many species have conspicuously large and uniform cells in the hypoglossal nucleus. Stereological data obtained in *Boa* indicate similarity between these neurons and those of the brainstem, rather than the spinal motor neurons (Ulinski, 1973).

The hypoglossal motor neurons are medium to large, often spindle-shaped and horizontally oriented. The nucleus is situated medially in the ventral part of the medulla (Figs 1, 2, 4, 5, 14, 15). In turtles, it begins

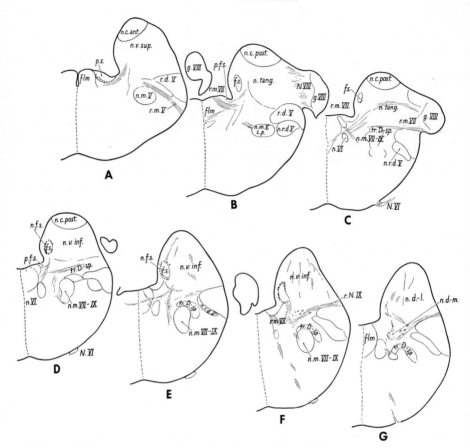

FIG. 2. Transverse sections through mid-medullary levels illustrating development of the cochlear and the vestibular nuclei of *Lacerta sicula*. The letter series proceeds from rostral to caudal. flm, Fasciculus longitudinalis medialis; f.s., fasciculus solitarius; g. VIII, ganglion of the VIIIth nerve; n.c.ant., nucleus cochlearis anterior; n.c.post., nucleus cochlearis posterior; n.d.-l., nucleus dorsolateralis; n.d.-m., nucleus dorsomedialis; n.f.s., nucleus of fasciculus solitarius; n.m.V, motor nucleus of the trigeminal; n.m.V,c.p., caudal part of motor trigeminal nucleus; n.m.VII–IX, motor nucleus of facial and glossopharyngeal nerves; n.r.d.V, nucleus of radix descendens V; n. tang.,nucleus tangentialis; n.v.inf., nucleus vestibularis inferior; n.v.sup., nucleus vestibularis superior; n.VI, nucleus of nervus abducens; N.VI, nervus abducens; N.VIII, nervus octavus; p.f.s., periventricular fiber system; p.s., periventricular system; r.d.V, radix descendens of the trigeminal nerve; r.m.V, motor root of the trigeminal nerve; r.m.VII, motor root of the facial nerve; r.N.IX, radix of the glossopharyngeal nerve; tr.D.-sp., tractus Deitero-spinalis.

caudal to the dorsomedial nucleus (Fig. 4), replacing the latter. In squamates, the rostral pole begins lateral to the dorsomedial nucleus

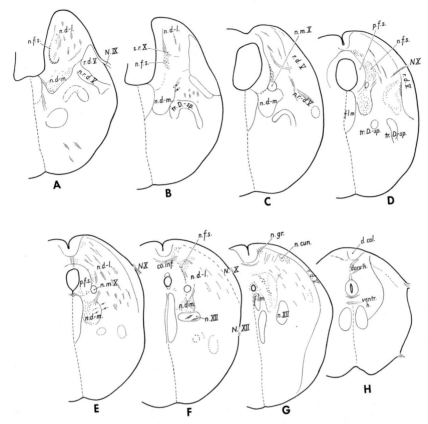

FIG. 3. Transverse sections through the caudal medulla of *Lacerta sicula*. The letter series proceeds from rostral to caudal. co.inf., Commissura infima; d.col., dorsal column of the spinal cord; dors. h., dorsal horn; flm, fasciculus longitudinalis medialis; n.cun., nucleus cuneatus; n.d.-l., nucleus dorsolateralis; n.d.-m., nucleus dorsomedialis; n.f.s., nucleus of fasciculus solitarius; n.gr., nucleus gracilis; n.m.X, motor vagal nucleus; n.r.d.V, nucleus of radix descendens V; N.IX, nervus glossopharyngeus; N.X, nervus vagus; n.XII, nucleus of nervus hypoglossus; N.XII, nervus hypoglossus; p.f.s., periventricular fiber system; r.d.V, radix descendens of the trigeminal nerve; s.r.X, sensory rootlets of the vagal nerve; tr.D.-sp., tractus Deitero-spinalis; ventr.h., ventral horn of spinal cord.

(Fig. 1). In lizards, replacement occurs at a more caudal level, while the hypoglossal nucleus retains its lateral position in snakes. In snakes, many turtles, and some lizards, the nucleus lies fairly close to the vagal motor nucleus. The rostral pole of the hypoglossal nucleus often lies slightly caudal to that of the vagal motor column. The caudal extension and the overall size of the nucleus exhibits considerable variation. In general, the nucleus is well developed in reptiles; it is of moderate size in crocodilians,

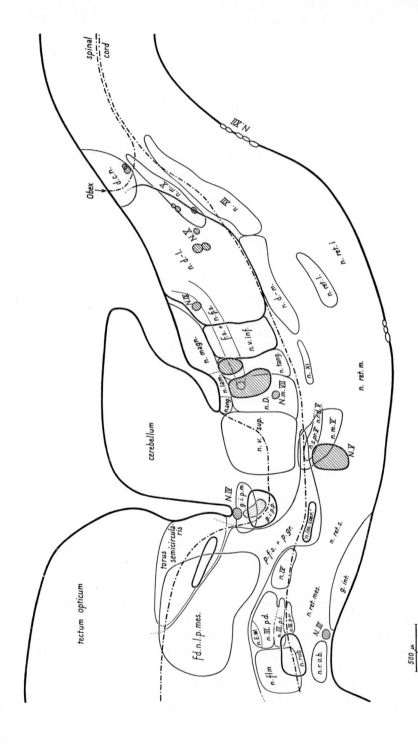

Fig 4—see facing page

500 μ

FIG. 4. Midsagittal reconstruction of the rhombencephalic nuclei of the painted turtle, *Chrysemys picta*. Hatched areas indicate positions of transected cranial nerve roots. d.c.n., Dorsal column nuclei; f.s. fasciculus solitarius; fd.n.l.p.mes., field of nucleus lateralis profundus mesencephali; g.i.p.m., ganglion isthmi pars magnocellularis; g.i.p.p., ganglion isthmi pars parvocellularis; g.int., ganglion interpeduncu- lare; n.ang., nucleus angularis; n.D., nucleus Deiters; n.d.-l., nucleus dorsolateralis; n.d.-m., nucleus dorsomedialis; n.E.W., nucleus Edinger-Westphal; n.f.s., nucleus of the fasciculus solitarius; n.flm., nucleus of fasciculus longitudinalis medialis; n.lam., nucleus laminaris; n.loc.coer., nucleus locus coeruleus; n.magn., nucleus magnocellularis; n.m.V, motor nucleus of the trigeminal; N.m.VII, motor facial nerve; n.m.X, motor vagal nucleus; n.r.d.V, nucleus of radix descendens of the trigeminal; n.r.o.b., nucleus of radix optica basalis; n.ret.i., nucleus reticularis inferior; n.ret.l., nucleus reticularis lateralis; n.ret.m., nucleus reticularis medius; n.ret.mes., nucleus reticularis mesen- cephali; n.ret.s., nucleus reticularis superior; n.rub., nucleus ruber; n.s.pr.V, principal sensory nucleus of the trigeminal; n.tang., nucleus tangentialis; n.v.inf., nucleus vestibularis inferior; n.v.sup., nucleus vestibularis superior; n.III p.d., nucleus oculomotorius pars dorsalis; n.III p.i., nucleus oculomotorius pars intermedia; n.III p.v., nucleus oculomotorius pars ventralis; N.III, nervus oculomotorius; n.IV, nucleus trochlearis; N.V, nervus trigeminis; n.VI, nucleus abducens; N.VI, nervus abducens; N.IX, nervus glossopharyngeus; N.X, nervus vagus; n.XII; nucleus of the hypoglossal nerve; N.XII; nervus hypoglossus; p.f.s., periventricular fiber system; p.gr., periventri- cular gray.

but remarkably large in many lizards and snakes. A quantitative assay in *Boa* yielded a mean of 942 ± 162 neurons per nucleus (Ulinski, 1973). A giant hypoglossal complex is found in chameleons. Many turtles and crocodilians, have the ventral part of the nucleus separated caudally.

The axons leave the hypoglossal nucleus medially, toward the medial longitudinal fasciculus, before turning ventrad. The nucleus appears to

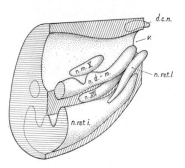

FIG. 5. Reconstruction of the nuclei of the caudal medulla of *Boa constrictor* (modified after Ulinski, 1973). d.c.n., Dorsal column nuclei; n.d.-m., nucleus dorsomedialis; n.m.X, vagal motor nucleus; n.ret.i., nucleus reticularis inferior; n.ret.l., nucleus reticularis lateralis; n.XII, nucleus of nervus hypoglossus; v., fourth ventricle.

form connections with the medial longitudinal fasciculus and the reticular formation. It may also connect with the periventricular fiber system and the vagal nuclei.

B. Accessory Nerve

Thin nerve rootlets leave the brain or the most rostral portion of the spinal cord, caudal to the vagal roots of many reptiles (Fig. 1). These fibers are heavily myelinated and, despite their exit dorsally, cannot be followed to the dorsal sensory column of the spinal cord. They can be traced to large cells in the ventral horn. The thin rootlets and their more ventral motor cells constitute an accessory nerve.

The mammalian accessory nerve (Addens, 1933), has both a bulbar component and a spinal component. The bulbar component arises originally from the vagal complex, innervates the larynx and is closely associated with the vagus. The spinal component is related to the trapezius muscles and consists of motor fibers leaving the brain dorsally in the first cervical segments. Many reptiles show the same pattern, to judge from my analysis and the descriptions of Soliman (1964). Snakes lack a spinal component as well as trapezius muscles.

VI. Facial, Glossopharyngeal and Vagal Systems

A. GENERAL

The caudal medulla oblongata is dominated by the nuclei associated with the VIIth, IXth and Xth cranial nerves (Figs 1–5, 7, 17). The nuclei of these three nerves are intimately related to each other. From an anatomical as well as functional viewpoint, the most appropriate subdivisions are: (a) two motor divisions, the facial and the glossopharyngeal, separated from the more caudal vagal motor nucleus, and (b) a sensory complex formed by the components of all three nerves. The medulla of all reptiles is characterized by high cell densities and poorly defined nuclear boundaries. Thus it is often difficult, if not impossible, to define nuclear boundaries accurately. Frequently, the nerves leave the brain as several fine rootlets, which presents many difficulties to an experimental approach. To date, there is only one study dealing with chromatolytic changes following sectioning of the facial nerve (Gillaspy, 1954). Its results agree closely with my own.

B. MOTOR NUCLEUS OF FACIAL AND GLOSSOPHARYNGEAL NERVES

In all reptiles, the facial nerve enters the brain together with the VIIIth nerve (Figs 1–4, 6, 7). Sensory and motor roots are always separated. In turtles, the motor root penetrates the descending trigeminal tract, often in two portions, immediately ventral to the VIIIth nerve. In all other reptiles, it barely slips over the trigeminal root that is associated with the most ventral part of the VIIIth root. The motor fibers course straight toward the ventricle where they turn caudally. They then pass dorsolaterally over the medial longitudinal fascicle as a small, compact tract. In some species, a rostral knee (genu) is formed (Ariëns Kappers, 1910; Black, 1920; Addens, 1933; Ariëns Kappers et al., 1936; Barnard, 1936). The suggested embryological origins of this rostral curvature were confirmed in my series of Lacerta sicula. A loop is formed by the crossing of the dorsal arcuate bundles of the cochlear complex over the facial root fibres. This is especially noticeable for the large fibers from the lateral vestibular nucleus. Rostral displacement and the formation of a genu are related to general shifts in the entire region during development.

The glossopharyngeal motor root, and often its sensory root fibers, enter the brain caudal to the VIIth root (Figs 1, 3, 4). The bundle is small and runs just above the descending trigeminal root where it turns medially.

In all reptiles investigated, a single motor nuclear complex exists for the VIIth and IXth nerves, and there are no indications of contact with the motor trigeminal nucleus. Subdivisions may occur, but the facial and glosso-pharyngeal divisions are invariably in close contact and, in most species, indistinguishable. Although the nucleus extends from a level slightly caudal to the VIIIth root to the entrance of the IXth root, the facial fibers join the nucleus at the more caudal level where they enter a more or less compact column of medium-sized, polygonal cells.

The highest cytoarchitectonic differentiation of the VII–IX motor nucleus occurs in crocodilians. In these taxa, the facial nucleus consists of dorsal, intermediate and ventral parts (Addens, 1933; Ariëns Kappers et al., 1936; Gillaspy, 1954). Degeneration studies (Gillaspy, 1954) in *Alligator* reveal that the dorsal part of the facial motor nucleus gives rise to the fibers supply-ing the depressor mandibulae, while the intermediate group supplies the constrictor colli oralis. The ventral part innervates the constrictor colli aboralis and the more rostral part the interhyoideus. The whole complex lies medial to the superior olive and is separated from the latter by the lateral vestibulospinal tract. This condition contrasts to that observed in lizards, in which the lateral vestibulospinal tract forms a cap over the VII–IX motor column. Moreover, in lizards, the nucleus is characterized by a regular and dense fiber plexus, which is quite different from the picture observed in other species. In turtles, as well as in snakes, the VII–IX motor nucleus is poorly defined. A column of more or less sparse cells can be found in the corresponding position, but delimitation from tegmental cell groups is often difficult. The facial and glossopharyngeal motor systems seem of no great significance in these groups.

C. MOTOR NUCLEUS OF THE VAGUS NERVE

The vagus nerve enters the brain dorsally as several small rootlets (Figs 1, 4). These rootlets penetrate the descending trigeminal tract, often after following it tangentially for a short distance just beneath the surface of the brainstem. The motor nucleus consists of a compact column of relatively large polygonal to round, intensely staining neurons. The nucleus lies dorsal to the lateral angle of the IVth ventricle immediately dorsal to the peri-ventricular fiber system. The rostral pole appears together with the first vagal root. Caudally, it extends into the first cervical segments, but at a slightly more dorsal level. The motor nucleus of the vagus occurs in all of the reptiles investigated. Some species have a closely associated lateral part, but this occurs irregularly (Black, 1920). Snakes have a well developed vagal motor column.

Nothing is known of the function or possible functional subdivisions of the vagal motor nucleus in reptiles, in contrast to the situation in birds

(Cohen *et al.*, 1970) and mammals. Presumably the vagal nucleus plays an important parasympathetic role as in the latter forms.

My observations permit only a cursory picture of the fiber connections of these two nuclear complexes. Prominent bundles interconnect the VII–IX motor nucleus with the tegmental and reticular system of the medulla. Well developed fiber bundles from the cochlear and vestibular regions run into and through the VIIth to IXth motor nuclei. The vagal motor nucleus appears to possess widespread connections with the adjacent sensory fields of the most caudal medulla oblongata.

D. THE SOLITARY FASCICULUS

Like the motor nucleus of the facial nerve, the sensory nucleus of the facial nerve lies far caudal to the entrance of the sensory nerve into the brain. The sensory facial root enters the brain together with the vestibular root fibers of the VIIIth nerve. It courses medially toward the ventricle and then turns sharply caudally. Running caudally, the root forms the so-called "prevagal" part of the solitary tract (fasciculus solitarius) Fig. 2. The compact root lies immediately over the periventricular fiber system and is often surrounded by cells forming the nucleus of the solitary tract. These cells may be absent when the system as a whole is poorly developed, as in many snakes. Caudal to the vestibular region, the sensory root of the glosso-pharyngeal nerve—which may enter together with the motor root, or separately—joins the solitary tract. The tract continues in a dorsal direction, the nucleus becoming more conspicuous (Fig. 3). With the arrival of vagal sensory roots, the system reaches its greatest extent immediately anterior to the obex. At this level, many of the fibers cross in the commissura infima. The nucleus of the solitary tract is continuous with the commissural nucleus. Anatomically as well as functionally, the latter may be regarded as closely associated with the solitary fasciculus.

E. DORSOLATERAL AND DORSOMEDIAL NUCLEI

Two additional large nuclear fields are found in the caudal medulla. A poorly defined cell mass, termed nucleus dorsolateralis by de Lange (1916) and Ariëns Kappers *et al.* (1936), begins caudal to the inferior vestibular nucleus and runs along the lateral edge of the solitary fascicle. In the region of the obex, it occupies the entire dorsolateral part of the dorsal medulla oblongata (Figs 1–5). Caudally, the dorsolateral nucleus merges with the dorsal horn of the spinal cord. The area contains small to medium-sized neurons, as well as a few fairly large nerve cells, often with intensely staining, rounded perikarya. These cells closely resemble ones in the nucleus of the descending trigeminal tract. The cytoarchitectonic boundaries of the dorso-lateral nucleus are ill-defined and the nucleus is traversed by numerous fiber tracts of varied origin, making it virtually impossible to describe the connections and possible functions of this cell mass.

The nucleus dorsomedialis (de Lange, 1916; Ariëns Kappers et al., 1936; nucleus parvocellularis medialis: Ebbesson, 1967, 1969) is located ventral to the vagal motor nucleus, beneath the floor of the IVth ventricle (Figs 1–5). The nucleus begins caudad to that of the abducens nucleus, but can be clearly separated. At its caudal end it is often replaced by hypoglossal neurons (Fig. 1). The nucleus dorsomedialis is conspicuous by its intricate fiber plexus and unusually high cell density, except in turtles. Often the cells of the nucleus are somewhat smaller than the normal medium-sized cells of the other sensory nuclei. Caudally, the nucleus shows a broad cytoarchitectonic connection with the dorsolateral nucleus. The two cell masses are almost continuous at this level in many groups of reptiles. Ebbesson (1967, 1969) has reported spinal input to the dorsomedial nucleus via the lateral funiculus, but other connections are unknown.

V. Statoacoustic System

A. General

The static and acoustic senses mediated by the labyrinth are clearly separated in the peripheral organ and this separation is maintained centrally in the ganglia of the statoacoustic nerve and centrally in its terminal nuclei within the medulla.

The vestibular labyrinth is far less variable in reptiles than is the acoustic labyrinth; this is also reflected centrally in the statoacoustic nuclei of the medulla. All reptiles have four vestibular nuclei, with little variation in their arrangement and differentiation. On the other hand, the cochlear nuclei are highly variable in number and in differentiation.

B. Statoacoustic Organ and Nerve

The reptilian labyrinth consists of three semicircular canals, each containing an ampulla and a sensory epithelial crista, plus the sacculus, utriculus, lagena and cochlear duct. The sacculus, utriculus and lagena each possess otolithic organs (maculae). The cochlear duct contains the final otic sensory receptor, a papilla basilaris, which consists of an elongated strip of hair cells that run the length of the cochlear duct.

The ampullary crista and the saccular and utricular maculae constitute the static receptor organs. The papilla basilaris is the acoustic receptor and varies greatly among reptiles (Evans, 1935; Wever, 1965; Miller, 1966, 1967, 1968, 1975; Baird, 1970). The function of the lagenar macula is unclear. Its fibers exit with the cochlear root of the statoacoustic nerve and appear to terminate in the cochlear region of the medulla. Thus the lagena may also possess an auditory function.

The statoacoustic nerve of reptiles consists of two roots (radices). Each root possesses its own ganglion and each root enters the medulla as a distinct bundle (Fig. 6). The anterior root and ganglion innervate the anterior and horizontal cristae, the utriculus and most of the sacculus. Thus, the anterior root and ganglion only contain vestibular fibers. The posterior root and ganglion innervate the posterior crista, the lagenar macula, the papilla basilaris, and a small part of the sacculus. The posterior root is frequently termed the cochlear root, but it obviously carries vestibular fibers as well. Both statoacoustic ganglia and roots contain fibers and cell bodies of various sizes. The different classes of neurons appear to be related to specific end organs (Beccari, 1912; Landmann, 1972).

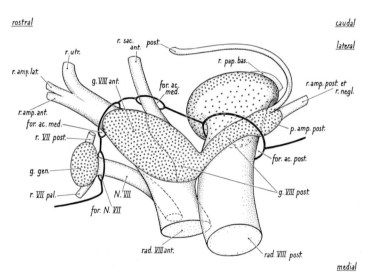

Fig. 6. Reconstruction of the ganglia, rami and roots of the eighth cranial nerve in *Caiman crocodilus* (after Glatt, 1975a). for.ac.med., Foramen acusticum mediale; for.ac.post., foramen acusticum posterius; for.N.VII, foramen nervi facialis; g.gen., ganglion geniculatum; g.VIII ant., ganglion VIII anterius; g.VIII post., ganglion VIII posterius; N.VII, nervus facialis; p.amp. post., pars ampullae posterioris; r.VII pal., ramus palatinus of VIIth nerve; r.VII post., ramus posterior of VIIth nerve; r.amp.ant., ramus ampullae anterioris; r.amp.lat., ramus ampullae lateralis; r.amp.post., ramus ampullae posterioris; r.negl., ramus maculae neglectae; r.pap.bas., ramus papillae basilaris; r.sac.ant.post., ramus sacculi, anterior and posterior; r.utr., ramus utriculi; rad.VIII ant., radix VIII anterior; rad.VIII post., radix VIII posterior.

C. Vestibular Nuclei

The vestibular region of the reptilian medulla is usually considered to consist of four nuclei. In rostrocaudal sequence they are the superior vestibular nucleus, ventrolateral vestibular nucleus (Deiters' nucleus), tangential nucleus and inferior vestibular nucleus (Figs 1–4, 7–9). However, the exact number of vestibular nuclei in reptiles and their nomenclature is often disputed due to the difficulty of defining precise boundaries within

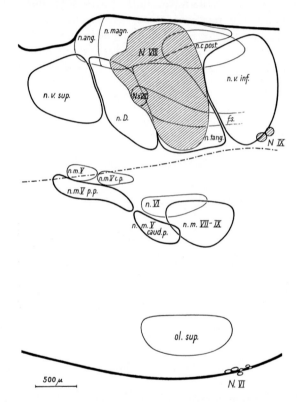

FIG. 7. Midsagittal reconstruction of the mid-medullary region of the tegu lizard, *Tupinambis nigropunctatus*. f.s., Fasciculus solitarius; N.VI, nervus abducens; N.s.VII, sensory facial nerve; n.VI, nucleus abducens; N.VIII, nervus statoacousticus; N.IX, nervus glossopharyngeus; n.ang., nucleus angularis; n.c.post., nucleus cochlearis posterior; n.D., nucleus Deiters; n.m.V, motor trigeminal nucleus; n.m.V.c.p., central part of motor trigeminal nucleus; n.m.V.caud.p., caudal part of motor trigeminal nucleus; n.m.V.p.p., peripheral part of motor trigeminal nucleus; n.m.VII–IX, motor nucleus of the facial and glossopharyngeal nerves; n.magn., nucleus magnocellularis; n.tang., nucleus tangentialis; n.v.inf., nucleus vestibularis inferior; n.v.sup., nucleus vestibularis superior; ol.sup., oliva superior.

the vestibular region. A final nomenclature will only emerge as the specific connections of the vestibular nuclei are determined in a number of reptilian orders.

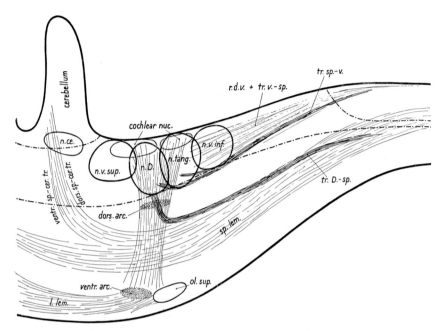

FIG. 8. Schematic representation of the main fiber tracts coursing through the vestibular region of the reptilian medulla. dors.arc., Dorsal arcuates; dors.sp.-cer.tr., dorsal spinocerebellar tract; l.lem., lateral lemniscus; n.ce., cerebellar nuclei; n.D., nucleus Deiters; n.tang., nucleus tangentialis; n.v.inf., nucleus vestibularis inferior; n.v.sup., vestibularis superior; ol.sup., oliva superior; r.d.v., radix descendens vestibularis; sp.lem., spinal lemniscus; tr.D.-sp., tractus Deitero-spinalis; tr.sp.-v., tractus spinovestibularis; tr.v.-sp., tractus vestibulospinalis; ventr.arc., ventral arcuates; ventr.sp.-cer.tr., ventral spinocerebellar tract.

The vestibular region of turtles is elongated compared to that of crocodilians and squamates. The vestibular nuclei are even more compressed in amphisbaenians, burrowing snakes and some burrowing lizards (scincids). In these lizards the cochlear area is greatly hypertrophied and the vestibular nuclei are compressed medially and ventrally. The cell density of the vestibular nuclei is much lower in turtles than in other taxa. The vestibular nuclei are most differentiated in crocodilians.

The superior vestibular nucleus (Beccari, 1912; de Lange, 1916; Schepman, 1918; Larsell, 1926, 1932; Hindenach, 1931; Ariëns Kappers et al., 1936; Stefanelli, 1944; Landmann, 1972; part of the anterior vestibular nucleus, van Hoevell, 1911; de Lange, 1916; dorsolateral vestibular nucleus, Weston, 1936) lies beneath the cerebellum (Figs 1–4, 7–9). Dorsally, the nucleus is in close contact, often almost fused, with the lateral cerebellar nucleus. More caudally, it is bounded dorsally by the cochlear area except in turtles, where the latter begins at a more caudal level. A rostral continuation of the nucleus into the isthmus, described as the superior vestibular

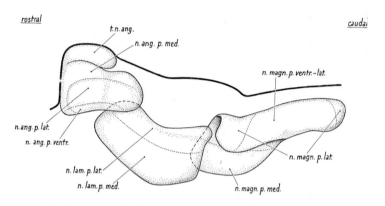

Fig. 9. Midsagittal reconstruction of the cochlear nuclei of *Caiman crocodilus* (after Glatt, 1975a). n.ang.p.lat., Nucleus angularis, pars lateralis; n.ang.p.med., nucleus angularis, pars medialis; n.ang.p.ventr., nucleus angularis, pars ventralis; n.lam.p.lat., nucleus laminaris, pars lateralis; n.lam.p.med., nucleus laminaris, pars medialis; n.magn.p.lat., nucleus magnocellularis, pars lateralis; n.magn.p.med., nucleus magnocellularis, pars medialis; n.magn.p.ventr.-lat., nucleus magnocellularis, pars ventrolateralis; t.n.ang., tongue of nucleus angularis.

nucleus of turtles (Weston, 1936) could not be identified. Caudally, the superior vestibular nucleus is in contact with Deiters' nucleus. Two main cell types can be recognized in the superior vestibular nucleus of all reptiles. Medium-sized, polygonal cells lie in the middle and caudal part. The main cell mass is comprised of smaller cells of various shapes. The cell density is highest in crocodilians, high in snakes, and rather low in turtles.

The ventrolateral vestibular nucleus, or Deiters' nucleus (Beccari, 1912; van Hoevell, 1911; de Lange, 1916; Schepman, 1918; Ariëns Kappers et al., 1936; Stefanelli, 1944; Landmann, 1972; rostral part of ventral nucleus, Holmes, 1903; lateral vestibular nucleus, Larsell, 1926, 1932; ventrolateral vestibular nucleus, Weston, 1936) is the most conspicuous vestibular nucleus (Figs 1–4, 7–9). It lies at, and rostral to, the level of the entering statoacoustic roots. In turtles, the nucleus extends over a long rostro-caudal distance. In crocodilians, it is long, whereas in lizards and snakes it is somewhat compressed. It is bounded dorsally by the cochlear region and where this is present, by a nucleus laminaris. An often indistinct ventra, boundary consists of the nucleus of the descending trigeminal tract and/or the principal trigeminal sensory nucleus. Medially, Deiters' nucleus contacts the periventricular system. Subdivision of Deiters' nucleus presents several difficulties. Frequently it is divided into central, dorsal, and ventrocaudal parts (Beccari, 1912; Ariëns Kappers, 1921; Ariëns Kappers *et al.*, 1936; Landmann, 1972). However, these individual parts may not be homologous in all reptiles, as the typical giant cells of this nucleus are not always located in the same subdivision. Thus, Stefanelli (1944) described different subdivisions in various turtles and squamates, but was unable to homologize single cell groups.

The tangential nucleus (Beccari, 1912; de Lange, 1916; Schepman, 1918; Ariëns Kappers *et al.*, 1936; Weston, 1936; Stefanelli, 1944; Landmann, 1972; caudal part of ventral nucleus, Holmes, 1903) is situated immediately at the entrance of the statoacoustic roots. Caudally, it merges with the inferior vestibular nucleus at an ill-defined boundary. Dorsally, the tangential nucleus is bordered by the caudal part of the cochlear area and ventrally by the principal sensory trigeminal nucleus or the descending trigeminal tract and nucleus. Frequently, the most caudal, periventricular part of Deiters' nucleus reaches as far as this level. The main cell mass of the tangential nucleus is located laterally, between the entering statoacoustic root fibers. These fibers arise from the ampullae (Beccari, 1912; Landmann, 1972). Beccari (1912) divided the tangential nucleus into four parts: anterior, medial, posterior and lateral. The anterior and medial parts are situated more dorsally and receive afferents from the posterior ampulla via the posterior ramus of the VIIIth nerve. The posterior and lateral subdivisions receive afferents via the anterior ramus from the lateral and anterior ampullae and from the utriculus. The tangential nucleus in *Lacerta sicula* may be divided into anterior, lateral and posterior parts based on afferents from the three ampullae (Landmann, 1972). Two main cell types are found within the tangential nucleus. Medium-sized and, occasionally, small cells are present in great numbers, especially in crocodilians and squamates. The small cells are concentrated in the medial part of the nucleus and are rarely seen among the root fibers. Large polygonal to spindle-shaped cells are located more laterally and receive the "spoonlike" synapses of ampullary fibers.

The inferior vestibular nucleus (Ariëns Kappers *et al.*, 1936; Stefanelli, 1944; Landmann, 1972; descending vestibular nucleus, Weston, 1936) is the most poorly defined of all vestibular nuclei; it is often regarded as a caudal continuation of the tangential nucleus (Figs 1–4, 7–9). Two factors justify its recognition as a separate nuclear field: the lack of spindle-shaped cells characteristic of the tangential nucleus, and the presence of a dense fiber plexus with relatively uniform cell distribution. The inferior vestibular nucleus is bounded ventrolaterally by the descending trigeminal tract and nucleus and dorsally by the extreme caudal end of the cochlear region; caudally it merges with the visceral sensory fields. Its cells are of medium and small size.

D. VESTIBULAR CONNECTIONS

In reptiles, the vestibular fibers entering the brain give off terminals to the tangential nucleus and then divide into ascending and descending roots (DeFina and Webster, 1974; Leake, 1974; Foster and Hall, 1978). The fibers of the ascending vestibular root terminate in the superior and ventro-lateral vestibular nuclei, whereas fibers of the descending vestibular root terminate in the inferior vestibular nucleus. In *Caiman*, vestibular fibers enter via both statoacoustic roots. They project ipsilaterally to the cerebellar nuclei as well as bilaterally to the granular layer of the cerebellum (Leake, 1974).

Other afferents to the vestibular nuclei have also been described in reptiles. Among these are spinovestibular projections via the dorsal funiculus and spinal lemniscus to the inferior and ventrolateral vestibular nuclei (Ebbesson, 1969) as well as cerebellar projections to the superior, ventro-lateral and tangential nuclei (Senn and Goodman, 1969).

Efferents of the vestibular nuclei pass to the cerebellum, medulla and spinal cord (Robinson, 1969; Cruce, 1975; ten Donkelaar, 1976a, b). The ventrolateral vestibular nucleus is the only vestibular nucleus that projects to the spinal cord (ten Donkelaar, 1976a, b).

In mammals, efferent fibers course with the various branches of the vestibular nerve to the sensory epithelia; the cell bodies of these fibers lie in the vestibular nuclei (Rasmussen and Gacek, 1958; Gribenski, 1970). Similar efferent vestibular fibers are known in *Rana* (Caston, 1972), but comparable information does not exist for reptiles.

E. COCHLEAR NUCLEI

The cochlear (acoustic) root of the statoacoustic nerve arises from the basilar papilla and lagenar macula. Its fibers enter the medulla more dorsally than the vestibular fibers, frequently they enter as the most caudal part of the statoacoustic nerve. Many of the cochlear fibers bifurcate on entering the medulla and form ascending and descending cochlear tracts (Beccari, 1912; Schepman, 1918).

The reptilian cochlear nuclei and cochlear ducts exhibit marked variation. Anatomical (Miller, 1966, 1967, 1973; Baird, 1970) and functional (Evans, 1935; Wever and Vernon, 1957, 1960; Wever and Peterson, 1963; Wever,

1965; Gans and Wever, 1972; Wever and Gans, 1972) details of variation in the reptilian cochlear duct are extensive. However, there is no general agreement regarding the nature of variation in the cochlear nuclei of reptiles (DeFina and Webster, 1974; Leake, 1974; Miller, 1975; Foster and Hall, 1978). My analysis of the species of reptiles listed in Table I suggests the following summary of cochlear variation.

All turtles have an anterior nucleus angularis and a posterior nucleus magnocellularis. Many turtles also possess a poorly developed third cochlear nucleus (nucleus laminaris) that appears to differentiate from a rostral pole of nucleus magnocellularis (Fig. 4). *Sternotherus minor*, *Testudo hermanni*, and *Platemys spixii* lack a recognizable nucleus laminaris.

Crocodilians exhibit the most differentiated cochlear nuclei, and well-developed angular and magnocellular nuclei. A well-developed laminar nucleus (Fig. 9) also occurs as in birds.

Cochlear variation in lizards exhibits two distinct patterns. Agamids, chamaeleonids, iguanids, teiids, and varanids possess an angular and magnocellular nucleus, but there is no distinct laminar nucleus. In these taxa, a third nucleus (posterior cochlear nucleus) differentiates caudal to the magnocellular nucleus (Fig. 7). The other families of lizards and the amphisbaenians possess a cochlear region divided into anterior and posterior cochlear nuclei (Fig. 1). The anterior cochlear nucleus of these taxa appears homologous to the angular and magnocellular cochlear nuclei of agamids, chamaeleonids, iguanids, teiids and varanids.

Snakes have a single cochlear nucleus which cannot at present be homologized with those of lizards. The basilar papilla of advanced snakes is small compared to their lagenar macula, and the cochlear nucleus of snakes may largely represent the lagenar portions of the cochlear nuclei of lizards.

The nucleus angularis (de Lange, 1916; Schepman, 1918; Huber and Crosby, 1926; Weston, 1936; Stefanelli, 1944; Glatt, 1975a, b; dorsal nucleus, Holmes, 1903) constitutes the rostral pole of the cochlear region of reptiles. In crocodilians and lizards, but not in turtles, it protrudes into the fourth ventricle forming the acoustic eminence (Holmes, 1903). The medium-sized cells of nucleus angularis are scattered among the thick cochlear fibers. The nucleus angularis is highly differentiated in crocodilians; thus lateral, medial and ventral subdivisions are recognized in *Caiman* (Fig. 9; Glatt, 1975a). Similar subdivisions are recognizable in birds (Boord and Rasmussen, 1963; Boord, 1968).

The nucleus laminaris (Holmes, 1903; de Lange, 1916; van Hoevell, 1911; Schepman, 1918; Ariëns Kappers, 1921; Huber and Crosby, 1926; Weston, 1936; Glatt, 1975a, b) is recognized as a distinct cochlear nucleus in crocodilians and many turtles. In crocodilians it occupies the middle third of the rostrocaudal length of the cochlear region (Fig. 9) as a broad band of spindle-shaped, polygonal cells bordered dorsally and ventrally by a distinct fiber plexus.

The nucleus magnocellularis (de Lange, 1916; Schepman, 1918; Huber and Crosby, 1926; Weston, 1936; Stefanelli, 1944; Glatt, 1975a, b; pars posterior of nucleus laminaris, Holmes, 1903) constitutes the most caudal cochlear nucleus in turtles and crocodilians (Figs 4, 9). It is conspicuous due to its large polygonal cells concentrated in the medial half of the nucleus. Its cells are never arranged into laminae as are those of the more rostral nucleus laminaris. In crocodilians, the magnocellular nucleus shows lateral, medial, and ventrolateral subdivisions (Glatt, 1975a, b), as does that of birds (Boord and Rasmussen, 1963; Boord, 1968).

In those lizards having a distinct magnocellular nucleus (agamids, chamaeleonids, iguanids, teiids and varanids) it is characterized by its large, oval, darkly staining cells. A descending division frequently reaches the caudal end of the vestibular region. This caudal division of the magnocellular nucleus of lizards is homologous to the medial magnocellular division of *Caiman*. In *Tupinambis* and *Varanus*, the rostral pole of the magnocellular nucleus is differentiated as a dense fiber plexus that is semilunar in outline and contains peripherally located polygonal and round cells. This portion of the magnocellular nucleus has been interpreted as a nucleus laminaris (Ebbesson, 1967).

The nucleus cochlearis anterior (Beccari, 1912; anterior and posterior cochlear nuclei, Glatt, 1975b) of most lizards occupies the position of the rostrocaudal extent of nucleus angularis and the nucleus magnocellularis of other reptiles. The anterior cochlear nucleus consists of fairly large polygonal cells, scattered in a dense fiber plexus, and forms a dorsomedially directed acoustic eminence. At present it is difficult to homologize the anterior cochlear nucleus of lizards with the cochlear nuclei of other reptiles. The cells in the rostral part of the nucleus are similar to those of the nucleus angularis in crocodilians and turtles, and the caudal part is similar to the magnocellular nucleus of these taxa. However, the caudal part of the anterior cochlear nucleus lacks the large cells characterizing the magnocellular nuclei of crocodilians, turtles and some lizards.

The nucleus cochlearis posterior of lizards (Beccari, 1912; lagenar nucleus of Glatt, 1975b) is the most caudal cochlear nucleus (Figs 1–3, 7). It often extends lateral to the magnocellular nucleus (Fig. 7), from which it can be distinguished by a fine, dense fiber plexus. The posterior cochlear nucleus consists of medium, star-shaped cells distributed throughout the fiber plexus. This nucleus is particularly well developed in *Anniella*, burrowing skinks, burrowing snakes, and amphisbaenians.

All snakes that I have examined, with the exception of *Cylindrophis*, possess a single cochlear nucleus. The cochlear region of *Cylindrophis* is divided into anterior and posterior nuclei as is that of most lizards. Most other snakes possess a cochlear nucleus that does not protrude into the fourth ventricle to form an acoustic eminence; however, the burrowing snakes (Uropeltidae, Aniliidae and Xenopeltidae) do have an eminence. The cochlear nucleus of snakes consists of medium and large cells embedded among heavily myelinated fibers. The cochlear nucleus of advanced snakes appears slightly reduced in comparison to the size of the other medullar nuclei. The homology of this nucleus in snakes with the cochlear nuclei of other reptiles requires experimental data on the termination of basilar and lagenar fibers in these taxa.

F. COCHLEAR CONNECTIONS

Experimental studies on the projections of the cochlear fibers only exist for *Caiman* (Leake, 1974), *Tupinambis* (DeFina and Webster, 1974), *Ameiva* (Miller, 1975) and *Iguana* (Foster and Hall, 1978). In *Caiman*, the ipsilateral cochlear projections terminate in nucleus angularis, nucleus magnocellularis and in the neuropil above nucleus laminaris. Miller (1975) recognized four subdivisions in the cochlear area of *Ameiva* (nucleus angularis, nucleus laminaris, and lateral and medial divisions of nucleus magnocellularis) and reported that all four of these nuclei received direct ipsilateral cochlear terminals. DeFina and Webster (1974) and Foster and Hall (1978) recognized three subdivisions in *Tupinambis* and *Iguana* (nucleus angularis, nucleus laminaris, and nucleus magnocellularis). Both studies reported ipsilateral cochlear projections to the nucleus angularis and the nucleus magnocellularis, but not to the nucleus laminaris.

Traditionally, three additional rhombencephalic nuclei have been considered to form cochlear connections of higher order; namely the nucleus of the lateral lemniscus, the superior olive and the nucleus (ganglion) isthmi. In most reptiles, fibers are traced ventrolaterally from the cochlear nuclei into the tegmentum where they take up a superficial position and turn rostrally to enter the torus semicircularis of the midbrain. This fiber bundle is termed the lateral lemniscus. At the entry of the lateral lemniscus into the caudal midbrain (isthmus) it shows one to two small nuclear groups embedded within it. These are termed the nuclei of the lateral lemniscus (Figs 1, 14) and, in *Iguana*, receive afferents from the contralateral cochlear nuclei and form reciprocal connections with the torus semicircularis (Foster and Hall, 1978).

Most reptiles have a superior olivary cell group (Figs 7, 8, 14) lying in the tegmentum ventral to the entry of the statoacoustic nerve (van Hoevell, 1911; Tuge, 1932; Gillaspy, 1954, 1958; Ebbesson, 1967). This nucleus receives an ipsilateral projection from the cochlear nuclei in *Caiman* (Leake,

1976) and in *Iguana* (Foster and Hall, 1978). In *Iguana*, the superior olive projects bilaterally to the central nucleus of the torus semicircularis (Foster and Hall, 1978).

The ganglion or nucleus isthmi, a prominent nucleus of the caudal midbrain (Figs 1, 4), is divided into a superficial magnocellular and an inner parvocellular part. The nucleus isthmi is reduced in snakes in which it may retain only a few cells. In all reptiles, the nuclei appear interconnected by a commissure that passes immediately caudal to the trochlear decussation. Nucleus isthmi was earlier believed to receive terminals from the lateral lemniscus and was homologized with the medial geniculate nucleus of mammals (Papez, 1935). However, recent experimental studies have not revealed such cochlear connections (Leake, 1976; Foster and Hall, 1978) but have demonstrated reciprocal connections with the optic tectum (Foster and Hall, 1975).

In most mammals, the cochlear root of the statoacoustic nerve contains efferent as well as afferent fibers (Rasmussen, 1946). The periolivary nuclei of mammals are medullary nuclei that receive projections from the auditory portion of the inferior colliculus and give rise to efferents that terminate in the cochlear nucleus and on hair cells. These fibers are believed to be inhibitory and to enhance the discrimination of a particular frequency (Fex, 1968). An efferent cochlear bundle has been identified in *Alligator* (Gillaspy, 1958) and birds (Boord, 1961). In *Alligator* the cells of origin are believed to lie in the superior olive (Gillaspy, 1958).

VI. Trigeminal System

A. GENERAL

The nuclei of the trigeminal nerve consist of both motor and sensory nuclei. The motor nucleus is relatively simple and compact. The sensory nuclei consist of a principal sensory nucleus at the entrance of the nerve, a mesencephalic nucleus located in the optic tectum and a descending nucleus running caudally to the cervical level of the spinal cord.

The trigeminal nerve enters the rhombencephalon between the isthmus and the entrance of the VIIIth nerve. In all reptiles, except turtles, the Vth and the VIIIth nerves lie close together (Fig. 4).

Most of the trigeminal nuclei are situated within the region of the nerve entrance, occupying a medial position in the brain wall. The caudal portion of the trigeminal complex is bounded dorsally by the vestibular nuclei and ventrally by the reticular and tegmental systems. The isthmal region rostral to the trigeminal nuclei is termed the pretrigeminal part of the rhombencephalon (Figs. 1–4).

B. Trigeminal Motor Nucleus

The trigeminal motor nucleus innervates a large part of the head and jaw muscles and is well developed in all reptiles. This nucleus is easily identified by its large and typical motor neurons. Cytoarchitectonic differentiation is greatest in crocodilians. In addition to the large motor neurons, there are many small and medium-sized cells. Among all other reptilian groups, but especially in those taxa comprising species with small body size, the nucleus consists almost exclusively of polygonal motor neurons. The trigeminal motor nucleus of many reptiles has two divisions (Ariëns Kappers, 1910; de Lange, 1916; Black, 1920; Huber and Crosby, 1916; Ariëns Kappers *et al.*, 1936; Woodburne, 1936; Gillaspy, 1954; Ulinski, 1973). A central part (Woodburne, 1936) lies near the ventricle, immediately lateral to the periventricular system (Figs 1, 2, 7). The cells of the central part are often somewhat smaller than those of the peripheral one, which lies ventrolaterally. The cells of the peripheral part are arranged more or less radially, with strong fiber connections to the most lateral, longitudinal fiber tracts (spinocerebellar and tectobulbar tracts). In turtles, these subdivisions are absent or only rudimentary (*Chrysemys*, *Sternotherus*) (Fig. 4).

The greatest variation of the motor nucleus occurs in lizards. Central and peripheral divisions can be identified although they are often in close contact. The nucleus is further subdivided and varies in many species. Frequently, there is a caudal division containing smaller cells. Burrowing snakes (Uropeltidae, Aniliidae and Xenopeltidae) have central and peripheral divisions, whereas typhlopids and leptotyphlopids resemble the other snakes in having a single, compact column of motor neurons.

C. Principal Sensory Trigeminal Nucleus

The principal sensory nucleus is located immediately dorsal to the trigeminal motor nucleus and occupies approximately the same rostrocaudal extent as the entering trigeminal root. The nucleus consists of small to medium-sized, spindle-shaped cells. The caudal boundary between the principal nucleus and the nucleus of the descending tract is indistinct; if it exists at all, it can only be defined functionally. A close relationship between the principal sensory nucleus and nucleus of the descending tract must be assumed. In turtles, the principal sensory nucleus is poorly developed and diffuse. Crocodilians have a large, compact nucleus. In lizards, the nucleus is moderate to large. In snakes, the nucleus is large, often diffuse yet densely packed. In crotalid snakes, the sensory nuclei have hypertrophied, as the pit organs are innervated by the trigeminal nerve (Molenaar, 1978a, b). An unusual feature of the principal nucleus in many squamates is the presence of large, polygonal cells in the caudal and dorsal part of the nucleus. Lizards possess few of these large cells, but in snakes these cells are conspicuous and occur in groups. Their function is presently unknown.

D. DESCENDING TRIGEMINAL TRACT AND NUCLEUS

Upon entering the brain, a major portion of the trigeminal sensory fibers turn caudally and course down the medulla as a prominent semilunar-shaped bundle (Figs 2, 3). This descending trigeminal tract is traced to the caudal sensory fields of the Xth nerve; here it turns dorsally, intermingling with the caudal medullary nuclei. Some fibers may continue as far caudally as rostral, cervical spinal levels (de Lange, 1916; Huber and Crosby, 1926; Ariëns Kappers et al., 1936; Woodburne, 1936; Kruger and Witkovsky, 1961; Robinson, 1969).

A descending trigeminal nucleus lies medially along the entire rostro-caudal length of the descending trigeminal tract. Both nucleus and tract fuse with the caudal medullary sensory fields. Boids and crotalids have an additional lateral nucleus associated with the pit organs (Molenaar, 1974, 1978a, b).

The sensory fibers arising from the skin of the posterior aspect of the head (vagus nerve) do not terminate in the sensory vagal nucleus (nucleus solitarius) but within the descending trigeminal nucleus. In mammals, such components are also seen in the facial and glossopharyngeal nerves (Torvik, 1950; Taren, 1964; Culberson and Kimmel, 1972; Iwata et al., 1972). The entire descending tract and its nucleus, as well as the principal sensory nucleus, are concerned with the primary integration of sensory information from the surface of the head. Tactile and joint responses have been demonstrated electrophysiologically in *Alligator* (Kruger and Witkovsky, 1961). Responses to temperature and pain have also been recorded in mammals, as has proprioceptive input from the muscle spindles of the eye muscles to the rostral portion of the descending trigeminal nucleus (Manni et al., 1972).

Somatotopic representation via the different branches of the trigeminal nerve and their sensory fields is well known in mammals. In *Alligator*, a somatotopic pattern comparable to that for cats is reported by Kruger and Witkovsky (1961). The three trigeminal divisions are arranged in lamellae. The mandibular division is represented dorsally and medially in the nucleus and occupies the largest part of the nucleus. Maxillary and ophthalmic branches are presented successively ventrally.

E. TRIGEMINAL CONNECTIONS

No experimental information presently exists for the efferents of the trigeminal sensory nuclei. The older descriptive literature has been summarized by Huber and Crosby (1926) and Woodburne (1936). Connections are believed to exist to the cerebellum, the vestibular nuclei and the underlying tegmental cellular fields. The trigeminal motor nucleus connects to the caudal medulla and spinal cord.

A trigeminal lemniscus arising from the principal and descending nucleus is believed to form in the ventrolateral tegmentum, medial to the lateral lemniscus, and to ascend to higher centers. Connections are believed to exist with the torus semicircularis and optic tectum. It is not known whether a quinto-frontal tract exists in reptiles as in birds, in which the principal trigeminal nucleus projects directly into a basal telencephalic nucleus (Cohen and Karten, 1974).

F. Mesencephalic Trigeminal System

The fibers of the mesencephalic trigeminal root enter the brain with the trigeminal motor branches. Upon entering the rhombencephalon, the bundle courses toward the ventricle where it turns rostrally, continuing through the pretrigeminal region toward the isthmus. The tract then passes through the decussating trochlear nerve, without decussating itself, and continues toward the torus semicircularis. There it splits into small fiber bundles ascending over the caudal surface or, lateral to the tori, into the optic tectum. The cell bodies of the mesencephalic trigeminal nucleus lie along the sagittal axis of the tectum as far rostrally as the posterior commissure. The cells of the mesencephalic trigeminal nucleus are located within the periventricular gray of the tectum, mostly adjacent to the stratum album centrale. Their heavily myelinated fibers run within the central fiber layer ventrally and caudally, often in association with the tectobulbar bundles. The mesencephalic trigeminal cells are larger than the normal periventricular cells and stain intensely.

This nucleus is divided into medial and lateral divisions in reptiles (Huber and Crosby, 1926; Weinberg, 1928; Ariëns Kappers et al., 1936; Woodburne, 1936; Goldstein and Jacobs, 1969). The cells of the lateral division are often somewhat larger than those of the medial. Variation in cell number, cell density and topography of the two divisions are illustrated in Figs 10–13. Crocodilians possess an intermediate part, just caudal to the posterior commissure, in addition to lateral and medial divisions. Turtles have a medial division with high cell density and a weakly developed lateral division. Snakes present the reverse picture. In lizards, the lateral and medial divisions are always well developed but vary greatly among different species. At present, there is no functional explanation for the striking variation observed in this nucleus among reptiles.

Earlier descriptions of the mesencephalic trigeminal nucleus are sum-

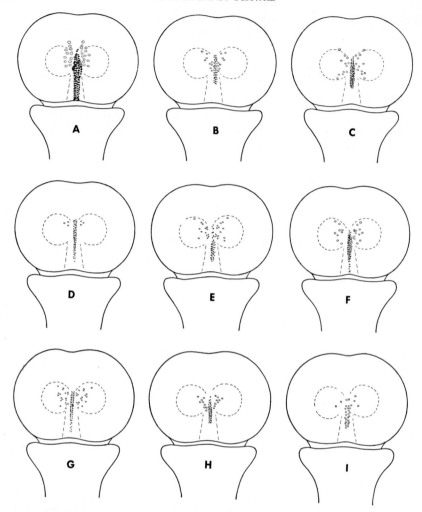

FIG. 10. Distribution of the cells of the mesencephalic trigeminal nucleus in lizards: (A) *Heloderma suspectum*; (B) *Ptyodactylus hasselquistii*; (C) *Cordylus cordylus*; (D) *Anolis carolinensis*; (E) *Gerrhosaurus nigrolineatus*; (F) *Platysaurus guttatus*; (G) *Basiliscus* sp.; (H) *Gerrhosaurus validus*; (I) *Gekko gecko*.
In Figs 10–13, open and solid circles indicate, respectively, the lateral and medial divisions of the nucleus.

marized by Weinberg (1928) and Ariëns Kappers *et al.* (1936). More recently, electrophysiological and degeneration data have accumulated (Goldstein and Jacobs, 1969; Desole *et al.*, 1970). The mesencephalic trigeminal system is concerned mainly, if not exclusively, with jaw proprioceptive functions. Direct responses of mesencephalic trigeminal cells occur to

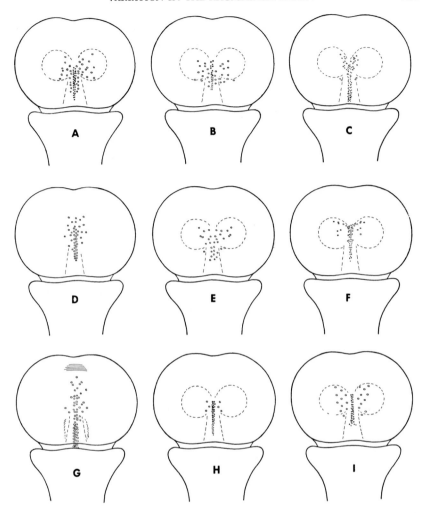

Fig. 11. Distribution of the cells of the mesencephalic trigeminal nucleus in lizards (A–C, E, F, H and I), an amphisbaenian (D) and a snake (G): (A) *Varanus indicus*; (B) *Chalcides ocellatus*; (C) *Dipsosaurus dorsalis*; (D) *Amphisbaena caeca*; (E) *Cnemidophorus tigris*; (F) *Iguana iguana*; (G) *Cylindrophis rufus*; (H) *Tupinambis nigropunctatus*; (I) *Lacerta sicula*.

lowering of the jaw or stretching of the masseter muscle in *Caiman* (Desole *et al.*, 1970). This response demonstrates that at least a portion of the mesencephalic trigeminal cells are first-order afferent neurons from masseteric muscle spindles. A similar response occurs in mammals and birds. However,

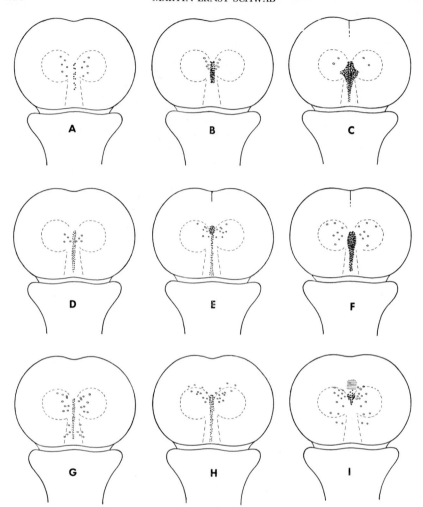

Fig. 12. Distribution of the cells of the mesencephalic trigeminal nucleus in lizards (A, D, E, G and H), the tuatara (B), turtles (C and F) and a crocodilian: (A) *Gerrhonotus multicarinatus*; (B) *Sphenodon punctatus*; (C) *Chelydra serpentina*; (D) *Anniella pulchra*; (E) *Uromastyx* sp.; (F) *Chrysemys picta*; (G) *Chamaeleo chamaeleon*; (H) *Agama mutabilis*; (I) *Caiman crocodilus*.

it remains to be determined which individual reptilian muscles are involved, and whether they possess somatotopic representation in the mesencephalic nucleus, as do those of cats and squirrel monkeys (Smith *et al.*, 1967).

Axons of the mesencephalic trigeminal neurons and their collaterals are believed to form contacts with tectal cells and with the trigeminal sensory

FIG. 13. Distribution of the cells of the mesencephalic trigeminal nucleus in snakes: (A) *Nerodia sipedon*; (B) *Xenopeltis unicolor*; (C) *Leptotyphlops humilis*; (D) *Vipera aspis*; (E) *Boa constrictor*; (F) *Typhlops vermicularis*; (G) *Natrix natrix*; (H) *Teretrurus rhodogaster*.

and motor nuclei in *Lacerta* (Goldstein and Jacobs, 1969). A small post-trigeminal bundle extends caudally giving off fibers to the facial motor nucleus, the nucleus of the descending trigeminal tract, and the vagal motor nucleus. However, these fiber contributions are very small, and the remainder of this small bundle distributes to the upper cervical spinal segments. There are no connections with the oculomotor or trochlear nuclei.

VII. Tegmental Regions

A. General

The mesencephalic and rhombencephalic floors consist of complex, longitudinal ascending and descending tracts and a series of more or less cytoarchitectonically distinct cell groups. This complex region is usually defined as the brainstem tegmentum and is divided into midbrain and medullary tegmental fields for purposes of description.

B. Nuclei of the Midbrain Tegmentum

The most rostrally occurring nuclei of the midbrain tegmentum are associated with the medial longitudinal fasciculus (Figs 1–4). A periventricular band of small to medium-sized cells, termed the nucleus of the medial longitudinal fasciculus, lies medially adjacent to the most rostral fibers of the medial longitudinal fasciculus in *Pseudemys* (Tuge, 1932). More laterally is a second population of larger polygonal cells, termed the interstitial nucleus of the medial longitudinal fasciculus. Both the medial and interstitial nuclei contribute axons to the medial longitudinal fasciculus, and both nuclei occur in all reptiles. Frequently these nuclei are not recognized as separate entities in many descriptions, and both names have been used to describe a composite of the two cellular groups.

At this same midbrain level in all reptiles, there is a more ventrolaterally located nucleus, termed the nucleus of the basal optic root. This nucleus is located immediately beneath the surface of the midbrain and consists of medium-sized cells embedded in a dense neuropil. The nucleus of the basal optic root receives a visual input via a distinct basal optic root which arises rostrally from the marginal optic tract (de Lange, 1913; Huber and Crosby, 1926; Senn, 1968). The axons of this nucleus are traced medially where they course toward the nucleus of the medial longitudinal fasciculus and the oculomotor nucleus. No experimental information is presently available for the efferents of this nucleus in reptiles.

A red nucleus is seen in all reptiles immediately adjacent to the nucleus of the basal optic root (Figs 1, 4). This nucleus lies in the middle of the midbrain floor, lateral to the rostral pole of the oculomotor nucleus. The red nucleus consists of large, multipolar cells and smaller reticular cells. A brief description of the ultrastructure of these cells exists for *Testudo* (Ovtscharoff, 1972). The reptilian nucleus is usually homologized to the magnocellular part of the mammalian nucleus. The red nucleus is well developed in most reptiles, except in snakes where it has only a few cells.

The red nucleus is believed to receive afferents from the cerebellum via the brachium conjunctivum. A descending uncrossed rubrospinal tract has been experimentally demonstrated in lizards and turtles, but appears to be absent in snakes (Robinson, 1969; ten Donkelaar, 1976a, b).

The caudal, lateral wall of the reptilian midbrain is characterized by a field of small, loosely scattered cells embedded in the ascending and descending tectal fibers. This field has been variously defined by different workers. Traditionally, this area has been divided into a dorsal area, termed nucleus lateralis profundus mesencephali, and a ventral area, termed the mesencephalic reticular nucleus (Figs 1, 4). In *Tupinambis*, the dorsal region has been called nucleus lateralis profundus (Ebbesson, 1967) and in *Iguana*, pars dorsolateralis of nucleus profundus mesencephali (Distel, 1973). In turtles and squamates, a dorsal portion of this region adjacent to the torus semicircularis, receives spinal input and is termed the intercollicular nucleus (Ebbesson, 1967, 1969).

The caudal midbrain floor of all reptiles is characterized by a distinct midline nucleus termed the interpeduncular ganglion or nucleus (Figs 1, 4). It generally consists of two cellular layers separated by a zone of fine fibers and its main input appears to arise from the habenula via a massive tract (fasciculus retroflexus) which enters the rostral pole of the nucleus. The fasciculus varies in size, as does the interpeduncular nucleus (Nagasaki, 1954; Tamura *et al.*, 1955). The nucleus is believed to possess extensive efferents terminating in the more caudal tegmentum, but no experimental studies exist for reptiles.

C. Medullary Tegmental System

The medullary tegmental fields consist of lateral paired reticular fields and midline raphé nuclei (Figs 1–4, 14). I have adapted a modified nomenclature after Van Hoevell (1911) to describe this area, as did Ebbesson (1967, 1969).

A dense reticular fiber system containing small scattered cells characterizes the medullary floor rostral to the trigeminal nuclei (superior reticular nucleus, Fig. 14). Rostrally, this pretrigeminal region grades over to the reticular field of the caudal mesencephalon. The rostral part of the pretrigeminal field lacks large polygonal cells, but very large polygonal cells begin to appear among the smaller cells of the caudal part (Fig. 14). At the level of the entry of the eighth cranial nerve, a medial reticular nucleus is distinguishable (Fig. 14), and contains giant cells seen toward the midline. More caudally, the large cells increase in density and this condensation is termed the inferior reticular nucleus (Fig. 14). The lateral reticular nucleus is a more lateral region of smaller cells lying along the rostrocaudal extent

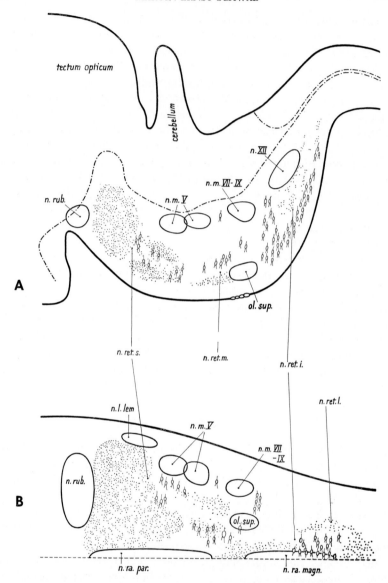

FIG. 14. Cell groups of the medullary tegmental nuclei of *Lacerta sicula* in lateral (A) and dorsal (B) views. The dots indicate small cell bodies and the stylized neurons giant ones. n.l.lem., Nucleus of lateral lemniscus; n.m.V, motor trigeminal nucleus; n.ra.magn., nucleus raphe magnocellularis; n.ra.par., nucleus raphe parvocellularis; n.ret.i., nucleus reticularis inferior; n.ret.l., nucleus reticularis lateralis; n.ret.m., nucleus reticularis medius; n.ret.s., nucleus reticularis superior; n.rub., nucleus ruber; n.m.VII–IX, motor nucleus of facial and glossopharyngeal nerves; n.XII, nucleus of nervus hypoglossus; ol.sup., superior olive.

of the larger, more medial cell group. The reticular cells have connections with all of the adjacent systems and many of the ascending and descending fiber tracts of the tegmentum. Connections of the large, polygonal cells with the medial longitudinal fasciculus are common. The superior and inferior reticular nuclei project ipsi- and contralaterally to the spinal cord, especially via the lateral funiculus (Robinson, 1969). Spinal input into the entire tegmental system is shown by degeneration studies (Goldby and Robinson, 1962; Ebbesson, 1967, 1969). A different nomenclature, proposed by Beccari (1922) and Stefanelli (1944), was used by Goldby and Robinson (1962) in their degeneration studies. These authors described a metencephalic tegmental center, which corresponds to the superior and medial reticular nuclei of the present account, and a myelencephalic center that corresponds to my inferior reticular nucleus. Tuge (1932) has extensively described the reticular nuclei in *Chrysemys* and, like Herrick (1930), proposed a distinction between motor tegmental nuclei and reticular nuclei with "correlation" functions. Such functional speculations cannot be evaluated until we have considerable experimental anatomical and physiological information regarding the organization of the reptilian reticular system.

Cellular accumulation in the midline, or raphé, is a consistent feature of the reptilian medulla oblongata. A gross topographical subdivision into a more rostral or parvocellular nucleus, and a more caudal or magnocellular nucleus is found throughout the class (Figs 1, 14). However, the subdivisions vary considerably.

The parvocellular nucleus of the raphé begins immediately caudal to the isthmus. Although the nucleus is characterized by a high cell density, the cells are small in lizards and turtles, but frequently larger than the pretrigeminal reticular cells of *Caiman* and snakes. A fine fiber plexus lies between the cells and along both sides of the nucleus. Frequently, these cells are arranged in two parallel vertical sheaths, rather than a single midline layer. This is a pattern reminiscent of the embryonic condition wherein the cells of the raphé nucleus migrate from the reticular fields of both sides (Schwab and Durand, 1974). The pars parvocellularis decreases in size and becomes continuous with the magnocellular nucleus near the level of the trigeminal region.

The more caudal magnocellular nucleus of the raphé is less pronounced than the parvocellular nucleus. At the level of the eighth nerve, few cells are present in the midline; more caudally, there is a cluster of giant neurons in the dorsal part of the raphe. At the level of the inferior reticular nucleus, large polygonal and medium-sized cells are concentrated in the raphé; however, the caudal raphé nucleus is more or less continuous laterally with the inferior reticular nucleus (Fig. 14).

In most reptiles, a group of spindle-shaped cells lies adjacent to the mesencephalic trigeminal root, within the pretrigeminal region immediately caudal to the isthmus. Van Hoevell (1911) called this cell group the nucleus loci coerulei, implying that it is homologous to the same-named nucleus in mammals; this idea still requires experimental confirmation. Locus coeruleus, and related monoaminergic systems are discussed in detail in Chapter 6.

D. Tegmental Fiber Systems

Based on descriptive material, the fiber systems coursing through the reptilian tegmentum can be divided into three general groups: (1) longitudinal tracts, (2) decussating systems or commissures, and (3) a periventricular fiber system.

The three major longitudinal tracts that characterize the reptilian tegmentum are: (i) the medial longitudinal fasciculus, (ii) reciprocal tracts between the spinal cord and the reticular formation, and (iii) the lemniscal systems. The medial longitudinal fasciculus may constitute the most important longitudinal tract. It begins rostrally, immediately caudal to the nucleus of the medial longitudinal fasciculus, and is joined by ascending and descending fibers from various medullary systems before coursing to the caudal end of the spinal cord (Figs 1–4, 15). In the ventral, more superficial, portion of the tegmentum, descending longitudinal tracts are efferent from the tectum, vestibular and reticular nuclei to other regions of the reticular nuclei and spinal cord. The most important ascending systems are the lemniscal tracts running more dorsally and laterally. These consist of fibers arising from the dorsal column nuclei, spinal cord, trigeminal sensory nuclei and auditory nuclei, and coursing to reticular, midbrain and thalamic centers.

Decussating fibers are observed at nearly all levels of the rhombencephalon (Fig. 15). The mesencephalic tegmentum is characterized by ventrally decussating tectobulbar and tectospinal tracts. A more dorsal band of decussating fibers, termed the dorsal arcuate fibers and associated with the nuclei of the eighth cranial nerve, characterize the medulla. These regions of complex decussating fibers and commissures are generally unlabeled in Fig. 15 because the several commissures or decussating fiber systems cannot be identified without experimental information. However, a general idea of the complexity of this region is gained when these fibers system are mapped.

Connections with the periventricular system are known for many of the systems of the rhombencephalon. A dense layer of fine fibers underlies the ependyma and varies in thickness in a rostrocaudal extent in the medulla, as well as among different taxa. The entire periventricular system is less developed in turtles than in other reptiles. Maximal development is seen in squamates, particularly in the larger species.

The periventricular fiber system is best developed in the mesencephalon, where it is continuous with the inner layers of the torus semicircularis and the periventricular zones of the optic tectum. The thick layer continues caudally through the isthmus and the pretrigeminal region where it decreases in size with the appearance of the otic system. More caudally, it consists of only a small fiber band. It continues caudally to the beginning of the vagal region where it again increases in volume. The floor and lateral walls of the fourth ventricle are characterized by a distinct periventricular fiber system, which appears to end at rostral cervical spinal levels.

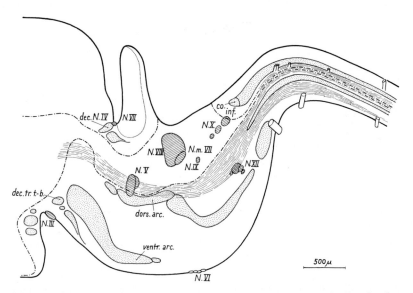

FIG. 15. Midsagittal reconstruction of the rhombencephalic commissures in *Lacerta sicula*. Hatched areas indicate transected cranial nerve roots and stippled areas the commissures. Most of the commissures are unlabeled because the exact sources of the decussating tracts are unknown. co.inf., Commissure infima; dec.N.IV, decussation of nervus trochlearis; dec.tr.t.-b., decussation of tractus tecto-bulbaris; dors.arc., dorsal arcuates; N.III through N.X., entry of the third through the tenth cranial nerves; N.XII, entry of the twelfth cranial nerve; N.m.VII, motor root of nervus facialis; ventr. arc., ventral arcuate fibers.

A clearly identifiable layer of smaller, round cells accompanies the periventricular fiber system in its rostral part, and these cells either form a layer or are distributed among the fibers. The cells of the periventricular gray may play an important role in mediating connections from the tegmental areas to the periventricular fiber system and vice versa (Huber and Crosby, 1926; Tuge, 1932). Following spinal cord hemisection in *Tupinambis*, the mesencephalic periventricular gray displays moderate terminal degeneration (Ebbesson, 1967).

The cells underlying the periventricular fiber system in the regions of the trigeminal and VIIIth nerves correspond, at least in part, to undifferentiated, pluripotent cells. They constitute a germinal layer, a remnant of the pro-liferating embryonic matrix (Kirsche, 1967). These cells retain their capacity for mitosis, and Kirsche and coworkers have shown their importance in regeneration processes among different vertebrates.

VIII. Extrinsic Eye Muscle Nuclei

The extrinsic eye muscles (superior and inferior oblique muscles and the anterior, superior, posterior and inferior rectus muscles) are innervated by three cranial nerves, the oculomotor (III), trochlear (IV), and abducens (VI). Most of the muscles are related to the oculomotor nerve. The superior oblique muscle is innervated by the trochlear nerve, while the posterior rectus muscle is supplied by the abducens. In addition to this well-known pattern, the abducens innervates the musculus retractor bulbi, and the oculo-motor nerve sends a branch to the ciliary ganglion of the eye. Further nerve supply to the ciliary ganglion arises from the ophthalmic ramus of the profundus nerve (Watkinson, 1906; Terni, 1921; Soliman, 1964).

The nuclei of these nerves are found at different levels of the rhombence-phalon. The oculomotor nucleus lies in the mesencephalic tegmentum together with the trochlear nucleus, which extends into the isthmic region. The cells of nucleus abducens are located at mid-medullary levels. The most remarkable common feature of the nuclei is their periventricular position. Each is closely associated with the medial longitudinal fasciculus. The unusual functional similarity of these nuclei would suggest an extremely well developed system of connections. From their consistent relation-ship with the medial longitudinal fasciculus, this fiber system would appear to be the internuclear pathway. In fact, many fibers from the eye muscle nuclei are seen coursing in the medial longitudinal fasciculus. Efferent vestibular fibers also ascend in the medial longitudinal fasciculus (Baker and Precht, 1972; Precht and Baker, 1972). It is unlikely that any of the medial longitudinal fascicular fibers are true internuclear connections effected by axons of corresponding nerve cells. Medullary input, especially from the vestibular nuclei, probably accounts for the majority of the fibers. However, information among all nuclei may be transmitted through col-laterals of these fibers. In mammals, afferents from the eye muscle spindles travel with the trigeminal, but not with eye muscle nerves (Baker and Precht, 1972; Manni et al., 1972). A similar condition likely exists in reptiles.

The oculomotor nucleus is a sharply delineated cell group in all reptiles, and consists of fairly large multipolar, often rounded motor neurons lying dorsal and medial to the medial longitudinal fasciculus. Its axons course ventrally, partly through the medial longitudinal fasciculus, and the nerve leaves the brain caudal to the plica ventralis, and anterior to, or at, the rostral pole of the interpeduncular nucleus. Most of the axons are uncrossed, but a small number of axons decussate and exit the contralateral oculomotor nerve.

The oculomotor nucleus consists of four divisions in all reptiles, except snakes (Tuge, 1932; Senn, 1966). The dorsal, intermediate and ventral parts are distinguished only by their position, as the cells are of nearly the same type (Fig. 16). The pars dorsalis constitutes the rostral and caudal

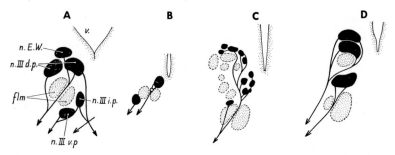

Fig. 16. Subdivisions of the oculomotor nucleus in: (A) a lizard, *Lacerta sicula*; (B) a uropeltid snake, *Teretrurus rhodogaster*; (C) a boid snake, *Boa constrictor*; and (D) a colubrid snake, *Malpolon monspessulanus* (modified after Senn, 1966). flm, Fasciculus longitudinalis medialis; n.III d.p., dorsal part of nucleus III; n.III i.p., intermediate part of nucleus III; n.III v.p., ventral part of nucleus III; n.E.W., nucleus Edinger–Westphal; v., ventricle.

pole of the nucleus, and is the largest division of the nucleus. The small intermediate part lies ventral and medial to the medial longitudinal fasciculus (Fig. 16A). Caudally, it often fuses with the ventral cell group. The ventral part lies ventral to the medial longitudinal fasciculus and often fuses with the contralateral pars ventralis of the nucleus. The Edinger–Westphal nucleus (nucleus III accessorius) comprises a fourth division of the oculomotor nucleus. This division is located dorsal and rostral to the remainder of the nucleus, and consists of smaller, round cells lying in a fine, dense fiber plexus. In mammals and birds, the accessory nucleus forms connections with the ciliary ganglion, as is probably true for reptiles (Ariëns Kappers *et al.*, 1936). Snakes lack an Edinger–Westphal nucleus, a condition probably correlated with reduction in size of the ciliary body (Senn, 1966; Walls, 1967). The same subdivisions of the oculomotor nucleus are seen in crocodilians and lizards. However, the nucleus of turtles is often of limited cell density and definition of subnuclei is often unclear.

Snakes do not show a similar pattern. In the burrowing forms (Aniliidae, Uropeltidae, Xenopeltidae), the eye muscle nuclei are reduced in size, but divisions comparable to those in lizards exist. In advanced snakes, nuclei attain a considerable size, but only one or two subdivisions—dorsal and ventral—can be identified (Fig. 16D). Homology with the oculomotor subdivisions of other reptiles is doubtful. These features in snakes closely agree with the phylogenetic theory of origin from burrowing ancestors with reduced vision (Senn, 1966; Walls, 1967).

The oculomotor nucleus receives an important input from the nucleus of the basal optic root. Fibers course horizontally through the tegmentum, from the superficial nucleus of the basal optic root to the oculomotor nucleus. The nucleus of the basal optic root receives a direct retinal input, thus this pathway serves as an important reflex pathway for eye movements.

The trochlear nucleus is located in the isthmic region caudal to the oculomotor complex (Figs 1, 4) and extends only a short distance. The cells of the trochlear nucleus are similar to those of the oculomotor nucleus, but are often a little larger. A dense fiber plexus, intimately related to the medial longitudinal fasciculus, is always present, as are connections with the periventricular fiber system and fibers running toward the tegmentum. A perplexing feature of the trochlear system is the exit of the nerve root, which proceeds dorsally from the nucleus. The heavily myelinated fibers are quite conspicuous and completely decussate where they exit the brain dorsally. No explanation has accounted for this unique decussation in vertebrates.

The abducens nucleus differs from the nuclei of the other eye muscles, both in position and cellular differentiation: however, like the other nuclei, it has a close relationship with the medial longitudinal fasciculus. The abducens nucleus extends through the rostral and middle portions of the medulla (Figs 1, 4, 7). In lizards and snakes, it is relatively compact; in crocodilians, it consists of scattered cells lying adjacent to the medial longitudinal fasciculus. In turtles, delimitation from tegmental cell groups is not always clear. The cells are multipolar motor neurons of medium size, the axons of which leave the brain ventrally as several small bundles.

An accessory abducens nucleus was reported in *Chalcides*, as well as in a number of other vertebrates (Terni, 1921; Addens, 1933). This nucleus is described as lying laterally, near the descending trigeminal tract, and is said to give rise to axons that exit with the principal abducens root and innervate the retractor bulbi muscle. I have been unable to recognise such an accessory nucleus in my material.

IX. Discussion and Summary

There are few existing data on the organization and variation of the reptilian rhombencephalon due, in large part, to lack of general surveys and the absence of a unified nomenclature. The present investigation has attempted to remedy this situation. During this study, attention focused on a comparison of many species spread over a wide systematic range. The results indicate only minor differences among species or families.

The squamates exhibit the greatest rhombencephalic variation, with the cochlear nuclei being the most variable rhombencephalic area. Turtles exhibit the most generalized pattern of rhombencephalic organization; whereas crocodilians possess the most differentiated rhombencephalon, comparable in most aspects—particularly cochlear development—to that of birds. Lizards exhibit two distinct patterns of cochlear development, namely a generalized pattern, consisting of anterior and posterior nuclei and a more specialized pattern characterizing agamids, chamaeleonids, iguanids, teiids and varanids. In the more specialized pattern, the anterior nucleus appears to have hypertrophied and subdivided, forming a condition similar to that in crocodilians where distinct rostral angular and magnocellular nuclei are seen. Amphisbaenians and *Cylindrophis* possess anterior and posterior cochlear nuclei similar to the generalized cochlear pattern of most lizards. All other snakes are characterized by a single cochlear nucleus, which suggests that ancestral snakes may have passed through a phase of cochlear regression and subsequent redevelopment. This possibility is further suggested by the ratio of the basilar papilla (small) to the lagenar macula (large). This condition is unique among reptiles. Snakes also exhibit reductions in the dorsal column system of the rhombencephalon, a condition likely related to the loss of limbs. Burrowing lizards with reduction or loss of limbs also exhibit similar trends. Such reductions are common; however, opposing trends also occur. Distinct subdivisions of the cochlear nuclei and trigeminal motor nucleus in crocodilians are most likely related to increased auditory sensitivity and fine motor control of jaw muscles in these taxa.

Continued sampling of the variation, particularly examinations utilizing increasingly sophisticated experimental neurobiological techniques, will likely reveal many such functional specializations in the reptilian rhombencephalon.

Acknowledgements

I am greatly indebted to Dr. R. G. Northcutt and Mrs. M. S. Northcutt (Ann Arbor) for their most helpful assistance in the preparation of the manuscript. Thanks are due to Mrs. M. Durand-Wenger for the histological preparations and to Drs C. Gans (Ann Arbor), D. G. Senn and W. Stingelin (Basel) for their support and encouragement. I am grateful to Mrs. S. Bousiani-Baur for preparing the drawings, and to Miss V. Forster for typing assistance.

MARTIN ERNST SCHWAB

References

Addens, J. L. (1933). The motor nuclei and roots of the cranial and first spinal nerves of vertebrates. Z. Anat. EntwGesch. 101, 307–410.

Ariëns Kappers, C. U. (1910). The migrations of the motor cells of the bulbar trigeminus, abducens and facialis in the series of vertebrates, and the differences in the course of the root fibers. Verh. K. Akad. Wet. 16, 1–195.

Ariëns Kappers, C. U. (1921). "Vergleichende Anatomie des Nervensystems." E. G. Bohn, Haarlem,

Ariëns Kappers, C. U., Huber, G. C. and Crosby, E. C. (1936). "The Comparative Anatomy of the Nervous System of Vertebrates, including Man." Hafner, New York.

Baird, I. L. (1970). The anatomy of the reptilian ear. In "Biology of the Reptilia." (C. Gans and T. S. Parsons, eds). Academic Press, London and New York, 2(2), 193–271.

Baker, R. and Precht, W. (1972). Electrophysiological properties of trochlear motoneurons as revealed by IVth nerve stimulation. Expl Brain Res. 14, 127–157.

Barnard, J. W. (1936). A phylogenetic study of the visceral afferent areas associated with the facial, glossopharyngeal, and vagus nerves, and their fiber connections. The efferent facial nucleus. J. comp. Neurol. 65, 503–602.

Beccari, N. (1912). La constituzione, i nuclei terminali e le vie di connessione del nervo acustico nella Lacerta muralis Merr. Archo. ital. Anat. Embriol. 10, 646–698.

Beccari, N. (1922). Studi comparativi sulla struttura del rombencefalo. Archo. ital. Anat. Embriol. 19, 122–291.

Bergquist, H. (1952). Transversal bands and migration areas in Lepidochelys olivacea. Kungl. Fysiogr. Sallsk. Handl. N.F. 63(13), 1–17.

Black, D. (1920). The motor nuclei of the cerebral nerves in phylogeny—a study of the phenomena of neurobiotaxis: reptiles. J. comp. Neurol. 32, 61–98.

Boord, R. L. (1961). The efferent cochlear bundle in the caiman and the pigeon. Expl Neurol. 3, 225–239.

Boord, R. L. (1968). Ascending projections of the primary cochlear nuclei and nucleus laminaris in the pigeon. J. comp. Neurol. 133, 523–542.

Boord, R. L. and Rasmussen, G. L. (1963). Projections of cochlear and lagenar nerves on the cochlear nuclei in the pigeon. J. comp. Neurol. 120, 463–475.

Caston, J. (1972). L'activité vestibulaire efférente chez la grenouille. Pflügers Arch. ges Physiol. 331, 365–370.

Cohen, D. H. and Karten, H. J. (1974). The structural organization of avian brain: an overview. In "Birds, Brain and Behavior." (J. I. Goodman and M. W. Schein, eds). Academic Press, New York and London, pp. 29–73.

Cohen, D. H., Schnall, A. M., Macdonald, R. L. and Pitts, L. H. (1970). Medullary cells of origin of vagal cardioinhibitory fibers in the pigeon. J. comp. Neurol. 140, 299–320.

Cruce, W. L. R. (1975). Termination of supraspinal descending pathways in the spinal cord of the tegu lizard (Tupinambis nigropunctatus). Brain, Behav. Evol. 12, 247–269.

Culberson, J. L. and Kimmel, D. L. (1972). Central distribution of primary afferent fibers of the glossopharyngeal and vagal nerves in the opossum, Didelphis virginiana. Brain Res. 44, 325–335.

DeFina, A. V. and Webster, D. B. (1974). Projections of the intraotic ganglion to the medullary nuclei in the tegu lizard, Tupinambis nigropunctatus. Brain, Behav. Evol. 10, 197–211.

de Lange, J. S. (1916). Das Hinterhirn, das Nachhirn und das Rückenmark der Reptilien. Folio neurobiol. 10, 385–422.

Desole, C., Palmieri, G. and Veggetti, A. (1970). Masticatory proprioception in reptilians (Caiman sclerops). Experientia 26, 376–377.

Distel, H. (1973). "Die Auslösbarkeit von Verhaltensreaktionen durch elektrische Hirnreizung bei *Iguana iguana* L., Reptilia." Doctoral dissertation, Ludwig-Maximilians Universität, Munich.

Ebbesson, S. O. E. (1967). Ascending axonal degeneration following hemisection of the spinal cord in the tegu lizard (*Tupinambis nigropunctatus*). *Brain Res.* 5, 178–206.

Ebbesson, S. O. E. (1969). Brain stem afferents from the spinal cord in a sample of reptilian and amphibian species. *Ann. N.Y. Acad. Sci.* 167, 80–101.

Evans, L. T. (1935). The development of the cochlea in the gecko, with special reference to the cochlea–lagena ratio and its bearing on vocality and social behaviour. *Anat. Rec.* 64, 187–201.

Fex, J. (1968). Efferent inhibition in the cochlea by the olivocochlear bundle. *In* "Hearing Mechanisms in Vertebrates." (A. V. S. de Rench and J. Knight, eds). J and A. Churchill, London, pp. 169–186.

Foster, R. E. and Hall, W. C. (1975). The connections and laminar organization of the optic tectum in a reptile (*Iguana iguana*). *J. comp. Neurol.* 163, 397–426.

Foster, R. E. and Hall, W. C. (1978). The organization of central auditory pathways in a reptile, *Iguana iguana. J. comp. Neurol.* 178, 783–832.

Gans, C. and Wever, E. G. (1972). The ear and hearing in Amphisbaenia (Reptilia). *J. exp. Zool.* 179, 17–34.

Gillaspy, C. C. (1954). Experimental study of the cranial motor nuclei in Reptilia. *J. comp. Neurol.* 100, 481–510.

Gillaspy, C. C. (1958). Superior olive in the alligator. *Proc. Soc. exp. Biol. Med.* 98, 492–494.

Glatt, A. (1975a). Vergleichend morphologische Untersuchungen am akustischen System einiger ausgewählter Reptilien. a. *Caiman crocodilus. Rev. Suisse Zool.* 82, 257–281.

Glatt, A. (1975b). Vergleichend morphologische Untersuchungen am akustischen System einiger ausgewählter Reptilien. b. Sauria und Testudines. *Rev. Suisse Zool.* 82, 469–494.

Goldby, F. and Robinson, L. R. (1962). The central connections of dorsal spinal nerve roots and the ascending tracts in the spinal cord of *Lacerta viridis. J. Anat.* 96, 153–170.

Goldstein, M. H. and Jacobs, V. L. (1969). The central projections of the mesencephalic root of the trigeminus in a lizard (*Lacerta viridis*). *Brain Res.* 14, 307–320.

Gribenski, A. (1970). L'innervation efferente du vestibule. *Ann. Otol. Rhinol.* 87, 77–92.

Herrick, C. J. (1899). The cranial and first spinal nerves of *Menidia*. A contribution upon the nerve components of the bony fishes. *J. comp. Neurol.* 9, 153–455.

Herrick, C. J. (1930). The medulla oblongata of *Necturus. J. comp. Neurol.* 50, 1–96.

Hindenach, J. C. R. (1931). The cerebellum of *Sphenodon punctatus. J. Anat. Physiol.* 65, 283–318.

His, W., Sr. (1888). Zur Geschichte des Gehirns sowie der centralen und peripherischen Nervenbahnen beim menschlichen Embryo. *Abh. math.-phys. Classe königl. Sächs. Ges. Wiss.* 14, 339–392.

Holmes, G. M. (1903). On the comparative anatomy of the nervus acusticus. *Trans. R. Irish Acad.* 32, 101–144.

Huber, G. C. and Crosby, E. C. (1926). On thalamic and tectal nuclei and fiber paths in the brain of the American alligator. *J. comp. Neurol.* 40, 97–227.

Iwata, N., Kitai, S. T. and Olson, S. (1972). Afferent component of the facial nerve: its relation to the spinal trigeminal and facial nucleus. *Brain Res.* 43, 662–667.

Johnston, J. B. (1902). An attempt to define the primitive functional divisions of the central nervous system. *J. comp. Neurol.* 12, 87–107.

Johnston, J. B. (1905). The morphology of the vertebrate head from the viewpoint of the functional divisions of the nervous system. *J. comp. Neurol.* **15**, 175–275.

Kirsche, W. (1967). Ueber postembryonale Matrixzonen im Gehirn verschiedener Vertebraten und deren Beziehung zur Hirnbauplanlehre. *Z. mikrosk.-anat. Forsch.* **77**, 313–406.

Kruger, L. and Witkovsky, P. (1961). A functional analysis in the dorsal column nuclei and the spinal nucleus of the trigeminal in the reptile (*Alligator mississippiensis*). *J. comp. Neurol.* **117**, 97–105.

Landmann, L. (1972). Bau und Ontogenese des vestibulären Systems bei *Lacerta sicula. Verh. naturf. Ges. Basel* **82**, 1–53.

Larsell, O. (1926). The cerebellum of reptiles: lizards and snakes. *J. comp. Neurol.* **41**, 59–94.

Larsell, O. (1932). The cerebellum of reptiles: chelonians and alligator. *J. comp. Neurol.* **56**, 299–345.

Leake, P. A. (1974). Central projections of the statoacoustic nerve in *Caiman crocodilus. Brain, Behav. Evol.* **10**, 170–196.

Leake, P. A. (1976). "Scanning Electron Microscopic Observations of Labyrinthine Sense Organs and Fiber Degeneration Studies of Secondary Vestibular and Auditory Pathways in *Caiman crocodilus.*" Doctoral Dissertation, Univ. Calif. San Francisco.

Manni, E., Palmieri, G. and Marini, R. (1972). Pontine trigeminal termination of proprioceptive afferents from eye muscles. *Expl Neurol.* **36**, 310–318.

Miller, M. R. (1966). The cochlear duct of lizards. *Proc. Calif. Acad. Sci.* **33**, 255–359.

Miller, M. R. (1967). Observations on the structure of the cochlear duct limbus of reptiles. *Proc. Calif. Acad. Sci.* **35**, 37–52.

Miller, M. R. (1968). The cochlear duct of snakes. *Proc. Calif. Acad. Sci.* **35**, 425–476.

Miller, M. R. (1972). A scanning EM study of the papilla basilaris of *Gekko gecko. Z. Zellforsch. mikrosk. Anat.* **136**, 307–328.

Miller, M. R. (1975). The cochlear nuclei of lizards. *J. comp. Neurol.* **159**, 375–406.

Molenaar, G. J. (1974). An additional trigeminal system in certain snakes possessing infrared receptors. *Brain Res.* **78**, 340–344.

Molenaar, G. J. (1978a). The sensory trigeminal system of a snake in the possession of infrared receptors. I. The sensory trigeminal nuclei. *J. comp. Neurol.* **179**, 123–136.

Molenaar, G. J. (1978b). The sensory trigeminal system of a snake in the possession of infrared receptors. II. The central projections of the trigeminal nerve. *J. comp. Neurol.* **179**, 137–152.

Nagasaki, T. (1954). On the fiber connection systems of the habenular nucleus in the ophidian brain. *Hirosh. J. med. Sci.* **4**, 113–135.

Ovtscharoff, W. (1972). Histochemie und Elektronen-mikroskopie des Nucleus ruber der Schildkröte (*Testudo hermanni*). *Histochemie* **29**, 240–247.

Papez, J. W. (1935). Thalamus of turtles and thalamic evolution. *J. comp. Neurol.* **61**, 433–475.

Precht, W. and Baker, R. (1972). Synaptic organization of the vestibulotrochlear pathway. *Expl Brain Res.* **14**, 158–184.

Rasmussen, G. L. (1946). The olivary peduncle and other fiber projections of the superior olivary complex. *J. comp. Neurol.* **84**, 141–219.

Rasmussen, G. L. and Gacek, R. (1958). Concerning the question of an efferent component of the vestibular nerve of the cat. *Anat. Rec.* **130**, 361–362.

Robinson, L. R. (1969). Bulbospinal fibers and their nuclei of origin in *Lacerta viridis* demonstrated by axonal degeneration and chromatolysis respectively. *J. Anat.* **105**, 59–88.

Schepman, A. M. H. (1918). "De Octavo-laterale Zintuigen en hun Verbindingen in de Hersenenen Vertebraten." Thesis, Amsterdam.

Schwab, M. E. (1973). Some new aspects about the prosencephalon of *Lampetra fluviatilis* (L.). *Acta anat.* **86**, 353–375.

Schwab, M. E. and Durand, M. (1974). An autoradiographic study about neuroblast proliferation in the rhombencephalon of a reptile, *Lacerta sicula. Z. Anat. EntwGesch.* **145**, 29–40.

Senn, D. G. (1966). Ueber das optische System im Gehirn squamater Reptilien. *Acta anat.* suppl. 52, **65**, 1–87.

Senn, D. G. (1968). Bau und Ontogenese von Zwischen-und Mittelhirn bei *Lacerta sicula* (Rafinesque). *Acta anat.* Suppl. 55, **71**, 1–150.

Senn, D. G. and Goodman, D. C. (1969). Patterns of localization in the cerebellar corticofugal projections of the alligator (*Caiman sclerops*). *In* "Neurobiology of the Cerebellar Evolution and Development." (R. Llinas, ed.). American Medical Association, Chicago, pp. 475–480.

Smith, R. D., Marcarian, H. Q. and Niemer, W. T. (1967). Bilateral relationships of the trigeminal mesencephalic nuclei and mastication. *J. comp. Neurol.* **131**, 79–92.

Soliman, M. A. (1964). Die Kopfnerven der Schildkröten. *Zt. wiss. Zool.* **169**, 215–312.

Starck, D. (1963). Die Metamerie des Kopfes der Wirbeltiere. *Zool. Anz.* **170**, 393–428.

Starck, D. (1965). "Embryologie." Thieme, Stuttgart, 2nd edn.

Stefanelli, A. (1944). I centri statici e della coordinazione motoria dei rettili. *Comment. pontif. Acad. Scient.* **8**, 147–294.

Tamura, J., Yashiki, K., Kondo, E. and Oki, H. (1955). On the fiber connections of the habenular nucleus in certain reptilian brains. *Hirosh. J. med. Sci.* **4**, 137–155.

Taren, J. A. (1964). The position of the cutaneous components of the facial, glossopharyngeal and vagal nerves in the spinal tract of V. *J. comp. Neurol.* **122**, 389–391.

ten Donkelaar, H. J. (1976a). Descending pathways from the brain stem to the spinal cord in some reptiles. I. Origin. *J. comp. Neurol.* **167**, 421–442.

ten Donkelaar, H. J. (1976b). Descending pathways from the brain stem to the spinal cord in some reptiles. II. Course and site of termination. *J. comp. Neurol.* **167**, 443–464.

Terni, T. (1921). Ricerche sul nervo abducente e in special modo intorno al significato del suo nucleo accessorio d'origine. *Folia neurobiol.* **12**, 277–327.

Torvik, A. (1956). Afferent connections to the sensory trigeminal nuclei, the nucleus of the solitary tract and adjacent structures. *J. comp. Neurol.* **106**, 119–145.

Tuge, H. (1932). Somatic motor mechanisms in the midbrain and medulla oblongata of *Chrysemys elegans* (Wied.). *J. comp. Neurol.* **55**, 185–271.

Ulinski, P. S. (1973). Quantitative studies on motoneurons: Hypoglossal neurons in the boa constrictor: *Constrictor constrictor. Anat. Rec.* **175**, 127–138.

van Hoevell, J. (1911). Remarks on the reticular cells of the oblongata in different vertebrates. *Proc. k. ned. Akad. Wet.* **13**, 1047–1065.

von Kupffer, K. (1906). Die Morphogenie des Centralnervensystems. *In* "Handbuch der vergleichenden und experimentellen Entwicklungslehre der Wirbeltiere." (O. Hertwig, ed.). Fischer, Jena, **2**, 1–272.

Walls, G. L. (1967). "The Vertebrate Eye and its Adaptive Radiation." Hafner, New York. Reprint of Walls (1942), Cranbrook Inst. Sci., Bloomfield.

Watkinson, G. B. (1906). The cranial nerves of *Varanus bivittatus. Morph. Jb.* **35**, 450–472.

Weinberg, E. (1928). The mesencephalic root of the fifth nerve, a comparative study. *J. comp. Neurol.* **46**, 249–405.

Weston, J. K. (1936). The reptilian vestibular and cerebellar gray with fiber connections. *J. comp. Neurol.* **65**, 93–199.

Wever, E. G. (1965). Structure and function of the lizards ear. *J. aud. Res.* **5**, 331–371.

Wever, E. G. and Gans, C. (1972). The ear and hearing in *Bipes biporus. Proc. natn. Acad. Sci. U.S.A.* **69**, 2714–2716.

Wever, E. G. and Peterson, E. A. (1963). Auditory sensitivity in three iguanid lizards. *J. aud. Res.* **3**, 205–212.

Wever, E. G. and Vernon, J. A. (1957). Auditory responses in the spectacled caiman. *J. cell. comp. Physiol.* **50**, 333–340.

Wever, E. G. and Vernon, J. A. (1960). The problem of hearing in snakes. *J. aud. Res.* **1**, 77–83.

Woodburne, R. T. (1936). A phylogenetic consideration of the primary and secondary centers and connections of the trigeminal complex in a series of vertebrates. *J. comp. Neurol.* **65**, 403–501.

CHAPTER 6

Monoaminergic Systems of the Brain

ANDRÉ PARENT

Laboratories of Neurobiology and Department of Anatomy,
Faculty of Medicine,
Laval University, Quebec, Canada

I. Introduction

Multiple biogenic amines occur in the central nervous system (CNS) of vertebrates (Cooper *et al.*, 1974). This chapter treats the regional distribution and cellular localization in the reptilian brain of (1) the primary catecholamines, norepinephrine and its immediate metabolic precursor dopamine, and of (2) the indolamine commonly known as serotonin or 5-hydroxytryptamine. The recent advances in the understanding of the overall role and importance of these two types of monoamines in the CNS derive mainly from two different methodological approaches. First, sensitive assay techniques have been developed that allow precise, quantitative measurement of the amount of various monoamines present in tissue extracts. Second, a more qualitative, but direct, visualization at the cellular level of monoamines in intact brain tissue has become possible through the development of highly sensitive histofluorescence methods.

The concentrations of monoamines were first estimated by bioassay procedures, which still remain among the most sensitive methods for the determination of biogenic amines. However, these techniques, using various biological preparations such as the rat uterus or stomach strip, have inherent problems of standardization and specificity. Consequently, they have been gradually replaced by chemical methods. The subsequent development of the less time-consuming fluorometric assay procedures is certainly a major cause of the rapid advancement of knowledge in the field of monoamines (see Cooper *et al.*, 1974). The fluorometric chemical methods utilize the observation that, after their extraction from tissue, the monoamines can be readily transformed into highly fluorescent products through a series of specific chemical reactions. For instance, the ethylene diamide condensation method for catecholamines involves the initial oxidation of catecholamines

247

to their intermediate quinone products; these products then react with ethylene diamide to form fluorophores. The amount of catecholamines may be estimated by comparing the intensity of the fluorescence produced by a given sample with that of standard samples containing known concentrations of catecholamines. Although fluorometric procedures are widely used for the routine assay of monoamines, it is difficult to estimate very small amounts of monoamines with these methods. Some very sensitive and specific radio-isotopic techniques are now available for the determination of minute amounts of monoamines in biological fluids and tissues. In these complex procedures the monoamines are transformed into radioactive derivatives after reaction or incubation with various labelled compounds. Prior to quantitative analysis the radioactive derivatives are subjected to a series of rigorous purification steps (see Cooper *et al.*, 1974).

Much information has been accumulated on the regional distribution of monoamines in the nervous systems with the help of these different bio-chemical techniques. Both the primary catecholamines and serotonin have been detected in the nervous systems of representatives of most animal phyla, even including the Platyhelminthes (see Welsh, 1970). In mammals, the various monoamines are not uniformly distributed in the CNS. For instance, dopamine is present in high concentration primarily in the basal ganglia, whereas norepinephrine and serotonin levels are especially high in the hypothalamus. The uneven distribution of monoamines suggested to the first workers in the field that the monoamines might subserve specialized functions, perhaps as central neurotransmitters.

However, it was not until Hillarp and co-workers had developed a histo-chemical, fluorescence microscopic method, that the monoamines could be directly related to morphologically recognizable neuronal structures in the CNS (Falck *et al.*, 1962). This procedure involves, first, the freeze-drying of the brain tissue and, second, the treatment of the freeze-dried tissue with formaldehyde vapors. Essentially, the method is based upon the conversion of various ring hydroxylated catecholamines and indolamines and their respective α-amino acids to highly fluorescent products in the presence of relatively dry formaldehyde vapors at 60 to 80°C. This reaction involves the condensation of the amino group of the monoamines with formaldehyde to form a new ring system. During the paraformaldehyde reaction, the catecholamines and serotonin are transformed into 3,4-dihydroisoquinoline and 3,4-dihydro-β-carboline derivatives, respectively. Each of these fluores-cent condensation products has its own characteristic excitation/emission spectra (maxima of 410/480 nm for catecholamine derivatives, and maxima of 410/525 nm for serotonin derivatives) and, hence, can be distinguished spectrally from one another (see Fuxe *et al.*, 1970). With the use of appro-priate excitation and emission filters, therefore, the primary catecholamines will display a bright green fluorescence whereas serotonin will appear yellow under the fluorescence microscope. It must be mentioned, however, that it is not possible to distinguish spectrally between the reaction products of the different catecholamines (dopamine, norepinephrine and epinephrine) because they all form a fluorophore with similar properties. Epinephrine as well as other secondary catecholamines can nevertheless be distinguished from primary catecholamines (dopamine, norepinephrine), mainly because their reaction with paraformaldehyde requires a much longer time for completion (Fuxe et al., 1970; Cooper et al., 1974). A certain distinction between dopamine and norepinephrine can also be achieved by the use of a pharmacological approach. For instance, pretreatment with inhibitors of dopamine-β-hydroxylase, the enzyme that transforms dopamine into norepinephrine, will progressively deplete the norepinephrine stores and hence will facilitate the identification of dopamine neurons, as the concentration of dopamine is not altered after such a treatment.

Recently, a modification of the original histofluorescence method has been introduced. In this procedure, glyoxylic acid is substituted for the paraformaldehyde as the reactive agent that transforms monoamines into fluorescent products. The capability of glyoxylic acid for transforming monoamines, especially catecholamines, into fluorophores is apparently much greater than is that of paraformaldehyde. In comparison to the classic Falck–Hillarp paraformaldehyde method, the glyoxylic acid procedure appears much more sensitive and allows a more complete and precise visualization of catecholamine neurons. This method, however, does not significantly improve the visualization of serotonin neurons (see Lindvall and Björklund, 1974a).

When the paraformaldehyde method and the more recent glyoxylic acid histofluorescence methods were applied to the CNS of vertebrates, they revealed monoamine neuronal pathways and cell bodies that were unrecognized by the conventional neuroanatomical techniques. Thus, the monoamine pathways in the brain have been extensively mapped (Ungerstedt, 1971; Lindvall and Björklund, 1974b). On the other hand, great advances toward a more complete understanding of the overall function of brain monoamines have been made possible by a combined use of histochemical and biochemical methods. At the present time, it is well accepted that dopamine, norepinephrine and serotonin might act as neurotransmitters or neuromodulators in the CNS. Many of the proposed criteria for neurotransmitters have been satisfactorily shown for these monoamines, both in the brains of mammals and in ganglia of invertebrates. It is well documented that the norepinephrine shown in the cerebellum and in the olfactory bulb and the dopamine in the caudate nucleus meet most, if not all, of these criteria (see Cooper et al., 1974). However, monoamines display certain peculiar features that suggest some differences from "typical" neurotransmitters, such as acetylcholine. For example, Descarries and his coworkers have shown that in rat frontal cortex very few norepinephrine and serotonin containing axon terminals (varicosities) appear to make typical synaptic contact. These authors have proposed, on the basis of the results of their radioautographic ultrastructural studies, that both norepinephrine and serotonin may have a rather diffuse and overall effect on cortical neurons, and that these substances might act more as neuromodulators than as true neurotransmitters (Lapierre et al., 1973).

Whether as putative neurotransmitters or as neuromodulators, the monoamines have been specifically involved in the control of many fundamental brain functions, such as endocrine and temperature regulation, control of sleep and wakefulness cycles, and control of motor activity. Monoamines are also involved in various affective disorders. Many studies suggest a crucial role for catecholamines and serotonin in the hypothalamic control of body temperature and reproductive cycles. For instance, intraventricular injection of microgram quantities of serotonin in diverse mammals will produce profound elevation of body temperature. The body temperature of a rat is also raised following electrical stimulation of the raphé nuclei, which contain most of the serotonin cell bodies. This effect can be prevented if the serotonin has first been depleted by reserpine. These data provided the basis for the amine theory of thermoregulation (Feldberg and Myers, 1964). On the other hand, the results of numerous biochemical, histochemical and pharmacological studies show that the tubero-infundibular dopamine system of the mammalian hypothalamus is involved in the control of gonadotropin secretion by the pituitary. This dopamine system, and possibly other monoamine hypothalamic circuits, appear to act by modulating the secretion of various releasing factors produced by the well-known neurosecretory peptidergic systems (Fuxe et al., 1974).

As mentioned above, monoamines and especially serotonin also appear to be intimately involved in the mechanisms that control the various states of sleep. When brain serotonin is increased by pharmacological manipulations, one sees electroencephalographic evidence of increased time spent in slow-wave sleep. In contrast, decreased brain serotonin, resulting either from lesion of the raphé nuclei or from pharmacological treatment, produces a marked decrease in the amount of slow-wave sleep time (Jouvet, 1972). Other brain monoamines appear also to play a role in sleep mechanisms. Jouvet and co-workers have suggested that norepinephrine as well as acetylcholine may be important in the transition from slow-wave sleep to rapid eye-movement (or paradoxical) sleep. On the other hand, an enormous amount of scientific literature dealing with the involvement of dopamine in the function of the extrapyramidal motor system has accumulated since the first demonstration that the highest concentration of dopamine in mammalian brains occur in the basal ganglia. Some of these studies have clearly shown that dopamine is elaborated within the nigrostriatal pathway. Moreover, the brains of human patients that have suffered from severe motor disturbances of the extrapyramidal type, such as Parkinson's disease, show an important degeneration of the substantia nigra and a marked decrease in brain dopamine level. Furthermore, the experimental interruption of the nigrostriatal dopamine pathway in monkeys induces tremor, a typical symptom of Parkinson's disease (Poirier et al., 1975). These various findings led to the use of L-dopa, the immediate metabolic precursor of dopamine, as an effective treatment for Parkinson's disease.

Beside this well-established role of dopamine in the function of the basal ganglia, numerous less well-established functions have been attributed to catecholamines and serotonin in the CNS. Among these are the possible involvement of catecholamines in emotion and human affective disorders. Recent biochemical and histochemical findings, establishing the existence of complex mesolimbic and mesocortical dopamine systems in the mammalian brain could well be of great significance to the so-called catecholamine theory of affective disorders (see Lindvall et al., 1977).

In comparison to our present-day knowledge of the central monoamine systems of mammals, very little is known about the structural and functional organization of monoamine neurons in the CNS of other vertebrates. Among the reptiles, only lizards had been studied by Baumgarten and Braak (1968) and Braak et al. (1968). Their Falck–Hillarp histofluorescence studies of lizards (Lacerta viridis and L. muralis) showed numerous catecholamine and serotonin neurons in the brainstem (Baumgarten and Braak, 1968; Braak et al., 1968). They postulated that these neurons give rise to the numerous monoamine axon terminals in the forebrain of these animals. The results of our own histofluorescence investigations of the brain of the turtle, Chrysemys picta, also done with the Falck–Hillarp method, have confirmed many of the findings of Baumgarten and Braak. In addition, it has been possible, by the use of an experimental lesion approach, to map out some of the ascending monoamine pathways originating in the brainstem of turtles (see below). This led us to investigate in detail the anatomical organization of monoamine neuronal systems in the brain of painted turtles (Chrysemys picta).

We chose turtles for at least two reasons. First, the fossil record suggests that reptiles occupy a crucial position in the phylogeny of vertebrates, and both birds and mammals are thought to originate from reptilian ancestors (Romer, 1966, 1967). Secondly, turtles offer perhaps the greatest potential for comparison with mammals (Goldby and Gamble, 1957; Riss et al., 1969; Northcutt, 1970; Hall and Ebner, 1970). Anatomical and physiological evidence suggests that the testudinian brain has retained features that were probably present in the brains of the reptilian ancestors of mammals (see Hall and Ebner, 1970). The histochemical approach has been of great help in establishing homologies of various structures in the vertebrates brain. In general, the cellular localization in vertebrate brains of different chemicals, particularly of substances related to neural transmission, such as acetylcholinesterase and monoamines have given us important clues to the understanding of the phylogeny of the vertebrate brain (see Baker-Cohen, 1968; Karten, 1969; Parent and Olivier, 1970).

This report compares the various histochemical, biochemical and neuro-anatomical findings relevant to reptilian monoamine systems. It is conceived essentially as a brief review of our present knowledge of the morphological organization of the monoamine-containing neuronal systems of the reptilian brain. The organization of central monoamine systems of reptiles will also be compared to those of amphibians and mammals in the hope that a comparative approach may reveal information on the evolution of monoamine systems and on the phylogenetic development of the vertebrate brain.

II. Distribution of Monoaminergic Neurons

A. General

It is well established that the amount of monoamine varies considerably in different portions of mammalian neurons. This is also true for the central neurons of most other vertebrates. The highest concentration (about 1000 to 3000 μg/g) of monoamine is usually found within the terminal portion of axons, which often display a varicose or beaded appearance, and each varicosity (axon terminal) is brightly fluorescent after paraformaldehyde treatment. Neuronal somata (cell bodies), on the other hand, contain a moderate amount of monoamine (about 100–300 μg/g), located exclusively in the cytoplasm, and display fluorescence of weak to moderate intensity after paraformaldehyde treatment. In contrast, the proximal portion of the axon contains very low amount of monoamine. Normally, this zone is barely visible with the Falck–Hillarp histofluorescence method.

B. Catecholamine-containing Cell Bodies and Axon Terminals

1. *Turtles*

The overall distribution of monoamine-containing cell bodies and axon terminals in the brain of *Chrysemys picta* is illustrated schematically in Figs 1 and 2.

In *Chrysemys*, the largest collection of catecholamine-containing perikarya is confined rostrocaudally within the middle third of the midbrain. It consists of a band of cells that is obliquely placed in the midbrain tegmentum and that appears immediately caudal to the typical large and multipolar

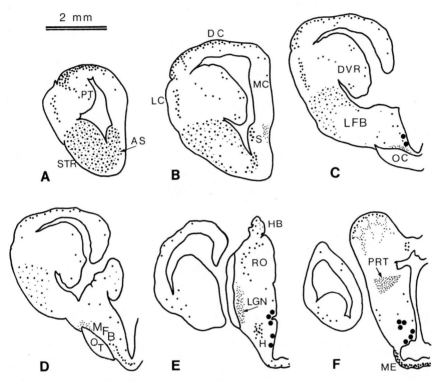

FIG. 1. Semischematic drawings of transverse sections through the left half of the forebrain of *Chrysemys picta* illustrating the distribution of catecholamine-containing axon terminals (large dots), cell bodies (full circles), serotonin-containing axon terminals (small dots). The sections (A–F) run in a rostrocaudal order. AS, nucleus accumbens septi; DC, dorsal cortex; DVR, dorsal ventricular ridge; H, hypothalamus; HB, habenula; LC, lateral cortex; LFB, lateral forebrain bundle; LGN, lateral geniculate nucleus; MC, medial cortex; ME, median eminence; MFB, medial forebrain bundle; OC, optic chiasma; OT, optic tract; PRT, pretectal nucleus; PT, pallial thickening; RO, nucleus rotundus; S, septum; STR, ventral striatum.

cells of the red nucleus (Fig. 2A–B). The cytology of the component neurons lets one subdivide this population of moderately fluorescent cells into a small, medial, and a larger, lateral, part that are continuous with one another. The catecholamine neurons located in the medial part (Fig. 3A) are of medium size and round or oval in shape (Fig. 3C), whereas most neurons

254 ANDRÉ PARENT

lying more laterally and dorsally in the tegmentum (Fig. 3A) are slightly larger in size (mean diameter of 35 μm) and multipolar (Fig. 3B). The catecholamine neurons of the lateral part are scattered obliquely in the tegmentum (Fig. 2B) in an area that closely corresponds to what has been identified as the "nucleus of the substantia nigra" in *Testudo graeca* (de Lange,

2 mm

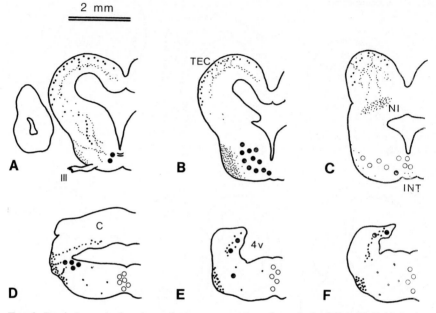

FIG. 2. Semischematic drawings of transverse sections through the left half of the brainstem of *Chrysemys picta* illustrating the distribution of catecholamine-containing axon terminals (large dots), cell bodies (full circles), serotonin-containing axon terminals (small dots) and cell bodies (empty circles). The sections (A–F) run in a rostrocaudal order. INT, nucleus interpeduncularis; NI, nucleus isthmi; TEC, optic tectum; 4v, fourth ventricle; III, oculomotor nerve.

1913) and in *Pseudemys scripta elegans* (Papez, 1935, Fig. 14). However, no "substantia nigra" could be identified in a more recent cytoarchitectural study of the brainstem of *Testudo hermanni* (Cruce and Nieuwenhuys, 1974). The midbrain catecholamine cell group described above lies mostly in the nucleus profundus mesencephali and partially in the red nucleus, according to the nomenclature of Cruce and Nieuwenhuys (1974). This group is best developed at levels 11 and 12 of the atlas of frontal sections published by these authors. The number of cells in this large midbrain catecholamine group is much greater than that of all the other catecholamine neurons located more caudally in the brainstem in *Chrysemys*.

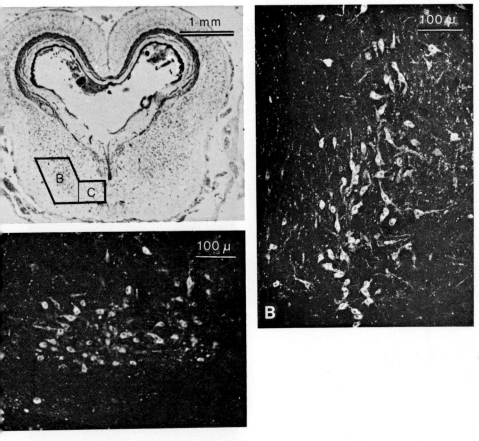

FIG. 3. A. Nissl-stained transverse section through the midbrain of *Chrysemys picta* at the level of maximal concentration of brain catecholamine-containing perikarya. The location and appearance of the lateral and medial parts of the large midbrain catecholamine cell group, is illustrated in B and C, respectively. B, C. Fluorescence photomicrographs of frontal sections through the midbrain showing typical catecholamine-containing cell bodies of the lateral (B) and medial (C) parts of the large midbrain catecholamine cell group.

The second largest group of catecholamine neuronal somata in the testudinian brainstem is found in the dorsolateral tegmentum of the isthmus (Figs 2D, 4A). It is worth mentioning that there is no direct continuity between this group and the large midbrain catecholamine group. The catecholamine group of the isthmus is composed of elongated and moderately fluorescent catecholamine cell bodies that are scattered in a rather small area corresponding approximately to, but extending more laterally than, the area labeled "locus coeruleus" by Cruce and Nieuwenhuys (1974,

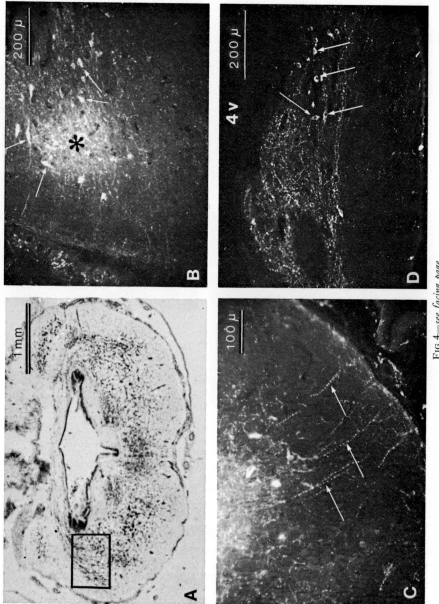

FIG 4—see facing page

Fig. 4. A. Nissl-stained transverse section through the isthmus of *Chrysemys picta*. The rectangle encloses the area where most catecholamine cell bodies of the second largest catecholamine cell group of the brainstem are located. B. Fluorescence photomicrograph of a transverse section of the catecholamine-containing neurons located in dorsolateral portion of the isthmus. The catecholamine cell bodies (arrows) surround numerous, closely packed, longitudinally coursing catecholamine fibers which form a highly fluorescent network (asterisk). C. Fluorescence photomicrograph of a transverse section through the isthmus illustrating catecholamine varicose processes (arrows) of the isthmal catecholamine cell groups that reach the lateral border of the brainstem. D. Fluorescence photomicrograph of an horizontal section through the dorsal portion of the medulla showing the green fluorescent neurons of the small medullary catecholamine cell group. The small-sized cell bodies (arrows) are intermingled with fine catecholamine varicose fibers near the fourth ventricle (4v).

for *Testudo*). The more laterally located catecholamine neurons of this group would indeed be lying in the area identified as "nucleus visceralis secundarius" by these two authors. The catecholamine group of the isthmus would be maximally developed at frontal plane 9 of Cruce and Nieuwenhuys (1974), but would not extend caudally as far as frontal plane 8, in contrast to what is indicated by Cruce and Nieuwenhuys. In frontal sections the catecholamine neurons of the isthmic group appear distributed around a brightly fluorescent bundle of transversely cut catecholamine fibers (Fig. 4B). These varicose catecholamine fibers course caudorostrally and appear to arise from catecholamine neurons in the medulla (see Section III). Some of the catecholamine perikarya of the tegmentum of the isthmus give rise to varicose processes that can be followed for a short distance into the anterior medullary velum, where they cross the midline (Fig. 2D). Other processes of the catecholamine neurons of the isthmus reach the ventrolateral border of the tegmentum (Fig. 4C) and can be followed far caudally into the medulla (see Figs 2D–F and Section III).

The last and smallest group of catecholamine cell bodies of the testudinian brainstem is composed of a few, small, catecholamine-containing neurons scattered within the dorsolateral quadrant of the medullary tegmentum (Figs. 2E–F). Most of these neuronal somata are round or oval in shape and are often embedded in a delicate network of catecholamine varicose fibers lying along the wall of the fourth ventricle (Fig. 4D). They are especially abundant immediately above the motor nucleus of the vagus nerve in an area identified as the nucleus of the solitary tract (Cruce and Nieuwenhuys, 1974). A few other catecholamine neurons occur more ventrally, in an area corresponding approximately to the nucleus ambiguus and to the spinal nucleus of the trigeminal nerve (in *Testudo*, Cruce and Nieuwenhuys, 1974). The medullary catecholamine group of *Chrysemys* would extend rostrocaudally from frontal planes 3 and 4 of the atlas of Cruce and Nieuwenhuys (1974).

Numerous catecholamine-containing cells also occur in the preoptico-hypothalamic complex. Most of these small catecholamine cells are unevenly distributed within the preoptico-hypothalamic periventricular gray. They are intimately associated with various specialized ependymal organs such as the preoptic recess organ (Fig. 1c) and the paraventricular organ (Fig. 1E). Most of them consist of very small, bipolar cells located immediately beneath the ependymal wall. Each cell has one short, clublike ventricular process that protrudes into the third ventricle and a more tenuous varicose process that either penetrates the underlying hypothalamic tissue or reaches the external layer of the median eminence. These catecholamine cells contact the cerebrospinal fluid (CSF) and are numerous, both along the highly vascularized ependymal wall of the small sulcus intrahypothalamicus, which forms the so-called paraventricular organ, and along the infundibular recess. In *Chrysemys* they are much less numerous, along and within the ependymal wall of the preoptic recess, than in amphibians (see Parent, 1979). Occasionally, thin "collaterals" may be seen to arise from a few ventricular processes of cells of the testudinian paraventricular organ and of the infundibular recess in material prepared by the Golgi–Cox method. In addition to the large number of CSF-contacting catecholamine cells that occurs in the testudinian hypothalamus, a small group (10 to 15 perikarya) of large catecholamine-containing neurons lies within the ventromedial area of the caudal hypothalamus. Even though these catecholamine neurons also lie close to the third ventricle, they do not show the typical CSF-contacting processes of the more abundant and smaller hypothalamic catecholamine cells. The complex organization of the numerous catecholamine cells of the testudinian hypothalamus tends to favor the above-outlined view, that catecholamines play an important role in the function of the hypothalamus.

No catecholamine cell bodies could be visualized in the telencephalon of turtles, even though this part of their brain is densely innervated by catecholamine axons. However, these terminals are not uniformly distributed in the telencephalon. They are prevalent in the ventral striatum and less frequent in the cerebral cortex. In comparison, the remaining portions of the telencephalon (including the dorsal ventricular ridge of Johnston, 1915) are sparsely innervated (Figs 1A–D). Due to its very high concentration of monoamine axon terminals, the whole ventral striatum (including the nucleus accumbens septi) fluoresces intensely and diffusely yellow-green (Fig. 11A–B). A biochemical study of the regional levels of monoamines in the brain of *Chrysemys picta* (fluorometric assay procedures of Maickel *et al.*, 1968 for serotonin and norepinephrine; Welch and Welch, 1969, for dopamine), shows that the ventral striatum indeed contains the highest concentrations of dopamine and of serotonin in the brain (Table I). These

TABLE I

Regional levels of dopamine (DA), norepinephrine (NE) and serotonin (5-hydroxytryptamine, 5-HT) in the brain of the turtle (Chrysemys picta) *estimated by fluorometric assays*

Tissues*		DA	NE	5-HT
Whole brain	(3)	$1\cdot51 \pm 0\cdot21$	$1\cdot56 \pm 0\cdot64$	$2\cdot86 \pm 1\cdot26$
Brainstem	(6)	$1\cdot05 \pm 0\cdot34$	$2\cdot02 \pm 0\cdot23$	$3\cdot47 \pm 1\cdot13$
Prosencephalon	(2)	$1\cdot56 \pm 0\cdot22$	$1\cdot59 \pm 0\cdot16$	$2\cdot23 \pm 0\cdot11$
Telencephalon	(2)	$3\cdot12 \pm 0\cdot62$	$2\cdot39 \pm 0\cdot91$	$3\cdot79 \pm 0\cdot38$
Basal striatum	(3)	$6\cdot53 \pm 2\cdot30$	$2\cdot24 \pm 0\cdot34$	$4\cdot76 \pm 0\cdot41$

* The results are expressed in µg of amine per g of fresh tissue $\pm$ S.E.M.
( ) Number of biological determinations.

findings confirm the results of an earlier biochemical study of the distribution of dopamine in the brain of the tortoise *Geochelone chilensis* (Juorio, 1969). In this species the highest concentration of dopamine ($3 \cdot 66 \, \mu g/g$) occurs in the ventral striatum (referred to as nucleus basalis). The rest of the telencephalon contains little dopamine, indeed less than 20% of the concentration found in the ventral striatum. As most of the dopamine occurs in this part of the brain, Juorio suggests that the ventral striatum in *Geochelone* might be homologous, at least from the biochemical point of view, with the neostriatum of mammals (Juorio, 1969). In *Chrysemys*, catecholamine axon terminals are especially abundant in the rostral pole of the ventral striatum (Fig. 1A), but their number gradually decreases caudally through the strioamygdaloid complex (Fig. 1B–D). At midtelencephalic level the catecholamine varicosities are consistently more numerous in the lateral part of the ventral striatum (corresponding to "zone 9" of Riss et al., 1969; Fig. 1C). In the caudal tip of the telencephalon, this part merges progressively into the lateral half of the so-called "amygdala" (Fig. 1D–F). At this level, however, the number of catecholamine varicosities is strikingly smaller than that found in the rostral pole of the ventral striatum (Fig. 1A, E–F).

As mentioned above, a significant number of catecholamine axon terminals also occur in the cerebral cortex of *Chrysemys picta*, which can be easily divided into medial, lateral and dorsal areas (Fig. 1B). On the basis of their location and fiber connections, the medial and lateral cortices have been associated most commonly with the mammalian hippocampal and piriform cortices, respectively. The dorsal cortex receives a direct thalamic input (Hall and Ebner, 1970) and develops late during ontogenesis (Kirsche, 1972); this cortical area has consequently been regarded as a possible homolog of the mammalian neocortex by some authors. However, the testudinian dorsal cortex appears to be more simply organized than the neocortex of mammals. It consists essentially of a single cell layer located immediately above the ependyma of the lateral ventricle (Fig. 5D). The neurons have numerous spiny, apical dendrites that project towards the pial surface (Fig. 5D–E). The largest number of cortical catecholamine-containing varicosities is found in the rostral tip of the dorsal cortex (Fig. 5A). At this level, numerous linear, varicose profiles displaying a weak catecholamine-type fluorescence are intertwined one with another (Fig. 5B). However, as in the ventral striatum, the number of catecholamine axon terminals markedly decreases caudally and very few catecholamine terminals remain in the caudal-third of the cerebral cortex (Fig. 1). In frontal planes, the number of catecholamine varicosities also decreases progressively as the cortex is followed either medially, into the medial or hippocampal cortex, or laterally into the lateral or piriform cortex (Fig. 1). In both the dorsal and medial cortices the highest density of catecholamine terminals

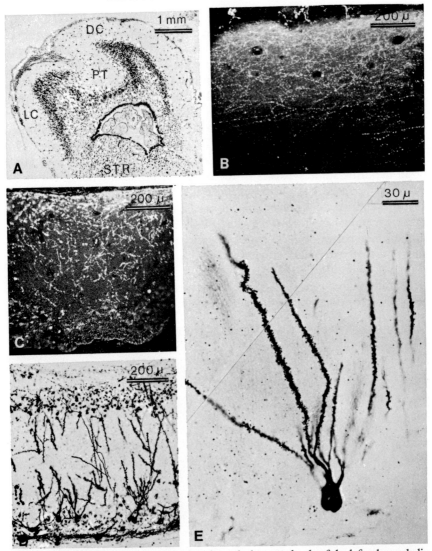

FIG. 5. A. Nissl-stained transverse section through the rostral pole of the left telencephalic hemisphere of *Chrysemys picta*. DC, dorsal cortex; LC, lateral cortex; PT, pallial thickening; STR, ventral striatum. B. Fluorescence photomicrograph of a transverse section showing numerous thin, catecholamine, varicose fibers intertwined at the level of the rostral dorsal cortex (same level as in A). C. The catecholamine-containing axon terminals are particularly abundant beneath the pial surface (upper portion of the figure) of the more caudal dorsal cortex (level B in Fig. 1). D. Golgi–Cox impregnated transverse section of the dorsal cortex taken at approximately the same level as that shown in C. E. High-power view of a Golgi–Cox impregnated neuron of the dorsal cortex. The pear-shaped cell body is located near the ependymal surface whereas the coarsely impregnated apical dendrites course toward the pial surface.

is found most superficially, immediately beneath the pial surface (Figs 5c, 6b). Their number decreases rapidly in the inner portion of the cortex so that very few catecholamine terminals occur in the vicinity of the cortical cell bodies. This suggests that most synaptic contacts of the catecholamine type occur along the outer segments of apical dendrites in the dorsal and medial cortices. Recent radioautographic investigations of the rat frontal neocortex have shown that more than 35% of the noradrenergic nerve endings occupy the outer molecular layer (Lapierre et al., 1973), a condition which appears similar to that found in the dorsal cortex of turtles. On the other hand, electron microscopic studies have revealed that over 60% of all dendritic spine synapses in the outer 100 μm of the dorsal cortex of *Pseudemys scripta* are found on organelle-filled spines (Ebner and Colonnier, 1975). Dendritic spines containing mitochondria or membranous sacs are rare in mammalian neocortex. Most of the catecholamine axon terminals in the lateral cortex occur in close proximity to the cortical cell bodies. This suggests that axosomatic catecholamine contacts may predominate here (Fig. 6a).

In addition to the cerebral cortex and ventral striatum, various other brain areas also receive a significant catecholamine input. For instance, numerous

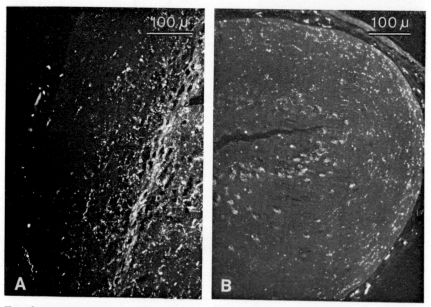

Fig. 6. A, B. Fluorescence photomicrographs of transverse sections through the lateral cortex (A) and the medial cortex (B) of *Chrysemys picta*. The catecholamine axon terminals in the lateral cortex closely surround the non-fluorescent cell bodies whereas they are scattered beneath the pial surface in the medial cortex.

catecholamine axon terminals occur in the optic tectum of turtles (Fig. 2A–C).

As seen in Fig. 7, several linear and varicose catecholamine profiles are ascending through the more internal layers of the tectum, i.e. the stratum fibrosum periventriculare, the stratum griseum periventriculare and the stratum album centrale of Huber and Crosby (1933). Most of these catecholamine afferent fibers appear to arborize mainly within the more external layers of the optic tectum, i.e. within the stratum opticum and the stratum fibrosum and griseum superficiale. In the stratum fibrosum and griseum superficiale, the catecholamine axon terminals are more abundant at intermediate depths in this layer (corresponding more or less to the zones 10–12 of P. Ramón, 1896).

The dorsolateral region of the septum, which slightly protrudes into the lateral ventricle, also contains fairly thick catecholamine axon terminals that closely surround the non-fluorescent cell bodies of this area. Many other catecholamine axon terminals are found within the nuclei dorsolateralis and dorsomedialis of the thalamus (Papez, 1935). These nuclei border the nucleus rotundus. The latter nucleus is, however, completely devoid of monoamine varicosities (see Parent, 1973a). Finally, a multitude of very fine catecholamine axon terminals are closely packed within the external layer of the median eminence of the hypothalamus, which thus appears as a zone of diffuse and intense green fluorescence, very similar to that found in median eminence of mammals. In *Chrysemys*, these terminals are apparently derived, at least in part, from the CSF-contacting catecholamine cells located along the infundibular recess (see above).

2. Lizards

Our knowledge of the distribution of catecholamine-containing nerve cell bodies and axon terminals in lizards is essentially derived from the histofluorescence study of Baumgarten and Braak (1968). These authors have shown that the tegmentum of the brainstem of both *Lacerta muralis* and *L. viridis* contains numerous catecholamine neurons in an area that extends caudorostrally from the level of the facial nerve to that of the oculomotor nerve. However, as in turtles, the largest number of these catecholamine neurons occurs in the midbrain tegmentum (nucleus reticularis mesencephali, Baumgarten and Braak, 1968), ventral and lateral to the nucleus of the oculomotor nerve. At this level, the catecholamine cells located medially are small and round, in contrast to the catecholamine neurons scattered more laterally in the tegmentum, which are larger in size. Although no catecholamine cell group of the isthmus has been identified as such in lizards, some catecholamine cells appear to occur in the brainstem caudal to the catecholamine cell group of the midbrain. These catecholamine

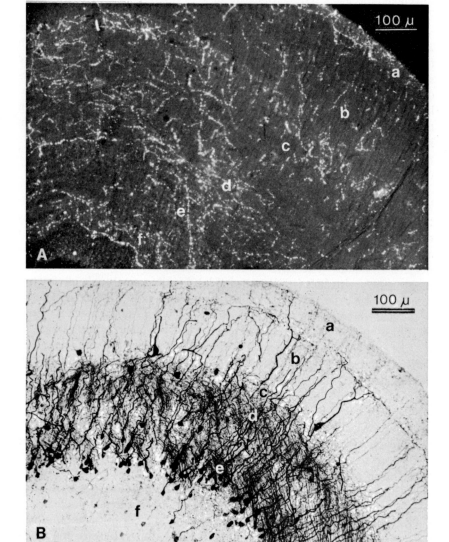

FIG. 7. A. Fluorescence photomicrograph of a transverse section through the optic tectum of *Chrysemys picta* illustrating the distribution of catecholamine axon terminals among the various layers numbered from a to f. a, stratum opticum; b, stratum fibrosum et griseum superficiale; c, stratum griseum centrale; d, stratum album centrale; e, stratum griseum periventriculare; f, stratum fibrosum periventriculare. B. frontal section through the optic tectum taken at the same level as in A, illustrating the morphology of some tectal neurons. In this preparation numerous neurons are completely filled with horseradish peroxidase following a massive injection of this enzyme into the midbrain tegmentum.

perikarya are apparently lying in an ill-defined area of the tegmentum, which according to the description of Baumgarten and Braak (1968) would be located immediately lateral to the raphé region in the so-called "nucleus reticularis medius". Numerous typical CSF-contacting catecholamine cells also occur in the hypothalamus of lizards. As in turtles, they are more abundant at the level of the paraventricular organ (nucleus ependymalis hypothalami, Baumgarten and Braak, 1968) and along the infundibular recess ("nucleus diffuses tuberi" of Baumgarten and Braak, 1968). However, no CSF-contacting catecholamine cells have been detected along the preoptic recess of lizards.

The pattern of the catecholamine innervation of the telencephalon in lizards appears strikingly similar to that disclosed in turtles. The largest number of catecholamine varicosities occurs in the parvocellular area of the so-called "paleostriatum". This region, which displays a diffuse and intense yellow-green fluorescence, appears to correspond to the "zone 9" of Riss et al. (1969), and thus may be considered homologous to the area identified above as "basal striatum" in *Chrysemys*. However, according to the results of their microspectrofluorometric and pharmaco-histochemical analysis, Baumgarten and Braak (1968) assume that the fluorescent substance in the paleostriatum of *Lacerta* is mainly norepinephrine. This finding differs markedly from the results of biochemical analysis of monoamine levels in the basal striatum in *Chrysemys* (see Table I). Although norepinephrine appears to occur in significant amounts in the basal striatum of turtles, dopamine occurs at more than twice the concentration of norepinephrine. The "hypopallial region" of lizards is similar to that of turtles in having only a few catecholamine axon terminals. The dorsolateral portion of the septum and medial and lateral cortical areas do show significant numbers of fairly thick catecholamine varicosities. As in turtles, the catecholamine axon terminals of lizards are concentrated beneath the pial surface in the medial or hippocampal cortex, whereas the terminals closely surround the cell bodies in the lateral or piriform cortex. Baumgarten and Braak (1968) did not identify the dorsal cortex as such in *Lacerta*.

C. SEROTONIN-CONTAINING CELL BODIES AND AXON TERMINALS

1. *Turtles*

Only at the level of the brainstem does the brain of *Chrysemys picta* have serotonin-containing cell bodies. Most of these are closely packed in the raphé or midline region where they form a nearly continuous cell column that extends rostrocaudally from the caudal midbrain tegmentum to the lower medulla (Figs 2C–F). These cells are thus confined to the nucleus raphes inferior and to the nucleus raphes superior, pars medialis (Cruce and Nieuwenhuys, 1974), which extend from frontal planes 2 to 10. However, numerous, elongate, serotonergic somata also invade the nucleus reticularis isthmi in the lateral tegmentum of the caudal midbrain and isthmus (Fig. 8).

The serotonin neurons innervate profusely a diversity of structures scattered throughout the central nervous system of turtles. In contrast to the catecholamine-type axon terminals, the serotonin varicosities are of very fine caliber. Hence, the serotonin terminals can be obscured easily by the larger catecholamine terminals in brain areas, such as the ventral striatum, where both catecholamine and serotonin varicosities occur. Furthermore, the weak yellow fluorescence displayed by the serotonin varicosities fades extremely rapidly under the fluorescence microscope. The serotonin axon terminals are thus much more difficult to document on photomicrographs than are the catecholamine varicosities.

It is nevertheless possible to identify various areas of the brains of turtles that receive a massive serotonin innervation. In some cases, the pattern of the serotonin innervation was documented on photomicrographs. This could be achieved mainly for areas having a very large number of serotonin varicosities and few or no catecholamine axon terminals. Among the serotonin-containing areas of the brains of turtles are optic relay nuclei, such as the lateral geniculate nucleus (Figs 1E, 9A), the pretectal nucleus of Papez (1935) (Figs 1F, 9B), the nucleus isthmi, pars parvo- and magnocellularis (Fig. 2C), and the optic tectum. Numerous serotonin varicosities also occur along the ventrolateral border of the midbrain tegmentum (Fig. 2B). In this area, the very fine serotonin axon terminals are closely packed lateral to the large catecholamine midbrain cell group; none is found in close contact with the catecholamine cell bodies themselves.

2. Lizards

The distribution of serotonin-containing cell bodies and axon terminals in the brains of lizards (*Lacerta muralis* and *L. viridis*) was studied in detail by Braak *et al.* (1968). According to these authors, the serotonin-containing perikarya lie almost exclusively in the so called "nucleus reticularis mesencephali" within the tegmentum of the midbrain. They are distributed immediately dorsal and lateral to the interpeduncular nucleus at the level of the nucleus of the trochlear nerve. In contrast to what has been found in turtles, no serotonin cells have been disclosed in the raphé region in lizards, caudal to the level of the mesencephalic–isthmic junction. Besides the large group of serotonin neurons in the midbrain, a certain number of small CSF-contacting cells of the paraventricular organ of the hypothalamus in *Lacerta* yields a fluorescence of the serotonin type. Such serotonin cells seem to be absent in the paraventricular organ of turtles (see above).

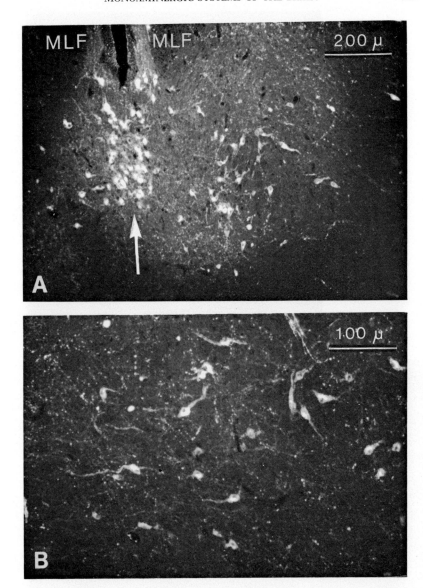

FIG. 8. A, B. Fluorescence photomicrographs of transverse sections showing serotonin-containing cell bodies in the caudal third of the midbrain tegmentum of *Chrysemys picta*. Numerous yellow fluorescent neurons are closely packed along the midline (arrow in A) whereas other serotonin neurons are scattered more laterally in the tegmentum. The laterally located neurons are shown at higher magnification in B. MLF, medial longitudinal fasciculus.

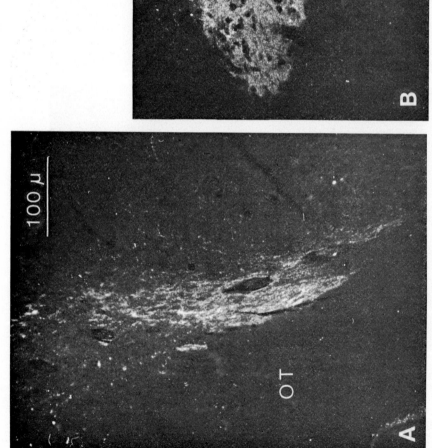

FIG. 9. A, B. Fluorescence photomicrographs of transverse sections through the thalamus (A) and pretectum (B) of *Chrysemys picta*. Numerous very fine, serotonin-containing axon terminals are present in the lateral geniculate nucleus (A) and in the pretectal nucleus (B). No catecholamine varicosities are found in these nuclei.

Despite these differences in the localization of serotonin cell bodies between lizards and turtles, the overall pattern of the distribution of the serotonin axon terminals in the brain is strikingly similar in both. As in turtles, the lateral geniculate nucleus, the pretectal and isthmi nuclei and the optic tectum of lizards receive a massive serotonin innervation. In addition, numerous very fine serotonin varicosities occur along the lateral border of the midbrain tegmentum in *Lacerta*, an area which is referred to as the "nucleus lateralis profundus mesencephali" by Braak *et al.* (1968). Abundant serotonin axon terminals occur in other structures of the lacertilian brain, such as in the interpeduncular nucleus, in the dorsomedialis and dorsolateralis nuclei of the thalamus and in the habenula.

In addition to the histochemical evidence outlined above, Braak *et al.* (1968) confirmed the occurrence of a large amount of serotonin in the brain of *Lacerta* with the help of fluorometric assays. Apparently, serotonin occurs in concentrations varying from 3·06 to 3·61 μg/g in the whole brain without the pineal gland of *Lacerta muralis*.

III. Catecholamine Pathways of Turtles

A. GENERAL

As mentioned in Section II, the proximal axons of monoamine neurons are barely visible under the fluorescence microscope because of their very low monoamine content. Mapping monoamine pathways in normal brain tissue is, therefore, difficult. This limitation can be overcome by lesioning monoamine bundles, because monoamine accumulates in the proximal segment of a lesioned axon, which thus becomes highly fluorescent, whereas the distal portion of the axon gradually disappears. This approach has been used successfully to map some of the main catecholamine pathways of the brains of turtles (Parent and Poitras, 1974). Following hemisections performed at various levels along the brainstem, three pathways have been identified thus far: (1) the mesostriatal pathway, (2) the isthmocortical pathway, and (3) the medullohypothalamic pathway. These three ascending catecholamine fiber systems, which are illustrated schematically in Fig. 10, are next described. Mention is also made of some descending catecholamine pathways that were observed in normal (unlesioned) turtles.

B. MESOSTRIATAL PATHWAY

In normal brains of *Chrysemys picta*, very weakly fluorescent catecholamine fibers are observed in the caudalmost segment of the medial forebrain bundle at the level of the mesodiencephalic junction (Fig. 11D). However,

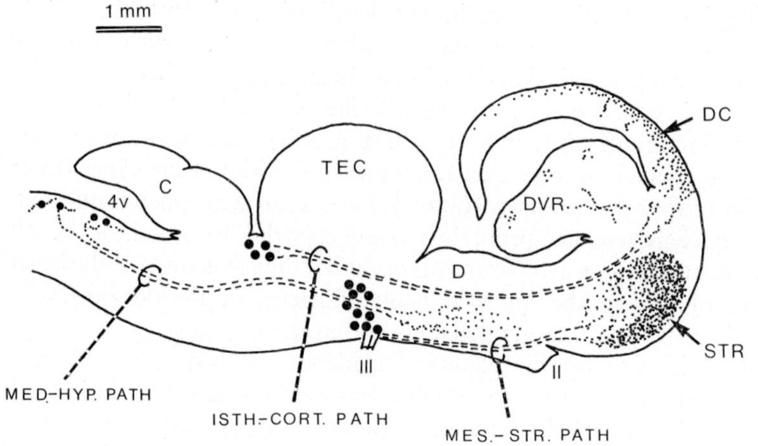

FIG. 10. Schematic drawing of a parasaggital section through the brain of *Chrysemys picta* illustrating the three major ascending catecholamine pathways: (1) the medullo-hypothalamic (MED.-HYP. PATH), (2) the isthmocortical (ISTH.-CORT. PATH), and (3) the mesostriatal (MES.-STR. PATH) pathways. The catecholamine cell bodies and axon terminals are illustrated as full circles and dots, respectively. C, Cerebellum; D, diencephalon; DC, dorsal cortex; DVR, dorsal ventricular ridge; STR, ventral striatum; TEC, tectum; II, optic nerve; III, oculomotor nerve; 4v, fourth ventricle. Rostral is to the right.

in this material no direct continuity can be shown unequivocally between these thin and varicose catecholamine fibers and the catecholamine neurons of the midbrain tegmentum located immediately caudad to them (Fig. 11E). The catecholamine fibers ascend rostrally within the lateral hypothalamic area where they are intermingled with the non-fluorescent fibers of the medial forebrain bundle. At the level of the preoptic area, they turn laterally and mingle with the non-fluorescent fibers of the lateral forebrain bundle (LFB; Fig. 11c). The catecholamine fibers continue rostrad and invade the ventral striatum, where they break up into numerous, highly fluorescent varicosities that intimately surround the non-fluorescent cell bodies of the ventral striatum (Fig. 11A, B). Shortly after the brainstem is completely hemisected at the level of the mesodiencephalic junction, green fluorescing material accumulates caudal to the lesion in the proximal portion of catecholamine axons and in their parent neuronal somata located in the tegmentum of the midbrain. However, rostral to the lesion both the catecholamine varicose fibers coursing in the lateral hypothalamus and their numerous axon terminals in the ventral striatum disappear. No comparable change can be observed after hemisections performed caudal to the large catecholamine cell group of the midbrain (Parent and Poitras, 1974).

The occurrence of a mesostriatal catecholamine pathway in the brains

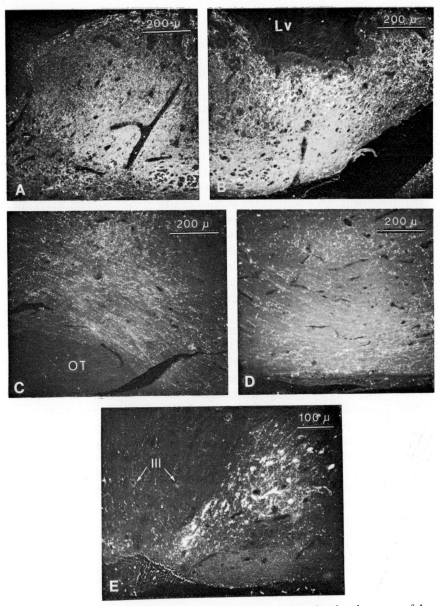

Fɪɢ. 11. Fluorescence photomicrographs of parasaggital sections showing the course of the mesostriatal catecholamine pathway in *Chrysemys picta*. The numerous catecholamine axon terminals present in the rostral and caudal portions of the ventral striatum are shown in A and B, respectively. The fine varicose catecholamine axons ascending in the rostral and caudal portions of the medial forebrain bundle are shown in C and D, respectively. Some of the catecholamine cell bodies of the lateral part of the midbrain CA cell group that appear to give rise to the pathway are shown in E. In all the photomicrographs, the rostral and caudal portions of the structure illustrated are found in the left- and right-hand side of the figure, respectively. Lv, lateral ventricle.

ANDRÉ PARENT

of turtles has been confirmed recently by a series of experimental studies with the horseradish peroxidase (HRP) tracing method. As shown in Fig. 12, small quantities (0·1 to 0·3 μl) of a 30% solution of HRP injected into the ventral striatum in *Chrysemys* (Fig. 12A) result in a typical retrograde labeling of a large population of neurons lying within the ipsilateral midbrain tegmentum (Fig. 12B, c). This collection of HRP positive neurons is strikingly similar to the lateral part of the large midbrain catecholamine cell group identified above, both in its location in the tegmentum of the midbrain and in the morphological characteristics of its neuronal somata (compare Figs 12B and 3B). However, HRP injection in the striatum, does not produce HRP-filled neuronal somata in the tegmental area of the midbrain where the green fluorescent neurons of the medial part of the midbrain catecholamine cell group were found earlier. After striatal injection, the caudalmost portion of the midbrain shows a few retrogradely labeled HRP neurons scattered in the lateral portion of the ipsilateral tegmentum. These neurons are morphologically very similar to, and found in the same area as, the serotonin-containing neurons located laterally in the tegmentum of the caudal midbrain (see above).

Besides labeled cell bodies, striatal injection also produces ipsilaterally numerous HRP-filled fibers in the lateral forebrain bundle (LFB; Fig. 12E). Labeled fibers occur in both the dorsal and ventral peduncles. The HRP-positive fibers of the dorsal peduncle can be easily followed caudally up to their origins in the retrogradely labeled cell bodies of the perirotundal nuclei (especially the "nuclei dorsomedialis anterior" and (centralis) "lateralis", Papez, 1935; see Parent, 1976). In contrast, the HRP-filled fibers of the ventral peduncle can be traced caudally down to their arborization in the ventrolateral border of the midbrain tegmentum (Fig. 12D). At this level, no direct contact could be demonstrated between the labeled fibers of the ventral peduncle and the HRP-positive neuronal somata lying more centrally in the tegmentum of the midbrain. The labeled fibers present within the ventral peduncle of the LFB could nevertheless represent a reptilian homologue of the well-documented strionigral pathway of mammals (see Section IV).

C. Isthmocortical Pathway

As mentioned above, a complete brainstem hemisection performed immediately caudal to the large midbrain catecholamine cell group does not produce a disappearance of catecholamine axon terminals in the ventral striatum. However, this type of lesion causes a marked ipsilateral loss of catecholamine varicosities within the cerebral cortex and in the preoptico-hypothalamic complex. In addition, caudal to such a lesion, a strong

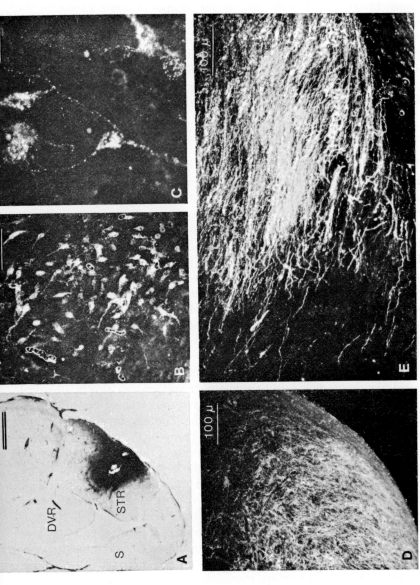

FIG. 12. A–E. Injection of horseradish peroxidase (0·3 μl, 30% solution) in the ventral striatum of *Chrysemys picta*. The injection site is seen in A, in bright field. Retrogradely labeled cell bodies present in the ipsilateral midbrain tegmentum are shown in B and C, in dark field. Numerous fine labeled axons present along the ventrolateral border of the midbrain tegmentum (D) and within the lateral forebrain bundle at a preoptic level (E) are shown in dark field. DVR, dorsal ventricular ridge; S, septum; STR, ventral striatum.

accumulation of green fluorescent material occurs within the proximal axon segments and in the cells bodies of the catecholamine cell group of the isthmus. In contrast, hemisections of the brainstem made caudal to the region of the isthmus do not alter the number of catecholamine axon terminals in the cerebral cortex (Parent and Poitras, 1974). These findings suggest that turtles have an isthmocortical catecholamine pathway that would be somewhat similar to the mammalian "coeruleocortical noradrenergic pathway" (see Section IV). The exact course of the isthmocortical pathway of turtles remains to be investigated in detail.

D. MEDULLOHYPOTHALAMIC PATHWAY

Although hemisections placed caudal to the region of the isthmus do not change the number of cortical catecholamine varicosities, all hemisections made at various levels in between the isthmus and the medullary catecholamine cell groups produce a significant loss of catecholamine axon terminals within the ipsilateral preoptico-hypothalamic complex. Caudal to these lesions the accumulation phenomenon can be observed in the axons and cell bodies of the catecholamine medullary group. According to the results of our mapping studies, the axons of this medullohypothalamic pathway (Fig. 10) ascend to the isthmus region within the central portion of the medulla and appear here to intermingle with the neurons of the catecholamine cell group of the isthmus (Parent and Poitras, 1974). The more rostral course of the pathway through the midbrain and diencephalon is still unknown.

In addition to the three ascending catecholamine pathways described above, some descending catecholamine fiber systems can also be observed in normal (unlesioned) brains of *Chrysemys picta*. One of the most conspicuous descending catecholamine bundles appears to arise from the neuronal somata of the catecholamine cell group of the isthmus. As mentioned above (Section IIA), some of the neurons of the catecholamine group of the isthmus have varicose processes which project toward the lateral border of the brainstem. More caudally in the medulla, these fluorescent fibers form a more compact bundle that courses along the ventrolateral border of the brainstem (Fig. 13A). Thus, the catecholamine cell group of the isthmus, much like the mammalian locus coeruleus, appears to have both ascending (cortical) and descending projections. However, the descending projections could well be more important in *Chrysemys* than they are in mammals. Finally, it is worth mentioning that numerous weakly fluorescent and varicose catecholamine fibers course longitudinally in the spinal cord of turtles (Fig. 13B). The exact origin of these spinal catecholamine fibers remains to be determined.

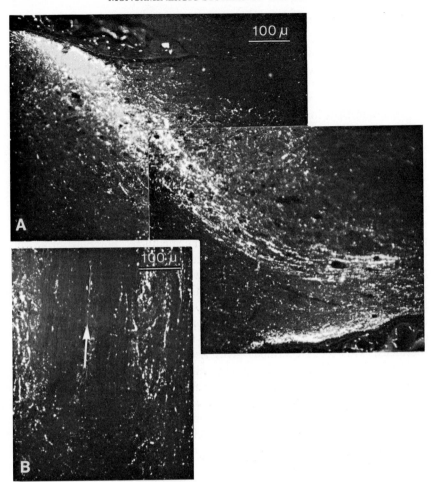

FIG. 13. A. Photomontage of a parasaggital section through the caudal brainstem of *Chrysemys picta* showing some descending catecholamine varicose axons. These axons arise from the isthmal catecholamine cell group, accumulate in the dorsolateral portion of the isthmal tegmentum (left-hand side of the figure), then course obliquely through the tegmentum, and descend along the ventrolateral border of the medulla (right-hand side of the figure). B. Fluorescence photomicrograph of a horizontal section through the cervical spinal cord of *Chrysemys picta* showing thick, catecholamine varicose axons coursing longitudinally on either side of the midline (arrow).

IV. Comparative Anatomy of Central Monoaminergic Systems

As a whole, the morphological organization of central monoamine neurons in *Chrysemys picta* appears in many aspects similar to the well-documented arrangement of mammalian brain monoamine neurons. For instance, the serotonin neuronal somata in the brain of turtles are mostly scattered within the raphé region of the entire brainstem, as is the case in the rat (Dahlström and Fuxe, 1964), the cat (Pin *et al.*, 1968) and the squirrel monkey (Di Carlo *et al.*, 1973). As in mammals, however, precise information on the projections of the reptilian serotonin neurons is lacking, mainly because the histofluorescence methods yet available are much less sensitive for serotonin than for catecholamine fluorophores.

The three groups of catecholamine cell bodies disclosed in the brainstem of turtles appear to correspond, at least in part, to the catecholamine cell groups located in similar areas of the mammalian brainstem. For instance, its location, the morphological characteristics of its cell bodies and its ascending projections suggest that the medullary catecholamine cell group of turtles, may be homologous to the groups of norepinephrine-containing neurons located in the caudal portion of the tegmentum of the medulla in rats (see Dahlström and Fuxe, 1964). The medullary norepinephrine cell groups in rats are known to give rise to the so-called "ventral noradrenergic bundle" which densely innervates the whole hypothalamus (Ungerstedt, 1971). Such a pathway appears similar to the medullohypothalamic catecholamine pathway identified in turtles. On the other hand, the isthmus catecholamine cell group of turtles is, on the basis of its location, fiber connections and catecholamine content, similar to the mammalian locus coeruleus. This locus coeruleus gives rise to the so-called "dorsal noradrengegic bundle" which essentially innervates the whole mammalian cerebral cortex (Ungerstedt, 1971; Lindvall and Björklund, 1974). Like the locus coeruleus, the isthmus catecholamine neurons also give rise to descending fibers in the caudal brainstem and contribute fibers that cross over the midline within the anterior medullary velum. The isthmus catecholamine neurons in *Chrysemys*, however, do not appear to project to the cerebellum as do those of mammals.

The numerous catecholamine-containing neuronal somata present in the tegmentum of the midbrain of turtles can also be related to well-characterized mammalian catecholamine cell groups. For instance, the lateral part of the large midbrain catecholamine cell group in turtles appears, in many aspects, to be similar to the pars compacta of the mammalian substantia nigra. In mammals, the dopamine-containing neurons of the pars compacta give rise to the well-documented nigrostriatal dopaminergic pathway, which courses in the medial forebrain bundle and arborizes profusely within the neostriatum (caudate nucleus and putamen). The mammalian nigrostriatal pathway thus appears somewhat equivalent to the mesostriatal catecholamine pathway disclosed in turtles. On the other hand, the neuropil area located along the ventrolateral border of the midbrain tegmentum in *Chrysemys*, lateral to the catecholamine cell bodies, can also be compared to a part of the mammalian substantia nigra. This neuropil area has been identified as the neuropil of the "nucleus of the substantia nigra" in turtles (Papez, 1935). The dendrites of the cells of the nucleus of the substantia nigra (corresponding to the lateral part of the large midbrain catecholamine cell group of the present study) would synapse in this neuropil area (Papez, 1935). The area of the lateral border of the midbrain tegmentum also receives fibers from the ventral striatum in *Chrysemys* (see above) and in *Tupinambis nigropunctatus* (Lohman *et al.*, 1973; Hoogland, 1977), and receives a massive input from serotonin neurons of the caudal brainstem (see above). In the mammalian brain, the strio-nigral fibers enter the midbrain tegmentum through a lateroventral course. Apparently they do not make direct synaptic contact on the catecholamine cell bodies of the substantia nigra, pars compacta, but instead on the long radiating dendrites of these cells, whose processes arborize ventrolaterally in the tegmentum. They thus terminate within the pars reticulata of the substantia nigra (see Nauta and Mehler, 1966). Because the pars recticulata of mammals contains many more dendrites and vastly more synaptic endings than the pars compacta, the pars reticulata should perhaps be regarded as the "plexiform layer of the substantia nigra" (Schwyn and Fox, 1974). On this basis, the neuropil area of the ventrolateral midbrain tegmentum of turtles, which also receives a striatal input and contains most of the dendrites of the cells of the "nucleus of the substantia nigra", could be homologous to the pars reticulata of the mammalian substantia nigra. This view is further supported by the fact that both the pars reticulata of the mammalian substantia nigra and the neuropil area of the testudinian midbrain contains numerous serotonin axon terminals (Fuxe, 1965). In any event, this neuropil area appears to represent an important point of convergence where numerous fiber systems (including striatal and serotonin afferents) could interact in order to modulate the activity of the catecholamine neurons of the lateral part of the catecholamine cell group of the testudinian midbrain.

In contrast to the catecholamine neurons of the lateral part, HRP studies (Parent, 1976) suggest that catecholamine cell bodies of the medial part of the catecholamine cell group in the midbrain of turtles do not project to the ventral striatum (see above). Owing to their location and amine content, the catecholamine neurons of the medial tegmentum of turtles could be homologous to the various perinigral catecholamine cell groups located near the midline in the mammalian midbrain tegmentum (Dahlström and Fuxe, 1964). These dopamine-containing neurons in mammals give rise to the so-called "mesolimbic dopamine pathway" that innervates the septal and olfactory tubercle areas (Ungerstedt, 1971). Although both the septum and the olfactory tubercle of turtles are densely innervated by catecholamine axons, the existence of such a mesolimbic catecholamine pathway remains to be confirmed experimentally in this group.

With regard to monoamine systems in avian brains, the few data presently available suggest that the overall organization of monoamine neuronal systems in birds is, in many ways, similar to that found in turtles and various mammals. In the chicken brain, for instance, the serotonin cell bodies are located within the raphé region whereas the catecholamine cell bodies are scattered more laterally in the tegmentum of the brainstem, as in turtles and mammals (Fuxe and Ljungren, 1965; Ikeda and Gotoh, 1971). Moreover, lesion experiments performed in two birds (*Columba livia* and *Melopsittacus undulatus*) have shown that some of the catecholamine neurons of the brainstem here appear to project to various areas of the telencephalon (Bertler *et al.*, 1964; Tohyama *et al.*, 1974). The detailed organization of these presumed catecholamine telencephalic afferents in birds remains, however, to be thoroughly investigated.

If one compares the distribution of monoamine neurons in the brain of turtles with that found in the brain of some frogs (*Rana pipiens* and *R. temporaria*), both similarities and dissimilarities emerge (Parent, 1973b). First, the arrangement of serotonin neurons in frogs is very similar to that in *Chrysemys* (see schematic drawing in Fig. 14). In frogs, the serotonin neurons are located mostly within the raphé region of the brainstem (Fig. 14D), except at caudal midbrain levels where the serotonin cell bodies also invade the lateral portion of the tegmentum (Fig. 14B). The distribution of catecholamine neurons in the anuran brainstem, in contrast, differs from that found in turtles. Although a small medullary catecholamine cell group, which is similar to that of turtles, has been found in both *Rana pipiens* and *R. temporaria* (Fig. 14C), no catecholamine neurons could be visualized with certainty at the level of the isthmus region in these two species. Moreover, only a very small population of catecholamine neurons occurs within the tegmentum of the anuran midbrain. These midbrain catecholamine cell bodies are closely packed along the midline at the level of the mesodiencephalic junction (Fig. 14A) and do not invade the lateral tegmentum, as is the case in turtles.

Such a difference in distribution of the catecholamine neurons at brainstem levels between frogs and turtles is reflected in the pattern of the catecholamine innervation of the telencephalon. The catecholamine neurons of the lateral part of the midbrain cell group in *Chrysemys* give rise to the mesostriatal pathway that innervates the structures lying in the ventrolateral quadrant of the telencephalon, especially the ventral striatum (Fig. 15). In contrast, no catecholamine neurons occur in the lateral midbrain tegmentum of frogs and the anuran striatum is, compared to that of turtles, very poorly innervated by catecholamine axons (Fig. 15; see also Parent, 1975). The

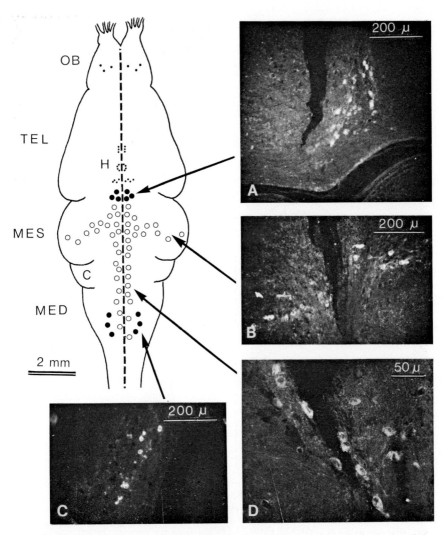

Fig. 14. A–D. Semischematic drawing of an horizontal section through the brain of the frog, *Rana temporaria*, showing the distribution of catecholamine and serotonin-containing cell bodies illustrated as full circles and empty circles, respectively. The fluorescence photomicrographs surrounding the drawing show catecholamine neurons lying in the rostral midbrain tegmentum (A), in the medulla oblongata (C), serotonin neurons occurring in the caudal midbrain tegmentum (B) and in the medulla oblongata (D). Transverse sections in A, B, and D and horizontal section in C. C, cerebellum; H, hypothalamus; MED, medulla oblongata; MES, mesencephalon; OB, olfactory bulb; TEL, telencephalon.

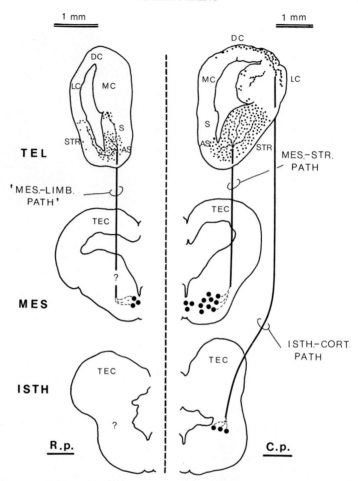

FIG. 15. Semischematic drawings of transverse half sections through the telencephalic hemisphere (TEL), mesencephalon (MES) and isthmus (ISTH) of the frog, *Rana pipiens* (R.p.) and of the turtle, *Chrysemys picta* (C.p.) comparing the distribution of catecholamine cell bodies (full circles) and axon terminals (dots). The postulated mesolimbic catecholamine pathway ('MES.-LIMB.PATH') of frogs is shown on the left-hand side of the figure. The mesostriatal (MES.-STR.PATH) and isthmocortical (ISTH.-CORT. PATH) catecholamine pathways of turtles are illustrated on the right-hand side. AS, nucleus accumbens septi; DC, dorsal cortex; LC, lateral cortex; MC, medial cortex; S, septum; STR, ventral striatum; TEC, optic tectum.

ventromedial quadrant (especially nucleus accumbens septi and nucleus lateralis septi) of the anuran telencephalon receives the strongest catecholamine innervation (Fig. 15). This observation is consistent with the fact that the monoamine oxidase activity appears stronger in the ventromedial part than in the ventrolateral part of the telencephalon of *Rana catesbeiana* (Northcutt, 1974). If we postulate that the midbrain catecholamine neurons (most of which are located near the midline) give rise to most of the catecholamine axon terminals that occur within the ventral half of the anuran telencephalon, as appears to be the case in reptiles, birds and mammals, then the midbrain telencephalic catecholamine connection could well represent an amphibian homologue of the above defined mammalian mesolimbic catecholamine pathway. If a catecholamine midbrain striatal connection exists in frogs (see Gruber and Ambros, 1974; Kicliter and Northcutt, 1975), it would be poorly developed in comparison to a mesolimbic catecholamine pathway.

On the other hand, there is the difficulty of finding a well-characterized isthmus catecholamine cell group in the anuran species investigated thus far. It is interesting to note that the anuran pallium seems devoid of catecholamine axon terminals when examined with the Falck–Hillarp method (Fig. 15). Thus, an homolog of the isthmocortical catecholamine pathway of turtles could be lacking or poorly developed in ranid frogs. However, our knowledge of the anatomy of monoamine systems in frogs is still scant, and further studies of anuran brains must be undertaken with the more sensitive glyoxylic acid method as well as with other neuroanatomical techniques, before any final conclusion on the different hypotheses formulated above can be reached.

It would also be premature, at this stage, to speculate on the significance of any findings that could emerge from the comparison between the organization of monoamine systems in turtles with those in fishes. Our knowledge of the monoamine neurons in all of these vertebrate groups is still too meager. Thus, results from detailed histofluorescence studies of the cellular localization of monoamines in the brains of fishes would obviously be of great help in reaching an overall understanding of the structural and functional organization of monoamine-containing neuronal systems in the brain of vertebrates.

V. Conclusion and Summary

This chapter has reviewed our knowledge of the organization of monoaminergic neurons in reptiles and compared the organization of these systems in the brains of vertebrates. Studies on reptiles have been confined to a turtle, *Chrysemys picta*, and the lizards *Lacerta muralis* and *L. viridis*.

In both turtles and lizards, the largest number of catecholaminergic neurons occurs in the midbrain tegmentum ventrolateral to the oculomotor nucleus. Turtles also have a distinct group of catecholaminergic neurons in the isthmus; it is apparently not present in lizards. Some catecholaminergic cells are present lateral to the raphé region, caudal to the midbrain, in lizards. Catecholamine neurons which contact the cerebrospinal fluid are present in the hypothalamus, particularly within the paraventricular organ, in both species. Catecholaminergic axon terminals are prevalent in the striatum of both groups, but the particular transmitter involved may vary between species. Fluorescent varicosities are also found in dorsal ventricular ridge and in the cortex in both groups.

Serotonin neurons are located in the raphé region in turtles and lizards, but there appear to be differences in their rostrocaudal distribution. Serotonin axon terminals are abundant in several nuclei in the thalamus, epithalamus, and midbrain.

Experimental studies suggest the presence of at least three catecholaminergic pathways in turtles. Neurons in the midbrain tegmentum project to the ventral striatum via a mesostriatal pathway. Neurons in the isthmus project to the cortex, and medullary cell groups project to the hypothalamus.

The overall organization of monoaminergic systems appears to be similar in the brains of reptiles, birds and mammals. A major difference between the pattern in these groups and that seen in frogs is the absence of a well-defined mesostriatal system in anurans.

There is a striking lack of information on monoaminergic systems in reptiles. There is no information on crocodilians and snakes, and all of the information available so far has been obtained with the Falck–Hillarp technique. It will be important to confirm these observations using the more sensitive glyoxylic acid method and to study the projections of monoamine cell groups with autoradiographic tracing techniques. Although studies on mammals make it likely that these systems are functionally very important, there have been no behavioral studies on reptiles.

Acknowledgement

This investigation was supported by the Medical Research Council of Canada.

References

Baker-Cohen, K. F. (1968). Comparative enzyme histochemical observations on sub-mammalian brains. *Ergebn. Anat. EntgwGesch.* 40, 1–70.
Baumgarten, H. G. and Braak, H. (1968). Catecholamine im Gehirn der Eidechse (*Lacerta viridis* und *Lacerta muralis*). *Z. Zellforsch. mikrosk. Anat.* 86, 574–602.
Bertler, A., Falck, B., Gottfries, C.-G., Ljungren, L. and Rosengren, E. (1964). Some observations on adrenergic connections between the mesencephalon and the cerebral hemispheres. *Acta pharmac. tox.* 21, 283–289.
Braak, H., Baumgarten, H. G. and Falck, B. (1968). 5-Hydroxytryptamine im Gehirn

der Eidechse (*Lacerta viridis* und *Lacerta muralis*). *Z. Zellforsch. mikrosk. Anat.* **90**, 161–185.

Cooper, J. C., Bloom, F. E. and Roth, R. H. (1974). "The Biochemical Basis of Neuropharmacology." Oxford Univ. Press, New York, London, Toronto, 2nd edn.

Cruce, W. L. R. and Nieuwenhuys, R. (1974). The cell masses in the brain stem of the turtle *Testudo hermanni*; a topographical and topological analysis. *J. comp. Neurol.* **156**, 277–306.

Dahlström, A. and Fuxe, K. (1964). Evidence for the existence of monoamine-containing neurons in the central nervous systems. I. Demonstration of monoamines in the cell bodies of brain stem neurons. *Acta physiol. scand.* Suppl. **232**, 1–80.

de Lange, S. J. (1913). Das Zwischenhirn und das Mittelhirn der Reptilien. *Folia neurobiol.* **7**, 67–138.

Di Carlo, V., Hubbard, J. E. and Pate, P. (1973). Fluorescence histochemistry of monoamine-containing cell bodies in the brain stem of the squirrel monkey (*Saimiri sciureus*). IV. An atlas. *J. comp. Neurol.* **152**, 347–372.

Ebner, F. F. and Colonnier, M. (1975). Synaptic patterns in the visual cortex of turtle: an electron microscopic study. *J. comp. Neurol.* **160**, 51–70.

Falck, B., Hillarp, N.-A., Thieme, G. and Torp, A. (1962). Fluorescence of catecholamines and related compounds condensed with formaldehyde. *J. Histochem. Cytochem.* **10**, 348–354.

Feldberg, W. and Myers, R. D. (1964). Effects on temperature of amines injected into the cerebral ventricles. A new concept of temperature regulation. *J. Physiol., Lond.* **173**, 226–237.

Fuxe, K. (1965). Evidence for the existence of monoamine-containing neurons in the central nervous system. IV. The distribution of monoamine terminals in the central nervous system. *Acta physiol. scand.* Suppl. **247**, 39–85.

Fuxe, K. and Ljungren, L. (1965). Cellular localization of monoamines in the upper brain stem of the pigeon. *J. comp. Neurol.* **125**, 355–382.

Fuxe, K., Hökfelt, I., Jonsson, G. and Ungerstedt, U. (1970). Fluorescence microscopy in neuroanatomy. *In* "Contemporary Research Method in Neuroanatomy." (W. J. H. Nauta and S. E. O. Ebbesson, eds). Springer Verlag, New York, Heidelberg, Berlin, pp. 275–314.

Fuxe, K., Goldstein, M., Hökfelt, T., Jonsson, G. and Lidbrink, P. (1974). Dopaminergic involvement in hypothalamic function: extrahypothalamic and hypothalamic control. A neuroanatomical analysis. *In* "Advances in Neurology." (F. H. McDowell and A. Barbeau, eds). Raven Press, New York 5, 405–419.

Goldby, F. and Gamble, H. J. (1957). The reptilian cerebral hemispheres. *Biol. Rev.* **32**, 383–420.

Gruber, E. R. and Ambros, V. R. (1974). A forebrain visual projection in the frog (*Rana pipiens*). *Expl Neurol.* **44**, 187–197.

Hall, W. C. and Ebner, F. F. (1970). Thalamotelencephalic projections in the turtle (*Pseudemys scripta*). *J. comp. Neurol.* **140**, 101–122.

Hoogland, P. V. J. M. (1977). Efferent connections of the striatum in *Tupinambis nigropunctatus*. *J. Morph.* **152**, 229–246.

Huber, G. C. and Crosby, E. C. (1933). The reptilian optic tectum. *J. comp. Neurol.* **57**, 57–164.

Ikeda, H. and Gotoh, J. (1971). Distribution of monoamine-containing cells in the central nervous system of the chicken. *Japan. J. Pharmac.* **21**, 763–784.

Johnston, J. B. (1915). The cell masses in the forebrain of the turtle, *Cistudo carolina*. *J. comp. Neurol.* **25**, 393–468.

Jouvet, M. (1972). The role of monoamines and acetylcholine-containing neurons in the regulation of sleep-waking cycle. *Ergebn. Physiol.* 64, 166–307.

Juorio, A. V. (1969). The distribution of dopamine in the brain of a tortoise, *Geochelone chilensis* (Gray). *J. Physiol., Lond.* 204, 503–529.

Karten, H. J. (1969). The organization of the avian telencephalon and some speculations on the phylogeny of the amniote telencephalon. *Ann. N.Y. Acad. Sci.* 167, 164–179.

Kicliter, E. and Northcutt, R. G. (1975). Ascending afferents to the telencephalon of ranid frogs: an anterograde degeneration study. *J. comp. Neurol.* 161, 239–254.

Kirsche, W. (1972). Die Entwicklung des Reptilien und deren Beziehung zur Hirn-Bauplanlehre. *Nova Acta Leop.* 37, 1–78.

Lapierre, Y., Beaudet, A., Demianczuk, N. and Descarries, L. (1973). Noradrenergic axon terminals in the cerebral cortex of the rat. II. Quantitative data revealed by light and electron microscope radioautography of the frontal cortex. *Brain Res.* 63, 175–182.

Lindvall, O. and Björklund, A. (1974a). The glyoxilic acid fluorescence histochemical method: a detailed account of the methodology for the visualization of central catecholamine neurons. *Histochemistry* 39, 97–127.

Lindvall, O. and Björklund, A. (1974b). The organization of the ascending catecholamine neuron systems in the rat brain as revealed by the glyoxylic acid fluorescence method. *Acta physiol. scand.* Suppl. 412, 1–48.

Lindvall, O., Björklund, A. and Divac, I. (1977). Organization of mesencephalic dopamine neurons projecting to neocortex and septum. *Adv. Biochem. Psychopharmac.* 16, 39–46.

Lohman, A. H. M., Hoogland, P. V. J. M. and van Woerden-Verkley, I. (1973). Experimental studies on the efferent telencephalic and connections in the tegu lizard. *Anat. Rec.* 175, 374–375.

Maickel, R. P., Cox, R. H. Jr, Saillant, J. and Miller, F. P. (1968). A method for the determination of serotonin and norepinephrine in discrete areas of the rat brain. *Int. J. Neuro-pharmac.* 7, 275–281.

Nauta, W. J. H. and Mehler, W. R. (1966). Projections of the lentiform nucleus in the monkey. *Brain Res.* 1, 3–42.

Northcutt, R. G. (1970). The telencephalon of the western painted turtle (*Chrysemys picta belli*). *Univ. Illinois biol. Monogr.* (43), 1–113.

Northcutt, R. G. (1974). Some histochemical observations on the telencephalon of the bullfrog, *Rana catesbeiana Shaw. J. comp. Neurol.* 157, 379–389.

Papez, J. W. (1935). Thalamus of turtles and thalamic evolution. *J. comp. Neurol.* 61, 433–475.

Parent, A. (1973a). Distribution of monoamine-containing nerve terminals in the brain of the painted turtle, *Chrysemys picta. J. comp. Neurol.* 148, 153–166.

Parent, A. (1973b). Distribution of monoamine-containing neurons in the brain stem of the frog, *Rana temporaria. J. Morphol.* 139, 67–78.

Parent, A. (1975). The monoaminergic innervation of the telencephalon of the frog, *Rana pipiens. Brain Res.* 99, 35–47.

Parent, A. (1976). Striatal afferent connections in the turtle (*Chrysemys picta*) as revealed by retrograde axonal transport of horseradish peroxidase. *Brain Res.* 108, 25–36.

Parent, A. (1979). The anatomical organization of monoamine and acetylcholinesterase-containing neurons in the vertebrate hypothalamus. *In* "Handbook of the Hypothalamus." (P. J. Morgane and J. Pankseep, eds). M. Dekker, New York (in press).

Parent, A. and Olivier, A. (1970). Comparative histochemical study of the corpus striatum. *J. Hirnforsch.* 12, 73–81.

Parent, A. and Poitras, D. (1974). The origin and distribution of catecholaminergic axon terminals in the cerebral cortex of the turtle (*Chrysemys picta*). *Brain Res.* 78, 345–358.

Pin, D., Jones, B. and Jouvet, M. (1968). Topographie des neurones monoaminergiques du tronc cérébral du chat: étude par histofluorescence. *C. r. Séanc. Soc. Biol.*, **162**, 2136–2141.

Poirier, L. J., Parent, A. and Roberge, A. G. (1975). The striopallidal system: its implication in motor disorders. *In* "Pathobiology Annual." (H. L. Ioachim, ed.). Appleton-Century-Crofts, New York, **5**, 339–367.

Ramón, P. (1896). Estructura del encéfalo del caméleon. *Rev. trimestr. micrograf.* **1**, 46–82.

Riss, W., Halpern, M. and Scalia, F. (1969). The quest for clues to forebrain evolution—the study of reptiles. *Brain Behav. Evol.* **2**, 1–50.

Romer, A. S. (1966). "Vertebrate Paleontology." Univ. Chicago Press, Chicago, 3rd edn.

Romer, A. S. (1967). Early reptilian evolution reviewed. *Evolution* **21**, 821–833.

Schwyn, R. C. and Fox, C. A. (1974). The primate substantia nigra: a Golgi and electron microscopic study. *J. Hirnforsch.* **15**, 95–126.

Tohyama, M., Maeda, T., Hashimoto, J., Shrestha, G. R., Tamura, O and Shimuzu, N. (1974). Comparative anatomy of the locus coeruleus. I. Organization and ascending projections of the catecholamine-containing neurons in the pontine region of the bird, *Melopsittacus undulatus*. *J. Hirnforsch.* **15**, 319–330.

Ungerstedt, U. (1971). Stereotaxic mapping of the monoamine pathways in the rat brain. *Acta physiol. scand.* Suppl. **367**, 1–48.

Welch, A. S. and Welch, B. L. (1969). Solvent extraction method for simultaneous determination of norepinephrine, dopamine, serotonin and 5-hydroxyindolacetic acid in a single mouse brain. *Analyt. Biochem.* **30**, 161–179.

Welsh, J. H. (1970). Phylogenetic aspects of the distribution of biogenic amines. *In* "Biogenic Amines as Physiological Regulators." (J. J. Blum, ed.). Prentice-Hall, Englewood Cliffs, New Jersey, pp. 75–94.

CHAPTER 7

Neurophysiology of the Forebrain

M. G. BELEKHOVA

Sechenov Institute of Evolutionary Physiology and Biochemistry,
U.S.S.R. Academy of Sciences, Leningrad, U.S.S.R.

I. Introduction

Comparative neurobiology is now in a period of rapid advancement due, in part, to widespread reinvestigation of neuronal connections. Modern silver impregnation, electron microscopical, horseradish peroxidase and autoradiographic techniques have yielded much new data for neuroanatomists. However, electrophysiological studies during the past two decades have also contributed to the progress of comparative neurobiology. Bremer *et al.* (1939) were the first to study afferent representations in the forebrain of reptiles and birds with physiological methods. In the 1950s and 1960s, similar investigations on reptiles, amphibians and fishes were performed in the USSR and the USA. It was these electrophysiological experiments which first suggested non-olfactory functions for the telencephalons of non-mammalian vertebrates.

Most electrophysiological studies on reptiles have been "electroanatomical", in the sense that they have established afferent and efferent connections by recording evoked activity. At the same time, electrophysiological methods can display some advantages over hodological methods. Simple application of direct connectional criteria in the study of some afferent systems (e.g. the olfactory representation in the telencephalons of non-mammalian vertebrates) can result in erroneous conclusions concerning their extent and properties. Electrophysiology permits the study of both monosynaptic and polysynaptic connections, as well as conduction velocity, synaptic activation, correlation between excitatory and inhibitory processes, and the interaction of converging afferents on single units. Electrophysiological techniques can also be used to determine the manner in which information is processed through successive centers in a pathway. Studies of this type have barely begun in reptiles, although several amphibian studies have followed the initial investigations of Lettvin, Maturana and Grüsser (Lettvin *et al.*, 1959;

Maturana *et al.*, 1960; Ewert, 1968, 1970, 1972; Grüsser and Grüsser–Cornehls, 1968, 1972; Ingle, 1970, 1973). Some investigations of the role of different brain structures in reptilian behavior have also been carried out (Hertzler and Hayes, 1967, 1969; Eldarov, 1969; Hertzler, 1972; Morlock, 1972; Bass *et al.*, 1973).

These technical advances in comparative neurobiology have paralleled a growing tendency to view comparative anatomical and physiological data within the framework of evolutionary theory (Biryukov, 1960; Anokhin, 1964; Diamond, 1967; Karamian, 1966, 1967; Senn, 1969; Batuev, 1973), thus promoting new insights into evolutionary changes in vertebrate nervous systems. Two major approaches have been used in this regard.

The first approach has tried to establish homologies between structures in different organisms. However, this approach has several major limitations. Evolving brain structures may lose or acquire connections, thus making it difficult to establish homologies by connectional criteria alone (Holmgren, 1925). The problem is aggravated by the significant variability of telence-phalic afferent projections among different vertebrates. This variation results from the adaptive specializations of different taxa. Physiological methods are also limited, as the function of a structure may change during the course of evolution (Holmgren, 1925). For example, "neopallial functions" in primitive vertebrates are at least partly the property of the somatic striatum in sharks (Holmgren, 1925) or medial pallium of amphibians (Gusel'nikov, 1965); but this does not imply a homology between these structures. Thus, all available criteria must be used in establishing homologies (Nieuwenhuys and Boden-heimer, 1966; Campbell and Hodos, 1970; Northcutt, 1970).

The second approach stems from the work of Orbeli (1934, 1942, 1958), one of the founders of evolutionary physiology as a distinct science. He pursued phylogenetic, ontogenetic and clinical lines of investigation and stressed the importance of their synthesis. His work and that of C. J. Herrick (1930, 1956) on the evolutionary stages of vertebrate brains generated a new approach to the evolutionary development of brain functions. This approach focused on the formation and development of individual functional systems and sought to establish major stages in the development of neural inte-grative capacities throughout vertebrate evolution (Karamian, 1956–76).

This chapter emphasizes the second approach in reviewing neurophysio-logical studies on reptiles. The functional organization of sensory systems is emphasized. Sections II, III, and IV deal with the representations of the major sensory systems at mesencephalic, diencephalic, and telencephalic levels, respectively. Section V treats thalamotelencephalic systems which are non-specific in that they do not process information restricted to a single sensory modality. Wherever possible, neural organization in reptiles is compared to that of other vertebrates. The last two sections return to the two theoretical approaches to evolution of the central nervous system. Section VI evaluates various attempts to establish homologies between forebrain structures in reptiles and mammals. Section VII summarizes our current concept of the reptilian stage of brain organization.

A number of neurophysiological studies have utilized various subdivisions (often the cerebellum) of reptilian brains as models for studying general problems regarding the organization of nervous centers (Llinas et al., 1968; Llinas and Hillman, 1969; Llinas and Nicholson, 1969; Kennedy et al., 1970; Manteifel', 1966; Bantil, 1972; Gusel'nikov et al., 1973; Walsh et al., 1973; Tsitolovsky and Pivovarov, 1974, 1975a, 1975b). Such studies are beyond the scope of the present review.

II. Mesencephalon

A. VISUAL REPRESENTATIONS

1. General

The optic tectum has traditionally been considered the main sensory correlation center in reptiles and other non-mammalian vertebrates. It was believed that the tectum received projections from several sensory modalities and, in particular, that it received the majority of retinal fibers. More recent work (see Sections IIIB and IVC) has indicated that the forebrain also plays important roles in the analysis of sensory information. However, the studies reviewed in this section suggest that the traditional view is correct to the extent that the tectum is involved in processing both visual and non-visual sensory information related to the guidance of movement.

Visual information is carried from the retina to the tectum via the axons of retinal ganglion cells. The way in which information is processed in the tectum is determined initially by the organization of the retinotectal projection and the manner in which it terminates in the tectum. Subsequent processing is effected by neuronal interactions within the tectum itself and with afferents from other regions of the brain. These interactions are considered important in the guidance of movement.

2. Retinotectal Projections

The retinotectal projection is organized so as to preserve the map of the visual world. Electrophysiological mapping experiments on the tectum in alligators (*Alligator mississippiensis*), turtles (*Emys orbicularis*) and snakes (*Agkistrodon halys brevicaudus, A. caliginosus*) reveal a precise retinotopic organization, similar to that present in other non-mammalian vertebrates (Heric and Kruger, 1965; Gusel'nikov et al., 1970; Terashima and Goris, 1975). Differences occur mainly in the geometry of the projection, and relate to specialized adaptations of the retina (Kruger, 1970).

The axons of retinal ganglion cells terminate primarily in the superficial layers of the tectum. Thus, multicomponent electrical responses have been recorded from the tectal surface following light flashes or electrical stimulation of the optic nerve in *Alligator mississippiensis*, *Emys orbicularis*, *Testudo horsfieldii*, *Agama caucasica*, and *Ophisaurus apodus* (Smirnov, 1961; Smirnov and Manteifel', 1962; Voronin and Gusel'nikov, 1963; Mazurskaya *et al.*, 1964; Gusel'nikov, 1965; Heric and Kruger, 1965; Karamian *et al.*, 1966, 1968; Manteifel', 1966; Belekhova and Kosareva, 1967; Kruger, 1969; Isabekova, 1969; Belekhova and Safarov, 1976). More detailed analyses indicate that retinal fibers are distributed differentially within the superficial layers according to fiber size, degree of myelinization, and synaptic type (Heric and Kruger, 1966; Manteifel', 1966; Kruger, 1969; Davydova and Mazurskaya, 1973). Some retinal fibers terminate in the stratum opticum and stratum zonale (Huber and Crosby, 1933) on the apical dendrites of cells, the somata of which, are situated in deeper layers. However, the main contingent of retinal afferents terminate in the stratum fibrosum et griseum superficiale on both dendrites and perikarya (Armstrong, 1950, 1951; Burns and Goodman, 1967; Knapp and Kang, 1968a, b; Butler and Northcutt, 1971; Davydova, 1973; Davydova and Smirnov, 1973; Braford, 1973; Butler, 1974; Northcutt and Butler, 1974a, b; Northcutt *et al.*, 1974; Bass and Northcutt, 1975; Cruce and Cruce, 1975; Repérant, 1975, 1976). A few authors have also observed terminal degeneration in the stratum griseum centrale following enucleation (Kosareva, 1967; Davydova and Mazurskaya, 1973). According to Foster and Hall (1975), cells in this layer have dendrites which reach into the overlying strata and are contacted by retinal afferents. Concurrent electrophysiological and electron microscopic investigations reveal synchronic correlations between different types of tectal degeneration and the properties of tectal responses elicited by optic nerve stimulation following enucleation in turtles (Boiko and Davydova, 1975). This differential distribution of retinotectal fibers resembles that seen in amphibians and fishes (Scalia *et al.*, 1968; Lazar and Szekely, 1969; Rubinson, 1969; Maximova *et al.*, 1971; Szekely, 1973; Manteifel', 1974; Gusel'nikov and Loginov, 1976).

3. *Intratectal Processing*

A significant portion of the analysis of visual information in reptiles is performed in the deeper layers of the optic tectum, as it is in other nonmammalian vertebrates (Ewert, 1968, 1970, 1972; Grüsser and Grüsser-Cornehls, 1968; Gusel'nikov, 1970; Gusel'nikov *et al.*, 1970; Ingle, 1970, 1973; Gusel'nikov and Loginov, 1976; Revzin, 1970). Thus, the properties of tectal neurons in *Emys orbicularis* and *Chrysemys scripta elegans* and their reactions to visual stimuli are found to differ as one passes a recording electrode from superficial to deep tectal layers. Specifically: (i) the receptive fields of neurons driven by a light spot or a moving pattern become larger and more complex (Gusel'nikov et al., 1970; Boiko and Davydova, 1973; Boiko, 1976); (ii) responsiveness to moving stimuli and directional sensitivity increases (Gusel'nikov et al., 1970; Robbins, 1972); (iii) the number of spontaneously active cells increases (Mazurskaya et al., 1964; Gusel'nikov et al., 1970; Robbins, 1972); (iv) the latency of on–off responses to diffuse light increases (Gusel'nikov et al., 1970); (iv) neuronal habituation increases, i.e. there are more "newness" neurons (Gusel'nikov et al., 1970; Robbins, 1972; Boiko, 1976); (v) deep tectal, mainly periventricular, layers reveal some multimodal cells with variable receptive fields, activated binocularly (Gusel'-nikov et al., 1970; Robbins, 1972; Boiko and Davydova, 1973; Boiko, 1976). These observations suggest increased complexity in the processing of visual information in the deeper layers of the tectum. The tectum of turtles shows vertical or columnar organization, as well as a correlation between the dimension of receptive fields and the pattern of dendritic branching (Boiko and Davydova, 1973).

Analysis of evoked potentials and single unit activity reveal that the reptilian optic tectum processes intensity and wavelength information (Heric and Kruger, 1966; Zagorul'ko, 1968; Robbins, 1972). The spectral sensitivities of the optic tectum and the retina are similar; their maximum is at the longer wavelength, the red region of the spectrum. There are some discrepancies at the shorter wavelengths. The optic tectum has a second peak of sensitivity in the blue region, which is poorly expressed in the retina (Granda and Stirling, 1965; Muntz and Sokol, 1967; Zagorul'ko, 1968). Variations in spectral sensitivity correlate largely with ecological adaptation (Granda and O'Shea, 1972).

4. Interaction with Non-tectal Afferents

a. *Forebrain Afferents.* In contrast to visual inputs, information from the forebrain and other sensory modalities terminates in the deeper layers of the optic tectum. Reptiles have few, if any, direct corticotectal connections (Karamian et al., 1968); rather, corticotegmental paths predominate (J. Hall and Ebner, 1974). Telencephalic influence on tectal functions in reptiles, as in amphibians (Halpern, 1972; Ingle, 1973; Szekely, 1973; Trachtenberg and Ingle, 1974), is probably conveyed through the thalamus and mesencephalic tegmentum. Cortical stimulation in *Emys orbicularis* inhibits flash-evoked activity (Zagourl'ko, 1967; Karamian et al., 1968). In anuran amphibians, modulation of the retinotectal channel occurs via the pretectum, thalamus and telencephalon (Ewert, 1968, 1970, 1972; Ingle, 1970, 1973).

b. *Somatosensory and Auditory Afferents.* Direct spinal projections to the tectum are poorly developed in reptiles, as in amphibians. Spinal afferents are confined mainly to the tegmentum (Goldby and Robinson, 1962; Ebbesson,

1967, 1969; Szekely, 1973). Representation of non-visual afferents in the reptilian optic tectum has not been systematically studied by physiological methods. Evoked potentials and single unit responses to auditory and tactile stimulation in turtles and alligators predominate in periventricular tectal layers. A crude somatotopic projection has also been shown here. The periventricular layers possess some multimodal units, with convergence of visual, somatosensory and auditory impulses in different combinations (Moore and Tschirgi, 1962; Heric and Kruger, 1966; Gusel'nikov et al., 1970). The response characteristics of the mesencephalic trigeminal nucleus (located in the deep tectal layers) to proprioceptive impulses from the masticatory muscles have been studied in *Caiman crocodilus* (Vegetti and Palmieri, 1969; Desole et al., 1970). In mammals, auditory and somatosensory projections to deep tectal layers are topographically organized, though not as precisely as are visual projections (Sprague, 1966; Gordon, 1973; Ingle, 1973; Stein et al., 1975).

c. *Infrared Receptor Information.* Representation of infrared receptor organs, situated in facial pits and innervated by the trigeminal nerve, was found in the optic tectum of the pit vipers *Trimeresurus flavoviridis, Agkistrodon halys brevicaudus* and *A. caliginosus* (Goris and Terashima, 1973; Terashima and Goris, 1975, 1976). These are the so-called infrared "eyes" that let the snake locate warm, moving prey, especially in the dark. The tectal projection of these infrared receptors is similar to that of the retina: it is contralateral, occupies the superficial tectal layers, and has a topographic organization, though the receptive fields of corresponding neurons are much wider than those of visual tectal units. Tectal neurons do not exhibit convergence or interaction of visual and thermal impulses. Thus, behavioral correlation probably occurs in some other brain division.

5. *Lesion Studies*

Physiological studies demonstrate that the optic tectum of reptiles plays a significant role in processing visual information. Attempts at elucidating this role by studying the deficits in visual behavior produced by lesions of the optic tectum have produced contradictory results. On the one hand, studies by Hertzler and Hayes (1967) and Hertzler (1972) report that bilateral tectal ablation in the turtle, *Terrapene carolina*, fails to produce blindness and results only in slight impairment on a visual cliff task. On the other hand, Bass et al. (1973) showed profound disturbance of natural visual behavior and learned pattern discrimination in the turtle, *Podocnemis unifilis*, after bilateral tectal ablation. Ablated turtles were incapable of locating or identifying objects, though they could discriminate crude differences in luminosity. These results could reflect differences in the extent of tectal damage or in the nature of the visual tasks tested. In the future, it will be important to use tests of visual function which are performed in natural environments and which are as natural as is possible. At present, tectal mechanisms for orienting responses are known for other vertebrate groups (Schneider, 1967; Ingle, 1970, 1973). In studying optokinetic nystagmus in turtles (*Terrapene carolina, Chrysemys scripta*) after tectal ablation, the optic tectum was shown to be the highest integrative center involved in movement detection (Hertzler and Hayes, 1969; Hertzler, 1972).

B. Somatosensory Representations

Somatosensory representation in the tegmentum of the turtle, *Emys orbicularis*, coincides with the intercollicular nucleus and the periventricular gray (Belekhova, 1973a), which receive direct spinal afferents (Ebbesson, 1967, 1969; Pedersen, 1973). Similar structures form a locus of overlap for the spinal and lemniscal projections from dorsal column nuclei in mammals (Schroeder *et al.*, 1968; Schroeder and Jane, 1971; Walsh and Ebner, 1973). The majority of somatic responsive, mesencephalic neurons in alligators (*Alligator mississippiensis*) display non-specific, extralemniscal properties. However, a small number of more specialized cells are activated either bilaterally or ipsilaterally (Moore, 1961). In turtles, electrical stimulation of the tegmental somatosensory region elicits short-latency responses in the ventral part of the ventrocaudal thalamus (see Section IIIC), suggesting that this part of the tegmentum may be a source of somatic impulses to the thalamus (Belekhova, 1973a). High-frequency stimulation (50–300 Hz) of the tegmentum in turtles produces EEG activation, although this arousal response is different from that in mammals (Voronin *et al.*, 1961; Belekhova, 1965). Also, see Section VB.

C. Auditory Representations

Some species of crocodilians and gekkonid lizards are sensitive to sounds in the middle frequency range, but all other species of reptiles are sensitive to sounds at relatively restricted ranges of frequency, with low-range sounds being most easily detected (Wever and Vernon, 1956a, 1956b; Karimova, 1958; McGill, 1960; Baru, 1962; Wever, 1965, 1968; Baird, 1970; Manley, 1970, 1974). Turtles respond to tones ranging from 100–700Hz while, 700–3000 Hz is the most effective range in *Crocodylus acutus* (Wever and Vernon, 1956a; Wever, 1971). Electrophysiological experiments show an auditory representation in the torus semicircularis of caimans (*Caiman crocodilus*) and gekkonid lizards (*Gekko gecko*) (Manley, 1971; Kennedy, 1974). The central nucleus of the torus semicircularis receives auditory projections through the lateral lemniscus. The peripheral region of the central nucleus is responsible for vocalizations related to alarm reactions (Kennedy, 1975). The torus semicircularis in caimans, as well as the primary acoustic nuclei (cochlear nuclei), possess a tonotopic organization similar to that of birds and mammals. Single units of the torus semicircularis are responsive to sound ranging from 70 to 1850 Hz, with maximum sensitivity at 1000 Hz (Manley, 1970, 1971). In lizards (Gekkonidae, *Coleonyx variegatus*), two peaks of frequency sensitivity are found, one at 400–800 Hz and a second at 1500 Hz. These reptiles show a sharpening effect around the optimum frequency as one records from higher auditory centers; however, this sharpening effect is more pronounced in mammals (Suga and Campbell, 1967).

III. Diencephalon

A. THALAMIC ZONES

1. *General*

The dorsal thalamus of reptiles is greatly elaborated and contains nuclear groups similar to the anterior, medial, ventral and posterior thalamic areas of mammals (Papez, 1935; Kappers *et al.*, 1936). These nuclei will be analyzed here in terms of three zones which can be distinguished on the basis of afferent connections in the thalami of *Emys orbicularis* and *Testudo horsfieldii*. These zones roughly coincide with the thalamic distribution of principal sensory systems (Ebbesson *et al.*, 1972; Riss *et al.*, 1972), and are termed: (1) lateral, (2) mediocentral, and (3) ventrocaudal (Belekhova and Kosareva, 1971; Belekhova, 1973a, 1977). The nomenclature of Papez (1935) is utilized for the nuclei in turtles. The general features of each thalamic zone are presented in this section. Sections IIIB, IIIC and IIID analyze the properties of sensory inputs to the three zones in more detail. The systems discussed in these sections are summarized in Fig. 1.

FIG. 1. A generalized scheme of the representation of the visual, somatic and auditory systems in a turtle brain. Connections in the visual system are indicated by solid lines, those in somatosensory systems by dotted lines and those in the auditory system by small dotted lines. Sections through the mesencephalon, diencephalon, and telencephalon are shown. In the diencephalon, the three thalamic zones are marked by horizontal shading (the lateral zone), the symbol v (the mediocentral zone) and dotted horizontal and vertical shading (the ventrocaudal zone). c. dors., dorsal (= general) cortex; c. lat., lateral cortex; c. med., medial cortex; d.v.r., dorsal ventricular ridge; ic., nucleus intercollicularis; l.f.b., lateral forebrain bundle; m.f.b., medial forebrain bundle; n.(c)l., nucleus (centralis) lateralis; n.GL(d), dorsal lateral geniculate nucleus; n.GL(v), ventral lateral geniculate nucleus; n.hab.l., lateral habenular nucleus; n.hab.m., medial habenular nucleus; n.mgc. th., magnocellular nucleus of the thalamus; n.re., nucleus reuniens; n.rot., nucleus rotundus; n.spped., nucleus suprapeduncularis; n.v., nucleus ventralis; pa.th., pallial thickening; ped.d., dorsal peduncle of the lateral forebrain bundle; ped.v., ventral peduncle of the lateral forebrain bundle; p.h., primordium hippocampi; str.d., dorsal striatum; str.v., ventral striatum; teg., mesencephalic tegmentum; t.o., optic tectum; tr.op., optic tract; t.s., torus semicircularis; tr.t.-th., tectothalamic tract.

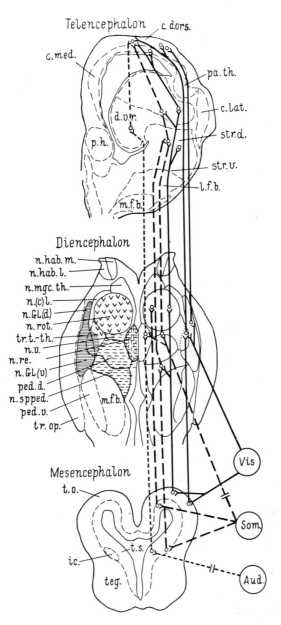

FIG. 1

2. Lateral Thalamic Zone

The lateral zone is primarily visual and includes the lateral geniculate nucleus, nucleus ovalis, triangular area and nucleus of the dorsal supraoptic decussation. All these nuclei (except the nucleus of the supraoptic decussation) receive direct retinal afferents, which are especially abundant in the lateral geniculate in most reptiles (Armstrong, 1950, 1951; Burns and Goodman, 1967; Kosareva, 1967; Knapp and Kang, 1968a, 1968b; Hall and Ebner, 1970a; Butler and Northcutt, 1971; Repérant, 1972, 1975, 1976; Braford, 1973; Halpern, 1973; Halpern and Frumin, 1973a, 1973b; Butler, 1974; Northcutt and Butler, 1974a, 1974b; Northcutt et al., 1974; Bass and Northcutt, 1975; Cruce and Cruce, 1975; Platel et al., 1975). The majority of single units in the lateral zone respond to light flashes, but not to electrical stimulation of the skin.

3. Mediocentral Thalamic Zone

The mediocentral zone is occupied by nucleus rotundus, the largest nucleus of the dorsal thalamus, and by the adjacent magnocellular and central lateral (= n. dorsolateralis anterior) nuclei. While nucleus rotundus does not receive a direct retinal input according to morphological experiments, more than half its units respond to visual stimuli; one-fifth of them reveal convergence of visual and somatic impulses. In the upper half of the dorsal thalamus, units respond to somatic stimuli but not to flashes of light. The exact location of these units was not determined (Belekhova, 1977); however, this dorsal thalamic region is known to receive direct spinal projections. Different authors have recognized this somatic sensory region under different names. In Tupinambis, it is nucleus intermedius dorsalis thalami, located rostral and dorsal to nucleus rotundus and regarded as a possible homologue of the intralaminar nuclei of mammals (Ebbesson, 1969; Ebbesson et al., 1972). In Iguana, this region corresponds to part of nucleus dorsolateralis anterior (Butler and Northcutt, 1973). In turtles, it is probably nucleus ovalis (Pedersen, 1973). Riss et al. (1972) describe a similar somatic sensory region located between the dorsal lateral geniculate and nucleus rotundus in turtles. This thalamic area receives somatic sensory input via the optic tectum and may be homologous to the mammalian posterior nucleus.

4. Ventrocaudal Thalamic Zone

The third thalamic zone includes such heterogeneous structures as the ventral nucleus, nucleus reuniens, suprapeduncular nucleus (which probably correspond to the ventrolateral area in Podocnemis unifilis, Riss et al., 1972) and the region related to the posterior commissure. Further investigations of this zone will probably reveal functional differentiation. The nuclei of the ventrocaudal thalamic zone all contribute to somatosensory representation, and together they contain four-fifths of all somatic responsive units in the thalamus of turtles. Experimental morphological studies indicate that the lateral part of the ventrocaudal thalamic zone receives somatic projections (Riss *et al.*, 1972; Pedersen, 1973). Somatic representation in this area largely overlaps visual representation, both topographically and at the level of single units. One-third of the units respond to both somatic and visual stimuli (Belekhova and Kosareva, 1971). Overlap of somatic and auditory projections might also be expected in this area. Papez (1936) suggested that the posterior part of nucleus reuniens is homologous to the medial geniculate, an auditory nucleus in mammals. The topographical relationships of nucleus reuniens are also similar to those of nucleus ovoidalis, an auditory thalamic relay nucleus in birds (Papez, 1936; Karten, 1969; Riss *et al.*, 1972). Nucleus reuniens in caimans and lizards and nucleus Z in alligators correspond to the medial geniculate nucleus of turtles (Huber and Crosby, 1926) and receive an auditory projection from the torus semicircularis (Pritz, 1974a; Foster, 1975).

B. Sources and Properties of Thalamic Visual Representations

1. *Retinothalamic and Tectothalamic Channels*

Visual information can reach the reptilian thalamus through two principal channels. Retinal information can reach the dorsal and ventral lateral geniculate nuclei directly (see Section IIIA1). In addition, retinal information may be conveyed through the optic tectum to the nucleus rotundus (see Section IIIB3). Nucleus rotundus and the dorsal lateral geniculate project to the forebrain (see Section IVC2), thereby forming tectothalamic and retinothalamic visual pathways to the forebrain. Interaction between the two pathways can also occur in the thalamus in that the optic tectum projects to the geniculate complex as well as nucleus rotundus (Hall and Ebner, 1970a). Thus, retinal and tectal information can converge in the geniculate complex.

2. *Thalamic Responses to Visual Stimuli*

Initial analyses of thalamic visual processing have been carried out by recording electrical activity in the thalamus while visual stimuli are presented to the anesthetized subject (Belekhova and Zagorul'ko, 1964; Karamian *et al.*, 1966, 1971, 1975a; Belekhova, 1967, 1970a, b, 1972a, 1973a; Belekhova and Kosareva, 1967; Karamian, 1967, 1969a). These studies demonstrate that light-evoked potentials and single unit responses in lateral geniculate and nucleus rotundus are similar due to their common retinal origin. Flash responses have similar patterns and consist of an initial component and a series of subsequent components, with some decrease in frequency compared to responses in the optic nerve. The lateral geniculate nucleus and nucleus rotundus are also similar in their responses to varying flash intensity and the presentation of steady light. The different pathways to the two structures are reflected in the latency of the geniculate and rotundal single unit responses and in their behavior during rhythmic flash stimulation. In the geniculate, initial components can follow 1–5/s stimulation, with later components becoming habituated; whereas in nucleus rotundus, the initial component of a flash-evoked potential is habituated during stimulation, and later components are facilitated or even driven by repetitive stimulation. Rhythmic stimulation reveals similar response patterns in lateral geniculate nucleus and dorsal cortex, and in nucleus rotundus and the optic tectum.

Two types of flash-evoked responses are found in the ventrocaudal thalamic zone. One type possesses short latencies and is presumably related to the entrance of large-size fibers of the accessory optic system (Kosareva, 1967; Knapp and Kang, 1968b); the other type possesses latencies similar to those in nucleus rotundus. Only part of the visual responses in this zone are mediated through the optic tectum (Belekhova and Kosareva, 1971; Morenkov and Pivovarov, 1973, 1975).

Little is known of other thalamic visual properties, except for the topographic organization of tectal projections to nucleus rotundus in turtles (Morenkov and Pivovarov, 1973, 1975). A large number of rotundal units demonstrate on–off responses to diffuse light, but about one-third of these units react only to moving stimuli. The receptive fields of these units cover the entire visual field with a zone of higher excitability below the horizontal meridian. Some units respond binocularly.

3. Tectal Contribution to Thalamic Responses

The visual responses in the thalamus of an intact animal are due to both retinal and tectal contributions. The tectal contribution to the total response has been studied by determining the effects of electrical stimulation of the tectum or of tectal lesions.

Electrical stimulation of the optic tectum in turtles reveals tectal representation in all three thalamic zones, though each zone possesses different characteristics. The greatest number of units responding to tectal stimulation are concentrated in nucleus rotundus and in the part of the lateral geniculate which overlaps the tecto-thalamic tract. Light flashes and tectal stimulation elicit similar response patterns in these units. Fewer units in the ventrocaudal thalamic zone respond to tectal stimulation (Belekhova and Akulina, 1970; Belekhova and Kosareva, 1971; Belekhova, 1973a). These findings correlate with morphological data on the differential density of tecto-thalamic projections in turtles and other reptiles (Hall and Ebner, 1970a; Belekhova and

Kosareva, 1972; Butler and Northcutt, 1971; Braford, 1972; Foster et al., 1973; Kosareva, 1974; Foster and Hall, 1975).

Unilateral ablation of the optic tectum destroys the heterogenity of neuronal receptive fields in nucleus rotundus and their response to stimuli moving in the contralateral visual field in that the thresholds of response to light and movement are raised. Restricted lesions of the optic tectum disturb rotundal unit responses to stimulus movement only in corresponding parts of the visual field (Morenkov and Pivovarov, 1973, 1975). After total, bilateral tectal ablation, visually driven units in nucleus rotundus decrease so significantly that the cells of this nucleus become essentially indifferent to light flashes. After unilateral tectal ablation, visual responses in nucleus rotundus are preserved due to contralateral tectorotundal projections (Belekhova and Kosareva, 1971).

4. *Comparisons with other Vertebrates*

The main retinofugal pathways, retinotectal and retinothalamic, are present in the visual systems of all vertebrates (Polyak, 1957; Karamian et al., 1966, 1972, 1975a; Ebbesson, 1970, 1972a; Doty, 1973; Northcutt and Przybylski, 1973). Telencephalic visual representation, demonstrated electrophysiologically, occurs in all anamniotes and in reptiles (Zagorul'ko, 1957; Supin and Gusel'nikov, 1964; Vesselkin, 1966; Karamian et al., 1966, 1969a; Belekhova and Vesselkin, 1969; Vesselkin and Kovačević, 1973a, 1973b; Vesselkin and Agayan, 1970; Vesselkin et al., 1971; Cohen et al., 1973).

However, the pathway by which visual impulses reach the telencephalon in anamniotes is as yet unknown. Morphological data indicate that the degree of overlap of tectofugal and thalamofugal visual pathways may be greater in anamniotes than in amniotes, as sharks, some teleosts and some amphibians show convergence of retinal and tectal projections at the level of the lateral geniculate and/or nucleus rotundus (Ebbesson and Ramsey, 1968; Ebbesson, 1971, 1972b; Ebbesson et al., 1972; Sharma, 1972). In frogs, the two pathways overlap considerably in the thalamus (Rubinson, 1968; Lazar, 1969; Scalia and Gregory, 1970). Although the two pathways are not as specialized as in reptiles, electrophysiological experiments reveal that the relationship between them is similar to that in reptiles (Belekhova, 1973b).

In birds, the two visual pathways (retino-tecto-rotundo-ectostriate and retino-thalamo-hyperstriate) are discrete at all neural levels (Karten and Nauta, 1968; Karten, 1969; Karten and Hodos, 1970; Karten et al., 1973; Meier et al., 1974; Mihailović et al., 1974).

Segregation and specialization of these pathways (retino-tecto-thalamo-cortical and retino-geniculo-striate) have occurred in mammals (Altman and Carpenter, 1961; Hall and Diamond, 1968a; Diamond and Hall, 1969;

Martin, 1969; Ablanalp, 1970; Benevento and Ebner, 1970; Diamond *et al.*, 1970; Rafols and Matzke, 1970; Ward and Masterton, 1970; Mathers, 1971; Harting *et al.*, 1972, 1973; Snyder, 1973; Lin *et al.*, 1974). Functional differentiation of these pathways has occurred with the separation of pattern and position visual analyses (Schneider, 1967, 1969; Teuber, 1970; Diamond, 1971) and with the integration of both types of information at cortical levels (Dubrovsky and Garcia-Rill, 1971), although this does not hold true for some primitive mammals (Cowey and Weiskrantz, 1971; Casagrande *et al.*, 1972; Jane *et al.*, 1972). Some overlap of retinotectal and retinothalamic pathways at thalamic relay levels is retained in mammals. The dorsal lateral geniculate, LP–pulvinar complex, ventral lateral geniculate and pretectum receive afferents from superficial, visual, layers of the superior colliculus (Myers, 1963; Hayashi and Sumitomo, 1967; Ablanalp, 1971; Blum *et al.*, 1972; Graybiel and Nauta, 1971; Ebbesson *et al.*, 1972; Hall, 1972; Harting *et al.*, 1973. In the tree shrew, tecto-dorsal lateral geniculate projections are retinotopically organized (Casagrande, 1974a). In the gray squirrel, a rather differentiated, topically organized, pathway exists from the upper part of the stratum griseum superficiale of the superior colliculus to the C-layer of the dorsal lateral geniculate (Robson and Hall, 1976). In insectivores, overlap occurs in the projections to the primary and secondary visual cortices (Hall and Diamond, 1968a; Kaas *et al.*, 1970; Benevento and Ebner, 1971; Ebbesson, 1972a). The degree of overlap of retinotectal and retinothalamic projections (as well as that of other sensory projections) may be determined by adaptive specialization, as suggested by Ebbesson *et al.*, (1972). Herrick (1948), Karamian *et al.* (1966, 1972), and Riss *et al.* (1972) have not regarded this interpretation as conclusive, however, and further study is necessary to understand the adaptive significance of this overlap.

C. Sources and Properties of Thalamic Somatosensory Representations

1. *Properties of Somatosensory Units*

Somatosensory representation in the reptilian thalamus has been investigated electrophysiologically in turtles (Belekhova and Kosareva, 1971; Belekhova, 1973a, 1977) and alligators (Berkowitz and Tschirgi, 1960; Moore, 1961; Moore and Tschirgi, 1960, 1962), though its topography was not determined in the latter. Somatic representation in the thalamus is bilateral in both groups, and responses to ipsi- and contralateral somatic stimuli are virtually identical in configuration and latency. Latency of response to fore- and hindlimb stimulation differs, however, due to conduction time. Most thalamic somatosensory units in turtles and alligators exhibit distinct extra-lemniscal properties: large receptive fields, often including all the body sur-face; rapid attenuation of responses to repetitive somatic stimuli; and response to tactile, pressure, or joint movement stimuli, with nociceptive stimuli being most effective. Over one-third of the somatic units display multimodal convergence: somatic and visual impulses in turtles; somatic, acoustic, vibratory and visual impulses in alligators. In alligators, few thalamic units possess specific lemniscal properties: more restricted receptive fields, slow adaptation to repetitive stimulation, and specific activation by tactile or proprioceptive stimuli. Similar units are identified in nucleus ventralis and nucleus reuniens in turtles; however, their thalamic location is unknown in alligators. In addition to somatoauditory convergent neurons, unimodal units in the alligator thalamus respond only to acoustic or vibratory stimuli (Moore, 1961). The exact location of these units is unknown, but morphological data (Pritz, 1974a, Foster, 1975) indicates that the region of auditory representation includes nucleus reuniens posterior and nucleus Z.

2. Sources of Somatosensory Information

a. *Spinal and Lemniscal Sources.* (i) Reptiles. Moore (1961) concludes that somatosensory representation in the alligator thalamus is related to the ventrolateral system of the spinal cord. Spinal pathways to the thalamus suggested in the literature include a spino-cervico-thalamic system (Ebbesson, 1969), direct spinal pathways (Ebbesson, 1967, 1969; Pedersen, 1973) and spino–reticulo–thalamic systems (Mehler, 1969). The dorsal column nuclei in alligators have a highly specialized organization (Kruger and Witkovsky, 1961) and a medial lemniscus pathway may be a source of somatic impulses to the reptilian thalamus.

(ii) Comparisons with other vertebrates. The dorsal column system of the spinal cord is known to project to nuclei of the medulla in amphibians and sharks (Joseph and Whitlock, 1968a; Ebbesson, 1972a; Nieuwenhuys and Cornelisz, 1971) as in reptiles (Goldby and Robinson, 1962). A medial lemniscus (bulbothalamic pathway) probably exists in amphibians (Joseph and Whitlock, 1968b).

Mammalian dorsal column systems also contain less specialized projections. These fibers relay in the dorsal column nuclei of the medulla oblongata and terminate in the ventrobasal thalamic complex, as well as in the subthalamus, pretectum, optic tectum and tegmentum, where they overlap with terminals of the direct spinal projections (Hand and Liu, 1966; Lund and Webster, 1967; Schroeder et al., 1968; Boivie, 1971; Jane and Schroeder, 1971; Schroeder and Jane, 1971; Hazlett et al., 1972; Gordon, 1973; Walsh and Ebner, 1973). This system probably arises in a non-specifically organized part of the mammalian dorsal column nuclei which exhibits extralemniscal properties Bowsher and Albe-Fessard, 1965; Winter, 1965; Lund and Webster, 1967; Tomasulo and Emmers, 1972; Dart and Gordon, 1973) and is probably also present in reptiles.

b. *Tectal Projections*. Other somatic impulses reach the reptilian thalamus after relay in the optic tectum via direct pathways to nucleus rotundus and the ventrolateral thalamic area. The anatomical bases of these pathways have been determined (Hall and Ebner, 1970a; Belekhova and Kosareva, 1971; Butler and Northcutt, 1971; Braford, 1972; Foster and Hall, 1975). Overlap of tectal and somatic projections occurs, therefore, in the ventrocaudal thalamic zone of reptiles. Somatic impulses occur mainly in the ventrocaudal thalamic zone, but also reach nucleus rotundus as well as the zone which probably corresponds to the dorsal part of the central lateral nucleus (nucleus dorso-lateralis anterior). Early morphologists (Huber and Crosby, 1926, 1943; LeGros Clark, 1932) believed that nucleus rotundus and the dorsolateral nucleus were the main somatic centers of the reptilian thalamus. Electro-physiology and experimental morphology do not support this idea, though the exact relationship of these nuclei to the trigeminal lemniscus remains undetermined.

c. *Tegmental Projections*. Somatosensory representation in the thalamus and telencephalon of turtles is not significantly altered by total, bilateral ablation of the optic tectum. Therefore, extratectal somatic impulses to the reptilian thalamus may originate in the dorsolateral region of the mesence-phalic tegmentum, including the intercollicular nucleus. Tegmental pro-jections to the turtle thalamus are confined mainly to the ventral thalamic area below nucleus rotundus, including the suprapeduncular nucleus, where short latency evoked potentials and single unit activity occur on electrical stimula-tion of the dorsolateral tegmentum (Belekhova, 1973a, 1977). This thalamic region corresponds to the ventrolateral area according to Riss *et al.* (1972).

3. *Summary*

It is likely that somatosensory representation in the reptilian thalamus is supplied from many sources, including lemniscal and extralemniscal systems; further experimental analyses are needed. The loss of specificity of the peri-pheral sensory volley as it ascends to higher neural centers may be due to increasing convergence of different sensory modalities. This would explain the nonspecific character of telencephalic responses to stimulation of the dorsal column nuclei in turtles (Moore, 1961; Orrego, 1961a). A similar decrease in somatic specificity exists in a somatic part of the mammalian posterior thalamic complex, where extralemniscal properties predominate in spite of a strong lemniscal input (Curry, 1972; Curry and Gordon, 1972).

D. Other Systems

Other afferent representations in the reptilian thalamus, including limbic and cerebellar, have not been studied electrophysiologically. The afferent supply to the reptilian hypothalamus is unknown except for olfactory bulb and tubercle input to the anterior and lateral hypothalamus (Sollertinskaya, 1972). The preoptic area of lizards contains neurons sensitive to temperature shifts (Cabanac *et al.*, 1967). Visual, somatic, and auditory representations in the cerebellum of lizards and turtles have been demonstrated, though their origins are unknown (Crepax and Parmeggiani, 1958; Gusel'nikov and Ivanova, 1958; Karamian *et al.*, 1969; Karamian, 1970). Unlike the cerebellum of fishes, the cerebellum of reptiles (like that of amphibians) does not play an essential role in the integration sensory information (Karamian, 1956, 1970).

IV. Telencephalon

A. General Comments

The amphibian–reptilian transition is characterized by marked transformations in the structural organization of the forebrain. Neuronal arrangement becomes more differentiated in both the subpallium and the pallium. The lateral, as opposed to medial, forebrain wall becomes predominant with the differentiation of the striatum in the subpallium. A cortical plate emerges in the pallium. It consists of distinct dorsal, lateral, and medial cortices. In addition, the characteristic dorsal ventricular ridge is formed. A topographic segregation of olfactory and non-olfactory exteroceptive representations occurs within the pallium in reptiles. Such segregation does not occur in anuran amphibians (Belekhova and Vesselkin, 1969; Karamian *et al.*, 1969a; Vesselkin and Agayan, 1970).

Reptiles are unique among vertebrates in having two, essentially different pallial areas in receipt of non-olfactory sensory projections. In some sauropsids (particularly agamid and varanid lizards), non-olfactory systems project primarily to the dorsal division of the medial cortex in the midposterior region of the hemisphere, and secondarily to the dorsal cortex (Gusel'nikova and Gusel'nikov, 1963; Gusel'nikov, 1965; Kulikov and Safarov, 1969; Karamian, 1970; Belekhova and Safarov, 1976; Belekhova, 1963, 1973a, 1977) (Fig. 2A). Turtles and alligators, have non-olfactory sensory representation mainly in the midrostral region of dorsal cortex and, to a lesser extent, in the medial cortex (Kruger and Berkowitz, 1960; Orrego, 1961a; Moore and Tschirgi, 1962; Orrego and Lisenby, 1962; Mazurskaya and Smirnov, 1965; Mazurskaya *et al.*, 1966; Belekhova and Kosareva, 1967; Pivovarov and Trepakov,

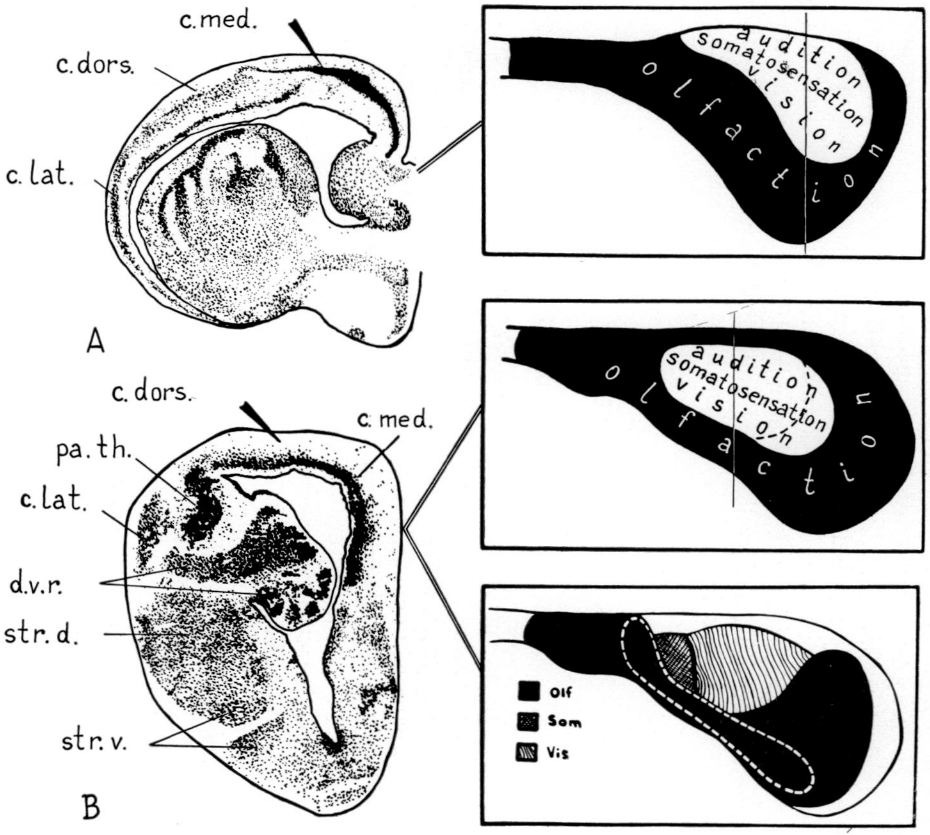

Fig. 2—see facing page

FIG. 2. Cortical representations of olfaction, vision, audition and somato-sensation in a lizard (A) and a turtle (B). Transverse sections through a lizard brain (*Varanus griseus*) and a turtle brain (*Emys orbicularis*) are shown to the left of the figure. The planes of the sections are indicated on the schematic dorsolateral views of the hemispheres to the right of the figure. The areas over which electrical activity can be evoked by each sensory modality are shown on these figures (arrows on the sections of the hemispheres). The figures are based on the results of: Gusel'nikov (1965), Belekhova (1963) (A); Karamian *et al.* (1966), Mazurskaya *et al.* (1966), Belekhova and Kosareva (1967) (B, upper scheme); Orrego (1961a) (B, lower scheme). c.dors, dorsal cortex; c.lat., lateral cortex; c.med., medial cortex; d.v.r., dorsal ventricular ridge; pa.th, pallial thickening; str.d., dorsal striatum; str.v., ventral striatum.

1972; Pivovarov, 1973; Gusel'nikov *et al.*, 1974; Belekhova and Akulina, 1975; Karamian, 1965, 1970, 1976; Belekhova, 1970a, 1973a, 1977) (Fig. 2B). In these zones, visual, somatic and acoustic stimuli evoke mainly surface negative potentials in turtles and alligators. These potentials are consistent with morphological data on the cortical distribution of dorsal thalamic projections (Hall and Ebner, 1970b; Kosareva and Nomokonova, 1972) and with other electrophysiological experiments (Karamian and Belekhova, 1963; Akulina, 1971; Karamian, 1965, 1970, 1976; Belekhova, 1963, 1967, 1973a, 1977) (see Section VA). Dorsal and medial cortices are also the foci of maximum electrical background activity (Kruger and Berkowitz, 1960; Belekhova, 1963).

B. OLFACTORY REPRESENTATIONS

1. General Features

Evoked potentials are recorded in the lateral, medial, and posterior dorsal cortices, following stimulation of the olfactory bulb or tract in turtles and alligators. Potentials are absent only from the relatively small anterior and middle regions of dorsal cortex, and in the pallial thickening, where the number of olfactory responsive neurons is insignificant (Orrego, 1961a, b, 1962; Orrego and Lisenby, 1962; Mazurskaya *et al.*, 1964, 1966; Karamian, 1967, 1970; Pivovarov and Trepakov, 1972; Belekhova, 1970b, 1973a; Karamian *et al.*, 1975b; Trepakov, 1976) (Fig. 2).

Olfactory representation in the telencephalon is bilateral. Electrophysiological studies indicate that the olfactory pathways to the contralateral hemisphere and olfactory bulb in turtles do not run through the anterior commissure (as do those of mammals), but through the habenular commissure. Some fibers probably terminate in the habenular nuclei. Electrical stimulation of these nuclei elicits hemispheric responses similar to those resulting from olfactory bulb stimulation. Lesion of the habenular complex produces marked suppression of olfactory responses in the contralateral hemisphere (Belekhova, 1970b, 1973a, 1977). These findings are corroborated by morphological data for turtles and other reptiles (Gamble, 1952, 1956; Heimer, 1969; Scalia *et al.*, 1969; Northcutt, 1970; Halpern, 1973).

2. Lateral Cortex

The characteristics of evoked olfactory activity differ in various cortical areas. In the lateral cortex, which receives direct afferents from the olfactory bulb, olfactory evoked potentials have the lowest threshold and the shortest latency. They retain a negative–positive configuration within the superficial plexiform layer, where terminal degeneration is seen following olfactory bulb ablation. The potentials are reversed at the level of the cellular layer, where a small number of terminals are seen (Karamian *et al.*, 1975b). Such a laminar distribution of secondary olfactory fibers in the lateral cortex ensures mono-synaptic activation of the principal neurons of this cortex. This activation is, in turn, responsible for secondary activation of the interneurons in the deeper layer. Two negative components of olfactory evoked potentials (recorded from the cortical surface) correspond to EPSPs of these two groups of neurons; the late positive component reflects their summated IPSPs (Gusel'nikova and Gusel'nikov, 1976). Single units in the lateral cortex are unimodal and are not responsive to non-olfactory exteroceptive stimuli (Karamian *et al.*, 1975b; Belekhova, 1973a, 1977).

The lateral cortex of turtles is similar to the prepyriform cortex of mammals in a number of respects—heterogeneity of afferents with slow conduction velocities, a rostrocaudal gradient of afferent bulbar input, axo-dendritic synapses of superficial olfactory fibers in the cortical plexiform layer, the manner of synaptic activation, and the characteristics of response to rhythmic stimulation (MacLean *et al.*, 1957; Cragg, 1959; Orrego, 1961a; Orrego and Lisenby, 1962; Mascitti and Ortega, 1966; Wenzel and Sieck, 1966; Biedenbach and Stevens, 1969; Karamian *et al.*, 1975b; Gusel'nikova and Gusel'nikov, 1976; Belekhova, 1970d, 1973a, 1977).

Orrego (1962) describes superficial and deep olfactory fiber systems in the lateral cortex of turtles, regarding them, respectively, as projectional and associative. The posterior dorsal cortex (marked by the dotted line in Fig. 2B upper hemisphere) receives olfactory impulses relayed by the lateral cortex; overlap of olfactory and long-latency visual and somatic evoked potentials occurs in this region. Therefore, some correlation of corresponding sensory volleys must occur in this cortical region (Orrego, 1961a, 1962; Belekhova, 1970a). This pattern is characteristic of the entire dorsal pallium of frogs (Belekhova and Vesselkin, 1969; Vesselkin and Agayan, 1970).

3. *Medial Cortex*

a. *Olfactory Inputs.* In turtles, high threshold, long-latency olfactory evoked potentials are recorded in medial cortex which, like dorsal cortex, receives no secondary olfactory projections (Gamble, 1956; Northcutt, 1970; Karamian *et al.*, 1975b). The main surface negative component of these evoked potentials reverses as the cellular layer is reached. One- to two-thirds of medial cortical neurons in turtles and lizards respond to olfactory stimulation and display convergence of visual and/or somatic impulses (Gusel'nikova and Gusel'nikov, 1963; Voronin *et al.*, 1964; Pivovarov and Trepakov, 1972; Belekhova, 1973a; Karamian *et al.*, 1975b). However, olfactory afferents to medial cortex of turtles predominate over non-olfactory (at least visual) afferents. More units react to olfactory, rather than to visual, stimulation, particularly in the medial division of the medial cortex. The latency and pattern of olfactory responses are less variable than those of visual responses (Pivovarov and Trepakov, 1972; Belekhova, 1973a; Karamian et al., 1975b). Unfortunately, no comparison of olfactory and non-olfactory medial cortex imputs was made in lizards, whose medial cortex is most responsive to non-olfactory exteroceptive afferents (see Section B). The medial division of the medial cortex of turtles appears more specialized for olfaction than its dorsal division. In both medial cortical formations, mainly inhibitory responses (IPSP or EPSP–IPSP) are recorded. Less frequently, only EPSPs are observed in conjunction with olfactory bulb stimulation. In the medial division of the medial cortex, however, there is less convergence of olfactory and visual stimuli than in the dorsal region, while there are more unimodal olfactory neurons (Pivovarov and Trepakov, 1972; Trepakov, 1976).

b. *Hypothalamic Inputs.* Nauta methods reveal direct hypothalamo–medial cortical connections via the fornix (Motorina, 1965). Hippocampal response to visceral stimulation has been recorded in turtles (Moiseeva, 1972) and at least some hypothalamic afferents are related to the visceral modality. Mammals reveal similar afferent input to the hippocampus (Green, 1964). There are three afferent inputs to the hippocampus in primates, but only fornix projections (from the hypothalamus and septum) are specific. These projections terminate on hippocampal cells close to the trigger zone, on the perikarya or the basal dendrites. The two other inputs, olfactory and visual, drive neurons through activation of apical dendrites and, therefore, are less effective (Gergen and MacLean, 1964).

c. *Comparisons with Other Vertebrates.* The role of the medial cortex in olfaction is of particular interest, and is the focus of the present tendency to separate the "rhinencephalon" into olfactory brain proper and limbic brain, reflecting phylo- and ontogenetic development (Brodal, 1947, 1963; Heinz, 1964; White, 1965a, b; Stephan, 1966; Riss et al., 1969a; Karamian, 1970, 1972).

Olfactory responses have been recorded in the medial cortex of most non-mammalian vertebrates (Karamian et al., 1969a; Vesselkin and Agayan, 1970; Bruckmoser, 1971, 1973; Bruckmoser and Dobrylko, 1972). The less differentiated the telencephalon, the greater the similarity of olfactory responses in the lateral and medial pallial regions. Such responses are most similar in lampreys and less so in frogs; in reptiles (and primitive mammals) lateral and medial olfactory responses differ greatly. Hippocampal involvement in olfaction has decreased during mammalian evolution (Cragg, 1959, 1960; Girgis, 1970). It is also apparent from embryological stages of mammals (Humphrey, 1966). Modern connectional data, however, indicate that the internal arrangement of the medial cortex in reptiles is quite different from that in mammals (Lohman and van Woerden-Verkeley, 1976); thus, these structures are probably not strictly homologous. Olfactory afferents probably played a role in the phylogensis of the medial cortex; it is likely, however, that hypothalamic afferents via the medial forebrain bundle have assumed a dominant role (Humphrey, 1966; Girgis, 1970; Karamian, 1969b, 1970, 1972). In reptiles (*Varanus*), most stable, short-latency, low-threshold, medial cortex potentials occur in response to hypothalamic stimulation (Belekhova, 1963; Karamian, 1969b, 1970; Karamian and Sollertinskaya, 1964, 1972; Sollertinskaya, 1967, 1973; Karamian *et al.*, 1975b).

Thus, the vertebrate medial cortex has developed as a multisensory correlative structure related to three afferent inputs: hypothalamic (guiding), olfactory and non-olfactory (exteroceptive). Evolutionary development of lateral cortex appears to reflect a more specialized monosensory center.

4. *Trends in Olfactory Representation*

Morphological and electrophysiological data on olfactory afferentation in vertebrates lead to different conclusions. Morphological data (Heimer, 1969; Ebbesson and Heimer, 1970; Ebbesson, 1972a) indicate an enlargement, from sharks to reptiles, of the secondary olfactory projection zone in the forebrain. In contrast, electrophysiological data support the traditional concept of decreased olfactory involvement of the forebrain throughout vertebrate evolution. This contradiction may result from the lack of differentiation in the olfactory system as in other central sensory pathways in anamniotes. Specialization and isolation of diffuse olfactory connections have evolved in most amniotic vertebrates. There has also been a decrease in the number of relays for mitral cell axons within the olfactory bulb itself, and within the retrobulbar formation en route to the main, secondary olfactory target in the telecephalon. Reptiles—and, to an even greater extent, mammals —reveal fewer structures involved in olfaction than do anamniotes (Crosby and Humphrey, 1939; Meyer and Allison, 1949; Allison, 1953; Nieuwenhuys, 1967; Scalia, 1968; Scalia *et al.*, 1969).

C. Visual Representations

1. *General Features*

Central visual and somatosensory representations show striking changes en route from the thalamus to the telencephalon (Moore, 1961; Moore and Tschirigi, 1962; Mazurskaya and Smirnov, 1965; Karamian, 1965, 1967, 1970; Karamian *et al.*, 1971; Belekhova, 1970a, 1972c, 1973a). In the thalamus, there are specialized visual relay stations for thalamofugal pathways (lateral geniculate nucleus) and tectofugal pathways (nucleus rotundus). The lateral geniculate, in particular, contains mainly visually specific neurons. In telencephalic structures (dorsal cortex, pallial thickening, dorsal ventricular ridge), however, only one-third of all visually responsive units are modality specific, and the majority are multimodal (Mazurskaya and Smirnov, 1965; Belekhova and Akulina, 1970, 1975). The retino–thalamo–cortical pathway in turtles does not exhibit temporal sharpening of the afferent volley, increase in its synchronization and strength, or shortening of conduction time (Belekhova, 1968, 1973a, 1977). Most mammalian visual systems do exhibit these features (Doty, 1958; Shevelev, 1971), and they are considered basic to higher analytical processes. Evoked potentials in cat striate cortex occur $1 \cdot 1–2 \cdot 1$ ms after stimulation of the optic nerve (Clare *et al.*, 1969); while in turtle dorsal cortex, potentials occur $21 \cdot 5 \pm 0 \cdot 5$ ms (mean $\pm$ S.E.M.) after stimulation (Belekhova and Kosareva, 1967). In turtles, the long-latency component of a visually evoked potential survives up to four months after optic nerve section (Belekhova, 1973a), indicating small, slowly conducting fibers in the visual pathways. Such fibers have been confirmed by electron microscopy in turtles and alligators (Kruger and Maxwell, 1969; Bishop and Smith, 1964; Davydova and Boiko, 1976).

2. Sources of Visual Input to the Telencephalon

a. *General.* Impulses to the forebrain via the tectofugal pathway are relayed in two thalamic structures, nucleus rotundus and the lateral thalamic zone (see Section IIIB). Additional pathways relay tectal impulses to the forebrain; one such pathway is mediated by the mesencephalic tegmentum and, subsequently, by the ventral peduncle of the lateral forebrain bundle, which responds to tectal stimulation (Belekhova, 1973a).

b. *Nucleus Rotundus.* Evoked potentials and neuronal responses to electrical stimulation of the optic tectum have been recorded in dorsal cortex and subcortical structures (pallial thickening, dorsal ventricular ridge, striatum) of turtles, and in medial cortex and lateral subcortical structures in the telencephalon of lizards. Following partial lesion of nucleus rotundus, the first main components in flash-evoked and tectal stimulation responses are drastically suppressed in dorsal ventricular ridge; but responses in dorsal cortex do not change significantly, except for some later components. However, after extensive lesions of the lateral thalamic zone (including the largest part of the lateral geniculate), flash-evoked and tectally elicited potentials disappear in dorsal cortex (except for late components), but remain unchanged in dorsal ventricular ridge and striatum (Belekhova, 1977). These data are consistent with degeneration studies indicating direct projections of nucleus rotundus to dorsal ventricular ridge and direct projections of the dorsal lateral geniculate to dorsal cortex (Hall and Ebner, 1970b; Kosareva, 1974; Hoogland *et al.*, 1975; Pritz, 1975; Parent, 1976). Thus, visual impulses reach dorsal ventricular ridge after relaying in the optic tectum and nucleus rotundus; they ultimately reach dorsal cortex where they provide the later components of visually and tectally elicited responses.

c. *Lateral Thalamus*. Retinal impulses, and some impulses mediated by the optic tectum, reach dorsal cortex after relaying in the lateral thalamic zone (probably in the lateral geniculate). Bilateral enucleation in turtles results in atrophy of the superficial layers of the optic tectum, and conduction of impulses via the tecto–geniculo–cortical pathway ceases approximately two years after such enucleation. The latency of cortical responses to tectal stimulation in enucleated turtles is twice as long as in normal animals. Tectally elicited responses in dorsal ventricular ridge and striatum, however, are not significantly altered by enucleation (Belekhova, 1977). These data correlate, in part, with the two reptilian patterns of tectothalamic connections: superficial tectal projections to the lateral geniculate, and deep tectal projections to nucleus rotundus (Foster *et al.*, 1973; Foster and Hall, 1975).

d. *Interactions between Tectal and Retinal Channels*. Many telencephalic units respond to both flash and tectal stimuli. Evoked cortical responses in turtles are blocked during paired stimulation of the optic tectum and the optic nerve, or the optic tectum and the lateral thalamic zone, including the lateral geniculate (Karamian, 1965, 1970; Mazurskaya and Smirnov, 1966; Belekhova, 1970a, 1973a; Belekhova and Akulina, 1970). Responses in the dorsal ventricular ridge of turtles are also blocked during paired stimulation of nucleus rotundus and the optic tectum (Belekhova, 1977).

3. *Characteristics of Visual Representations*

a. *General*. Study of the functional organization of telencephalic visual representations is only beginning. Differences in cortex, dorsal ventricular ridge and striatum are known; but unlike the situation in birds there are insufficient data to support complete separation of retino–thalamo–cortical and retino–tecto–thalamo–telencephalic pathways in reptiles.

b. *Dorsal Cortex*. Visual evoked potentials in reptilian cortex closely resemble mammalian reticulocortical responses in their surface negative configuration, their long latency, and their extreme sensitivity to anesthetics (Karamian and Belekhova, 1963; Belekhova and Zagorul'ko, 1964; O. A. Karamian, 1965; Zagorul'ko *et al.*, 1965; Mazurskaya *et al.*, 1966; Belekhova and Kosareva, 1967; Karamian, 1966, 1969b, 1970; Karamian *et al.*, 1966, 1968, 1971). Visual potentials in turtle cortex more closely resemble those in mammalian primary visual cortex in other features: cycle recovery, poorly expressed posttetanic potentiation, logarithmic correlation with varying intensity of light stimuli, potentiation in steady light, the facilitatory effect of nociceptive stimulation on potentials of central origin, and flash-evoked potential variation during wakefulness and sleep (Zagorul'ko, 1968; Isabe-kova, 1969; Karamian, 1968, 1969b, 1970; Karamian et al., 1968, 1971; Karmanova et al., 1971; Belekhova, 1968, 1970a, d, 1973a).

Dorsal cortex in turtles reveals a crude retinotopic organization with extensive convergence of retinal impulses and a larger representation of the nasal retina. In the superficial plexiform layer (100 μm below the surface), there are distinct visual units (probably visual fibers) with small, round or ovoid receptive fields (2–5°), as well as units with extensive, complex receptive fields. The vast majority of cortical plate cells (200–1000 μm) have large receptive fields ("observer" cells), often covering the entire visual field of one or both eyes. As a rule, cortical units respond to stationary light and patterned stimuli, but respond maximally to moving stimuli (Gusel'nikov et al., 1971; Mazurskaya, 1971, 1972). Single units of the upper (200–300 μm) and lower (800–1000 μm) cortical plate differ in response to visual stimuli. Units of the upper plate respond poorly, or not at all, to local light stimuli, but display on–off responses to diffuse illumination. Some of these units have restricted receptive fields (10–40°) and exhibit directional sensitivity. Deeper units usually respond to a light spot anywhere in the visual field, but are not activated by diffuse illumination. These units are sensitive to moving stimuli regardless of direction. Deeper units respond to novel stimuli, but habituate after a few repetitions (Mazurskaya, 1971, 1972). It is possible that receptive fields of deep cortical units form in the cortex itself by convergence of visual afferents and cells with more restricted receptive fields; however, cortical visual fibers with complex receptive fields are a more likely source of complex inputs to deep cells. Visual projections in the dorsal cortex of turtles reveal features typical of associative cortex in mammals (Mazurskaya, 1972).

c. *Subcortical Structures.* Dorsal ventricular ridge and striatum respond to visual stimuli in a manner similar to that of cortical units. However, subcortical units respond more intensively to moving stimuli than to stationary stimuli or diffuse illumination. Receptive fields of subcortical cells, as well as those of nucleus rotundus, cover the entire visual field, but many of these units possess a zone of higher excitability in the lower parts of the visual field. There are fewer binocularly activated units in subcortical structures than in the cortex. Latency of visual responses is shorter in the subcortical structures than in cortex, responses are less variable and habituation is slower and less complete. Both cortical and subcortical units discriminate illumination intensity, movement velocity, and object dimension; however, subcortical responses vary more readily to stimulus characteristics. These properties are more often observed in the striatum, where single unit responses closely resemble fiber response in the dorsal peduncle of the lateral forebrain bundle (Gusel'nikov et al., 1971; Morenkov and Pivovarov, 1973). After tectal ablation or dorsal thalamic lesions, subcortical units respond to movements of larger objects and movements of greater velocity than in unlesioned turtles (Morenkov and Pivovarov, 1973).

4. Functional Studies

a. *General.* Thus, the functional characteristics of telencephalic visual projections indicate a tecto–rotundo–telencephalic (dorsal ventricular ridge) pathway responsible for analyzing specific visual features and, possibly, regulating such motor acts as attack and avoidance responses (Gusel'nikov *et al.*, 1971; Morenkov and Pivovarov, 1973). Dorsal cortex also processes visual information in reptiles, but is regarded as an associative structure based on its properties of multimodal convergence, rapid habituation of evoked responses, prolonged after effects and plasticity. It correlates volleys of different sensory modalities, and is essential for integrated perception of objects (Mazurskaya *et al.*, 1966; Gusel'nikov *et al.*, 1971; Mazurskaya, 1971, 1972). This view of dorsal cortex is only partly compatible with data on cortical and subcortical motor functions in reptiles.

b. *Electrical Stimulation.* Electrical stimulation of subcortical areas in anesthetized turtles and lizards (Goldby, 1937; Bremer *et al.*, 1939) and in unanesthetized turtles and free-moving caimans results in coordinated locomotor activity influenced by environmental changes. Stimulation of dorsal cortex does not elicit expressed movement, though it exerts some influence on motor functions related to the animal's head (Koppany and Pearcy, 1925; Shapiro and Goodman, 1969). Earlier reports that cortical stimulation resulted in motor responses in turtles and alligators probably resulted from current spread to underlying structures (Johnston, 1916; Bagley and Richter, 1924; Bagley and Langworthy, 1926).

c. *Ablation Studies.* The above description of reptilian telencephalic visual organization is in striking contrast to behavioral studies. Bilateral ablation of dorsal cortex, dorsal cortex and part of dorsal ventricular ridge, or the entire forebrain in turtles (*Chrysemys scripta elegans, C. picta picta, Podocnemis unifilis, Testudo horsfieldii, Emys orbicularis*) and in lizards (*Lacerta strigata, L. trilineata*) does not abolish visual cliff performance (Hertzler and Hayes, 1967), two-choice spatial discrimination (Morlock, 1972), food-conditioned response to light stimuli (Sikharulidze, 1972a, b; Beritashwili, 1974) or learned pattern discrimination for food reward (Bass *et al.*, 1973; Safarov, 1974a). General locomotor activity and feeding do not change after cortical ablations in turtles.

Lesions extending into the pallial thickening result in a decline in general activity and some impairment of climbing responses; but only combined cortical and tectal lesions produce significant deficits in visually guided behavior (Hertzler and Hayes, 1967; Safarov, 1974b). In lizards (*Ophisaurus apodus*) and snakes (*Coluber karelini, C. ravergieri*), neither extensive cortical ablation involving dorsal ventricular ridge nor entire forebrain ablation disturbs previously learned spatial orientation behavior visually and aurally cued for heat/food reward (Safarov, 1971, 1974b). However, reflexes conditioned by alimentary reward gradually disappear, as the forebrain ablated animals refuse to feed. Such conditioned behavior is irreversibly abolished in grass snakes (*Natrix tessellata*) (Safarov, 1971).

Reptiles require more trials to learn habits after cortical ablation, suggesting a facilitatory role for dorsal cortex (Morlock, 1972; Bass *et al.*, 1973). However, rudimentary visual behavior is retained after tectal ablation, suggesting that the thalamotelencephalic visual system in turtles assumes the remaining visual functions. This is supported by the fact that lesions of dorsal cortex, in addition to tectal ablation, result in more significant deficits in visual behavior than does tectal ablation alone (Hertzler and Hayes, 1967). More sensitive behavioral tests are needed to evaluate the significance of telencephalic structures in reptilian behavior (Granda, 1972; Morlock, 1972).

Entire forebrain ablation in turtles (*Emys orbicularis, Mauremys caspica*) does not interfere with alimentary conditioning to light signals, but it does abolish color discrimination and disrupts both short-term memory and delayed conditioned responses. For instance, turtles in which the forebrain has been ablated only approach a conditioned visual signal within 20 seconds after its presentation, whereas normal turtles approach the signal up to 5 minutes after presentation. Conditioned responses to stimuli of other modalities are also disrupted, as are responses to nociceptive stimuli (Sikharulidze, 1972a; Beritashwili, 1974). Ablation of only the anterior one-third of dorsal cortex in *Emys orbicularis* does not interfere with visually conditioned responses or color discrimination; however, the ability to make delayed responses disappears and is not recovered (Eldarov, 1969). Such turtles cannot follow movement of a food stimulus behind a screen; lesion of the posterior part of dorsal cortex does not produce this deficit (Ochinskaya and Rubtsova, 1976). Thus, the reptilian forebrain influences some forms of visual behavior, but its main function (and the function of dorsal cortex) is the perception of certain visual features and the integration of complex behaviors, such as searching for food objects (Eldarov, 1969; Beritashwili, 1974; Ochinskaya and Rubtsova, 1976). These functions of dorsal cortex correlate with electrophysiological data indicating that dorsal cortex is a multisensory field, in which prolonged excitability traces are maintained after stimulation of its mesencephalic and diencephalic afferent pathways (see Section VA).

d. *Comparisons with other Vertebrates.* Ablation of reptilian dorsal cortex produces an effect similar to that of accessory and dorsal hyperstriatal (Wulst) lesions in birds and striate cortical lesions in some mammals. Lesions of the avian Wulst or of the anterior dorsolateral thalamic nuclei (thalamofugal visual pathway) cause little, if any, impairment of intensity and pattern discrimination (Hodos *et al.*, 1973). However, damage to the ectostriatum or nucleus rotundus (tectofugal visual pathway) produces severe deficits in learned responses and color discrimination (Hodos and Karten, 1966, 1970; Hodos, 1970; Hodos and Bonbright, 1974). Lesions of the thalamofugal pathway in birds reveal deficits in response to difficult visual tasks, such as discrimination of stimuli approaching the threshold of discriminability, or reversal of learned discriminations (Stettner and Schulz, 1967; Pritz *et al.*, 1970; Hodos *et al.*, 1973; Maier and Tanaka, 1973). Deficits resulting from lesions of reptilian dorsal cortex are more similar to deficits produced by lesions of the avian Wulst than they are to deficits resulting from lesions of mammalian striate cortex.

The geniculostriate system is significant for pattern vision in mammals (Schneider, 1969; Teuber, 1970); however, ablation of the striate cortex in the tree shrew does not alter pattern discrimination, nor do corresponding lesions in reptiles and birds (Snyder and Diamond, 1968; Jane *et al.*, 1969; Killackey *et al.*, 1971, 1972; Ware *et al.*, 1972. Similar results have also been reported for cats (Doty, 1973) and ground squirrels (Levy *et al.*, 1973). Removal of reptilian dorsal cortex, avian hyperstriatum, or mammalian striate cortex aggravates visual impairment in animals with tectal ablation or other lesions of the tectofugal pathway (Sprague, 1966; Hertzler and Hayes, 1967; Maier and Tanaka, 1973; Hodos and Bonbright, 1974). These behavioral data, as well as morphological and electrophysiological findings (Section IIIB), indicate dual visual pathways (tectal and thalamofugal) to the telencephalon in reptiles, birds and mammals. They also suggest certain vertebrate homologies: reptilian dorsal cortex—avian Wulst—mammalian striate cortex; and reptilian dorsal ventricular ridge—avian ectostriatum—mammalian peristriate cortex; but further data are needed to confirm these homologies.

Recent data indicate that the optic tectum (superior colliculus) of birds and mammals is significant for pattern discrimination as well as for orienting visual attention (Sprague, 1966; Sprague *et al.*, 1971; Casagrande *et al.*, 1972; Jane *et al.*, 1972; Casagrande, 1974b; Hodos and Fletscher, 1974; Hodos and Karten, 1974; Keating, 1974). Additional studies are needed to resolve telencephalic and tectal functions in pattern discrimination among vertebrates.

This telencephalic pattern varies among anamniotes. The telencephalic visual area, rather than the optic tectum, is essential for pattern discrimination in sharks (Graeber and Ebbesson, 1972; Graeber *et al.*, 1973); however, the reverse is the case for frogs (Ingle, 1973).

D. SOMATOSENSORY REPRESENTATION

1. General Features

In turtles, the somatosensory system is less specialized than the visual system at thalamic levels (see Section III), the discrepancy between the two systems increases in the telencephalon. Somatic evoked potentials in dorsal cortex are much more variable in composition and latency than are visual potentials. The latency difference between thalamic and cortical responses to electrical stimulation of the skin can be 70 ms (Belekhova, 1973a; Belekhova and Akulina, 1975). Somatic evoked potentials are more stable and synchronized in the dorsal ventricular ridge and striatum, and they have latencies 30 ms shorter than in the cortex. The number of somatically sensitive units is greater in subcortical structures than in the cortex (Belekhova and Akulina, 1975; Karamian, 1976).

2. Sources of Somatosensory Input to the Telencephalon

The ventrocaudal somatic zone in turtles evidently does not project directly to dorsal cortex, as the latency of cortical responses to electrical stimulation of the ventrocaudal thalamic zone is long—$72 \pm 6\cdot4$ ms (mean $\pm$ S.E.M.) (Belekhova, 1973a, 1977). Horseradish peroxidase studies in turtles indicate that ventral nucleus (the probable homologue of the somatic relay nuclei) projects to the striatum and dorsal ventricular ridge (Parent, 1976). Thus, somatic impulses may synapse several times in subcortical telencephalic structures before reaching the cortex (Fig. 1). Somatic representation in subcortical divisions of the reptilian telencephalon requires further study.

3. Characteristics of Somatosensory Representations

The non-specific, extralemniscal properties of single units are more pronounced in the telencephalon than in the thalamus. Almost all somatically responsive units in dorsal cortex, pallial thickening, dorsal ventricular ridge, and striatum also respond to light flashes; while only one-third of such units in the thalamus are somatovisually convergent. No somatotopic organization occurs in dorsal cortex of turtles (Mazurskaya and Smirnov, 1965; Mazurskaya et al., 1966; Belekhova, 1973a; Karamian, 1976). A crude somatotopic map exists in dorsal cortex of alligators; the head is represented caudally and the legs more rostrally (Kruger and Berkowitz, 1960). The somatosensory system is represented bilaterally in dorsal cortex. Most cortical single units in turtles and alligators have large receptive fields, often covering the entire surface of the body and limbs, and nociceptive stimuli drive these units most effectively. Somatosensory responses to repetitive (especially natural) stimulation attenuate rapidly and are extremely susceptible to anesthesia. Non-specific properties of cortical somatic potentials are well expressed in turtles (*Emys orbicularis, Testudo horsfieldii*; Belekhova, 1973a; Belekhova and Akulina, 1975) and less so in alligators (*Alligator mississippiensis*; Kruger and Berkowitz, 1960; Moore, 1961; Moore and Tschirgi, 1962) and lizards (*Varanus griseus, Ophisaurus apodus*; Belekhova, 1963; Belekhova and Safarov, 1976), indicating various degrees of somatosensory specialization among reptiles.

4. Comparisons with other Vertebrates

As indicated above, the reptilian thalamic somatosensory zone receives both lemniscal and extralemniscal afferents. Thus, it is likely that telencephalic somatosensory areas also receive both types of pathways (as is the case for the reptilian visual system), though lemniscal and extralemniscal somatosensory projections are practically inseparable at the level of the telencephalon. Somatic volley specificity declines from the periphery to the forebrain due to increasing rostral convergence of impulses of different origin (heterotopic, heterosensory, heterosubmodal) suggesting "incomplete lemniscal" afferent systems in non-mammalian vertebrates (Noback and Shriver, 1966). Mammalian somatosensory systems reveal functional specializations (Bowsher and Albe-Fessard, 1965; Brodal, 1969; Mehler, 1969; Durinyan and Rabin, 1971), but lemniscal and extralemniscal projections overlap in the mesencephalon, the posterior thalamic complex, and even in the thalamic somatic relay nucleus, VPL (Bava *et al.*, 1966; Bowsher, 1971; Schroeder and Jane, 1968, 1971; Curry, 1972; Curry and Gordon, 1972; Jabbur *et al.*, 1972). Extralemniscal somatic systems are relatively stable in vertebrate evolution, while lemniscal pathways have undergone extensive development, resulting in highly specialized, rapidly conducting projection systems related to fine sensory discrimination.

E. AUDITORY REPRESENTATIONS

There are few electrophysiological studies of auditory representation in the reptilian telencephalon. In crocodilians (*Alligator mississippiensis, Caiman crocodilus*), evoked responses to click, vibration and sound (70–1000 Hz) stimuli occur in the dorsal ventricular ridge; their distribution coincides, in part, with the terminal field of nucleus reuniens (Moore, 1961; Weisbach and Schwartzkopff, 1967; Pritz, 1974b). A three-dimensional tonotopic projection, with maximal sensitivity at 1500–2000 Hz, is present in the telencephalic dorsal ventricular ridge of caimans (Weisbach and Schwartzkopff, 1967). Auditory responses in dorsal cortex and pallial thickening of alligators, turtles (*Emys orbicularis*) and lizards (*Ctenosaura pectinata*) are weaker than responses evoked by visual and somatic stimuli (Moore and Tschirgi, 1962; Gusel'nikov, 1965; Mazurskaya and Smirnov, 1965; Mazurskaya *et al.*, 1966;

Tauber *et al.*, 1968). In lizards (*Agama caucasica, Ophisaurus apodus*), auditory responses to clicks and tones occur in the mediodorsal cortex, as do responses to visual and somatic stimuli. Impulses of all three modalities converge there on common neurons (Gusel'nikova and Gusel'nikov, 1963; Voronin *et al.*, 1964; Gusel'nikov, 1965; Belekhova and Safarov, 1976), as they also do in the dorsal cortex of turtles and alligators (Moore and Tschirgi, 1962; Mazurskaya and Smirnov, 1965).

Little is known about the role of the forebrain in reptilian auditory functions. Avoidance and alimentary conditioned responses to auditory signals are retained in lizards following removal of the entire forebrain. New postoperative responses are acquired with difficulty, however, and are preserved only 3–5 days, as opposed to 3–4 weeks in unablated lizards (Safarov, 1971; Sikharulidze, 1972b; Beritashwili, 1974).

F. Reciprocal Relationships

Thalamocortical interrelationships of reptiles are reciprocal. The dorsal cortex lacks specialized patterns, but the cortex differentially influences the lateral geniculate and mediocentral (nucleus rotundus) thalamic zones in turtles (Belekhova, 1972b). Thus, the reptilian geniculocortical pathway is similar to the geniculostriate path in mammals, as both possess corticofugal projections to the lateral geniculate. Nucleus rotundus of turtles does not possess reciprocal connections with dorsal cortex. Nucleus rotundus has no direct projections to the cortex; but, as in the lateral geniculate, relatively short-latency activity occurs in response to cortical stimulation, suggesting direct or oligosynaptic projections of dorsal cortex to nucleus rotundus. At the same time, nucleus rotundus and dorsal cortex are connected by bilateral, polysynaptic projections mediating long-latency recruiting responses (Belekhova, 1972b). Direct corticofugal projections to the lateral geniculate nucleus and nucleus rotundus are known from anterograde degeneration studies (Karamian *et al.*, 1968; Riss *et al.*, 1972; Hall and Ebner, 1974; Gaidaenko, 1977); but the main telencephalic input to nucleus rotundus originates in subcortical telencephalic structures and is conveyed via the dorsal peduncle of the lateral forebrain bundle (Lohman *et al.*, 1973).

V. Non-specific Thalamotelencephalic Systems

A. Non-specific Pathways

1. *General Comments*

In turtles (*Emys orbicularis, Testudo horsfieldii*), cortical projections from the epithalamus (habenular nuclei and commissure) and several thalamic nuclei (lateral geniculate nucleus, nucleus rotundus and suprapeduncular nucleus) have been studied by direct electrical stimulation. Projections of the habenular complex are confined to lateral and medial cortices. Three other systems (geniculo-, rotundo-, and suprapedunculo-cortical) project to the same area of dorsal cortex (Fig. 3) (Belekhova and Kosareva, 1971; Belekhova, 1970a, b, 1973a).

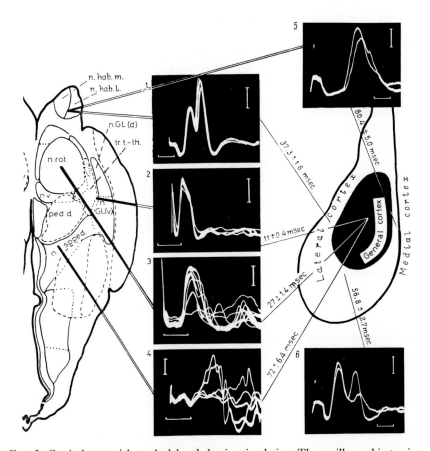

FIG. 3. Cortical potentials evoked by thalamic stimulation. The oscillographic tracings show the form of electrical activity elicited from the cortex by stimulation of the following diencephalic nuclei: tracings 1, 5 and 6, habenular nuclei; tracing 2, lateral geniculate complex; tracing 3, nucleus rotundus; tracing 4, suprapeduncular nucleus. The numbers indicate response latencies (mean ± S.E.M.). The initial positive potential in 1, 5 and 6 is a field artifact. Negative is upward. Calibration: 200 mV, 40 ms. n.GL(d), dorsal lateral geniculate nucleus; n.GL(v), ventral lateral geniculate nucleus; n.hab.m., medial habenular nucleus; n.hab.l., lateral habenular nucleus; n.rot., nucleus rotundus; n.spped., suprapeduncular nucleus; n.v., nucleus ventralis; ped.d., dorsal peduncle of the lateral forebrain bundle; tr.t.-th., tectothalamic tract.

Only one of the three pathways, the geniculocortical, is solely sensory, and it likely conveys the shortest latency impulses from the lateral geniculate to dorsal cortex. It terminates in the superficial cortical layer on apical dendrites of cells whose somata are situated more deeply. This pathway is apparently a sensory projection system which was probably present in the earliest mammals. In modern mammals, it is evident in both primitive and advanced species (Walsh and Ebner, 1968; Ebner, 1969; Rossignol and Colonnier, 1969; Benevento and Ebner, 1971; Garey and Powell, 1971; Polley, 1971; Adrianov and Polyakova, 1972; Benevento, 1972; Killackey, 1972; Lund, 1973; Rosenquist et al., 1974). These primitive parts of the mammalian sensory projection system develop earlier ontogenetically than more recent terminations in the main cortical receptive layers (Laemle et al., 1972; Anker and Cragg, 1974). In newborn mammals, cortical sensory responses, mediated via thalamic relay nuclei, are similar to reptilian cortical sensory responses in surface negative polarity, long latency, rapid attenuation during rhythmic stimulation, and high susceptibility to anesthetics (Purpura, 1961a; Scherrer, 1965; Karamian, 1966; Karamian et al., 1966; Farber, 1969; Mysliveček, 1969). The earliest cortical responses in neonate mammals may depend on the more primitive pathways (Anokhin, 1961; Rose and Lindsley, 1968; Rose and Ellingson, 1970; Ata-Muradova and Belova, 1971).

Thalamotelencephalic evolution in reptiles is not limited to the origin and development of sensory projection systems. Two other thalamotelencephalic pathways (rotundo- and subthalamotelencephalic) convey sensory impulses to the telencephalon; however, these pathways are not solely sensory, as both receive strong input from the mesencephalon: the optic tectum projects to both nucleus rotundus and the subthalamic suprapeduncular nucleus; the tegmentum also projects to subthalamic nuclei. Both pathways modulate forebrain sensory responses.

2. Rotundotelencephalic Pathway

The rotundotelencephalic pathway selectively influences one or two of the components which immediately follow cortical potentials evoked by flashes or tectal stimulation; the subthalamotelencephalic pathway affects later components of these potentials (Fig. 4). As stated above, neither thalamo-telencephalic pathway connects directly with dorsal cortex, and they may reach it only after synapsing in subcortical telencephalic structures. Afferents appear to terminate on apical dendrites of cells in the superficial plexiform layer of the cortex, and represent maximum "integrative" properties of synapses (Andersen and Lømo, 1967). Nucleus rotundus provides a relay for tectal impulses and for complex integrative or modulatory functions (Kosareva et al., 1973). Some single units in rotundus are plastic: they respond variably to the same flash or tectal stimulation and reproduce a patterned response several times after removal of the stimulus. Within nucleus rotundus, synapses of tectal afferents and those of rotundocortical projections display: (i) considerable facilitation of recruiting activity in the course of rhythmic (1–20 Hz) stimulation; and (ii) prolonged (up to 6 min) preservation of enhanced synaptic efficacy after prior tectal or rotundal tetanization,

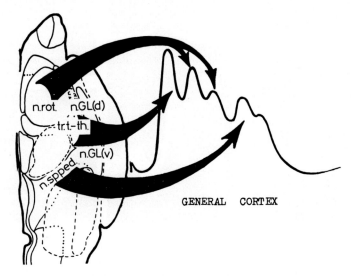

FIG. 4. Visual response in turtle general cortex. The right part of the figure shows a waveform recorded from turtle cortex following a visual stimulus. The identity of each of the components of the waveform is indicated by the arrows leading from specific diencephalic structures. n.GL(d), dorsal lateral geniculate nucleus; n.GL(v), ventral lateral geniculate nucleus; n.spped., suprapeduncular nucleus; n.rot., nucleus rotundus; tr.t.-th., tectothalamic tract.

similar to posttetanic potentiation (Fig. 5) (Belekhova, 1967, 1968b, 1970a, 1973a, 1977). Single electric shocks applied to nucleus rotundus of quiet turtles elicit bursts of spindle activity in the dorsal cortex (Servit and Strejčková, 1972). High-frequency (50–300 Hz) stimulation of nucleus rotundus produces an EEG reaction in dorsal cortex characterized by enhancement of amplitude and synchronization of EEG components predominantly at 12–24 Hz. This response is virtually identical to that elicited by natural stimuli, such as object movement before the eyes, and accompanies an orienting response (Fig. 6) (Belekhova, 1965). The reptilian tecto–rotundo–telencephalic system combines sensory, integrative and modulatory functions related to vigilance. Visual input to nucleus rotundus, via the optic tectum, appears to trigger a modulatory function.

An homologous system in birds exhibits analogous relay (Belekhova, 1966; Karten and Revzin, 1966; Revzin and Karten, 1966; Revzin, 1967; Karten and Hodos, 1970) and modulatory (Belekhova, 1965, 1966) functions, the latter relating to the dorsolateral surface of the forebrain hemisphere.

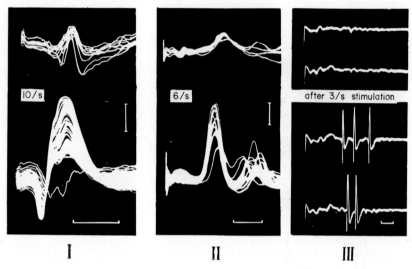

FIG. 5. Rhythmic and posttetanic facilitation of evoked activity in the tecto-rotundo-telencephalic system in turtles. I. Evoked responses in nucleus rotundus following stimulation of the optic tectum. II and III. Evoked responses in general cortex following stimulation in nucleus rotundus at various stimulation frequencies. Calibration: 200 mV, 40 ms.

3. Subthalamotelencephalic Pathway

The reptilian subthalamotelencephalic system resembles the rotundo-telencephalic system, but is slower conducting and reveals more multimodal convergence. As part of the somatic zone, it is probably triggered mainly by somatic impulses. The subthalamotelencephalic pathway is closely connected with the mesencephalic tegmentum, and directly controls background electrical activity in the forebrain. Prolonged preservation of EEG changes, after cessation of electrical stimulation of nucleus suprapeduncularis, is typical of this pathway (Belekhova, 1963, 1973a).

4. Interactions between the Three Pathways

The geniculocortical, rotundotelencephalic and subthalamotelencephalic pathways all terminate on apical dendrites of cells in the superficial cortical layer. Reptilian cortex is characterized by lophodendritic (Ramón-Moliner,

1967) or extraverted (Sanides, 1972) neurons, with apical dendrites oriented to the cortical surface and poorly developed basal dendrites (Gieseman, 1964; Poliakov, 1964; Minelli, 1966, 1967; Ebner and Colonnier, 1975). Thus, cortical responses to stimulation of the three thalamocortical systems have a surface negative–positive character, suggesting primary activition of apical dendrites and secondary activation of perikarya in the cortical plate.

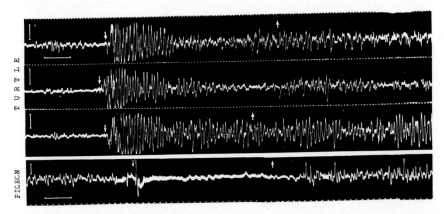

FIG. 6. Electroencephalographic arousal reaction in reptiles and birds. The top three traces show responses recorded from turtle general cortex to the stimulation of nucleus rotundus at 100 Hz (top), to a moving object, and to stimulation of the mesencephalic tegmentum at 100 Hz (bottom). The bottom trace shows responses recorded from the forebrain of a pigeon to stimulation of nucleus rotundus at 100 Hz. The beginning and end of the stimulation are marked by arrows. Calibration: 200 mV, 0·5 s.

This interpretation is reinforced by data on the synaptic origin of visual evoked potentials, revealed by intracellular recordings in turtle dorsal cortex. The first EPSP is generated in more distal branches of apical dendrites; later EPSPs and IPSPs are generated closer to the perikarya (Pivovarov, 1973; Gusel'nikov et al., 1974). The dorsal cortex in turtles does not differ significantly from lateral and medial cortices in the genesis of elicited activity, though each area is morphologically distinct in reptiles (Smirnov, 1968; Davydova and Smirnov, 1969; Northcutt, 1970; Davydova and Goncharova, 1971; Goncharova, 1974; Ulinski, 1974).

5. Comparisons with Other Vertebrates

a. Rotundo-telencephalic Pathway. The tecto–rotundo–telencephalic system may be widely distributed among vertebrates, as a nucleus rotundus or other tectal recipient nucleus is found in sharks, teleosts, dipnoans and amphibians (Frontera, 1952: Schnitzlein and Crosby, 1968; Ebbesson, 1972a;

Kicliter and Northcutt, 1975; Ebbesson and Vanegas, 1976). Some sharks, teleosts, and frogs display direct retinal input to nucleus rotundus (Scalia and Gregory, 1970; Ebbesson *et al.*, 1972; Sharma, 1972). Other vertebrates show increased tectal input and loss of direct retinal input. The details of a rotundotelencephalic system are not known for mammals. Nucleus rotundus and its projections are specialized structures of the reptilian thalamus and reflect a main trend of vertebrate brain evolution: development of tecto-thalamo-telencephalic systems. The tectal input and telencephalic projections of nucleus rotundus and of the mammalian lateralis posterior nucleus are similar (Diamond and Hall, 1969; Hall and Ebner, 1970a; Karten and Hodos, 1970). Nucleus rotundus also bears some functional resemblance to non-specific thalamic nuclei in mammals (Belekhova, 1963; Karamian and Belek-hova, 1963; Karamian, 1970). Both possible homologies, however, rely on only one feature of nucleus rotundus (Belekhova and Kosareva, 1971). Jones and Powell (1971) note that in mammals the posterior thalamic group is similar in origin and function to the intralaminar thalamic nuclei; mammalian lateral posterior and non-specific thalamic nuclei may originate from the same neuronal population in ancestral reptiles. However, nucleus rotundus can not be homologized to a single nucleus of the mammalian thalamus: during vertebrate evolution the optic tectum has become less significant as a sensory correlative center, with concurrent modification of the thalamus.

   b. *Subthalamotelencephalic Pathway.* All vertebrates have a subthalamo-telencephalic system; it is a convergent, polysensory system, which is dominated by somatosensory input in mammals. The subthalamotelence-phalic system is an important part of the non-specific, ascending activating system (Starzl *et al.*, 1951; Adey and Lindsley, 1959; Crosby *et al.*, 1962; Denavit and Kosinski, 1968; Bach-y-Rita *et al.*, 1969; Lindsley *et al.*, 1970).

   c. *Cortical Terminations.* Mammalian pyriform and hippocampal cortices demonstrate activation patterns similar to those of reptilian dorsal cortex (Gergen and MacLean, 1964; Biedenbach and Stevens, 1969). However, mammalian neocortex shows a complex stratification that reveals differential afferentation and termination of most sensory fibers in layers III–IV (Bene-vento and Ebner, 1971; Hall, 1972), which contain neurons with equally developed apical and basal dendrites (Sanides, 1972). Very different evoked potentials result from various modes of neuronal activation. In turtles, cortical responses to stimulation of various thalamocortical pathways differ in latency and in capacity to follow rhythmic stimulation (Fig. 3). The geniculo-cortical pathway conducts most rapidly and projects directly from the dorsal lateral geniculate to dorsal cortex (Hall and Ebner, 1970b). The slowly conducting rotundocortical and suprapedunculocortical pathways are polysynaptic systems synapsing in subcortical structures before reaching the cortex.

tricular nucleus, or of the inhibitory (for spinal reflexes) zones of the brain stem, as well as after interoceptive stimulation, which has a different function than arousal (Berkowitz, 1957; Belekhova, 1963; Karamian and Sollertins-kaya, 1964; Tagiev, 1969). In all non-mammals, except birds, EEG activation in the form of electrical activity synchronization is probably due to poorly elaborated cortices (Voronin *et al.*, 1961; Novikova, 1962; Belekhova, 1965; Flanigan, 1972). The arousal response observed in reptiles (synchronization of α or θ rhythms) occurs in mammalian reticular formation, hippocampus, and immature postnatal cortex, on low level activation backgrounds, during initial stages of sleep and following deafferentation and other pathology (Green and Arduini, 1954; Danilov, 1959; Tokizane *et al.*, 1959; Anokhin, 1961; Purpura, 1961a, b; Iwamura and Kawamura, 1962; Novikova, 1962; Kaada *et al.*, 1963; Maiorchik, 1964).

VI. Homologies between Forebrain Structures in Reptiles and Mammals

A. CORTICAL STRUCTURES

Two different modes of corticalization exist within reptiles. In one mode afferent systems project to medial cortex; in the other mode, afferents project to dorsal cortex, probably the homologue of neocortex. The first type of corticalization is seen in anamniotes and in some squamate reptiles, and could be the basis for mammalian evolution of non-olfactory exteroceptive projections in the cortical division of the limbic system. The second type of corticalization—neocorticalization—is the source of thalamo-neocortical elaboration in mammals. Its existence in turtles is not surprising, as they share a common ancestor with mammals (Holmgren, 1925; Riss *et al.*, 1969b; Northcutt, 1970; Romer, 1970).

This view of two modes of corticalization within reptiles is valid only if medial and dorsal cortices are part of hippocampus and neocortex, respectively. However, several investigations indicate otherwise. The entire dorsal cortex, or its medial part, may be a differentiated region of archicortex or periarchicortex (Rose, 1923; Kruger and Berkowitz, 1960; Filimonov, 1963; Kruger, 1969; Platel, 1969; Lohman and van Woerden-Verkley, 1976); or a specialized reptilian structure (Goldby and Gamble, 1957). Only the dorso-lateral part of dorsal cortex, the pallial thickening in particular, may represent the neocortical precursor (Schepers, 1948; Northcutt, 1970; Kirsche, 1972). According to Northcutt (1970), only the dorsolateral component of dorsal cortex in *Chrysemys* is homologous to neocortex. Cells of the dorsolateral area have retained Golgi type I neurons, with long descending axons; whereas sauropsids have no Golgi type I neurons in the dorsolateral area. The medial cortex is the main pallial target of non-olfactory sensory projections in amphibians. It is doubtful, however, that this area is homologous to neocortex. The medial cortex of amphibians may be homologous to the dorsomedial part of the dorsal cortex in reptiles and to the parahippocampal cortex of mammals. Differences between medial and lateral parts of the reptilian dorsal cortex led Dart (1934) to assume it had a dual origin from archi- and paleopallium. This concept was extended by Sanides (1969, 1972, 1973), who stated that mammalian neocortex resulted from elaboration and differentiation of periarchicortex and peripaleocortex, and under the influence of increased thalamic sensory projections.

A particularly important criterion is the degree of segregation present in the cortical representation of sensory systems. However, contradictory results have been reported on this point. Orrego (1961a), Gusel'nikov (1965) and Voronin et al. (1965) have all described discrete zones receiving visual and somatic projections to turtle dorsal cortex (Fig. 2B lower hemisphere). Subsequent morphological experiments reveal that the part of the dorsal cortex (Hall and Ebner, 1970b) which receives projections from the dorsal lateral geniculate nucleus coincides with the zone of visual evoked potentials. However, Hall and Ebner did not completely destroy the dorsal lateral geniculate. Therefore, the entire terminal field may not have been revealed. On the other hand, most electrophysiological studies have failed to demonstrate separate sensory projections within the dorsal cortex of turtles and alligators (Fig. 2B upper hemisphere). Such zones may occur only in mammalian cortex (Bishop, 1958). Indeed, there is not only topographic overlap of visual, somatic and auditory projections in reptilian dorsal cortex, but convergence of different modalities on common neurons as well (Kruger and Berkowitz, 1960; Moore and Tschirgi, 1962; Mazurskaya and Smirnov, 1965; Mazurskaya et al., 1966; Akulina, 1971; Belekhova, 1973a; Belekhova and Akulina, 1970, 1975; Karamian, 1970, 1976).

The above data on the organization of the turtle dorsal cortex—absence of olfactory projections; representation of main sensory nonolfactory exteroceptive systems; direct geniculocortical connections; synaptic organization (Ebner and Colonnier, 1975) and histochemical characteristics (Baker-Cohen, 1968; Parent and Poitras, 1974) similar to mammalian neocortex; sensory evoked potentials similar to those in neocortex of newborn mammals—suggest that dorsal cortex in turtles is homologous to mammalian neocortex. Both sensory systems of several modalities and sensory—integrative—modulatory systems converge in the turtle dorsal cortex. Thus, it is doubtful that dorsal cortex is homologous to mammalian visual cortex alone, or to its primary (Hall and Ebner, 1970b; Ebner and Colonnier, 1975) or secondary (Hall and Diamond, 1968b; Kaas et al., 1970) projection zones, even though the secondary zone, especially, is similar to dorsal cortex in structure and function. Morphological data indicate that dorsal ventricular ridge and the tectofugal pathway are homologous to the secondary visual zone in mammals. These considerations apply mainly to turtles, the dorsal cortex of which is more developed and differentiated (Platel *et al.*, 1973; Davydova and Goncharova, 1971, 1974), than is that of lizards (Gieseman, 1964) and crocodilians (Platel *et al.*, 1973). Ascending pathways to dorsal cortex in lizards have not been sufficiently studied to propose homologies (Belekhova, 1963; Butler and Ebner, 1972).

From this point of view, sauropsid and theropsid reptiles, with their differently organized cortical areas, may exhibit two different stages in the process of neocortical differentiation. The dorsal cortex in turtles represents an earlier stage in the development of neocortex, a stage prior to the segregation of discrete projectional sensory zones which combines sensory and primitive associative functions. However, in some ways the dorsal cortex of turtles is a specialized structure with some neocortical features likely due to convergent evolution. Thus, it appears unreasonable to search for its homologue in a distinct neocortical area of mammals. To some extent, the dorsal cortex of turtles may be closer to the periallocortex stage in mammalian neocortical evolution (Sanides, 1969) or to the proisocortex stage (Kirsche, 1972). A dorsal cortex corresponding to these stages might have existed in mammal-like reptiles (Sanides, 1969). In some lizards, dorsal cortex probably does not reach a level of organization comparable to that in turtles. Lizards may have diverged from turtles by continuing an amphibian-like line of cortical development.

B. Subcortical Structures

1. *General*

Sensory representation in the reptilian "subpallium" has been studied far less intensively than has that of the cortex. At present, it is difficult to establish the significance of reptilian "subpallial" structures. Their phylogenetic history is unknown; and their homologies with mammalian telencephalic structures are in dispute. Part of the so-called "subpallium" may actually be homologous to the pallium of other vertebrates. Three separate cell groups have traditionally been considered to be subpallium (Fig. 2B). In this review, these cell groups will be termed—from dorsal to ventral—dorsal ventricular ridge, dorsal striatum, and ventral striatum. Earlier workers homologized all of the nuclei of the lateral telencephalic wall (except for the pallial thickening) to the striatum of mammals. The term "striatum" for these reptilian forebrain structures is retained in some recent morphological studies and reviews (Hewitt, 1967; Webster and Webster, 1964), and is used extensively in physiology.

2. *Dorsal Ventricular Ridge* (*DVR*)

Several homologies have been proposed for the reptilian dorsal ventricular ridge. The pallial thickening and dorsal ventricular ridge have been homologized to the dorsal and ventral claustrum of mammals (Holmgren, 1925; Filimonov, 1963; Crosby *et al.*, 1966; Carey, 1967; Schnitzlein *et al.*, 1973). This interpretation does not exclude the possibility that part of dorsal ventricular ridge is homologous to putamen (Crosby *et al.*, 1966) or to part of the caudate nucleus (Baker-Cohen, 1968). A similar conclusion was reached by Hewitt (1967), who homologized reptilian dorsal ventricular ridge with the intermedial and lateral striatal elevations of the human embryo. More recently, the reptilian dorsal ventricular ridge and its avian homologues, despite their non-laminar organization, have been homologized to parts of mammalian neocortex, based on similarities in their embryology (Källén, 1951; Northcutt, 1970), afferent connections (Karten, 1969; Hall and Ebner, 1970b; Karten and Hodos, 1970; Nauta and Karten, 1970; Pritz, 1974b, 1975), and histochemistry (Parent and Olivier, 1970; Parent, 1976).

The dorsal ventricular ridge of turtles and caimans receives sensory projections from the thalamus; and these sensory zones of the dorsal ventricular ridge occupy different segments of the ridge. A thalamic nucleus (nucleus reuniens) receives auditory afferents from the torus semicircularis and projects to a caudomedial portion of the ridge. This ridge area in reptiles is believed to be homologous to a similar region of the avian neostriatum (field L) and to auditory cortex in mammals (Karten, 1969; Pritz, 1974b). Another thalamic nucleus, nucleus rotundus, receives tectal afferents and projects to an anterolateral region of the dorsal ventricular ridge in turtles and caimans. This region of the reptilian dorsal ventricular ridge is believed to be homologous to the avian ectostriatum and to mammalian peristriate cortex (Karten, 1969; Hall and Ebner, 1970a, b; Pritz, 1975).

The hypothesis that the reptilian dorsal ventricular ridge is homologous to parts of mammalian neocortex is supported by afferent similarities, but is not definitely proven. It is possible that dorsal ventricular ridge in birds and reptiles represents a telencephalic specialization in these taxa without mammalian homologies. At any rate, it is no longer feasible to consider all reptilian subcortical structures as "striatum".

3. *Striatum*

Interpretations of the "ventral striatum" are more uniform, and many investigators consider only this structure as striatal (Holmgren, 1925; Hall and Ebner, 1970b). The ventral striatum consists of dorsal and ventral divisions (str.d., str.v. at Fig. 2B). These divisions have been homologized to part of mammalian caudoputamen and globus pallidus, respectively (Johnston, 1923;

Crosby *et al.*, 1966). This interpretation is also supported by recent histochemical findings (Baker-Cohen, 1968; Parent and Olivier, 1970).

There are few data concerning afferent connections of the striatum. Cells in both nucleus rotundus and reuniens project to dorsal ventricular ridge, but also terminate in the striatum. This is not the case with lateral geniculate fibers (Hall and Ebner, 1970b; Hall, 1972; Pritz, 1974b). Parent (1976) injected horseradish peroxidase separately into the dorsal ventricular ridge and striatum of turtles. After striatal injections, retrograde transport was evident in nucleus ventralis and reuniens, which probably represent somatosensory and auditory relays (Papez, 1935; Pritz, 1974b). However, far more labeled cells in these and other perirotundal nuclei were evident after injections in dorsal ventricular ridge.

Electrical stimulation of the lateral thalamic zone evokes short-latency potentials in dorsal ventricular ridge and striatum of turtles (Belekhova, 1977). Parent (1976) observed a few labeled cells in the dorsal lateral geniculate after horseradish peroxidase injection of striatum, the rostral tip of dorsal ventricular ridge and the ventral part of the pallial thickening. This suggests that lateral geniculate efferents to dorsal cortex give off collaterals that terminate in both subcortical structures. This is not the primary pathway for visual impulses to these structures, as lesions of the lateral thalamic zone do not abolish flash-evoked and tectal stimulation responses in dorsal ventricular ridge and the striatum (Belekhova, 1977).

C. Encephalization in Vertebrates

There is some indication that visual and somatic impulses, including those relaying in the thalamus, project to striatum in sharks and amphibians (Ebbesson and Schroeder, 1971; Ebbesson, 1972a, b; Vesselkin and Kovaȝević, 1973a, b; Nomokonova, 1971, 1976; Kicliter and Northcutt, 1975). Dorsal ventricular ridge in amphibians is, at most, rudimentary (Crosby *et al.*, 1966; Schnitzlein *et al.*, 1973; Northcutt, 1974). Afferent supply to the striatum via thalamic relay nuclei decreases in mammals, but is retained as a system of collateral projections for auditory medial geniculate, somatosensory (VPL), and vestibular relay nuclei (Crosby *et al.*, 1962; Brodal, 1969; Carreras and Eager, 1969; Ebner, 1969; Copack *et al.*, 1972).

Thus, reptilian thalamo-sensory projections have shifted rostrally from the striatum (as in amphibians) to the dorsal ventricular ridge and cortex (Ebner, 1969; Kicliter and Northcutt, 1975). Accordingly, the striatal sensory representation in non-mammalian vertebrates may be considered as a stage of encephalization en route to their complete corticalization. However, the matter is not so simple, as not only the precursors of the relay nuclei, but also other structures—nucleus rotundus, perirotundal nuclei, ventrocaudal thalamic zone—project to the telencephalon. Connections of these structures with the striatum do not decrease, but are likely retained and augmented. The separation of afferent thalamic inputs to sensory neocortex and striatum becomes very definite in mammals. The cortex receives its input via specific thalamic nuclei, the striatum via non-specific intralaminar nuclei (Brodal, 1969; Jones and Leavitt, 1974). The enigma of the vertebrate striatum requires further study.

According to Herrick's (1930, 1956) classic concept, the sensory thalamus is the main factor determining the evolution of the telencephalic cortex. However, their evolutionary rates are different; the thalamus develops in advance of the cortex with respect to the degree of differentiation and specialization of various functional systems (Karamian, 1967, 1968, 1970; Belekhova, 1970a, 1973a). This discrepancy is even seen in living insectivores (Schroeder and Jane, 1971). In reptiles, differences in specialization between thalamic and telencephalic levels are revealed in the organization of the separate afferent systems.

VII. Summary

Neurophysiological data help us to understand the functional organization of reptilian brains. Neurophysiology and experimental morphology of reptiles contribute, in turn, to our understanding of the evolution of vertebrate nervous systems. Such data allow us to identify trends in CNS adaptations and attempt to relate these trends to other features of vertebrate evolution.

The following features characterize reptiles:

1. Thalamic afferents consist of two types of pathways for a given modality, with partial functional overlap. Some pathways are multisynaptic (extralemniscal somatosensory, retino–tecto–thalamo–telencephalic) and are considered more primitive; other pathways are more direct (lemniscal somatosensory, retino–geniculo–telencephalic) and are regarded as more recently derived. Pathways of both types undergo telencephalization. Some afferent thalamotelencephalic systems receive input after relaying in the midbrain, and project directly to the subcortical region of the forebrain (dorsal ventricular ridge); other sensory systems project directly to the cortex. Both types of systems ultimately converge on a single cortical area. Thus, functions do not merely shift from primitive systems to more recently evolved ones.

2. Thalamic and telencephalic organization in reptiles and birds reflects development of the optic tectum as the main sensory-correlative center, while more direct projection systems provide thalamic and telencephalic

afferents in mammals. Important differences occur in pallial projections from thalamic nuclei, and these projections vary considerably among reptiles and other non-mammalian vertebrates.

3. Rostral areas of reptilian brains are less specialized than caudal centers, though reptilian brains are generally more specialized than those of fishes or amphibians. Afferent zones are segregated in the reptilian thalamus, and each zone contains two types of pathways. Olfactory and non-olfactory pallial projections are separate, and non-olfactory extero-ceptive afferents converge on a common zone in dorsal cortex (turtles); however, specific unimodal neurons do appear in dorsal cortex. Projections of different modalities overlap in both the thalamus and telencephalon. Sensory representations appear to receive specific information but display non-specific organization.

4. Mixed sensory-integrative-modulatory systems are significant in the organization of reptilian brains. These systems conduct sensory information to higher forebrain centers and regulate electrical activity in the telencephalon, thus controlling arousal levels. Mammalian thalamo-telencephalic systems reveal sensory pathways. Mammalian sensory systems are specialized for refined analysis of unimodal impulses and integration of converging impulses of different modalities.

The non-specific character of many reptilian brain systems does not necessarily imply their homology with an anatomically distinct non-specific system in mammals. Specific brain systems may pass through a non-specific stage during evolutionary development, or may retain unspecialized features which dominated some earlier stage. Adaptive specializations at different evolutionary stages involve the dominance of one or another afferent system, but do not alter the general trend in brain evolution—the development of discrete patterns from a diffuse mode of organization. Evolution of the dominant system accelerates, but all of the systems follow the general trend.

Comparative neurophysiology attempts to combine the electrophysiological analysis of behavior with an understanding of behavioral mechanisms. Not all neurophysiological techniques have been applied to reptiles; and there is certainly need for an eclectic approach involving experimental morphology and embryology in investigating many neurobiological problems. These include: encephalization of lemniscal and extralemniscal somatosensory systems; differential function of dorsal and ventral lateral geniculate nuclei; the functional significance of dual sensory projections to reptilian cortex and dorsal ventricular ridge; and the interaction of afferents in separate brain structures. The method of antidromic stimulation effectively reveals direct connections, as well as their cells of origin, but this method has not been utilized in studies of reptilian brains.

Both Herrick (1939, 1956) and Orbeli (1934) stated that the study of analytical brain functions requires quite different approaches than the study of integrative functions. Electrophysiologists have had scanty means for investigating integrative aspects and convergent processes. Statistical methods will probably allow investigators to recognize minute functional shifts in nervous centers. Thus, these methods offer a propitious approach for investigating changes in integrative brain systems.

References

Ablanalp, P. (1970). Some subcortical connections of the visual system in tree shrews and squirrels. *Brain, Behav. Evol.* 3, 155–168.

Ablanalp, P. (1971). The neuroanatomical organization of the visual system in the tree shrew. *Folia primatol.* 16, 1–34.

Adey, W. R. and Lindsley, D. F. (1959). On the role of subthalamic areas in the maintenance of brainstem reticular excitability. *Expl Neurol.* 1, 407–426.

Adrianov, O. S. and Polyakova, A. G. (1972). Peculiarities of connections of the thalamic ventrobasal complex with the parietal and somatosensory cortical areas of the cat's brain. *Zh. Vyssh. Nerv. Deyat. Pavlova* 22, 1039–1045. (In Russian.)

Akulina, M. M. (1971). Electrophysiological studies on thalamotelencephalic interrelations in turtles. *Zh. Evol. Biokhim. Fiziol.* 7, 543–545. (In Russian.)

Allison, A. C. (1953). The morphology of the olfactory system in the vertebrates. *Biol. Rev.* 28, 195–244.

Altman, J. and Carpenter, M. B. (1961). Fiber projections of the superior colliculus in the cat. *J. comp. Neurol.* 116, 157–178.

Andersen, P. and Lømo, T. (1967). Mechanisms of control of pyramidal cell activity. *In* "Contemporary Problems of the Electrophysiology of the Central Nervous System". (V. S. Rusinov, ed.). Nauka, Moscow, pp. 5–13. (In Russian.)

Andry, M. L., Luttges, M. W. and Gamov, C. J. (1971). Temperature effects on spontaneous and evoked neural activity in the garter snake. *Expl Neurol.* 31, 32–44.

Anker, R. L. and Cragg, B. G. (1974). Development of the extrinsic connections of the visual cortex in the cat. *J. comp. Neurol.* 154, 29–42.

Anokhin, P. K. (1961). The multiple ascending influences of the subcortical centers on the cerebral cortex. *In* "Brain and Behavior". (M. Brazier, ed.). *Amer. Inst. Biol. Sci.*, Washington, pp. 139–170.

Anokhin, P. K. (1964). Systemogenesis as a general regulator of brain development. *Progr. Brain Res.* 9, 54–86.

Ariëns, Kappers, C. U., Huber, G. C. and Crosby, E. C. (1936). "The Comparative Anatomy of the Nervous System of Vertebrates Including Man." Macmillan, London and New York.

Armstrong, J. A. (1950). An experimental study of the visual pathways in a reptile (*Lacerta vivipara*). *J. Anat.* 84, 146–167.

Armstrong, J. A. (1951). An experimental study of the visual pathways in a snake (*Natrix natrix*). *J. Anat.* 85, 275–288.

Ata-Muradova, F. A. and Belova, T. I. (1971). Phylo-ontogenetic regularities of the maturation of corticopetal projections of optic cortex. *Dokl. Ak. Nauk SSSR* 200, 1483–1487. (In Russian.)

Bach-y-Rita, G., Baurand, C. and Cristolomme, A. (1969). A comparison of EEG modifications induced by coagulation of subthalamus, preoptic region, and mesencephalic reticular formation. *Electroenceph. clin. Neurophysiol.* **26**, 493–502.

Bagley, C., Jr. and Langworthy, D. R. (1926). The forebrain and midbrain of the alligator with experimental transection of the brain stem. *Archs Neurol. Psychiat.* **16**, 154–166.

Bagley, C., Jr. and Richter, C. P. (1924). Electrically excitable region of the forebrain of the alligator. *Arch. Neurol. Psychiat.* **11**, 257–263.

Baird, J. L. (1970). The anatomy of the reptilian ear. *In* "Biology of the Reptilia". (C. Gans and T. S. Parsons, eds). Academic Press, London and New York, **3**, 193–275.

Baker-Cohen, K. F. (1968). Comparative enzyme histochemical observations on sub-mammalian brains. Striatal structures in reptiles and birds. Basal structures of the brainstem in reptiles and birds. *Ergebn. Anat. EntwGesch.* **40**, 7–70.

Bantil, H. (1972). Multielectrode analysis of field potentials in turtle cerebellum: an electrophysiological method for monitoring continuous spatial parameters. *Brain Res.* **44**, 676–679.

Baru, A. V. (1962). Characteristics of audition in various vertebrates. *Uspekhi Sovrem. Biol.* **54**, 174–192. (In Russian.)

Bass, A. H. and Northcutt, R. G. (1975). Retinal projections in the Atlantic loggerhead sea turtle (*Caretta caretta*); an autoradiographic study. *Anat. Rec.* **181**, 308.

Bass, A. H., Pritz, M. B. and Northcutt, R. G. (1973). Effects of telencephalic and tectal ablations on visual behaviour in the side-necked turtle, *Podocnemis unifilis. Brain Res.* **55**, 455–460.

Batuev, A. S. (1973). On regularities of evolution of brain associative systems in mammals. *Uspekhi Fisiol. Nauk* **4**, 103–123. (In Russian.)

Bava, A., Fadiga, E. and Manzoni, T. (1966). Deafferentazione cronica e proprieta funzionali dei nuclei thalamici di relais somatico. *Atti Accad. naz. Lincei Re.* **40**, 912–920.

Belekhova, M. G. (1963). Electrical activity in cerebral hemispheres of *Varanus* evoked by diencephalic stimulation. *Fiziol. Zh. SSSR Sechnova* **59**, 1318–1329; (1965) *Fed. Proc. Trans.* Suppl. **24**, T159–T165.

Belekhova, M. G. (1965). Characteristics of cerebral activation response in reptiles and birds. *Zh. Evol. Biokhim. Fiziol.* **1**, 183–191. (In Russian.)

Belekhova, M. G. (1966). On subcortico-cortical interrelations in birds. *Fiziol. Zh. SSSR Sechenova* **52**, 677–686; (1968) *Neurosci. Transl.* **2**, 195–203.

Belekhova, M. G. (1967). Posttetanic potentiation and recruitment in the cerebral cortex of turtles. *Zh. Vyssh. Nerv. Deyat. Pavlova* **17**, 513–522; (1967–68) *Neurosci. Transl.* **2**, 204–212.

Belekhova, M. G. (1968). The recovery cycle of recruiting potentials in the cortex of hemispheres in the brain of the turtle (*Emys orbicularis*). *Bull. exp. Biol. Med.* **5**, 11–15. (In Russian.)

Belekhova, M. G. (1970a). Peculiarities of the organization of the thalamocortical system in turtles. *In* "Electrophysiological Studies on The Central Nervous System of Vertebrates". (A. I. Karamian, ed.). *Zh. Evol. Biokhim. Fiziol.* Suppl., pp. 137–146. (In Russian.)

Belekhova, M. G. (1970b). Projections of the olfactory system to the forebrain cortex in tortoises. *In* "Electrophysiological Studies on the Central Nervous System of Vertebrates" (A. I. Karamian, ed.). *Zh. Evol. Biokhim. Fiziol.* Suppl., pp. 137–146. (In Russian.)

Belekhova, M. G. (1970c). Properties of potentials in the forebrain cortex evoked by stimulation of the olfactory bulbs and habenular nuclei in tortoises. *In* "Electro-physiological Studies on the Central Nervous System of Vertebrates". (A. I. Karamian, ed.). *Zh. Evol. Biokhim. Fiziol.* Suppl., 147–151. (In Russian.)

Belekhova, M. G. (1970d). The influence of constant light on light flash-evoked activity in the turtle optic system. *Dokl. Akad. Nauk SSSR* **190**, 241–244. (In Russian.)

Belekhova, M. G. (1972a). The effect of light flash intensity on cell responses in the turtle thalamic visual center. *Fiziol. Zh. SSSR Sechenova* **58**, 1300–1305. (In Russian.)

Belekhova, M. G. (1972b). Corticothalamic projections in *Emys orbicularis* (electrophysiological investigation). *Dokl. Akad. Nauk SSSR* **206**, 1018–1021. (In Russian.)

Belekhova, M. G. (1972c). A *propos* a principle of encephalization of brain afferent systems in vertebrate evolution. *Proc. 6th Sci. Conf. on Evolutionary Physiology*, 20 Leningrad. (In Russian.)

Belekhova, M. G. (1973a). "Thalamotelencephalic System of the Turtle. Its Afferent Organization and the Place in the Brain Evolution in Vertebrates." Doctoral Thesis, Leningrad.

Belekhova, M. G. (1973b). An electrophysiological study of tecto-thalamo-telencephalic interrelations in frog. *Neurofiziologia (Kiev)* **5**, 147–154.

Belekhova, M. G. (1977). "Thalamotelencephalic System of Reptiles." Nauka, Leningrad. (In Russian.)

Belekhova, M. G. and Akulina, M. M. (1970). The tecto-thalamotelencephalic system of the turtle (electrophysiological study). *Neurofiziologia (Kiev)* **2**, 296–306. (In Russian.)

Belekhova, M. G. and Akulina, M. M. (1975). Comparative electrophysiological characteristics of afferent representation in cortical and striatal sections of the turtle forebrain. *Neurofiziologia (Kiev)* **7**, 184–193. (In Russian.)

Belekhova, M. G. and Kosareva, A. A. (1967). Morphophysiological characteristics of visual representation in the forebrain, diencephalon and midbrain of the turtle *Emys orbicularis*. *Zh. Evol. Biokhim. Fiziol.* **3**, 248–257. (In Russian.)

Belekhova, M. G. and Kosareva, A. A. (1971). Organization of the turtle thalamus: visual, somatic and tectal zones. *Brain, Behav. Evol.* **4**, 337–375.

Belekhova, M. G. and Safarov, Kh. M. (1976). On telencephalic afferent projections in the lizard *Ophisaurus apodus*. *Zh. Evol. Biokhim. and Fiziol.* **12**, 95–98.

Belekhova, M. G. and Vesselkin, N. P. (1969). Afferent system characteristics in the frog brain. *In* "Mechanisms of Nervous Activity." (D. A. Biryukov *et al.*, eds). *Fiziol. Zh. SSSR Sechenova* Suppl., pp. 162–171. (In Russian.)

Belekhova, M. G. and Zagorul'ko, T. M. (1964). Correlations between background electrical activity, afterdischarge and EEG activation response to photic stimulation in tortoise brain (*Emys lutaria*). *Zh. Vyssh. Nerv. Deyat. Pavlova* **14**, 1079–1089; (1965) *Fed. Proc. Trans.* Suppl. 24(6), T1028–T1032.

Benevento, L. A. (1972). Thalamic terminations in the visual cortex of the rhesus monkey and opossum. *Anat. Rec.* **172**, 268.

Benevento, L. A. and Ebner, F. F. (1970). Pretectal, tectal, retinal and cortical projections to thalamic nuclei of the Virginia opossum in stereotaxic coordinates. *Brain Res.* **18**, 171–175.

Benevento, L. A. and Ebner, F. F. (1971). The contribution of the dorsal lateral geniculate nuclei to the total pattern of thalamic terminations in striate cortex. *J. comp. Neurol.* **143**, 243–260.

Benevento, L. A. and Fallon, J. H. (1975). The ascending projections of the superior colliculus in the rhesus monkey (*Macaca mulatta*). *J. comp. Neurol.* **160**, 339–362.

Beritashwili, J. S. (1974). "The Memory of Vertebrates, its Characteristics and Origin." Nauka, Moscow. (In Russian.)

Berkowitz, E. C. (1957). Stimulation of the central brain stem of the alligator. *Anat. Rec.* **123**, 285.

Berkowitz, E. C. and Tschirgi, R. D. (1960). Functional organization of left and right afferent inputs in the brain of *Alligator mississippiensis*. *Anat. Rec.* 136, 163.

Bert, J. and Godet, R., (1963). Réaction d'éveil télencéphalique d'un Dipneuste. *C. r Séanc. Soc. Biol.* 157, 1787–1790.

Biedenbach, M. A. and Stevens, Ch. F. (1969). Electrical activity in cat olfactory cortex produced by synchronous orthodromic volleys. *J. Neurophysiol.* 32, 193–203.

Biryukov, D. A. (1960). "Ecological Physiology of the Nervous Activity." Medzig, Leningrad. (In Russian.)

Bishop, G. H. (1958). The place of cortex in a reticular system. In "Reticular formation of the brain." (H. Jasper and L. D. Proctor, eds). Little, Brown, Boston, pp. 413–422.

Bishop, G. H. and Smith, J. M. (1964). The sizes of nerve fibers supplying cerebral cortex. *Expl Neurol.* 9, 483–501.

Blum, B., Godel, V., Gitter, S. and Stein, R. (1972). Impulse propagation from photically discharged neurons in the visual system. *Pflügers Arch. ges.Physiol.* 331, 38–43.

Boiko, V. P. (1976). Neuronal receptive fields in mesencephalic visual center of the tortoise *Emys orbicularis*. In "Comparative Neurophysiology and Neurochemistry." (E. M. Kreps, ed.). *Zh. Evol. Biokhim. Fiziol.* Suppl. pp. 89–96. (In Russian.)

Boiko, V. P. and Davydova, T. V. (1973). Comparative study of functional and morphological characteristics of neurons in turtle mesencephalic visual center. *Zh. Evol. Biokhim. Fiziol.* 9, 541–544. (In Russian.)

Boiko, V. P. and Davydova, T. V. (1975). Morphofunctional changes in the turtle mesencephalic visual centre after enucleation. *Neurofiziologia (Kiev)* 7, 172–177. (In Russian.)

Boivie, J. (1971). The termination in the thalamus and zona incerta of fibers from the dorsal column nuclei in the cat. An experimental study with silver impregnation methods. *Brain Res.* 28, 459–490.

Boldyreva, G. N. and Grindel, O. M. (1959). Study of electrical activity in different areas of the frog brain. *Fiziol. Zh. SSSR Sechenova* 55, 1037–1044. (In Russian.)

Bowsher, D. (1971). Properties of ventrobasal thalamic neurons in cat following interruption of specific afferent pathways. *Archs ital. Biol.* 109, 59–74.

Bowsher, D. and Albe-Fessard, D. (1965). The anatomophysiological basis of somatosensory discrimination. *Int. Rev. Neurobiol.* 8, 37–69.

Braford, M. R. (1972). Ascending efferent tectal projections in the South American spectacled caiman. *Anat. Rec.* 172, 275.

Braford, M. R. (1973). Retinal projections in *Caiman crocodilus*. *Am. Zool.* 13, 1345.

Bremer, F., Dow, R. S. and Moruzzi, G. (1939). Physiological analysis of the general cortex in reptiles and birds. *J. Neurophysiol.* 2, 473–488.

Brodal, A. (1947). The hippocampus and the sense of smell (a review). *Brain* 70, 179–222.

Brodal, A. (1963). Discussion. *Progr. Brain Res.* 3, 237–244.

Brodal, A. (1969). "Neurological Anatomy in Relation to Clinical Medicine." Oxford Univ. Press, London and New York.

Bruckmoser, P. (1971). Elektrische Antworten im Vorderhirn von *Lampetra fluviatilis* (L.) bei Reizung des Nervus olfactorius. *Z. vergl. Physiol.* 75, 69–85.

Bruckmoser, P. (1973). Beziehungen zwischen Structur und Funktion in der Evolution des Telencephalon. *Verhandl. dt. zool. Ges.* 66, 219–229.

Bruckmoser, P. and Dobrylko, A. K. (1972). The evoked potentials in the telencephalon of the lamprey *Lampetra fluviatilis* during stimulation of the olfactory nerve. *Zh. Evol. Biokhim. Fiziol.* 8, 558–560. (In Russian.)

Bullock, T. H. (1945). Problems in the comparative study of brain waves. *Yale J. Biol. Med.* 17, 657–679.

Burns, A. H. and Goodman, D. C. (1967). Retinofugal projections of *Caiman sclerops*. *Expl Neurol.* **18**, 105–115.

Burr, W. and Lange, H. (1973). Spontaneous brain activity in some species of amphibians and a reptile: differential structures of frequency distribution. *Electroenceph. clin. Neurophysiol.* **34**, 735.

Butler, A. B. (1974). Retinal projections in the night lizard, *Xantusia vigilis* Baird. *Brain Res.* **80**, 116–121.

Butler, A. B. and Ebner, F. F. (1972). Thalamotelencephalic projections in the lizard *Iguana iguana*. *Anat. Rec.* **172**, 282.

Butler, A. B. and Northcutt, R. G. (1971). Retinal projections in *Iguana iguana* and *Anolis carolinesis*. *Brain Res.* **26**, 1–13.

Butler, A. B. and Northcutt, R. G. (1973a). Architectonic studies of the diencephalon of *Iguana iguana* (Linnaeus). *J. comp. Neurol.* **149**, 439–462.

Butler, A. B. and Northcutt, R. G. (1973b). Visual projections in *Natrix siepdon sipedon* (L.). *Anat. Rec.* **175**, 282.

Cabanac, M., Hammel, T. and Hardy, J. D. (1967). *Tiliqua scincoides:* Temperature-sensitive units in lizard brain. *Science, N.Y.* **158**, 1050–1051.

Campbell, C. B. G. and Hodos, W. (1970). The concept of homology and the evolution of the nervous system. *Brain. Behav. Evol.* **3**, 353–367.

Carey, J. H. (1967). The striatum in the box turtle, *Terrapene c. carolina*. *Ala. J. med. Sci.* **4**, 381–389.

Carreras, M. and Eager, R. P. (1969). Residual neurons in the ventrobasal complex of the cat after decortication. *Anat. Rec.* **163**, 297.

Casagrande, V. A. (1974a). The laminar organization and connections of the lateral geniculate nucleus in tree shrew (*Tupaia glis*). *Anat. Rec.* **178**, 323.

Casagrande, V. A. and Diamond, I. T. (1974). Ablation study of the superior colliculus in the tree shrew (*Tupaia glis*). *J. comp. Neurol.* **156**, 207–237.

Casagrande, V. A., Harting, J. K., Hall, W. C., Diamond, I. T. and Martin, G. G. (1972). Superior colliculus of the tree shrew: a structural and functional subdivision into superficial and deep layers. *Science, N.Y.* **177**, 444–447.

Caspers, H. and Winkel, K. (1952). Untersuchungen über die Bedeutung des Thalamus und Lobus opticus für die Grosshirnrhythmik beim Frosch. *Pflügers Arch. ges. Physiol.* **225**, 391–416.

Clare, M. H., Landau, W. M. and Bishop, G. H. (1969). The relationship of optic nerve fiber groups activated by electrical stimulation to the consequent central postsynaptic events. *Expl Neurol.* **24**, 400–420.

Cohen, D. H., Duff, Th. and Ebbesson, S. O. E. (1973). Electrophysiological identification of a visual area in shark telencephalen. *Science, N.Y.* **182**, 492–494.

Copack, P., Dafny, N. and Gilman, S. (1972). Neurophysiological evidence of vestibular projections to thalamus, basal ganglia and cerebral cortex. *In* "Corticothalamic Projections and Sensorimotor Activities." (T. L. Frigyesi, E. Rinvik and M. D. Yahr, eds). Raven Press, New York, pp. 309–335.

Cowey, A. and Weiskrantz, L. (1971). Contour discrimination in rats after frontal and striate cortical ablations. *Brain Res.* **30**, 241–252.

Cragg, B. G. (1959). A specific response in the hippocampus of the rabbit to olfactory stimulation. *Nature, Lond.* **184**, 1697–1699.

Cragg, B. G. (1960). Responses of the hippocampus to stimulation of the olfactory bulb and various afferent nerves in five mammals. *Expl Neurol.* **3**, 547–572.

Crepax, P. and Parmeggiani, P. L. (1958). Analisi della risposte elettriche del cervelleto di Lucertola a stimolozioni periferiche. *Atti. Accad. Naz. Lincei Rc.* **24**, 446–449.

Crosby, E. C. and Humphrey, T. (1939). Studies on the vertebrate telencephalon. I. The nuclear configuration of the olfactory formations and the nucleus olfactorius anterior of certain reptiles, birds and mammals. *J. comp. Neurol.* 71, 121–213.

Crosby, E. C., Humphrey, T. and Lauer, E. W. (1962). "Correlative Anatomy of the Nervous System." Macmillan, New York.

Crosby, E. C., De Jonge, B. R. and Schneider, R. C. (1966). Evidence for some of the trends in the phylogenetic development of the vertebrate telencephalon. *In* "Evolution of the Forebrain." (R. Hassler and H. Stephan, eds). Plenum Press, New York, pp. 117–135.

Cruce, J. A. F. (1974). A cytoarchitectonic study of the diencephalon of the tegu lizard, *Tupinambis nigropunctatus*. *J. comp. Neurol.* 153, 215–238.

Cruce, W. L. R. and Cruce, J. A. F. (1975). Projections from the retina to the lateral geniculate nucleus and mesencephalic tectum in a reptile (*Tupinambis nigropuntactus*): a comparison of anterograde transport and anterograde degeneration. *Brain Res.* 85, 221–228.

Curry, M. J. (1972). The exteroceptive properties of neurons in the somatic part of the posterior group (PO). *Brain Res.* 44, 439–462.

Curry, M. J. and Gordon, G. (1972). The spinal input to the posterior group in the cat. An electrophysiological investigation. *Brain Res.* 44, 417–437.

Danilov, I. V. (1959). Changes in patterns of electrical activity of the brain evoked by photic stimulation in young dogs reared in darkness. *Fiziol. Zh. SSSR Sechenova* 45, 1060–1066. (In Russian.)

Dart, A. M. and Gordon, G. (1973). Some properties of spinal connections of the cat's dorsal column nuclei which do not involve the dorsal column. *Brain Res.* 58, 61–68.

Dart, R. A. (1934). The dual structure of the neopallium: Its history and significance. *J. Anat.* 69, 1–19.

Davydova, T. V. (1973). Ultrastructure of normal and degenerated visual terminals in the turtle optic tectum. *Cytology* 15, 150–155. (In Russian.)

Davydova, T. V. and Boiko, V. P. (1976). Morphofunctional characteristics of the optic nerve in the tortoise *Emys orbicularis*. *In* "Comparative Neurophysiology and Neurochemistry." (B. M. Kreps, ed.). *Zh. Evol. Biokhim., Fiziol.* Suppl., pp. 97–101. (In Russian.)

Davydova, T. V. and Goncharova, N. V. (1971). Comparative study of neuronal organization of main cortical zones in the turtle forebrain. *Archs Anat. Histol. Embryol.* 60, 28–36. (In Russian.)

Davydova, T. V. and Mazurskaya, P. Z. (1973). Ultrastructural peculiarities of degenerated nervous terminals in the turtle optic tectum after enucleation. *Cytology* 15, 22–30. (In Russian.)

Davydova, T. V. and Smirnov, G. D. (1969). Neuronal organization of cortical plate in the turtle hemispheres. *Archs Anat. Histol. Embryol.* 57, 3–11. (In Russian.)

Davydova, T. V. and Smirnov, G. D. (1973). Retinotectal connections in the tortoise: An electron microscopic study of degeneration in optic nerve and midbrain tectum. *J. Hirnforsch.* 14, 473–492.

Denavit, M. and Kosinski, E. (1968). Somatic afferents to the cat subthalamus. *Archs ital. Biol.* 106, 391–410.

Desole, C., Palmieri, G. and Veggetti, A. (1970). Mesencephalic trigeminal nucleus and jaw muscle proprioception in reptilians. *Archs ital. Biol.* 108, 121–129.

Diamond, I. T. (1967). The sensory neocortex. *In* "Contributions to Sensory Physiology." (W. D. Neff, ed.). Academic Press, London and New York, 2, 51–98.

Diamond, I. T. (1971). Two visual systems in tree shrews (*Tupaia glis*) and squirrels (*Sciurus carolinensis*). *Proc. 25th Int. Congr. Physiol. Sci.*, pp. 225–226.

Diamond, I. T. and Hall, W. C. (1969). Evolution of neocortex. *Science, N.Y.* **164**, 251–262.

Diamond, I. T., Snyder, M., Killackey, H., Jane, J. and Hall, W. C. (1970). Thalamacortical projections in the tree shrew (*Tupaia glis*). *J. comp. Neurol.* **139**, 273–306.

Doty, R. W. (1958). Potentials evoked in cat cerebral cortex by diffuse and by punctiform photic stimuli. *J. Neurophysiol.* **21**, 347–464.

Doty, R. W. (1973). Ablation of visual areas in the central nervous system. *In* "Handbook of Sensory Physiology." (R. Jung, ed.). Springer Verlag, Berlin and New York, Vol. VII/3, Part B, pp. 483–529.

Dubrovsky, B. and Garcia-Rill, E. (1971). Convergence of tectal and visual cortex inputs to pericruciate neurons. *Expl Neurol.* **33**, 475–484.

Durinyan, R. A. and Rabin, A. G. (1971). Problem on double representation of brain projection systems. *Uspekhy Fiziol. Nauk* **2**, 3–25. (In Russian.)

Ebbesson, S. O. E. (1967). Ascending axon degeneration following hemisection of the spinal cord in the tegu lizard (*Tupinambis nigropunctatus*). *Brain Res.* **5**, 178–206.

Ebbesson, S. O. E. (1969). Brainstem afferents from the spinal cord in a sample of reptilian and amphibian species. *Ann. N.Y. Acad. Sci.* **167**, 80–101.

Ebbesson, S. O. E. (1970). On the organization of central visual pathways in vertebrates. *Brain, Behav. Evol.* **3**, 178–194.

Ebbesson, S. O. E. (1971). Projections of the optic tectum in the nurse shark (*Ginglymostome cirratum* Bonnaterre). *Proc. 1st Annual Meet. Soc. Neurosci.* 109.

Ebbesson, S. O. E. (1972a). A proposal for a common nomenclature for some optic nuclei in vertebrates and the evidence for a common origin of two such cell groups. *Brain, Behav. Evol.* **6**, 75–91.

Ebbesson, S. O. E. (1972b). New sights into the organization of the shark brain. *Comp. Biochem. Physiol.* **42A**, 121–129.

Ebbesson, S. O. E. and Heimer, L. (1970). Projections of the olfactory tract fibers in the nurse shark (*Ginglymostoma cirratum*). *Brain Res.* **17**, 47–55.

Ebbesson, S. O. E. and Ramsey, J. S. (1968). The optic tract of two species of sharks (*Galeocerdo cuvier* and *Ginglymostoma cirratum*). *Brain Res.* **8**, 36–53.

Ebbesson, S. O. E. and Schroeder, D. M. (1971). Connections of the nurse shark's telencephalon. *Science, N.Y.* **173**, 254–256.

Ebbesson, S. O. E. and Vanegas, H. (1976). Projections of the optic tectum in two teleost species. *J. comp. Neurol.* **165**, 161–180.

Ebbesson, S. O. E., Jane, J. A. and Schroeder, D. (1972). A general overview of major interspecific variations in thalamic organization. *Brain, Behav. Evol.* **6**, 92–130.

Ebner, F. F. (1969). A comparison of primitive forebrain organization in metatherian and eutherian mammals. *Ann. N.Y. Acad. Sci.* **167**, 241–257.

Ebner, F. F. and Colonnier, M. (1975). Synaptic patterns in the visual cortex of turtle: An electron microscopic study. *J. comp. Neurol.* **160**, 51–80.

Eldarov, A. L. (1969). On the functional significance of the forebrain dorsal cortex in turtle. *Proc. of the 22nd Conf. on Higher Nervous Activity Problem*, 272, Ryazan'. (In Russian.)

Enger, S. (1957). The electroencephalogram of the goldfish (*Gadus callarias*). Spontaneous electrical activity and reaction to photic and acoustic stimulation. *Acta physiol. scand.* **39**, 53–72.

Ewert, J.-P. (1968). Der Einflus von Zwischenhirn-defekten auf die Visuomotorik in Beute -und Fluchtverhalten der Erdkröte (*Bufo bufo* L.). *Z. vergl. Physiol.* **61**, 41–70.

Ewert, J.-P. (1970). Neural mechanisms of prey-catching and avoidance behavior in the toad (*Bufo bufo* L.). *Brain Behav. Evol.* 3, 36–56.

Ewert, J.-P. (1972). Zentralnervöse Analyse und Verarbeitung visueller Sinnesreize. *Naturwiss. Rundsch.* 25, 1–11.

Farber, D. A. (1969). "Functional Maturation of Brain in Early Ontogenesis." Prosvestchenye, Moscow. (In Russian.)

Filimonov, I. N. (1963). "Comparative Anatomy of Reptilian Cerebrum." Akad. Nauk SSSR, Moscow. (In Russian.)

Flanigan, W. F. (1972). Behavioral states and electroencephalograms of reptiles. *In* "The Sleeping Brain." (M. H. Chase, ed.). Brain Inform. Service, Los Angeles, pp. 14–19.

Flanigan, W. F. (1973). Sleep and wakefulness in iguanid lizards, *Ctenosaura pectinata* and *Iguana iguana*. *Brain Behav. Evol.* 8, 401–436.

Flanigan, W. F. (1974). Sleep and wakefulness in chelonian reptiles. II. The red-footed tortoise, *Geochelone carbonaria*. *Archs ital. Biol.* 112, 227–252.

Flanigan, W. F., Knight, C. P., Hartse, K. M. and Rechtschaffen, A. (1974). Sleep and wakefulness in chelonian reptiles. I. The box turtle, *Terrapene carolina*. *Archs ital. Biol.* 112, 199–226.

Flanigan, W. F., Wilcox, R. H. and Rechtschaffen, A. (1973). The EEG and behavioral continuum of the crocodilian *Caiman sclerops*. *Electroenceph. clin. Neurophysiol.* 34, 521–538.

Foster, R. E. (1975). The ascending brainstem auditory pathways in a reptile, *Iguana iguana*. *Anat. Rec.* 178, 357.

Foster, R. E. and Hall, W. C. (1975). The connections and laminar organization of the optic tectum in a reptile (*Iguana iguana*). *J. comp. Neurol.* 163, 397–425.

Foster, R. E. and Hall, W. C. (1978). The organization of central auditory pathways in a reptile, *Iguana iguana*. *J. comp. Neurol.* 178, 783–832.

Foster, R. E., Lymberis, M. E. B. and Hall, W. C. (1973). The laminar organization of the projections from the optic tectum in a reptile *Iguana iguana*. *Anat. Rec.* 175, 322.

Frontera, J. G. (1952). A study of the anuran diencephalon. *J. comp. Neurol.* 96, 1–71.

Gaidaenko, G. V. (1977). On descending connections of the dorsal cortex in turtles. *Zh. Evol. Biokhim. Fiziol.* 13, 416–418. (In Russian.)

Gamble, H. J. (1952). An experimental study of the secondary olfactory connections in *Lacerta viridis*. *J. Anat.* 86, 180–196.

Gamble, H. J. (1956). An experimental study of the secondary olfactory connections in *Testudo graeca*. *J. Anat.* 90, 15–29.

Garey, L. J. and Powell, T. P. S. (1971). An experimental study of the termination of the lateral geniculocortical pathway in the cat and monkey. *Proc. R. Soc.* B179, 41–63.

Gergen, J. A. and MacLean, P. D. (1964). The limbic system: photic activation of limbic cortical areas in the squirrel monkey. *Ann. N.Y. Acad. Sci.* 117, 69–87.

Gilbert, P. W., Hodgson, E. S. and Mathewson, R. F. (1964). Electroencephalogram of sharks. *Science N.Y.* 145, 949–951.

Girgis, M. (1970). The rhinencephalon. *Acta anat.* 76, 157–199.

Goldby, G. (1937). An experimental investigation of the cerebral hemispheres of *Lacerta viridis*. *J. Anat.* 71, 332–355.

Goldby, F. and Gamble, H. J. (1957). The reptilian cerebral hemispheres. *Biol. Rev.* 32, 383–420.

Goldby, F. and Robinson, L. R. (1962). The central connection of dorsal spinal nerve roots and the ascending tracts in the spinal cord of *Lacerta viridis*. *J. Anat.* 96, 153–170.

Gordon, B. (1973). The superior colliculus of the brain. *Scient. Am.* 227, 72–82.

Goris, R. C. and Terashima, S. (1973). Central response to infrared stimulation of the pit receptors in a crotaline snake, *Trimeresurus flavoviridis*. *J. exp. Biol.* **58**, 59–76.

Graeber, R. C. and Ebbesson, S. O. E. (1972). Visual discrimination learning in normal and tectal-ablated nurse sharks (*Ginglymostoma cirratum*). *Comp. Biochem. Physiol.* **42A**, 131–139.

Graeber, R. C., Ebbesson, S. O. E. and Jane, J. A. (1933). Visual discrimination in sharks without optic tectum. *Science, N.Y.* **180**, 413–415.

Granda, A. M. (1972). Summary and conclusions. *Brain, Behav. Evol.* **5**, 264–273.

Granda, A. M. and O'Shea, P. J. (1972). Spectral sensitivity of the green turtle (*Chelonia mydas mydas*) determined by electrical responses to heterochromatic light. *Brain, Behav. Evol.* **5**, 143–154.

Granda, A. M. and Stirling, C. E. (1965). Differential spectral sensitivity in the optic tectum and eye of the turtle. *J. gen. Physiol.* **48**, 901–917.

Granda, A. M. and Yazulla, S. (1971). The spectral sensitivity of single units in the nucleus rotundus of pigeon, *Columba livia*. *J. gen. Physiol.* **57**, 363–384.

Graybiel, A. M. and Nauta, W. J. H. (1971). Some projections of superior colliculus and visual cortex upon the posterior thalamus in the cat. *Anat. Rec.* **169**, 328.

Green, J. D. (1964). The hippocampus. *Physiol. Rev.* **44**, 561–608.

Green, J. D. and Arduini, A. A. (1954). Hippocampal electrical activity in arousal. *J. Neurophysiol.* **17**, 533–557.

Grüsser, O.-J. and Grüsser-Cornehls, U. (1968). Neurophysiologische Grundlagen visueller angeborener Auslösemechanismen beim Frosch. *Z. vergl. Physiol.* **59**, 1–24.

Grüsser, O.-J. and Grüsser-Cornehls, U. (1972). Comparative physiology of movement-detecting neuronal systems in lower vertebrates (Anura and Urodela). *Bibl. Ophthalmol.* **82**, 260–273.

Gusel'nikov, V. I. (1956). On electrophysiological characteristics of some forebrain subdivisions in turtle. *Zh. Vyssh. Nerv. Deyat. Pavlova.* **6**, 898–904. (In Russian.)

Gusel'nikov, V. I. (1960). On mechanisms of generalized reactions in the electrogram of the reptilian cortex. *Fiziol. Zh. SSSR Sechenova* **56**, 537–543. (In Russian.)

Gusel'nikov, V. I. (1965). "Electrophysiological Study of Analyzer Systems in Phylogeny of Vertebrates." Moscow Univ. Press, Moscow. (In Russian.)

Gusel'nikov, V. I. (1970). Contribution to the study on the evolution and functional organization of the visual analyzer in vertebrates. I. On the role of the retina in processing of the visual information in submammalian vertebrates. *Vestnik Moskovsk. Univ., Biol. Pochvoved* **3**, 3–16. (In Russian.)

Gusel'nikov, V. I. and Ivanova, V. I. (1958). Electrical reactions of the cerebellum to various stimuli in fishes, turtles and pigeons. *Fiziol. Zh. SSSR Sechenova* **44**, 119–125. (In Russian.)

Gusel'nikov, V. I. and Loginov, V. V. (1976). "Visual Analyzer in Fishes (Electrophysiological Studies)." Moscow Univ. Press, Moscow. (In Russian.)

Gusel'nikov, V. I. and Poletaeva, I. I. (1962). On the analysis of generalized reactions in the electrogram of lizard forebrain cortex. *Fiziol. Zh. SSSR Sechenova* **48**, 1195–1202. (In Russian.)

Gusel'nikov, V. I. and Supin, A. Ya. (1963). Representation of visual and auditory analyzers in forebrain hemispheres of the lizard. *Fiziol. Zh. SSSR Sechenova* **49**, 919–927. (In Russian.)

Gusel'nikov, V. I. and Supin, A. Ya. (1964). Representation of somatosensory and olfactory analyzers in forebrain hemispheres in the lizard (*Agama caucasica*). *Fiziol. Zh. SSSR Sechenova* **50**, 129–137. (In Russian.)

Gusel'nikov, V. I., Morenkov, E. D. and Pivovarov, A. S. (1970). On functional organization of the visual system of the tortoise (*Emys orbicularis*). *Fiziol. Zh. SSSR Sechenova* 56, 1377–1385. (In Russian.)

Gusel'nikov, V. I., Morenkov, E. D. and Pivovarov, A. S. (1971). Peculiarities of neuron reactions to visual stimulation in the turtle forebrain. *Fiziol. Zh. SSSR Sechenova* 57, 1455–1463. (In Russian.).

Gusel'nikov, V. I., Pivovarov, A. S. and Tsitolovsky, L. E. (1973). Postsynaptic inhibition in the general cortex of the tortoise forebrain. *Neurofiziologia* (*Kiev*) 5, 383–390.

Gusel'nikov, V. I., Pivovarov, A. S. and Tsitolovsky, L. F. (1974). Synaptic processes in the neurons of the forebrain general cortex of the turtle to visual stimulation. *Zh. Vyssh. Nerv. Deyat. Pavlova* 24, 800–810. (In Russian.)

Gusel'nikova, K. G. and Gusel'nikov, V. I. (1963). Investigation of electrical activity of archicortical neurons in the lizard. *Fiziol. Zh. SSSR Sechenova* 49, 277–280. (In Russian.)

Gusel'nikova, K. G. and Gusel'nikov, V. I. (1976). "Electrophysiology of the Olfactory Analyzer in Vertebrates." Moscow Univ. Press, Moscow. (In Russian.)

Hall, J. A. and Ebner, F. F. (1974). The efferent projections of general cortex to the brainstem in the turtle, *Pseudemys scripta*. *Anat. Rec.* 178, 513.

Hall, W. C. (1972). Visual pathways to the telencephalon in reptiles and mammals. *Brain, Behav. Evol.* 5, 95–113.

Hall, W. C. and Diamond, I. T. (1968a). Organization and function of the visual cortex in hedgehog. I. Cortical cytoarchitecture and thalamic retrograde degeneration. *Brain, Behav. Evol.* 1, 181–214.

Hall, W. C. and Diamond, I. T. (1968b). Organization and function of the visual cortex in hedgehog. II. An ablation study of pattern discrimination. *Brain, Behav. Evol.* 1, 215–243.

Hall, W. C. and Ebner, F. F. (1970a). Parallels in the visual afferent projections to the thalamus in the hedgehog (*Paraechinus hypomelas*) and the turtle (*Pseudemys scripta*). *Brain, Behav. Evol.* 3, 125–154.

Hall, W. C. and Ebner, F. F. (1970b). Thalamotelencephalic projections in the turtle (*Pseudemys scripta*). *J. comp. Neurol.* 140, 101–122.

Hall, J. A., Foster, R. E., Ebner, F. F. and Hall, W. C. (1977). Visual cortex in a reptile, the turtle (*Pseudemys scripta* and *Chrysemys picta*). *Brain Res.* 130, 197–216.

Halpern, M. (1972). Some connections of the telencephalon of the frog *Rana pipiens*. *Brain, Behav. Evol.* 6, 32–68.

Halpern, M. (1973a). Olfactory bulb and accessory bulb projections in the snake *Thamnophis sirtalis*. *Anat. Rec.* 175, 337.

Halpern, M. (1973b). Retinal projections in blind snakes. *Science, N.Y.* 182, 390–391.

Halpern, M. and Frumin, N. (1973). Retinal projections in a snake, *Thamnophis sirtalis*. *J. Morph.* 141, 359–382.

Hand, P. J. and Liu, C. N. (1966). Efferent projections of the nucleus gracilis. *Anat. Rec.* 154, 353.

Harting, J. K., Hall, W. C. and Diamond, I. T. (1972). Evolution of the pulvinar. *Brain, Behav. Evol.* 6, 424–452.

Harting, J. K., Diamond, I. T. and Hall, W. C. (1973). Anterograde degeneration study of the cortical projections of the lateral geniculate and pulvinar nuclei in the tree shrew. *J. comp. Neurol.* 150, 393–440.

Hayashi, Y. and Sumitomo, I. (1967). Activation of lateral geniculate neurons by electrical stimulation of superior colliculus in cats. *Jap. J. Physiol.* 17, 638–651.

Hazlett, J. C., Dom, R. and Martin, G. F. (1972). Spinobulbar, spinothalamic and medial lemniscal connections in the American opossum *Didelphis marsupiails virginiana*. *J. comp. Neurol.* **146**, 95–118.

Heimer, L. (1969). The secondary olfactory connections in mammals, reptiles and sharks. *Ann. N.Y. Acad. Sci.* **167**, 129–146.

Heinz, St. (1964). Die kortikalen Anteile des limbischen Systems (Morphologie und Entwicklung). *Nervenarzt.* **35**, 396–401.

Heric, Th. M. and Kruger, L. (1965). Organization of the visual projection upon the optic tectum of a reptile (*Alligator mississippiensis*). *J. comp. Neurol.* **124**, 101–112.

Heric, Th. M. and Kruger, L. (1966). The electrical response evoked in the reptilian optic tectum by afferent stimulation. *Brain Res.* **1**, 187–199.

Herman, H., Jouvet, M. and Klein, M. (1964). Analyse poligraphique du sommeil de la tortue. *C. r. Séanc. Acad. Sci., Paris* **258**, 2175–2178.

Herrick, C. J. (1930). "Brains of Rats and Men." Hafner, New York.

Herrick, C. J. (1948). "The Brain of the Tiger Salamander (*Ambystoma tigrinum*)." Univ. Chicago Press, Chicago.

Herrick, C. J. (1956). "The Evolution of the Human Nature." Univ. Texas Press, Austin.

Herrick, C. J. and Bishop, G. H. (1958). A comparative survey of the spinal lemniscus system *In*. "Reticular Formation of the Brain." (H. Jasper and L. O. Proctor, eds). Little, Brown, Boston, pp. 353–360.

Hertzler, D. R. (1972). Tectal integration of visual input in the turtle. *Brain, Behav. Evol.* **5**, 240–255.

Hertzler, D. R. and Hayes, W. N. (1967). Cortical and tectal function in visually guided behavior. *J. comp. physiol. Psychol.* **63**, 444–447.

Hertzler, D. R. and Hayes, W. N. (1969). Effects of monocular vision and midbrain transection on movement detection in the turtle. *J. comp. physiol. Psychol.* **64**, 473–478.

Hewitt, W. (1967). The basal ganglia of *Testudo graeca*. *J. comp. Neurol.* **131**, 605–614.

Hobson, J. A., Goin, O. B. and Goin, C. J. (1968). Electrographic correlates of behavior in tree frogs. *Nature, Lond.* **220**, 386–387.

Hodos, W. (1970). Evolutionary interpretation of neural and behavioral studies of living vertebrates. *In* "The Neurosciences: Second Study Program." (F. O. Schmidt, ed.). Rockfeller Univ. Press, New York, pp. 26–39.

Hodos, W. and Bonbright, J. C. (1974). Intensity difference in pigeons after lesions of the tectofugal and thalamofugal visual pathways. *J. comp. physiol. Psychol.* **87**, 1013–1031.

Hodos, W. and Fletscher, G. V. (1974). Effects of nucleus rotundus lesions on post-operative acquisition of visual intensity pattern discrimination. *Physiol. and Behav.* **13**, 501–506.

Hodos, W. and Karten, H. J. (1966). Brightness and pattern discrimination deficits in the pigeon after lesions of nucleus rotundus. *Expl Brain Res.* **2**, 151–167.

Hodos, W. and Karten, H. J. (1970). Visual intensity and pattern discrimination deficits after lesion of ectostriatum in pigeons. *J. comp. Neurol.* **140**, 53–68.

Hodos, W. and Karten, H. J. (1974). Visual intensity and pattern discrimination deficits after lesions of the optic lobe in pigeons. *Brain, Behav. Evol.* **9**, 165–194.

Hodos, W., Karten, H. J. and Bonbright, J. C. (1973). Visual intensity and pattern discrimination after lesions of the thalamofugal visual pathways in pigeons. *J. comp. Neurol.* **148**, 447–468.

Holmgren, N. (1925). Points of view concerning forebrain morphology in lower vertebrates. *J. comp. Neurol.* **34**, 413–477.

Hoogland, P., van Woerden-Verkley, I. and Lohman, A. H. M. (1975). Efferent and afferent connections of the striatial complex in the lizard, *Tupinambis nigropunctatus*. *Expl Brain Res.* **23**, Suppl. 93.

Huber, G. C. and Crosby, E. C. (1926). On thalamic and tectal nuclei and fiber paths in the brain of the American alligator. *J. comp. Neurol.* **40**, 97–227.

Huber, G. C. and Crosby, E. C. (1933). The reptilian optic tectum. *J. comp. Neurol.* **57**, 57–163.

Huber, G. C. and Crosby, E. C. (1943). A comparison of the mammalian and reptilian tecta. *J. comp. Neurol.* **78**, 133–168.

Huggins, S. E., Parsons, L. C. and Pena, R. V. (1968). Further study of the spontaneous electrical activity of the brain of *Caiman sclerops*. *Physiol. Zool.* **41**, 370–383.

Humphrey, T. (1966). The development of the human hippocampal formation correlated with some aspects of its phylogenetic history. *In* "Evolution of the Forebrain." (R. Hassler and H. Stephan, eds). Plenum Press, New York, pp. 104–116.

Hunsaker, D. and Lansing, R. W. (1962). Electroencephalographic studies of reptiles. *J. exp. Zool.* **149**, 21–32.

Isabekova, S. B. (1969). The effect of steady illumination of the evoked potentials of the turtle (*Emys orbicularis*) visual centers. *Neurofiziologia* (*Kiev*) **1**, 219–224. (In Russian.)

Ingle, D. J. (1970). Visuomotor functions of the frog optic tectum. *Brain, Behav. Evol.* **3**, 57–71.

Ingle, D. J. (1973). Evolutionary perspectives on the function of the optic tectum. *Brain Behav. Evol.* **8**, 211–237.

Iwamura, G. and Kawamura, H. (1962). Activation pattern in lower level in the neo-, paleo- and archicortices. *Jap. J. Physiol.* **12**, 494–505.

Jabbur, S. J., Baker, M. A. and Towe, A. L. (1972). Wide-field neurons in thalamic nucleus ventralis posterolateralis of the cat. *Expl Neurol.* **36**, 213–238.

Jane, J. A. and Schroeder, D. M. (1971). A comparison of dorsal column nuclei and spinal afferents in the European hedgehog (*Erinaceus europeans*). *Expl Neurol.* **30**, 1–17.

Jane, J. A., Carlson, J. J. and Levey, N. (1969). A comparison of the effect of lesions of striate cortex and superior colliculus on vision in the Malayan tree shrew (*Tupaia glis*). *Anat. Rec.* **163**, 306.

Jane, J. A., Levey, N. and Carlson, N. J. (1972). Tectal and cortical functions in vision. *Expl Neurol.* **35**, 61–77.

Johnston, J. B. (1915). The cell masses in the forebrain of turtle, *Cistudo carolina*. *J. comp. Neurol.* **25**, 393–468.

Johnston, J. B. (1916). Evidence of a motor pallium in the forebrain of reptiles. *J. comp. Neurol.* **26**, 475–480.

Johnston, J. B. (1923). Further contributions to the study of the evolution of the forebrain. *J. comp. Neurol.* **35**, 337–481.

Jones, E. G. and Leavitt, R. Y. (1974). Retrograde axonal transport and the demonstration of non-specific projections to the cerebral cortex and striatum from thalamic intralaminar nuclei in the rat, cat and monkey. *J. comp. Neurol.* **154**, 349–378.

Jones, E. G. and Powell, T. P. S. (1971). An analysis of the posterior group of thalamic nuclei on the basis of its afferent connections. *J. comp. Neurol.* **143**, 185–216.

Joseph, B. S. and Whitlock, D. G. (1968a). Central projections of brachial and lumbar dorsal roots in reptiles. *J. comp. Neurol.* **132**, 469–484.

Joseph, B. S. and Whitlock, D. G. (1968b). Central projections of selected spinal dorsal roots in anuran amphibians. *Anat. Rec.* **160**, 279–288.

Juan de A. O. R. and Segura, E. T. (1968/1969). Reaction hypersynchrone du telencephale chez les anoures. *C.r. Séanc. Soc. Biol.* **162**, 1607–1608.

Kaada, B. R., Thomas, F., Alnaes, E. and Wester, K. (1963). Synchronization in the electroencephalogram induced by high-frequency stimulation of the midbrain reticular formation in anesthetized cats. *Acta physiol. scand.* Suppl. **213**, 75–76.

Kaas, I., Hall, W. C. and Diamond, I. D. (1970). Cortical visual areas I and II in the hedgehog: relation between evoked potential maps and architectonic subdivision. *J. Neurophysiol.* 33, 595–615.

Källén, B. (1951). On the ontogeny of the reptilian forebrain. Nuclear structures and ventricular sulci. *J. comp. Neurol.* 95, 397–447.

Karamian, A. I. (1956). "Evolution of Functions of the Cerebellum and the Cerebral Cortex." Medgiz, Leningrad; (1962) Israel Program of Scientific Translation, Jerusalem.

Karamian, A. I. (1964). On the principle of stage development in the central nervous system of vertebrates. *In* "Evolution of Function." (E. M. Kreps, ed.). Nauka, Leningrad, pp. 35–44. (In Russian.)

Karamian, A. I. (1965). On the evolution of the integrative activity of the central nervous system in the vertebrate phylogeny. *Progr. Brain, Res.* 22, 427–447.

Karamian, A. I. (1966). On some correlations between phylo- and ontogenetic evolution of the central nervous system in vertebrates. *Zh. Evol. Biokhim. Fizio.* 2, 233–243. (In Russian.)

Karamian, A. I. (1967). On some regularities of the functional evolution of higher centers of the central nervous system. *Zh. Evol. Biolhim. Fiziol.* 3, 412–422. (In Russian.)

Karamian, A. I. (1968). "Development of Diencephalocortical Interrelationships in the Vertebrate Phylogenesis." Gagrskye Besedy (Gagra Symposium). Akad. Nauk Gruz. SSR, Tbilisi, 5, 221–232. (In Russian.)

Karamian, A. I. (1969a). On some peculiarities of the functional and structural organization of visual, somatic and olfactory afferent systems in submammalian vertebrates. *In* "Visual and Auditory Analyzers (Morphological, Physiological and Clinical Aspects)." (S. A. Sarkisov, ed.). Meditsina, Moscow, pp. 56–63. (In Russian.)

Karamian, A. I. (1969b). Principle of stagewise development of hypothalamocortical interrelationships in vertebrates. *Zh. Evol. Biolhim. Fiziol.* 5, 198–206. (In Russian.)

Karamian, A. I. (1970). "Functional Evolution of the Brain in Vertebrates." Nauka, Leningrad. (In Russian.)

Karamian, A. I. (1972). On the formation of structural and functional organization of paleo-, archi- and neocortex in submammalian vertebrates phylogeny. *Zh. Evol. Biokhim. Fizio.* 8, 324–333. (In Russian.)

Karamian, A. I. (1976). "The Functional Evolution of the Vertebrate Telencephalon." Nauka, Leningrad. (In Russian.)

Karamian, A. I. and Belekhova, M. G. (1963). On the functional evolution of the non-specific thalamocortical system. *Zh. Vyssh. Nerv. Deyat. Pavlova* 13, 904–915; (1964) *Fed. Proc. Trans.* Suppl. 23, 2, 1189–1194.

Karamian, A. I. and Sollertinskaya, T. N. (1964). On some peculiarities of the development of hypothalamotelencephalic interrelations in vertebrate phylogenesis. *Fiziol. Zh. SSSR Sechenova* 50, 962–972. (In Russian.)

Karamian, A. I. and Sollertinskaya, T. N. (1972). On comparative physiological peculiarities of functional interrelationships of hypothalamus, olfactory and limbic brain systems. *Fiziol. Zh. SSSR Sechenova* 58, 974–987. (In Russian.)

Karamian, A. I., Vesselkin, N. P., Belekhova, M. G. and Zagorulko, T. M. (1966). Electrophysiological characteristics of tectal and thalamocortical divisions of the visual system in lower vertebrates. *J. comp. Neurol.* 127, 559–576.

Karamian, A. I., Zagorul'ko, T. M., Belekhova, M. G., Kosareva, A. A. and Vesselkin, N. P. (1968). Morphofunctional peculiarities of corticosubcortical interrelations in submammalian vertebrates. *In* "Cortical Regulation of Subcortical Activity." (S. P. Narikashvili, ed.). Metsniereba, Tbilisi, pp. 96–114. (In Russian.)

Karamian, A. I., Belekhova, M. G. and Vesselkin, N. P. (1969a). Comparison of thalamo-telencephalic systems in amphibians and reptiles. *Fiziol. Zh. SSSR Sechenova* **55**, 997–986. (In Russian.)

Karamian, A. I., Fanardyan, V. V., Kosareva, A. A. (1969b). The functional and morphological evolution of the cerebellum and its role in behavior. *In* "Neurobiology of Cerebellar Evolution and Development." (R. Llinas, ed.). American Medical Association, Chicago, pp. 639–673.

Karamian, A. I., Belekhova, M. G. and Vesselkin, N. P. (1971). Peculiarities of afferent organization of the diencephalon and telencephalon in Amphibia and Reptilia. *In* "Mechanisms of Evoked Potentials." (A. S. Batuev, ed.). Nauka, Leningrad, pp. 69–79. (In Russian.)

Karamian, A. I., Belekhova, M. G. and Zagorul'ko, T. M. (1972). New concept on evolution of retino-geniculo-cortical and retino-tecto-thalamo-cortical optical systems in vertebrates. *Zh. Evol. Biokhim. Fiziol.* **8**, 166–172. (In Russian.)

Karamian, A. I., Zagorul'ko, T. M., Belekhova, M. G., Vesselkin, N. P. and Kosareva, A. A. (1975a). On the corticalization of two divisions of the visual system in the vertebrates evolution. *Neurofiziologia* (*Kiev*) **7**, 12–20. (In Russian.)

Karamian, A. I., Belekhova, M. G. and Kosareva, A. A. (1975b). On two trends in the phylogenetic development of the vertebrate archipaleocortex as exemplified by reptiles. *In* "The Brain Mechanism." (T. N. Oniani, ed.). Metsniereba, Tbilisi, pp. 307–317. (In Russian.)

Karamian, O. A. (1965). On mesencephalocortical connections in reptiles. *Dokl. Akad. Nauk SSSR.* **160**, 479–482. (In Russian.)

Karimova, M. M. (1958). On the conditioned reflex characteristics of the auditory analyser of turtles. *Zh. Vyssh. Nerv. Deyat. Pavlova* **8**, 103–108. (In Russian.)

Karmanova, I. G., Belekhova, M. G. and Churnosov, E. V. (1971). Specifics of behavioral and electrographic patterns of natural sleep and wakefulness in reptiles. *Fiziol. Zh. SSSR Sechenova* **57**, 504–511. (In Russian.)

Karmanova, I. G., Khomutetskaya, O. E. and Churnosov, E. V. (1972). On some neurophysiological aspects of the comparative study of sleep-like states, sleep and wakefulness in birds and reptiles. *In* "The Sleeping Brain." (M. H. Chase, ed.). Brain Inform Service, Los Angeles, pp. 49–51.

Karten, H. J. (1969). The organization of the avian telencephalon and some speculations on the phylogeny of the amniote telencephalon. *Ann. N.Y. Acad. Sci.* **167**, 164–179.

Karten, H. J. and Hodos, W. (1970). Telencephalic projections of the nucleus rotundus in the pigeon (*Columba livia*). *J. comp. Neurol.* **140**, 35–52.

Karten, H. J. and Nauta, W. J. H. (1968). Organization of retinothalamic projections in the pigeon and owl. *Anat. Rec.* **160**, 373.

Karten, H. J. and Revzin, A. M. (1966). The afferent connections of the nucleus rotundus in the pigeon. *Brain Res.* **2**, 368–377.

Karten, H. J., Hodos, W., Nauta, W. J. H. and Revzin, A. M. (1973). Neural connections of the "visual Wulst" of the avian brain. Experimental studies in the pigeon (*Columba livia*) and owl (*Speotyto cunicularia*). *J. comp. Neurol.* **150**, 253–278.

Keating, E. G. (1974). Impaired orientation after primate tectal lesions. *Brain Res.* **67**, 538–544.

Kennedy, D. T., Shimono, T. and Kitai, S. T. (1970). Parallel fiber and white matter activation of Purkinje cells in a reptilian cerebellum (*Lacerta viridis*). *Brain Res.* **22**, 381–385.

Kennedy, M. C. (1974). Auditory multiple-unit activity in the midbrain of the Tokay gecko (*Gekko gecko* L.). *Brain, Behav. Evol.* **10**, 257–264.

Kennedy, M. C. (1975). Vocalization elicited in a lizard by electrical stimulation of the midbrain. *Brain Res.* **91**, 321–325.

Kicliter, E. and Northcutt, R. G. (1975). Ascending afferents to the telencephalon of ranid frogs: an anterograde degeneration study. *J. comp. Neurol.* **161**, 239–254.

Killackey, H. P. (1972). Projections of the ventral nucleus to neocortex in the hedgehog. *Anat. Rec.* **172**, 345.

Killackey, H., Snyder, M. and Diamond, I. T. (1971). Function of striate and temporal cortex in the tree shrew. *J. comp. physiol. Psychol. Monogr.* **74**, 1–29.

Killackey, H. P., Wilson, M. and Diamond, I. T. (1972). Further studies of the striate and extrastriate visual cortex in the tree shrew. *J. comp. physiol. Psychol.* **81**, 45–63.

Kirsche, W. (1967). Über postembryonale Matrixzonen im Gehirn verschiedener Vertebraten und deren Beziehung zur Hirnbauplanlehre. *Z. mikrsosk.-anat. Forsch.* **77**, 313–406.

Kirsche, W. (1972). Die Entwicklung des Telencephalons der Reptilien und deren Beziehung zur Hirn-Bauplanlehre. *Nova Acta Acad. Leop.* **204**, 1–78.

Klein, M. (1963). "Étude Polygraphique et Phylogenetique des États de Sommeil." Thése de Medicine, Lyon.

Knapp, H. and Kang, D. S. (1968a). The visual pathways of the snapping turtle (*Chelydra serpentina*). *Brain, Behav. Evol.* **1**, 19–42.

Knapp, H. and Kang, D. S. (1968b). The retinal projections of the side-necked turtle (*Podocnemis unifilis*) with some notes on the possible origin of the pars dorsalis of the lateral geniculate body. *Brain, Behav. Evol.* **1**, 369–404.

Koppani, T. and Pearcy, J. F. (1925). Comparative studies on the excitability of the forebrain. *Am. J. Physiol.* **71**, 339–343.

Kosareva, A. A. (1967). Projection of optic fibers to visual centers in a turtle (*Emys orbicularis*). *J. comp. Neurol.* **130**, 263–275.

Kosareva, A. A. (1974). Afferent and efferent connections of the nucleus rotundus in the tortoise *Emys orbicularis*. *Zh. Evol. Biokhim. Fiziol.* **10**, 395–399. (In Russian.)

Kosareva, A. A. and Nomokonova, L. M. (1972). Thalamotelencephalic projections in Amphibia and Reptilia. *Proc. 6th Sci. Conf. on Evolutionary Physiology*, p. 108. (In Russian.)

Kosareva, A. A., Ozirskaya, E. V., Tumanova, N. L. and Gaidaenko, G. V. (1973). Structural organization of nucleus rotundus in the brain of the tortoise *Emys orbicularis Zh. Evol. Biokhim. Fiziol.* **9**, 195–201. (In Russian.)

Kovačević, N. and Šušiš V. (1971). Recording electric activity of sea turtle *Caretta caretta*. (Chelonia.) *Arh. biol. nauka, Beograd* **23**, 5P–6P.

Kruger, L. (1969). Experimental analysis of the reptilian nervous system. *Ann. N.Y. Acad. Sci.* **167**, 102–117.

Kruger, L. (1970). The topography of the visual projection to the mesencephalon: A comparative survey. *Brain, Behav. Evol.* **3**, 169–177.

Kruger, L. and Berkowitz, E. C. (1960). The main afferent connections of the reptilian telencephalon as determined by degeneration and electrophysiological methods. *J. comp. Neurol.* **115**, 125–142.

Kruger, L. and Maxwell, D. S. (1969). Wallerian degeneration in the optic nerve of a reptile: an electron microscopic study. *Am. J. Anat.* **125**, 247–270.

Kruger, L. and Witkovsky, P. (1961). A functional analysis of neurons in the dorsal column nuclei and spinal nucleus of the trigeminal in the reptile (*Alligator mississippiensis*). *J. comp. Neurol.* **117**, 97–106.

Kulikov, G. A. and Safarov, Kh. M. (1969). On the representation of afferent systems in fore- and midbrain of the lizard (*Ophiaurus apus* P.) *Dokl. Akad. Nauk SSSR* **187**, 952–955. (In Russian.)

Laemle, L., Benhamida, Ch. and Purpura, D. P. (1972). Laminar distribution of geniculocortical afferents in visual cortex of the postnatal kitten. *Brain Res.* **41**, 25–37.

Lazar, G. (1969). Efferent pathways of the optic tectum in the frog. *Acta biol. hung.* **20**, 171–183.

Lazar, G. and Szekely, G. (1969). Distribution of optic terminals in the different optic centers of the frog. *Brain Res.* **16**, 1–14.

Le Gros Clark, W. E. (1932). The structure and connections of the thalamus. *Brain* **55**, 406–470.

Lesny, I. and Vogel, Z. (1960). Elektroencephalogramm des Wüstenwarans (*Varanus griseus arabicus*). *Zool. Anat.* **69**, 163–168.

Lettvin, J. Y., Maturana, H. R., McCulloch, W. S. and Pitts, W. H. (1959). What the frog's eye tells the frog's brain. *Proc. inst. Radio Engr.* **47**, 1940–1951.

Levey, N. H., Harris, J. and Jane, J. A. (1973). Effects of visual cortical ablation on pattern discrimination in the ground squirrel (*Citellus tridecemilineatus*). *Expl Neurol.* **39**, 270–276.

Lin, C. S., Wagor, E. and Kaas, H. J. (1974). Projections from the pulvinar to the middle temporal visual area (MT) in the owl monkey, *Aotus trivirgatus*. *Brain Res.* **76**, 145–149.

Lindsley, D. F., Barton, R. J. and Atkins, R. J. (1970). Effect of subthalamic lesions on peripheral and central arousal thresholds in cats. *Expl Neurol.* **26**, 109–119.

Llinas, R. and Hillman, D. E. (1969). Physiological and morphological organization of the cerebellar circuits in various vertebrates. *In* "Neurobiology of Cerebellar Evolution and Development." (R. Llinas, ed.). American Medical Association, Chicago, pp. 43–73.

Llinas, R. and Nicholson, C. (1969). Electrophysiological analysis of alligator cerebellum cortex: a study on dendritic spikes. *In* "Neurobiology of Cerebellar Evolution and Development." (R. Llinas, ed.). American Medical Association, Chicago, pp. 431–465.

Llinas, R., Nicholson, C., Freeman, J. A. and Hillman, D. E. (1968). Dendritic spikes and their inhibition in alligator Purkinje cells. *Nature, Lond.* **160**, 1132.

Lohman, A. H. M. and van Woerden-Verkley, I. (1976). Further studies on the cortical connections of the tegu lizard. *Brain Res.* **103**, 9–28.

Lohman, A. H. M., Hoogland, P. and van Woerden-Verkley, I. (1973). Experimental studies of the efferent telencephalic connections in the tegu lizard. *Anat. Rec.* **175**, 374.

Lund, R. D. and Webster, K. E. (1967). Thalamic afferents from the dorsal column nuclei. An experimental anatomical study in the rat. *J. comp. Neurol.* **130**, 301–312.

Lund, J. S. (1973). Organization of neurons in the visual cortex, area 17, of the monkey (*Macaca mulatta*). *J. comp. Neurol.* **147**, 455–496.

Luttges, M. W. and Gamow, R. I. (1970). Garter snakes: Studies of spontaneous and evoked brain responses with electroencephalography. *Communs Behav. Biol.* **5**, 115–130.

MacLean, P. D., Rosner, B. S. and Robinson, F. A. (1957). Piryform responses to electrical stimulation of olfactory fila, bulb and tract. *Am. J. Physiol.* **189**, 395–398.

Maier, V. and Tanaka, M. (1973). Monocular pattern discrimination deficits in pigeons after unilateral lesions of the dorsolateral region of the thalamus. *Brain Res.* **49**, 497.

Maksimova, E. M., Orlov, O. Yu and Dimmentman, A. M. (1971). Study on visual system in several species of marine fishes. *Voprosy Ikhtiologyi* **11**, 892–899. (In Russian.)

Manley, G. A. (1970). Frequency sensitivity of auditory neurons in the caiman cochlear nucleus. *Z. vergl. Physiol.* **66**, 251–256.

Manley, G. A. (1971). Single unit studies in the midbrain auditory area of *Caiman*. *Z. vergl. Physiol.* **71**, 255–261.

Manley, G. A. (1974). Activity patterns in the peripheral auditory system of some reptiles. *Brain, Behav. Evol.* **10**, 244–256.

Maiorchik, V. E. (1964). Some theoretical problems of modern clinical electroencephalography. *In* "Contemporary Problems of Electrophysiological Studies of the Central Nervous System" Meditsina, Moscow, pp. 289–312. (In Russian.)

Manteifel', Y. B. (1966). Evoked potentials of the lizard tectum opticum. *Dokl. Akad. Nauk SSSR* **168**, 480–483. (In Russian.)

Martin, G. F. (1969). Efferent tectal pathways of the opossum. *J. comp. Neurol.* **135**, 209–224.

Mascitti, T. A. and Ortega, S. N. (1966). Efferent connections of the olfactory bulb in the cat. An experimental study with silver impregnation methods. *J. comp. Neurol.* **127**, 121–136.

Mathers, L. H. (1971). Tectal projections to the posterior thalamus of the squirrel monkey. *Brain Res.* **35**, 295–298.

Maturana, H. R., Lettvin, J. Y., McCulloch, W. S. and Pitts, W. H. (1960). Anatomy and physiology of vision in the frog (*Rana pipiens*). *J. gen. Physiol.* **43**, Suppl. 2, 129–175.

Mazurskaya, P. Z. (1971). Organization of neuronal receptive fields in the forebrain cortex of the tortoise (*Emys orbicularis*). *Zh. Evol. Biokhim. Fiziol.* **8**, 617–623. (In Russian.)

Mazurskaya, P. Z. (1972). Organization of neuronal receptive fields in the forebrain of the tortoise *Emys orbicularis*. *Zh. Evol. Biokhim. Fiziol.* **8**, 617–623. (In Russian.)

Mazurskaya, P. Z. and Smirnov, G. D. (1965). Functional features of exteroceptive projections to forebrain cortex dorsal in the turtle. *Zh. Evol. Biokhim. Fiziol.* **1**, 442–448. (In Russian.)

Mazurskaya, P. Z. and Smirnov, G. D. (1966). Some characteristics of visual projections in the turtle forebrain. *Dokl. Akad. Nauk SSSR* **167**, 1414–1417. (In Russian.)

Mazurskaya, P. Z., Manteifel', Y. B. and Smirnov, G. D. (1964). Comparative study of neuronal reactions in visual centers. *In* "Evolution of Functions." (E. M. Kreps, ed.). *Nauka*, Leningrad, pp. 45–54. (In Russian.)

Mazurskaya, P. Z., Davydova, T. V. and Smirnov, G. D. (1966), Functional organization of exteroceptive projections in the turtle forebrain cortex. *Fiziol. Zh. SSSR Sechenova* **52**, 1049–1057. (In Russian.)

McGill, T. (1960). A review of hearing in amphibians and reptiles. *Psychol. Bull.* **57**, 165–168.

McGinty, D. (1972). Sleep in amphibians. *In* "The Sleeping Brain." (M. H. Chase, ed.). Brain Inform. Service, Los Angeles, pp. 7–10.

Mehler, W. R. (1969). Some neurological species differences—a posteriori. *Ann. N.Y. Acad. Sci.* **167**, 424–469.

Meier, R. E., Mihailović, J. and Cuénod, M. (1974). Thalamic organization of the retino-thalamo-hyperstriatal pathway in the pigeon (*Columba livia*). *Expl Brain Res.* **19**, 351–364.

Meyer, M., Allison, A. C. (1949). An experimental investigation of the connections of the olfactory tracts in the monkey. *J. Neurol. Neurosurg. Psychiat.* **12**, 274–286.

Mihailović, J., Perisié, M., Bergonzi, R. and Meier, R. E. (1974). The dorsolateral thalamus as a relay in the retino-Wulst pathway in pigeon (*Columba livia*). An electro-physiological study. *Expl Brain Res.* **21**, 229–240.

Minelli, G. (1966). Architettura delle corteccie di alcuni Rettili (*Lacerta muralis, Lacerta viridis, Testudo graeca, Crocodylus acutus*). *Archs zool. ital.* **51**, 543–573.

Minelli, G. (1967). Considerazioni anatomocomparative sulle cortecci dei rettili. *Archs zool. ital.* **52**. 75–88.

Moiseeva, N. A. (1972). Electrical reactions to visceral stimulation in the brain of the tortoise *Testudo horsfieldi*. *Zh. Evol. Biokhim. Fiziol.* 8, 536–541. (In Russian.)

Moore, G. P. (1961). "Non-specific Responses to Somatic Stimuli in the Brain of *Alligator*." Thesis, Univ. of California, Los Angeles.

Moore, G. P. and Tschirgi, R. D. (1960). Bilateral organization of the somatic afferent system in lower vertebrates. *Physiologist* 3, 117.

Moore, G. P. and Tschirgi, R. D. (1962). Non-specific responses of reptilian cortex to sensory stimuli. *Expl Neurol.* 5, 196–209.

Morenkov, E. D. and Pivovarov, A. S. (1973). Peculiarities of the organization of the visual system in reptiles. *In* "Functional Organization and Evolution of the Vertebrate Visual System." (V. I. Gusel'nikov, ed.). *Nauka*, Leningrad, pp. 95–107. (In Russian.)

Morenkov, E. D. and Pivovarov, A. C. (1975). Peculiarities of cell reactions in turtle dorsal and ventral thalamus to visual stimuli. *Zh. Evol. Biokhim. Fiziol.* 11, 70–75. (In Russian.)

Morlock, H. C. (1972). Behavior following ablation of the dorsal cortex of turtles. *Brain, Behav. Evol.* 5, 256–263.

Motorina, M. V. (1965). Development of hypothalamocortical relationships. *Zh. Evol. Biokhim. Fiziol.* 1, 262–268. (In Russian.)

Muntz, W. R. and Sokol, S. (1967). Psychophysical thresholds to different wavelengths in light adapted turtles. *Vision Res.* 7, 729–741.

Myers, R. E. (1963). Projections of the superior colliculus in monkey. *Anat. Rec.* 145, 264.

Mysliveček, J. (1969). Significance of diencephalic specific nuclei for the formation of responses in auditory and visual cortex. *In* "Visual and Auditory Analyzers (Morphological, Physiological and Clinical Aspects)." (S. A. Sarkisov, ed.). Meditsina, Moscow, pp. 104–111. (In Russian.)

Nauta, W. J. H. and Karten, H. J. (1970). A general profile of the vertebrate brain with sidelights on the ancestry of cerebral cortex. *In* "The Neurosciences: Second Study Program." (F. O. Schmidt, ed.). Rockfeller Univ. Press, New York. pp. 7–26.

Nieuwenhuys, R. (1967). Comparative anatomy of olfactory centers and tracts. *Progr. Brain Res.* 23, 1–64.

Nieuwenhuys, R. and Bodenheimer, Th. S. (1966). The diencephalon of primitive bony fish *Polypterus* in the light of the problem of homology. *J. Morph.* 118, 415–450.

Nieuwenhuys, R. and Cornelisz, M. (1971). Ascending projections from the spinal cord in the Axolotl (*Ambystoma mexicanum*). *Anat. Reç.* 169, 388.

Noback, Ch. R. and Shriver, J. E. (1966). Phylogenetic and ontogenetic aspects of the lemniscal systems and the pyramidal system. *In* "Evolution of the Forebrain." (R. Hassler and H. Stephan, eds.). Plenum Press, New York, pp. 316–325.

Nomokonova, L. M. (1971). On thalamotelencephalic connections in the frog *Rana ridibunda*. *Zh. Evol. Biokhim. Fiziol.* 7, 546–547. (In Russian.)

Nomokonova, L. M. (1976). Connections of lateral thalamus opticus and adjacent nuclear structures with the telencephalon in the frog Rana ridibunda. *In* "Comparative Neurophysiology and Neurochemistry." (E. M. Kreps, ed.). *Zh. Evol. Biokhim. Fiziol.* Suppl., pp. 70–76. (In Russian.)

Northcutt, R. G. (1970). "The Telencephalon of the Western Painted Turtle (*Chrysemys picta belli*)." Univ. Illinios Press, Urbana, Illinois.

Northcutt, R. G. (1974). Some histochemical observations on the telencephalon of the bullfrog, *Rana catesbeiana* Shaw. *J. comp. Neurol.* 157, 379–390.

Northcutt, R. G. and Butler, A. B. (1974a). Retinal projections in the Northern water snake *Natrix sipedon sipedon* (L.). *J. Morph.* 142, 117–136.

Northcutt, R. G. and Butler, A. B. (1974b). Evolution of reptilian visual system: retinal projections in a nocturnal lizard *Gekko gecko* (Linnaeus). *J. comp. Neurol.* 157, 453–466.
Northcutt, R. G. and Przybylski, R. J. (1973). Retinal projections in the lamprey *Petromyzon marinus* (L.) *Anat. Rec.* 175, 400.
Northcutt, R. G., Braford, M. R. and Landreth, G. E. (1974). Retinal projections in the tuatara *Sphenodon punctatus*: An autoradiographic study. *Anat. Rec.* 178, 428.
Novikova, L. A. (1962). Mechanisms of changes of background activity in brain hemispheres. *In* "Principal Problems on Electrophysiology of the Central Nervous System." Kiev, pp. 201–216. (In Russian.)
Ochinskaya, E. I. and Rubtsova, N. B. (1976). Turtle extrapolation reaction after ablation of the forebrain dorsal cortex. *Zh. Vyssh. Nerv. Deyat. Pavlova* 26, 626–631. (In Russian.)
Orbeli, L. A. (1934). "Lectures on Physiology of the Nervous System." Leningrad-Moscow. (In Russian.)
Orbeli, L. A. (1942). Evolutionary principle as applied to the physiology of the central nervous system. *In* "Selected Works." USSR Acad. Sci., Moscow-Leningrad (1961), 1, 166–182. (In Russian.)
Orbeli, L. A. (1958). Principal problems and methods of evolutionary physiology. *In* "Selected Works." USSR Acad. Sci., Moscow-Leningrad (1961), 1, pp. 56–69. (In Russian.)
Orrego, F. (1961a). The reptilian forebrain. I. The olfactory pathways and cortical areas in the turtle. *Archs ital. Biol.* 99, 425–445.
Orrego, F. (1961b). The reptilian forebrain. II. Electrical activity in the olfactory bulb. *Archs ital. Biol.* 99, 446–465.
Orrego, F. (1962). The reptilian forebrain. III. Cross connections between the olfactory bulbs and the cortical areas in the turtle. *Archs ital. Biol.* 100, 1–16.
Orrego, F. and Lisenby, D. (1962). The reptilian forebrain. IV. Electrical activity in the turtle cortex. *Archs ital. Biol.* 100, 17–30.
Parent, A. (1976). Striatal afferent connections in the turtle (*Chrysemys picta*) as revealed by retrograde axonal transport of horseradish peroxidase. *Brain Res.* 108, 25–36.
Parent, A. and Olivier, A. (1970). Comparative histochemical study of the corpus striatum. *J. Hirnforsch.* 12, 73–81.
Parent, A. and Poitras, D. (1974). The origin and distribution of catecholaminergic axon terminals in the cerebral cortex of the turtle (*Chrysemys picta*). *Brain Res.* 78, 345–358.
Papez, J. W. (1935). Thalamus of turtles and thalamic evolution. *J. comp. Neurol.* 61, 433–475.
Papez, J. W. (1936). Evolution of the medial geniculate body. *J. comp. Neurol.* 64, 41–61.
Parsons, L. C. and Huggins, S. E. (1965a). A study of spontaneous electrical activity in the brain of *Caiman sclerops*. *Proc. Soc. exp. Biol. Med.* 119, 397–400.
Parsons, L. C. and Huggins, S. E. (1965b). Effects of temperature on the EEG of the caiman. *Proc. Soc. exp. Biol. Med.* 120, 422–426.
Pedersen, R. (1973). Ascending spinal projections in three species of side-necked turtle: *Podocnemis unifilis*, *Pelusius subniger* and *Pelomedusa subrufa*. *Anat. Rec.* 175, 409.
Peyrethon, J. (1968). "Sommeil et Evolution. Étude Polygraphique des États de Sommeil chez les Poissons et les Reptiles." Tixier et Fils, Lyon.
Peyrethon, J. and Dusan-Peyrethon, D. (1969). Étude polygraphique du cycle veille-sommeil chez troi genres de reptiles. *C. r. Séanc. Soc. Biol.* 163, 181–186.
Pivovarov, A. S. (1973). Synaptic origin of the evoked potential main components in the general cortex of the tortoise forebrain. *Neurofiziologia* (*Kiev*) 5, 261–271. (In Russian.)
Pivovarov, A. S. (1974). "Intracellular Analysis of Mechanisms of the Reactivity and Plasticity of the General Cortex Neurons in the Turtle." Thesis, Moscow. (In Russian.)

Pivovarov, A. S. and Trepakov, V. V. (1972). Unit activity in the general and hippocampal cortex of the turtle telencephalon during afferent stimulation. *Fiziol. Zh. SSSR Sechenova* **58**, 690–696. (In Russian.)

Platel, R. (1969). Étude cytoarchitectonique qualitative et quantitative des aires corticales d'un Saurien: *Scincus scincus* (L.) Scincides. *J. Hirnforsch.* **11**, 31–66.

Platel, R., Beckers, H. J. A. and Nieuwenhuys, R. (1973). Les champs corticaux chez *Testudo hermanni* (Reptile Chélonien) et chez *Caiman crocodylus* (Reptile Crocodilien). *Acta morph. neerl.-scand.* **11**, 121–150.

Platel, R., Raffin, J. P. and Repérant, J. (1975). The primary visual system in a lizard of the family Scincidae: *Scincus scincus* (L.) An experimental study. *Expl Brain Res.* **23**, Suppl., 162.

Poliakov, G. I. (1964). Development and complication of the cortical part of the coupling mechanism in the evolution of vertebrate. *J. Hirnforsch.* **7**, 253–273.

Polley, E. H. (1971). Intracortical distribution of lateral geniculate axons in cat and monkey. *Anat. Rec.* **169**, 404.

Polyak, S. (1957). "The Vertebrate Visual System." Univ. Chicago Press, Chicago.

Pritz, M. (1974a). Ascending connections of a midbrain auditory area in a crocodile, *Caiman crocodilus*. *J. comp. Neurol.* **153**, 179–198.

Pritz, M. (1974b). Ascending connections of a thalamic auditory area in a crocodile, *Caiman crocodilus*. *J. comp. Neurol.* **153**, 199–214.

Pritz, M. (1975). Anatomical identification of a telencephalic visual area in crocodiles: ascending connections of nucleus rotundus in *Caiman crocodilus*. *J. comp. Neurol.* **164**, 323–338.

Pritz, M. B., Mead, W. R. and Northcutt, R. G. (1970). The effects of Wulst ablations on color, brightness and pattern discrimination (*Columba livia*). *J. comp. Neurol.* **140**, 81–100.

Purpura, D. P. (1961a). Morphophysiological basis of elementary evoked response patterns in the neocortex of the newborn cat. *Ann. N.Y. Acad. Sci.* **92**, 840–859.

Purpura, D. P. (1961b). Structure and function of cortical synaptic organizations activated by corticopetal afferents in newborn cat. *In* "Brain and Behavior." (M. Brazier, ed.). *Amer. Inst. Biol. Sci.*, Washington **1**, 95–138.

Rafols, J. A. and Matzke, H. A. (1970). Efferent projections of the superior colliculus in the opossum. *J. comp. Neurol.* **138**, 147–160.

Ramón-Moliner, E. (1967). La differentiation morphologique des neurones. *Archs ital. Biol.* **105**, 149–188.

Rechtschaffen, A., Bassan, M. and Ledecky-Kanecek, S. (1968). Activity patterns in *Caiman sclerops*. *Psychophysiology* **5**, 201.

Repérant, J. (1972). Étude experimentale des projections visuelle chez la vipere (*Vipera aspis*). *C. r. Séanc. Acad. Sci., Paris* **275**, 695–697.

Repérant, J. (1975). Nouvelles donees sur les projections retiniennes chez *Caiman sclerops*. Étude radioautographique. *C. r. Séanc. Acad. Sci., Paris* **280**, 2881–2884.

Repérant, J. (1976). Retinal projections in *Vipera aspis*. A reinvestigation using light radioautographic and electron microscopic degeneration technnqiues. *Brain Res.* **107**, 603–609.

Revzin, A. M. (1967). Unit responses to visual stimuli in the nucleus rotundus of the pigeon. *Fed. Proc. Trans.* **26**, 656.

Revzin, A. M. (1969). A specific visual projection area in the hyperstriatum of the pigeon (*Columba livia*). *Brain Res.* **15**, 246–249.

Revzin, A. M. (1970). Some characteristics of wide-field units in the brain of the pigeon. *Brain, Behav. Evol.* **3**, 195–204.

Revzin, A. M. and Karten, H. J. (1966). Rostral projections of the optic tectum and nucleus rotundus in the pigeon. *Brain Res.* 3, 264–276.

Riss, W., Halpern, M. and Scalia, F. (1969a). Anatomical aspects of the evolution of the limbic and olfactory systems and their potential significance for behavior. *Ann. N.Y. Acad. Sci.* 159, 1096–1111.

Riss, W., Halpern, M. and Scalia, F. (1969b). The quest for clues to forebrain evolution— the study of reptiles. *Brain, Behav. Evol.* 2, 1–50.

Riss, W., Pedersen, R. A., Jackway, J. S. and Ware, C. B. (1972). Levels of function and their representation in the vertebrate thalamus. *Brain, Behav. Evol.* 6, 26–41.

Robbins, D. O. (1972). Coding of intensity and wavelength in optic tectal cells of the turtle. *Brain, Behav. Evol.* 5, 124–142.

Robson, J. A. and Hall, W. C. (1976). Projections from the superior colliculus to the dorsal lateral geniculate nucleus of the grey squirrel (*Sciurus carolinensis*). *Brain Res.* 113, 379–385.

Romer, A. S. (1970). "The Vertebrate Body." Saunders, Philadelphia, 4th edn.

Rose, G. H. and Ellingson, R. J. (1970). Ontogenesis of evoked potentials. *In* "Developmental Neurobiology." C. C. Thomas, Springfield, pp. 393–440.

Rose, G. H. and Lindsley, D. B. (1968). Development of visually evoked potentials in kittens: Specific and non-specific responses. *J. Neurophysiol.* 31, 607–623.

Rose, M. (1923). Histologische Lokalization des Vorderhirns der Reptilien. *J. Physiol. Neurol.* 29, 219–272.

Rosenquist, A. C., Edwards, S. B. and Palmer, L. A. (1974). An autoradiography study of the projections of the dorsal lateral geniculate nucleus and the posterior nucleus in the cat. *Brain Res.* 80, 71–93.

Rossignol, S. and Colonnier, M. (1969). Patterns of degeneration in the cerebral cortex of the cat after lesions of the lateral geniculate nucleus. *Anat. Rec.* 163, 253.

Rubinson, K. (1968). Projection of the tectum opticum of the frog. *Brain, Behav. Evol.* 1, 529–561.

Rubinson, K. (1969). Retinal projections in the toad, *Bufo marinus*. *Anat. Rec.* 163, 254.

Safarov, Kh. M. (1971). "On physiology of Space Analysis in Reptiles (Lizards, Snakes)." Thesis, Dushanbe.

Safarov, Kh. M. (1974a). Warm conditioning in *Ophisaurus apodus* to and after forebrain ablation. *Trans. Dept. Physiol. of Animals and Man* 2, 29–36. State Univ., Dushanbe. (In Russian.)

Safarov, Kh. M. (1974b). Learned pattern discrimination in reptiles. *Inform. of Acad. Sci. Tadz. SSR Sect. Biol. Sci. N4*, 58–64.

Sanides, F. (1969). Comparative architectonics of the neocortex of mammals and their evolutionary interpretation. *Ann. N.Y. Acad. Sci.* 167, 404–423.

Sanides, F. (1972). Representation in the cerebral cortex and its areal lamination patterns. *In* "The Structure and Function of Nervous Tissue." (G H. Bourne, ed.). Academic Press, New York and London 5, 330–349.

Sanides, F. (1973). The review of W. Kirsche's paper "Die Entwicklung des Telencephalons der Reptilien und deren Beziehung zur Hirn-Bauplanlehre." *J. Hirnforsch.* 14, 347–348.

Scalia, F. (1968). A review of recent experimental studies on the distribution of the olfactory tracts in mammals. *Brain, Behav. Evol.* 1, 101–123.

Scalia, F. and Gregory, K. (1970). Retinofugal projections in the frog: Location of the postsynaptic neurons. *Brain, Behav. Evol.* 3, 16–29.

Scalia, F., Knapp, H., Halpern, M. and Riss, W. (1968). New observations on the retinal projection in the frog. *Brain. Behav. Evol.* 1, 324–353.

Scalia, F., Halpern, M. and Riss, W. (1969). Olfactory bulb projections in the South American caiman. *Brain, Behav. Evol.* 2, 238–262.

Schadé, J. P. and Weiler, I. J. (1959). Electroencephalographic patterns of the goldfish (*Carassius auratus*). *J. exp. Biol.* 36, 435–452.

Schepers, G. W. H. (1948). "Evolution of the Forebrain." Maskew Miller, Cape Town.

Scherrer, J. (1965). Electrophysiological aspects of cortical development. *Prog. Brain Res.* 22, 480–489.

Schneider, G. E. (1967). Contrasting visiomotor functions of tectum and cortex in the golden hamster. *Psychol. Forsch.* 31, 52–62.

Schneider, G. E. (1969). Two visual systems. Brain mechanisms for localization and discrimination are dissociated by tectal and cortical lesions. *Science, N.Y.* 163, 895–902

Schnitzlein, H. N. and Crosby, E. C. (1968). The epithalamus and thalamus of the lungfish, *Protopterus. J. Hirnforsch.* 10, 352–371.

Schnitzlein, H. N., Hamel, E. G., Carey, J. H., Brown, J. W., Hoffman, H. H., Faucette, J. R. and Showers, M. J. C. (1973). The interrelations of the stratium with subcortical areas through the lateral forebrain bundle. *J. Hirnforsch.* 13, 409–455.

Schroeder, D. M. and Jane, J. A. (1971). Projection of dorsal column nuclei and spinal cord to brainstem and thalamus in the tree shrew, *Tupaia glis. J. comp. Neurol.* 142, 309–350.

Schroeder, D. M., Yashon, D., Becker, D. P. and Jane, J. A. (1968). The evolution of the primate medial lemniscus. *Anat. Rec.* 160, 424.

Segura, E. T. and de Juan, A. (1966). Electroencephalographic studies in toads. *Electroceph. clin. Neurophysiol.* 21, 373–380.

Senn, D. G. (1966). Über das optische System im Gehirn squamater Reptilien. Eine vergleichend morphologische Untersuchung, unter Berücksichtigung einiger Wühlschlangen. *Acta anat.* 65, Suppl. 52, 1–88.

Senn, D. G. (1969). Über die Bedeutung der Hirnmorphologie für die Systematick. *Verh. naturf. Ges. Basel* 80, 49–55.

Servit, Z. and Strejčkova, A. (1972). Thalamocortical relations and the genesis of epileptic electrographic phenomena in the forebrain of the turtle. *Expl Neurol.* 35, 50–60.

Shapiro, H. and Goodman, D. C. (1969). Motor functions and their anatomical basis in the forebrain and tectum of the alligator. *Expl Neurol.* 24, 187–195.

Sharma, S. C. (1972). The retinal projections in the goldfish: An experimental study. *Brain Res.* 39, 213–223.

Shevelev, I. A. (1971). "Dynamics of Visual Sensory Signal." Nauka, Moscow. (In Russian.)

Sikharulidze, N. I. (1972a). Participation of different brain structures in the behavior of lizards. *Zh. Vyssh. Nerv. Deyat. Pavlova* 22, 181–183. (In Russian.)

Sikharulidze, N. I. (1972b). On functions of cerebellum and forebrain in behavior of turtles (*Emys orbicularis, Clemmys caspica*). *Dokl. Akad. Nauk SSSR* 205, 1258–1260. (In Russian.)

Smirnov, G. D. (1961). Comparative approach to the neurophysiology of vision. *In* "Brain and Behavior" (M. Brazier, ed.). *Amer. Inst. Biol. Sci.*, Washington, pp. 263–286.

Smirnov, G. D. (1968). Comparative investigation of different formations in the brain cortex of turtles and monkeys. *In* "Gagrskye Besedy (Gagra Symposium)." Akad. Nauk Gruz. SSR, Tbilisi 5, 114–126. (In Russian.)

Smirnov, G. D. and Manteifel', Y. B. (1962). Comparative electrophysiological study of the brain over the phylogenetic scale of vertebrates. *Uspekhi Sovrem. Biol.* 54, 309–332. (In Russian.)

Snyder, F. (1966). Toward an evolutionary theory of dreaming. *Am. J. Psychiat.* **123**, 121–142.

Snyder, M. (1973). The evolution of mammalian visual mechanisms. *In* "Handbook of Sensory Physiology." Springer Verlag, Berlin and New York. Vol. VII/3, Part A, pp. 693–712.

Snyder, M. and Diamond, I. T. (1968). The organization and function of the visual cortex in the tree shrew. *Brain, Behav. Evol.* **1**, 244–288.

Sollertinskaya, T. N. (1967). Electrophysiological studies on the hypothalamocortical connections in reptiles. *Zh. Evol. Biokhim. Fiziol.* **3**, 55–65. (In Russian.)

Sollertinskaya, T. N. (1972). Electrophysiological data on hypothalamic projections from the olfactory system in the tortoise. *Fiziol. Zh. SSSR Sechenova* **58**, 17–27. (In Russian.)

Sollertinskaya, T. N. (1973). Hypothalamocortical connections in the vertebrate phylogenesis. *Uspekhi fiziol. nauk* **4**, 54–89. (In Russian.)

Sprague, J. M. (1966). Visual, acoustic and somesthetic deficits in the cat after cortical and midbrain lesions. *In* "The Thalamus." (D. P. Purpura and M. D. Jahr, eds). Columbia Univ. Press, New York, pp. 392–417.

Sprague, J. M., Berlucci, G., Levy, J. and Diberardino, A. (1971). The role of the pretectum and superior colliculus in form discrimination in the cat. *Anat. Rec.* **169**, 437.

Starzl, T. E., Taylor, C. W. and Magoun, H. W. (1951). Ascending conduction in reticular activating system with special reference to the diencephalon. *J. Neurophysiol.* **14**, 479–496.

Stein, B. E., Magalhaes-Castro, B. and Kruger, L. (1975). Superior colliculus: Visiotopic-somatotopic overlap. *Science, N.Y.* **189**, 224–226.

Stephan, H. (1966). Größenänderungen im olfactorischen und limbischen System während der phylogenetischen Entwicklung der Primaten. *In* "Evolution of the Forebrain." (R. Hassler and H. Stephan, eds). Plenum Press, New York, pp.377–388.

Stettner, L. J. and Schultz, W. J. (1967). Brain lesions in birds: effects on discrimination, acquisition and reversal. *Science, N.Y.* **155**, 1689–1692.

Suga, N. and Campbell, H. (1967). Frequency sensitivity of single auditory neurons in the gecko *Coleonyx variegatus*. *Science, N.Y.* **157**, 88–90.

Šušić, V. (1972). Electrographic and behavioral correlates of the rest–activity cycle in the sea turtle, *Caretta caretta* L. (Chelonia). *J. exp. Mar. Biol. Ecol.* **10**, 81–87.

Supin, A. Y. and Gusel'nikov, V. I. (1964). Representation of visual, auditory and somato-sensory analyzers in forebrain hemisphere of the frog (*Rana temporaria*). *Fiziol. Zh. SSSR Sechenova* **50**, 426–434. (In Russian.)

Szekely, G. (1973). Anatomy and synaptology of the optic tectum. *In* "Handbook of Sensory Physiology" (R. Jung, ed.). Springer Verlag, Berlin and New York, Vol. VII/3, pp. 1–26.

Tagiev, Sh. K. (1969). Interoceptive influence on electroencephalogram in animals of different phylogenetic levels. *Zh. Vyssh. Nerv. Deyat. Pavlova* **19**, 149–155. (In Russian.)

Tauber, E. S., Roffwarg, H. P. and Weitzman, E. D. (1966). Eye movements and electroencephalogram activity during sleep in diurnal lizard, *Chamaleo jacksoni* and *C. melleri*. *Nature, Lond.* **212**, 1612–1613.

Tauber, E. S., Rojas-Ramirez, J. and Hernandez-Peon, R. (1968). Electrophysiological and behavioral correlates of wakefulness and sleep in the lizard, *Ctenosaura pectinata*. *Electroenceph. clin. Neurophysiol.* **24**, 424–433.

Terashima, S. and Goris, R. C. (1975). Tectal organization of pit viper infrared reception. *Brain Res.* **83**, 490–494.

Terashima, S. and Goris, R. C. (1976). Receptive area of an infrared tectal unit. *Brain Res.* **101**, 155–159.

Teuber, H. L. (1970). Subcortical vision. *Brain, Behav. Evol.* **3**, 7–15.

Tokizane, T., Kawamura, M. and Gellhorn, E. (1959). Hippocampal and neocortical activity in different experimental conditions. *Electroenceph. clin. Neurophysiol.* **11**, 431–437.

Tomasulo, K. C. and Emmers, R. (1972). Activation of neurons in the gracile nucleus by two afferent pathways in the rat. *Expl Neurol.* **36**, 197–206.

Trachtenberg, M. C. and Ingle, D. (1974). Thalamo-tectal projections in the frog. *Brain Res.* **79**, 419–530.

Trepakov, V. V. (1976). Organization of the olfactory afferent input in the hippocampal cortex of the tortoise *Emys orbicularis*. In "Comparative Neurophysiology and Neurochemistry." (E. M. Kreps, ed.). *Zh. Evol. Biokhim. Fiziol.* Suppl. **10**, 9–11. (In Russian.)

Tsitolovsky, L. E. and Pivovarov, A. S. (1974). Economical inhibition of the neurons in the general cortex of the turtle forebrain. *Fiziol. Zh. SSSR Sechenova* **60**, 1170–1179. (In Russian.)

Tsitolovsky, L. E. and Pivovarov, A. S. (1975a). Economical inhibition and processes occurring in intracellular neuron structures. *Fiziol. Zh. SSSR Sechenova* **61**, 699–707.

Tsitolovsky, L. E. and Pivovarov, A. S. (1975b). Selective decrease of neuronal spike amplitude during habituation. *Neurofiziologia (Kiev)* **7**, 324–326. (In Russian.)

Ulinski, P. S. (1974). Cytoarchitecture of cerebral cortex in snakes. *J. comp. Neurol.* **158**, 243–266.

Van Twyver, H. (1973). Polygraphic studies of the American alligator. *Sleep Res.* **2**, 87.

Vasilescu, E. (1970). Sleep and wakefulness in the tortoise *Emys orbicularis. Rev. roum. Biol., Ser. Zool.* **15**, 177–179.

Vasilescu, E. (1972). Sleep in reptiles. *In* "The Sleeping Brain" (M. H. Chase, ed.). Brain Inform. Service, Los Angeles, pp. 1012.

Vegetti, A. and Palmieri, G. (1969). On the function of the mesencephalic nucleus in *Caiman sclerops. Sperimentale* **119**, 1–17.

Vesselkin, N. P. (1966). Visual projections in amphibian brain. *Zh. Evol. Biokhim. Fiziol.* **2**, 473–479. (In Russian.)

Vesselkin, N. P. and Agayan, A. L. (1970). Electrophysiological study on afferent projection in the brain of frogs. *In* "Electrophysiological Studies of the Central Nervous System in Vertebrates." (A. I. Karamian, ed.). *Zh. Evol. Biokhim. Fiziol.* Supp. pp. 154–162. (In Russian.)

Vesselkin, N. P. and Kovačević, N. (1973a). Non-olfactory projections of frog telencephalon. *Neurofiziologia (Kiev)* **5**, 537–544. (In Russian.)

Vesselkin, N. P. and Kovačević, N. (1973b). Non-olfactory afferent projections of telencephalon in Plagiostomes. *Zh. Evol. Biokhim. Fiziol.* **9**, 585–594. (In Russian.)

Vesselkin, N. P., Agayan, A. L., Nomokonova, L. M. (1971). A study of thalamo-telencephalic afferent systems in frogs. *Brain, Behav. Evol.* **4**, 295–306.

Voronin, L. G. and Gusel'nikov, V. I. (1959). Some comparative physiological data on bioelectrical reactions. *Zh. Vyssh. Nerv. Deyat. Pavlova* **9**, 398–408. (In Russian.)

Voronin, L. G. and Gusel'nikov, V. I. (1963). Phylogenesis of internal mechanisms of the analysis and integration in the brain. *Zh. Vyssh. Nerv. Deyat. Pavlova* **13**, 193–206; (1964) *Fed. Proc. Trans.* Suppl. **23**(1), T105-T112.

Voronin, L. G., Gusel'nikov, V. I. and Smirnov, G. D. (1961). Electroencephalographic study of the brain in relation to animal phylogenesis. *Excerpta med. Int. Congr. Ser. N37, Vth Int. Congr. of EEG and Clin. Neurophysiol.* **37**, Rome.

Voronin, L. G., Gusel'nikova, K. G. and Gusel'nikov, V. I. (1964). Some data on interrelationships of slow and impulse activities in the lizard archicortex. *Zh. Vyssh. Nerv. Deyat. Pavlova* **14**, 326–336. (In Russian.)

Voronin, L. G., Gusel'nikova, K. G., Gusel'nikov, V. I. and Supin, A. Y. (1965). On the problem of the evolution of the vertebrate afferent systems. *Progr. Brain Res.* 22, 541–465.

Walker, J. M. and Berger, R. J. (1973). A polygraphic study of the tortoise (*Testudo denticulata*). *Brain, Behav. Evol.* 8, 453–467.

Walsh, T. M. and Ebner, F. F. (1968). Organization of somaticomotor cortex in the opossum. *Anat. Rec.* 160, 446.

Walsh, T. M. and Ebner, F. F. (1973). Distribution of cerebellar and somatic lemniscal projections in the ventral nuclear complex of the Virginia opossum. *J. comp. Neurol.* 147, 427–446.

Walsh, J. V., Houk, J. C., Alturi, R. L. and Mugnaini, E. (1973). Synaptic transmission at single glomeruli in the turtle cerebellum. *Science, N.Y.* 178, 881–883.

Ward, J. P. and Masterton, B. (1970). Encephalization and visual cortex in the tree shrew (*Tupaia glis*). *Brain, Behav. Evol.* 3, 421–469.

Ware, C. B., Casagrande, V. A. and Diamond, I. T. (1972). Does the acuity of the tree shrew suffer from the removal of striate cortex? A commentary on the paper by Ward and Masterton. *Brain, Behav. Evol.* 5, 18–29.

Ware, C. B., Diamond, I. T. and Casagrande, V. A. (1974). Effects of ablating the striate cortex on a successive pattern discrimination: Further study of the visual system in the tree shrew (*Tupaia glis*). *Brain Behav. Evol.* 9, 237–316.

Webster, D. B. and Webster, M. (1974). "Comparative Vertebrate Morphology." Academic Press, New York and London.

Weisbach, W. and Schwartzkopff, J. (1967). Nervöse Antworten auf Schallreiz im Grosshirn von Krokodilen. *Naturwissenschaften* 54, 650.

Wenzel, B. M. and Sieck, M. H. (1966). Olfaction. *Ann. Rev. Physiol.* 28, 381–434.

Wever, E. G. (1965). Structure and function of the lizard ear. *J. auditory Res.* 5, 160–172.

Wever, E. G. (1968). The lacertid ear: *Eremias argus*. *Proc. natn. Acad. Sci. U.S.A.* 61, 1292–1299.

Wever, E. G. (1971). Hearing in Crocodilia. *Proc. natn. Acad. Sci. U.S.A.* 68, 1498–1500.

Wever, E. G. and Vernon, G. A. (1956a). The sensitivity of the turtle ear as shown by its electrical potentials. *Proc. natn. Acad. Sci. U.S.A.* 42, 213–220.

Wever, E. G. and Vernon, G. A. (1956b). Auditory responses in the common box turtle. *Proc. natn. Acad. Sci. U.S.A.* 42, 962–965.

White, L. E. (1965a). Olfactory bulb projections of the rat. *Anat. Rec.* 152, 465–480.

White, L. E. (1965b). A morphological concept of the limbic lobe. *Int. Rev. Neurobiol.* 8, 1–30.

Winkel, K. and Caspers, H. (1953). Untersuchungen an Reptilien über die Beeinflussung der Grosshirnrindenrhythmik durch Zwischenhirnreizungen unit besonderer Berücksichtigung des Thalamus. *Pflügers Arch. ges. Physiol.* 258, 22–37.

Winter, D. L. N. (1965). Nucleus gracilis of cat. Functional organization and corticofugal effects. *J. Neurophysiol.* 28, 48–70.

Zagorul'ko, T. M. (1957). On the localization of cerebral centers of the visual analyzer in the frog. *Fiziol. Zh. SSSR Sechenova* 43, 1156–1165. (In Russian.)

Zagorul'ko, T. M. (1967). Functional connections of the cerebral cortex with visual center in tectum opticum of the tortoise. *Zh. Evol. Biokhim. Fiziol.* 3, 342–351. (In Russian.)

Zagorul'ko, T. M. (1968). Effect of intensity and wavelength of photic stimulus on evoked responses of general cortex and optic tectum in turtles. *Fiziol. Zh. SSSR Sechenova* 54, 436–446; (1968–69) *Neurosci. Transl.* 6, 659–668.

Zagorul'ko, T. M., Belekhova, M. G. and Vesselkin, N. P. (1965). Peculiarities of evoked potentials in turtle brain cortex (to flash stimuli). *In* "Functional Evolution of the Nervous System" (E. M. Kreps, ed.). Nauka, Moscow and Leningrad, pp. 73–83. (In Russian.)

Author Index

A

Ablanalp, P., 300, *334*
Abzug, C., 63, *102*
Acolat, L., 13, *47*
Adams, W. E., 3, 4, 5, 8, 9, 10, 41, *47*
Addens, J. L., 186, *194*, 210, 211, 212, 240, 242
Adey, W. R., 324, *334*
Adrianov, O. S., 320, *334*
Agayan, A. L., 299, 303, 307, 308, *357*
Akers, T. K., 35, *47*
Akulina, M. M., 298, 306, 310, 311, 316, 317, 328, *334*, *336*
Alanis, J., 12, 18, *47*
Albé-Fessard, D., 77, *102*, 302, 317, *337*
Alexander, N. J., 43, *47*
Allison, A. C., 309, *334*, *350*
Alnaes, E., 327, *345*
Altman, J., 299, *334*
Alturi, R. L., 289, *358*
Ambache, N., 40, *47*
Ambros, V. R., 281, *283*
Andén, N.-E., 178, *194*
Andersen, P., 320, *334*
Anderson, S. D., 77, *104*
Ando, K., 36, *52*
Andry, M. L., 325, *334*
Anker, R. L., 320, *334*
Anokhin, P. K., 288, 320, 327, *334*
Appelrot, S., 20, *47*
Appert, H., 15, 17, *47*
Archangelsky, K., 36, *49*
Arduini, A. A., 327, *342*
Arinës Kappers, C. U., 59, 60, 63, 69, 74, 75, 78, 80, 82, *102*, 117, 118, 120, 121, 123, 128, *129*, 137, 167, 168, 173, 175, 179, 181, 182, *194*, 211, 212, 213, 214, 217, 218, 219, 221, 225, 226, 227, 228, 239, *242*, 294, *346*
Armstrong, J. A., 290, 296, *334*
Arnold, A. P., 63, *108*

A (continued)

Asanuma, H., 63, *108*
Ashman, R., 15, 18, *47*, *51*
Ata-Muradova, F. A., 320, *334*
Atkins, R. J., 320, *349*
Azuma, T., 10, 18, *47*

B

Bach-y-Rita, G., 324, *334*
Badano, F., 15, 20, *50*
Bagley, C. Jr., 313, *335*
Bagnara, J. T., 42, *47*
Baird, I. L., 215, 220, *242*
Baird, J. L., 293, *335*
Baker, L. A., 35, 36, 46, *57*
Baker, M. A., 317, *345*
Baker, R., 238, *242*, *245*
Baker-Cohen, K. F., 178, *194*, 252, *282*, 328, 330, 331, *335*
Banchi, A., 76, 77, 78, 80, 84, *102*, 118, *129*
Bantil, H., 289, *335*
Barboriak, J. J., 18, *54*
Barnard, J. W., 170, 190, *194*, 211, *242*
Barrera, E., 60, 70, *105*
Barton, R. J., 324, *349*
Baru, A. V., 293, *335*
Bass, A. H., 288, 290, 292, 296, 313, 314, *335*
Bassan, M., 326, *353*
Batuev, A. S., 288, *335*
Baumgarten, H. G., 251, 263, 265, 266, 269, *282*
Baurand, C., 324, *334*
Bava, A., 317, *335*
Beattie, M. S., 93, 94, 95, *106*
Beaudet, A., 250, 262, *284*
Beccari, N., 119, *129*, 171, 172, 177, 178, 181, 182, 183, 184, 187, *194*, 215, 217, 218, 219, 220, 222, 235, *242*
Becker, D. P., 293, 301, *355*
Beckers, H. J. A., 329, *353*

361

Subject Index

375